HUEY "PIANO" SMITH
and the Rocking Pneumonia Blues

HUEY "PIANO" SMITH
and the
Rocking Pneumonia
Blues

JOHN WIRT

Louisiana State University Press
Baton Rouge

Published by Louisiana State University Press
Copyright © 2014 by Richmond Book Company, LLC
All rights reserved
Manufactured in the United States of America
LSU Press Paperback Original
First printing

Designer: Michelle A. Neustrom
Typeface: Whitman
Printer and binder: Maple Press

Library of Congress Cataloging-in-Publication Data

Wirt, John, 1955–, author.
  Huey "Piano" Smith and the Rocking pneumonia blues / John Wirt.
    p. cm.
  Includes bibliographical references and index.
  ISBN 978-0-8071-5295-9 (pbk. : alk. paper) — ISBN 978-0-8071-
5296-6 (pdf) — ISBN 978-0-8071-5297-3 (epub) — ISBN 978-0-8071-
5298-0 (mobi) 1. Smith, Huey. 2. Pianists—United States—Biography.
3. Rhythm and blues musicians—United States—Biography. I. Title.
  ML417.S672W57 2014
  786.2'164092—dc23
  [B]
                                   2013041751

CONTENTS

Illustrations follow page 112.

PREFACE
A Rare Return

Among those who love the classic rhythm-and-blues of New Orleans, Huey "Piano" Smith is a lost legend from the city's golden age of rock 'n' roll and rhythm-and-blues. A pianist, composer, producer, and sometimes principal vocalist, he created songs that live among New Orleans and American music classics. The best known of these include 1957's contagious "Rocking Pneumonia and the Boogie Woogie Flu," 1958's comic call-and-response "Don't You Just Know It" and its pre-funk flipside, "High Blood Pressure," 1959's equally infectious "Sea Cruise," and the best of the cartoon character–based, early 1960s Popeye dance records, "Pop-Eye." For years people wondered where Huey was, how he was doing, why he dropped so completely from sight. Rumors placed the former star on street corners, dressed in the traditional garment of penitence, sackcloth, and clutching a raggedy Bible in one hand, a bottle of wine in the other. Others claimed he lived in a one-room shack, so broken and embittered by the music business that he wanted nothing more to do with it.

My job as music writer for the daily newspaper in Baton Rouge, Huey's city of residence since 1980, as well as his being named one of the Rhythm & Blues Foundation's Pioneer Awards recipients in 2000, opened the door for me to finally meet him. Unbeknownst to me, Huey had been reading my newspaper interviews with his peers, including Earl King, Dr. John, Allen Toussaint, Frankie Ford, Ellis Marsalis, Irma Thomas, and Deacon John Moore. And when the American sister label of England's Westside Records, Music Club, released a collection of his recordings for Johnny Vincent's Ace Records label in 1998, I praised these 1950s and 1960s classics and mentioned that, oh, by the way, Huey Smith, like so many songwriters and recording artists of his day, had not been properly paid for his often-played, performed, and re-recorded songs.

In September 2000, Huey, his wife Margrette, and their granddaughter, Tyra, flew to New York City to attend the Rhythm & Blues Foundation's Pioneer Awards ceremony. It was a well-deserved, much-publicized honor that included a $15,000 award. Financially devastated by years of legal conflict, Huey and his family needed the money. The honor put Huey in the public eye and on stage for the first time in nearly twenty years. It also gave me an opportunity to request an interview with Huey through the Rhythm & Blues Foundation. The foundation relayed the request to the Smiths in Baton Rouge, and Margrette called to say, yes, her husband would be glad to give the newspaper an interview once they'd returned from New York.

Back home after the gala, Huey had much to say, most of it totally unexpected by me. He spoke as if the lawyers and judges he'd encountered through years of haggling over his four most popular and valuable compositions had never heard anything he'd repeatedly tried to tell them, but perhaps this local reporter would listen. Speaking with sometimes dizzying velocity, the sixty-six-year-old Huey leapt year to year, decade to decade, place to place, and person to person with little regard for chronology or continuity. His epic accounts of unpaid royalties for his songwriting and recordings and of his recent bankruptcy filing illuminated the dark flipside of the music business. The man whose middle name is "Piano" had a piano bench but no piano to stand alongside it. Even that had been lost in court.

Two weeks before being feted at the music star–filled R&B Foundation awards, Huey was in a federal courthouse in Baton Rouge, attending the bankruptcy hearing that ultimately deprived him of much of the income generated by "Rocking Pneumonia and the Boogie Woogie Flu," "Don't You Just Know It," "High Blood Pressure," and "Sea Cruise." More than forty years after music-filled nights at New Orleans hotspots Club Tiajuana and the Dew Drop Café, recording sessions at Cosimo Matassa's French Quarter studio-incubator of rock 'n' roll, soul, and funk, appearances at the Apollo Theater in Harlem and Howard Theatre in Washington, D.C., an unprecedented bidding war over his 1958 hit "Don't You Just Know It," two national television appearances with Dick Clark, and the behind-the-scenes maneuvering that led to "Sea Cruise" being released as a Frankie Ford record, rock 'n' roll pioneer Huey's twelve-year legal battle with the New York City–based Artists Rights Enforcement Corporation culminated in a Louisiana courtroom on August 18, 2000. That day, his bankruptcy trustee, an impeccably groomed man in a fine suit, called the composer-pianist into a courthouse room big enough for a table and a few chairs. "I'm trying to help you," he said. "Now, you got to sign these things." "I'll sign them," Huey replied, "but if I read them I can't sign them, because I know what's in here is not the truth."

ACKNOWLEDGMENTS

Thanks first of all to the singers, songwriters, musicians, and music business people who made themselves available for interviews. Thanks to writer and musician Ben Sandmel for his frequent help and encouragement. Thanks to Rick Coleman for his early review of the manuscript and for providing research material and contacts for interviewees. Thanks to Cyril Vetter, Rob Payer, "Scarface" John Williams's daughter Deborah Williams, Ron Bartholomew, Alison Fensterstock, Suzanne Jones Myers, Tad Jones, Lynn Abbott and Bruce Raeburn at Tulane University's Hogan Jazz Archive, Rachel Lyons at the New Orleans Jazz and Heritage Foundation Archive, and Jennifer Navarre at the Historic New Orleans Collection, Williams Research Center. Thanks to Jason Berry, Jerry Brock, and Jim Scheurich. Thanks to attorney Stephen F. Armbruster for his review of the manuscript. Special thanks to John Broven, Jeff Hannusch, Jonathan Foose, Keith Spera, Bunny Matthews, Geraldine Wyckoff, and other chroniclers of New Orleans music. Thanks to LSU Press executive editor Rand Dotson, LSU Press senior editor Catherine Kadair, and freelance copy editor Derik Shelor. Most of all, thanks to Huey and Margrette Smith and their family.

AUTHOR'S NOTE

Much of the content of this book is based on first-person interviews that I conducted between 2001 and 2010. The interviews for the project began with Huey "Piano" Smith. We met on a weekly basis from January 2001 through September 2001. Our meetings typically lasted ninety minutes to two hours. I conducted a few additional, undated interviews with Huey in the months and years after the original meetings.

Most of the interviews with Huey's singers, musicians, and business associates were conducted from January 2001 through June 2003. These interviews were conducted by telephone or, to a lesser extent, in person.

In addition to Huey, I interviewed the surviving members of the Clowns, Gerri Hall and Jesse Thomas; Huey's music peers Dave Bartholomew, Earl Palmer, Eddie Bo, Earl King, Clarence "Frogman" Henry, Shirley Goodman, Carl Gardner, Robert Parker, James Rivers, Dr. John, Skip Easterling, George Porter Jr., Tex Liuzza, Deacon John Moore, Rudy Ray Moore, and Ike "Diz" Williams; music business people Billy Diamond, Jim Russell, Herb Holiday, S. J. Montalbano, Jonathan Foose, Diane M. Grassi, and Ed Arrow; writer and historian Tad Jones; and attorneys Clifford Levy, Suzette Becker Toledano, and Robert Arentson.

Other interviewees were Baton Rouge musician John Fred Gourrier; younger-generation New Orleans musicians Louis Kahl, Jon Cleary, John Boutte, and Davis Rogan; southern soul singer and Johnny Vincent associate Willie Clayton; the WWOZ-associated Billy Delle and Stephanie Lawrence; New Orleans writer-musician Ben Sandmel; Huey's New Orleans contemporary Herreast Harrison; and non–New Orleans musicians and Huey Smith fans Roy Loney and Steve Ripley.

Artists Rights Enforcement Corporation president Chuck Rubin, attorneys Richard Linn, Ralph Hood, Ellis J. Pailet, and Dwayne Murray, and former judge Louis Phillips either refused requests for interviews or did not respond to requests.

Because Huey and his peers often were such natural storytellers who recounted incidents and conversations from decades ago in vivid detail, I have, for the sake of readability and entertainment value, occasionally transposed their stories into dialogue format of the kind found in fiction. I *have not fictionalized or invented* stories, details, characters, or situations. The book is based on first-person interviews, firsthand observations, court transcripts and documents, and research from sources such as newspapers, magazines, and audio interviews. Details of the interviews and other sources can be found in the bibliography.

As for dialect, I have chosen to faithfully retain these mostly southern voices as I heard them. The fact that these talented musicians, songwriters, producers, and record and publishing company owners do not always speak what is considered "standard" English in no way betrays them as lacking intelligence. I found the opposite to be true, regardless of the level of formal schooling some of these musicians received. Considering the economic and social hardships they experienced in the years of Jim Crow and beyond, their accomplishments in music and culture stand out as even more impressive.

HUEY "PIANO" SMITH
and the Rocking Pneumonia Blues

Introduction
New Orleans

Have you ever been down to New Orleans?
Then you can understand just what I mean.
—LOUIS JORDAN

Upriver from where the Mississippi meets the Gulf of Mexico, steamy New Orleans sits precariously below sea level. A network of levees, canals, and pumping stations surround the city's French Quarter townhouses, St. Charles Avenue mansions, and the rows of shotgun houses and cottages that visitors don't usually see. The view from tourist-heavy riverboats on the Mississippi reveals that the dry side of the levee is indeed lower than the river. New Orleans also lies alongside massive Lake Pontchartrain. Locals knew that a well-aimed hurricane could drown the city that care forgot. Such a catastrophe happened following Hurricane Katrina's Gulf Coast landfall on August 29, 2005. The post-storm flood that drenched 80 percent of New Orleans scattered the city's population, including musicians, throughout the United States.

The calamity threatened New Orleans's distinctive culture. For three centuries, diverse rhythms and races mingled in the port city's tropical heat. Home to a large African American population since the arrival of slaves in the early 1700s, the city is particularly rich with their music. In slavery days, Congo Square, a grassy plain just beyond the French Quarter, served as an oasis of African musical expression. It was the only southern place where slaves were allowed, albeit only on Sundays, to sing, dance, and play their instruments.

Slavery and its painfully prolonged aftermath contributed to the creation of a powerful metaphor—the blues. "Yeah, blues is kind of a revenge," singer-pianist Memphis Slim told folklorist and musicologist Alan Lomax in 1946. "We all have had a hard time in life, and things we couldn't say or do, so we sing it."

1

A raggedy stepchild, the blues became a primary root of American music, particularly for jazz and rhythm-and-blues from New Orleans, a city where music is more than entertainment. It flows like life itself through the celebrating second-line dancers who follow parading brass bands, and in the rhythms and chants of the Mardi Gras Indians, those fantastically costumed urban tribes of tradition-honoring African Americans who mask in feathered and beaded suits and headdresses.

In the early twentieth century, New Orleans produced Louis "Satchmo" Armstrong, a brilliant trumpeter and charismatic vocalist who, via the phonograph and moving pictures, charmed audiences worldwide. Also from the city were cornetist Buddy "King" Bolden, possibly the first jazz star; Sidney Bechet, a volatile master of the clarinet and soprano saxophone; and Ferdinand "Jelly Roll" Morton, the pianist, composer, vaudevillian, and hustler who claimed he alone created jazz. Ingenious though Morton was, he was but one of the city's many jazz pioneers.

Like the blues, New Orleans's keyboard tradition grew in part from social and economic deprivation. Weekend nights in Louisiana, people of all colors kept roofs over their heads and food on their tables by opening their homes and selling fish and chicken dinners. Upright pianos in the tiny houses provided entertainment. Necessity spurred invention among the pianists who played these house parties. Having no drummer, they exploited the keyboard's percussive nature.

In the years before World War II, blues, jazz, and gospel performers and recording artists emerged from New Orleans and elsewhere. The music business dubbed recordings by these African American artists "race music" and "race records." By the late 1940s, Cosimo Matassa, a young man whose Italian-American family worked in the grocery, bar, jukebox, appliance, and used-records businesses, was recording African American artists in the 15-by-16-square-foot studio behind his J&M Music Shop on North Rampart Street. Drummer Earl Palmer called the room "the smallest you've ever seen." Symbolically, perhaps, the studio stood across the street from Congo Square. In 1947, Roy Brown cut the romping "Good Rockin' Tonight," often cited as the first rock 'n' roll record, at J&M. By December 1949, *Billboard,* the weekly magazine about and for the music business, had renamed "race music" as "rhythm-and-blues," and future star Fats Domino, a singer-pianist from the city's Lower Ninth Ward, had recorded his first hit, "The Fat Man," at Matassa's studio. By the mid-1950s, a young pianist from Uptown named Huey Pierce Smith was playing J&M sessions for local and visiting hit makers. Huey also participated in the rich local nightlife represented most obviously by the Dew Drop Café and Club Tiajuana, two African American nightclubs far removed from the French Quarter's Bourbon Street.

Huey and his peers called their music "blues" or "jump," but it soon got a new name. Rock 'n' roll records by white performers such as Elvis Presley, Pat Boone, and Gale Storm—often remakes of hits by black blues and rhythm-and-blues acts—dominated the pop charts during an era of segregated radio. While no individual deserves the title "king of rock 'n' roll," Huey played his part in the shift from mournful blues to joyful music with a beat that moved young people no matter what their color.

In a city filled with unique, creative personalities, Huey brought his special touch to the party. Casting singers in the manner of Phil Spector and preferring to be behind the scenes in the manner of Brian Wilson, he composed, arranged, performed, and recorded captivating, often comic songs wrapped in the pulse and sound of New Orleans. Countless piano players from the city and beyond recycled his intro for "Rocking Pneumonia and the Boogie Woogie Flu," a song the Rock and Roll Hall of Fame cited as one of five hundred songs that shaped rock 'n' roll. Beginning in the 1950s, Huey's songs were recorded and performed by dozens of major artists, including Aerosmith, the Beach Boys, the Grateful Dead, 1960s British invasion acts the Animals and Herman's Hermits, Creedence Clearwater Revival front man John Fogerty, Jimmy Buffett, French rock 'n' roll star Johnny Hallyday, and fellow New Orleans performers Professor Longhair, Dr. John, the Neville Brothers, Wynton Marsalis, and Allen Toussaint.

"When I was a kid, we did Huey Smith stuff," Robert Plant, the British rock star, Led Zeppelin singer, and New Orleans rhythm-and-blues devotee, told local disc jockey Billy Delle during a visit to the city in 1990. "'Don't You Just Know It,' stuff that was popular."

Huey's songs earned a fortune, little of which their creator received. Even so, the music business heartbreak he experienced can't erase the inescapable groove and joy in his songs.

"Listen," advised Huey's New Orleans songwriting, piano-playing peer, Dr. John, a five-time Grammy winner and 2011 Rock and Roll Hall of Fame inductee. "I credit Huey with opening the door for funk, basically as we know it, in some ridiculously hip way, and putting it in the mainstream of the world's music."

1

Robertson Street Boogie

People assumed Huey Pierce Smith's parents named him after Huey Pierce Long, the populist governor and U.S. senator who ruled Louisiana in the 1920s and 1930s. Long delivered his "Carry Out the Command of the Lord" speech from the Senate floor on February 5, 1934, ten days after Huey Smith's birth. The nation was at the bottom of the Depression, and Louisiana, economically and geographically, was at the bottom of the nation. "People of America," Long announced through radios across the land, "in every community get together at once and organize a share-our-wealth society—Motto: Every man a king."

Despite Senator Long's notoriety, Huey's parents actually named him after his uncle. Born January 26, Huey grew up at 2610 South Robertson Street in Uptown New Orleans, a neighborhood of frame cottages and shotgun duplexes where everyone played a song or two at the piano.

Huey's father, Arthur Smith Sr., moved from the small southeastern Louisiana town of Independence to the city famous for jazz and Mardi Gras. His mother, Carrie Victoria Scott, came from Scotlandville, ninety miles northwest of New Orleans in East Baton Rouge Parish.

Huey was a "daddy's boy." He dearly loved his father and sat on the front porch every day waiting for him to come home from work. Huey waited there especially if he'd done something his mother disapproved of. Mother and son were not close. She gave him frequent whippings, so many that he felt he'd best not enter the house until his father's return.

Although Huey never engaged in organized religion during his childhood and youth, his faith and reverence were strong. As a child of five or six, he gazed into the night sky and prayed. "But mostly because I had a fear that something might happen to my daddy," he remembered. "Those barrooms down there, he didn't go in them, but the people would be running out. Somebody done stabbed somebody. So I worry when my daddy be gone. I prayed that some kind of way Jehovah wouldn't let nothing happen to him."

Like other boys in New Orleans, Huey ran along St. Charles Avenue during Mardi Gras parades to catch beads thrown from the floats. He believed in Santa Claus, too. One rainy Christmas Eve, he cried after his mother told him to go to sleep. When she heard him crying, she entered his bedroom and pinched him. The next morning he didn't get the bicycle he'd wanted for Christmas. Instead, he got a tiny red bike that fell to pieces in a few days. "And this boy next door, Leonard, got a big, strong bicycle," Huey said. "I knew we couldn't really afford nothing like that, but my mama told me, 'Santa Claus heard you crying. That's why you didn't get a bicycle like Leonard!' For years and years and years, I was angry with myself for crying."

In Huey's neighborhood, people concocted home remedies. Next-door neighbor Mrs. Seaberry told Mrs. Smith that tea brewed from a cockroach would cure Huey's asthma. His mother made the cockroach tea, but luckily his daddy came home just in time to object to the noxious brew. The boy had no intention of drinking it anyhow.

Huey's mother worked in a New Orleans laundry in the years before air conditioning became common. He wondered how she could stand such extreme conditions and never miss a day of work. Mrs. Smith cleaned her own children's clothes at the laundry. He always had a fresh white shirt for school, a reflection of the importance his mother attached to getting a good education. Working mother though she was, Carrie Smith found time to cook a daily breakfast of smoked sausage, grits, and eggs for her family.

Huey's father was a roofer and laborer who also found employment cutting cane during Louisiana's sugarcane harvest. He'd stay in rural Louisiana during harvesttime and send money home. Arthur Smith's employers valued him for being someone who could accomplish things others couldn't. "I remember my daddy telling me, 'Whatever you do, do it good,'" Huey said.

The confetti-strewn World War II victory parades that rolled through New Orleans with generals Dwight D. Eisenhower and Douglas MacArthur made less of an impression on Huey than the fact that his third-grade teacher had married a black officer. In his letters home, the teacher's husband said things would be different for the black citizens of New Orleans after the war. The screens that separated blacks from whites on the city's streetcars, for instance, would be banished. Half of the day, the teacher talked about her husband, always referring to him as Lieutenant Williams. She told her students about a letter she'd received from him and the inscription he'd written on the envelope: "Mailman, mailman, do your duty. Deliver this letter to my brown-skin beauty."

Huey recalled going to the hospital with his uncle to pick up his newborn brother, Melvin. Seeing the light-skinned baby for the first time, wrapped in his blanket, alarmed Huey. "This is a white boy!" he exclaimed. But Melvin darkened with age. When Melvin was a small child, Huey let his little brother win foot races, so much so that Melvin thought he was the fastest boy on Robertson Street. Older boys in the neighborhood were kind to the younger children. Good boys in general, they didn't curse or steal.

At twelve, Huey joined his fellow Boy Scouts Alvin Smith and Willie Lee as they walked to the edge of the Industrial Canal in the Gentilly section of New Orleans. The heavily wooded area reminded him of the jungles in Tarzan movies. The boys couldn't swim, but they waded into the canal anyway, thinking it wasn't deep. As they headed to the middle of the waterway, the canal's bottom dropped from beneath their feet. Huey managed to put his hand in some mud and grab a small tree branch. Miraculously, he pulled himself from the canal. Alvin held on to Huey and he, too, escaped the muddy water. From the canal bank they looked for their friend, Willie. He was gone. A man who'd seen the boys struggling in the water told them Willie had been beneath the surface too long, that he was beyond help.

The survivors went home, leaving the lost Scout's short pants on the bank. Huey's father was working at night then, so Huey didn't tell anyone about the incident. "But I recall getting in the bed by my mother," he said. "I stayed just about all that night. I think she was surprised. I felt her caress me. Like a mother and a baby, that's how she was holding me. I know she must have sensed something."

In the middle of the night, some young men came to the Smiths' house looking for Willie Lee. "Ooh," Mrs. Smith told them, "it's three o'clock in the morning! He's not here." After Mrs. Smith went to work the next morning, Huey walked to Alvin's house. He wanted to tell Alvin's mother about Willie but didn't. Policemen came to the Smiths' house later. They questioned Alvin and

Huey and took them to the canal. A woman the boys didn't know was there, too. She argued with the officers, saying there had obviously been a struggle on the canal bank. But the white policemen—all New Orleans policemen were white at this time—dismissed her scenario. The gentleman who'd witnessed the incident was there, too. He told the officers that it was a wonder all three of the boys hadn't drowned.

The Smiths, like many Depression-era families, kept chickens. In wet New Orleans, the birds had to be kept off the ground and fed a diet of corn three or four weeks before slaughter. Otherwise they'd taste like mud. When Huey's mother decided to kill a particularly fierce rooster, she held the bird on the wooden steps as Huey wielded a hatchet. The rooster jumped to safety and, instead of chopping the bird's head off, the hatchet sliced into Mrs. Smith's thumb. Neighbors accused her son, who'd gotten a whipping earlier that day, of wounding her intentionally. She didn't believe them. "Ain't nobody in the world going to tell me you did that on purpose," she told him. "I know good and well that was an accident."

Though the rooster's day of execution came, the Smiths had one chicken they'd never harm: Nubby. When he hatched, Nubby was unusually small and his feet were turned downward. While every other chicken in the yard inevitably had an appointment with a pot, oven, or skillet, the misshapen Nubby became a family pet. Nubby was so cherished that his death via an opportunistic rat made the whole family cry.

Despite limited opportunities for blacks in the South, Arthur Smith hoped his children would grow up to be professionals—doctors, lawyers, or preachers—and ride around in Cadillacs. Huey, imitating hellfire preachers, would lie on the floor growling as he flipped through the Bible. His daddy encouraged him, saying, "Go ahead, Doc!"

A fascination for chemistry helped Huey get his Doc nickname. Like scientists in monster movies, he had a laboratory, located in the backyard. After paying twenty-five cents to a pharmacist at the Good Citizens drugstore for chemicals that he believed would ignite when combined, Huey mixed the ingredients in a matchbox. Nothing happened. Disappointed, he slipped the matchbox in his coat pocket. Sometime later he noticed his coat was aflame, the consequence of a delayed chemical reaction. He later found another, nearly as explosive reason for remembering this particular experiment. The pharmacist who sold the chemicals to him, Kermit A. Parker, became the first black man since Reconstruction to run for governor of Louisiana. Even while Louisiana and the South were deep in the grip of Jim Crow–era segregation and discrimination, Parker announced his candidacy for the state's top elected office on June 13, 1951. "In the United States of America, some of our national, state, and local public officials are doing everything they can to impress other nations that America is practicing the Democracy she is preaching," Parker told reporters in Baton Rouge. "However, I have had many occasion to observe many forms of injustice, many of which the general public has no idea that they are even in existence. We stress equality of opportunity and many other factors to show the world that we stand for justice."

"Black people really wasn't voting hardly at all at the time," Huey recalled. "I remember my uncle came from Washington, D.C. He said, '*He-eee* can run. . . .' He meant that's the farthest Parker can go."

The Smiths lived a few streets away from Shakespeare Park, located at Washington Avenue and Freret Street. From his back porch, Huey heard Dixieland bands playing at the park's swimming pool. He sat there listening, beating time with the band. The Dew Drop Café, a nightclub where he would become a regular performer in the early 1950s, was a block and a half away on LaSalle Street. The Sail Inn, a rough white bar that had a watermelon stand out front, stood across the street from the Smiths. Huey heard the bar's jukebox playing country-and-western music all night long. He particularly liked Hank Williams's "Lovesick Blues," the phenomenally popular country hit of 1949 that made Williams a star. Alabaman Williams likely based his rendition of "Lovesick Blues," including its show-stopping yodeling, upon a 1928 hit by Emmett Miller. A white entertainer from Macon, Georgia, Miller performed in blackface minstrel shows from 1919 through 1949.

Williams's rendition of "Lovesick Blues," released February 11, 1949, reached No. 1 on May 7 and remained there for sixteen weeks. Fifteen-year-old Huey heard the song playing in the bar as he lay in bed at night. "I got a feelin' that I'm blue-*ooh-ooh*," Williams sang. Getting up the next morning, Huey would go to the piano and play and sing, "I got a feelin' that I'm blue-*ooh-ooh*. . . ." "I liked it so much," he said. Another barroom, a black establishment named the Duck

Inn, also opened across the street. The jukebox in the new place played records through the night, too, especially the hits of Louis Jordan. Recordings by Jordan spent 113 weeks at No. 1 on *Billboard*'s rhythm-and-blues chart. That feat easily makes Jordan—a singer, saxophonist, and rhythm-and-blues pioneer originally from Arkansas—the genre's biggest star of the 1940s.

Huey, an avid moviegoer, enjoyed seeing Jordan and his band in short films shown at movie theaters. Huey and his friends never missed the Red Ryder western serials, starring Wild Bill Elliott as Red Ryder and young Bobby Blake as his Indian sidekick, Little Beaver. The peace-loving Red Ryder roamed the West, enforcing justice and protecting the innocent. In 1944's *The San Antonio Kid*, for instance, a bad guy named Ace plots with an oil company scout to defraud ranchers out of oil royalties. The scout intends to tell his company about the black gold he's found in Painted Valley, but only after Ace's thugs terrorize the ranchers into selling out cheap. The scheme-busting Red Ryder comes to the rescue.

Huey's by now religious-minded mother believed movies were an abomination. "So," Huey recalled, "not that my mother will say, 'You can't go to the movies,' but it's no good to ask her for to give you show fare. She's not go' send you there!" Bargain admission to the movies was a nickel on Thursdays, but Huey could earn thirty or forty cents cleaning for his aunt and then see a movie even on nonbargain days.

The boys in Huey's neighborhood ran to their destinations, whether they were going to the movies, the grocery store, or anywhere else. Huey's quick feet came in handy one evening after he'd seen the Universal Studios horror classic *The Mummy's Hand*. He'd gone to the show alone that day, as he often did. By the movie's end it was dark and deserted outside—no cars, no people, nothing but those big, scary oak trees so common in Louisiana, with limbs like tentacles. He hit the street running, not slowing until his feet reached the steps of his house.

Featuring a scenario prophetic for Huey's own life, 1947's *Body and Soul* became one of his favorite movies. The drama stars John Garfield as a prizefighter who falls under the control of a racketeer who demands 50 percent of the boxer's earnings. *My Foolish Heart*, a World War II melodrama, also made a powerful impact on Huey, even though he wasn't interested in the sad story. Huey and his friends wanted action, not kissing. It was the film's theme music that captivated him. "When that melody shot in there, everybody in the movie got tears in their eyes," he recalled. "The music did that. It almost scared you, and then it leveled off and it was beautiful."

Huey and his friends also loved comic books. Huey's favorites were science fiction, "going to the moon and stuff like that," he said. "They never thought of nothing like that in reality, but it was in the comic book. So, really, later the comic books came alive." He also grabbed the newspaper comics every Sunday. Medieval hero Prince Valiant was his favorite character. "And we always had Nancy. Later on, when the Afros came out, they said, 'Hey, Nancy was the first white girl with a bush!'"

He found more entertainment at Lee's Treat, a new tavern on Washington Avenue where his older sister, Oddress (pronounced Audrey), went with her friend, Rosalie. Underage though he was, the staff let him come in alone and play the jukebox. "They just looked the other way. I just sat there and put a nickel in the box when I wasn't with my sister and them." The jukebox selections he especially liked included the swinging "Fine Brown Frame," a 1947 hit by Nellie Lutcher. A singer-pianist from Lake Charles, Louisiana, Lutcher moved to Los Angeles and became a recording star. Huey also played records by another L.A.-based artist, the singer-pianist dubbed the queen of boogie, Hadda Brooks. His other favorites were Houston singer-pianist Amos Milburn's signature tune, "Chicken Shack Boogie," and tenor saxophonist Gene Ammons's warm and lyrical 1950 rendition of the movie theme "My Foolish Heart." Ammons's record was the debut release from a new Chicago label, Chess Records. The saxophonist was the son of the first boogie-woogie pianist Huey had ever heard, Albert Ammons.

Huey's own piano playing began when he was eight or nine years old. He and his siblings learned about the keyboard by observing their uncle and neighbor, Isidore Miller. Their uncle's repertoire included singer-pianist Leroy Carr's mournful "How Long—How Long Blues," recorded in 1928.

> Sometimes I feel so disgusted and I feel so blue,
> That I hardly know what in this world, baby, just to do.
> For how long, how long, baby, how long?

The Smiths' next-door neighbor, Dorothy Porter, knew "How Long," too. Between watching her and Uncle Isidore, Huey learned the song's eight-bar progression. He discovered, too, that he could use the identical progression to play hundreds of other blues songs. Blues was the dominant African American music of the time.

Smith sisters Oddress and Jackelee took lessons from piano teachers, known as professors, who rode bicycles through New Orleans neighborhoods. Huey bought sheet music for the girls at a music store on Jackson Avenue: "Amazing Grace," "What a Friend We Have in Jesus," and whatever else they might want. Unlike his sisters, he taught himself to play. He preferred simply playing to studying the fundamentals. And not spending the money his father gave him to take piano lessons at the Grunewald School of Music on Magazine Street— where many African American veterans back from World War II used their G.I. Bill benefits to finance music lessons—meant he could spend it on other things.

Huey's interest in the piano soon surpassed that of his sisters. "They wasn't even concerned about playing piano," he said. "But me, myself, I'm banging on the piano all day. Miss Thelma, next door, she beat on the wall that separated our houses. *Boom-boom, boom-boom.* 'Knock it off over there!' But as soon she quieted down, I'm back at it again." Arthur Smith Jr., Huey's older brother by five years, was even more enthusiastic about the piano than Huey. But because Arthur never learned more than one song, "How Long"—the blues standard that apparently everyone in New Orleans could sing and play at the piano—a future for him in music seemed unlikely.

Practicing the piano for hours, Huey attracted his first fan. As he played, a half-naked, curly-topped little boy about three years old peeped through the blinds on a daily basis. Three decades later, whenever Huey saw television commercials produced by the international charity organization Feed the Children, the doe-eyed, ragged children on the screen reminded him of the boy with no pants who'd watched him practice on South Robertson Street. That child's name was June "Curley" Moore Jr., and he'd grow up to sing in Huey's group, the Clowns. "Hu-ree raised me," Curley liked to say.

In addition to Huey's blooming piano skills, he began composing rhymes. "We played little games at school and put a beat and music to it," he said. The aspiring songwriter's first musical partner was a boy in the neighborhood, Percy Anderson. Percy's straight hair earned him the nickname "Slick." "Everybody sang, all the neighbors, but Percy, we be walking to school, he be singing. 'It was early one morning, on my way to school. Was that Monday morning, I broke my teacher's rule.' Percy and I used to always get by the piano and sing and play little things. We be sitting on the step making up songs, 'The Robertson Street Boogie' and stuff like that."

On the spur of the moment, Huey and Percy entered the Lincoln Theatre's weekly talent show. Billing themselves as Slick and Doc, they performed "The Robertson Street Boogie."

> Get hip everybody to a street that's all reet. It's not Canal, but it's
> Robertson Street.
>
> . . .
>
> The kastatacality was driving you mad. Say, "Hey little daddy, ain't I bad?"
> It's the Robertson Street boogie, Robertson boogie, Robertson boogie,
> Boogie-woogie all day long.

Huey got the song's invented word, "kastatacality," from Curley Moore's brother, Austin. "His vocabulary wasn't big, but he wanted to use some big words," Huey explained. "So he said 'the kastatacality,' something he made up out of his head."

Teenagers Huey, Percy, and "Grandpa" James Bailey tried to enlist in the U.S. Army. They saw military service as a chance to go to college and advance themselves in life. Huey altered his birth certificate because he was too young to enlist. The alteration didn't pass muster, but Percy and Grandpa were accepted. Percy saw action during the Korean War and survived machine-gun bullets in his chest. But another young man they knew, Leon, never returned. Huey guessed he was missing in action. In fact, Leon C. Irving Jr., a U.S. Army corporal from Orleans Parish, died August 27, 1951. The list of fatal U.S. military Korean War casualties cites Irving's remains as unrecovered. As the reality of serving in the military during wartime emerged, Huey and his peers lost their interest in enlisting. "When things like that start going, ain't nobody trying to get in the Army then," Huey said. "Nobody was interested after we knew about it."

On a more benign note, Huey also was too young to patronize the nearby Dew Drop Café, New Orleans's premier black nightclub. Nonetheless, neighbor Stella Mae Seaberry told him about Larry Darnell's dramatic performance of his 1949 hit, "I'll Get Along Somehow." "Well," the indignant Darnell says in the song's spoken intro, "you're right up on top now, and you want to be free. Why, you feel that you're too good, much too good for a nobody like me!" As he finished performing his emotion-wracked ballad and recitation, Darnell meticulously ripped up a letter from his ungrateful ex-lover before tossing the bits of paper in the air like confetti. His performance tore the house down every time.

The singer's extended stay at the Dew Drop launched his national stardom after Fred Mendelsohn, an artist and repertoire director from New Jersey's Regal Records, witnessed him performing the song and, as Mendelsohn put it, "dames screaming and hollering." The New Jersey–based label released many Darnell hits, starting with a No. 1 ballad, 1949's "For You My Love."

Huey's own entry into show business was soon to come. Still a student at Walter L. Cohen High School, he and some other young fellows formed the Joy Jumpers. The group played a few weekends on the black side of a segregated Canal Street music venue, Club Revere. The Joy Jumpers performed the hits of the day better than other bands featuring musicians their age. West Coast pianist Lloyd Glenn's jukebox favorite, "Old Time Shuffle Blues," was one example. "We played it identically to the record," Huey said. "That's why the people liked it."

After a Joy Jumpers rehearsal, tenor player Kermit Butler's older brother, the group's driver, and the boys stopped for snacks at a venue where Henry Roeland Byrd, aka Professor Longhair, was performing. Huey knew of Professor Longhair, the singer-pianist who recorded future Carnival classic "Mardi Gras in New Orleans" in 1949 and released the national rhythm-and-blues hit "Bald Head" in 1950. Longhair's idiosyncratic piano proficiency didn't just impress Huey; it inspired him to practice more. He noticed, too, that "Fess" kicked the piano in rhythm, making it his drum and, consequently, leaving his mark on every upright piano he played. Meanwhile, Joe Kenner, brother of future New Orleans recording star Chris Kenner ("Land of 1000 Dances," "I Like It Like That," "Sick and Tired"), had already schooled Huey in Longhair's boogie-blues-second line-Caribbean-barrelhouse style. Joe, a gifted piano player himself, and Longhair were friends.

Huey saw Professor Longhair another time during a neighborhood party at South Saratoga and Seventh streets. Jax beer, a local brand brewed in the French Quarter, sponsored the event. "I was just listening with admiration," he remembered. Longhair explained his genre-sweeping approach to New Orleans music historian Tad Jones in 1975. "I took up to tryin' to learnin' a variety of music other than just one individually styled. Like I say, I like my own style, but my own style is completely different than rhythm-and-blues, or calypso or any of that. It's just deep down funk."

In New Orleans's large African American community, the dapper Dr. Daddy-O served as the voice and face of Jax beer. Dr. Daddy-O was a pseudonym for Dillard University art professor Vernon Winslow, who became New Orleans's first black disc jockey in 1949. A man in the right place at the right time, he helmed WWEZ's *Jivin' with Jax* and wrote the "Boogie-Beat Jive" column for the *Louisiana Weekly*, an African American newspaper. The column covered such visiting stars as Count Basie and Amos Milburn as well as local talent Professor Longhair, Fats Domino, Dave Bartholomew, Smiley Lewis, and Mr. Google Eyes. Winslow's radio show popularized the city's fledgling recording artists. "Congratulations to all those youngsters who are making musical history for New Orleans and the nation," he enthused in his January 7, 1950, column. "You're great!! . . . mighty, mighty, great!!!"

Joe "Mr. Google Eyes" August was the first person Huey knew who made a record. After singing in New Orleans clubs with Roy Brown, Paul Gayten, and Annie Laurie, teenager August released the jump-blues number "Young Boy" and "Poppa Stoppa's Be-Bop Blues." Henry "Duke" Thiele, a white deejay who played black music and called himself Poppa Stoppa, inspired the latter song. August, known to his family as Boisie, was a nephew of Huey's neighbor, Mrs. Seaberry. The singer's cousin, Stella Mae, bragged that Boisie earned one hundred dollars a night. Despite his local star status, August would not learn the lyrics to his songs. "Every time he got on a stage, he didn't know what he was going to sing, from beginning to end," Huey said.

While Mr. Google Eyes made a local splash, Antoine "Fats" Domino, a five-foot-five, 224-pound, twenty-two-year-old singer-pianist from the Lower Ninth Ward, began a national career from New Orleans. Domino's first recording for Lew Chudd's Hollywood-based Imperial label, "The Fat Man," made its *Billboard* rhythm-and-blues chart debut on February 18, 1950. The song is a sped-up, cleaned-up rendition of "The Junkers Blues," a local standard that singer-pianist Champion Jack Dupree recorded in 1941 with its drug references intact. Domino's "The Fat Man"—popularized in his hometown by disc jockeys Dr. Daddy-O and Poppa Stoppa—was ascending the national charts when Huey ignored his mother's warning to stay away from Canal Street and attended a dance on New Orleans's main commercial thoroughfare with friends Percy Anderson and "Grandpa" James Bailey. The boys paid fifty cents each to see Domino and Tommy Ridgley sing with Dave Bartholomew's band. Bartholomew, a singer, trumpeter, and recording artist who'd grown up idolizing Louis Armstrong, was Imperial Records' artist and repertoire man in New Orleans. He'd led the "Fat Man" session at J&M Recording Studios. With the record on its way to selling a million copies, he and Domino were enjoying what would be the first of many hits.

Underage Huey got into the dance with no trouble. "If you had 50 cents, they didn't care," he recalled. "And I'm standing up there in front, at the front door, looking right at him at the piano. He is sitting there with an upright piano with no front on it. Because the record is hitting, for you to see this in person, that's a thrill." Domino's band leader Bartholomew had released his own hit the year before, 1949's "Country Boy." Huey encountered him another time when he competed in a talent show at Hayes' Chicken Shack on Louisiana Avenue and Saratoga Street. Said to be the best black restaurant in New Orleans, it advertised itself as "Just a Step Ahead in an Atmosphere of Refinement." The thirty-year-old Bartholomew sat at the Hayes bar in his sharp leather jacket while the fifteen-year-old Huey nervously fingered the riff from "Country Boy." Despite his stage fright, he won second prize, placing just behind a girl in his class who sang Oscar Rasbach's often performed and recorded musical setting of Alfred Joyce Kilmer's poem "Trees," featuring the famous opening lines, "I think that I shall never see, a poem as lovely as a tree." Both an applause meter and O. C. W. Taylor, educator, businessman, and cofounder of the *Louisiana Weekly*, determined the contest's winner.

Huey soon found a way to overcome his shyness. Seeking the courage to kiss his girlfriend goodnight, he drank a beer. "That was the reason I drank it, not because I wanted the beer," he said. "I never liked none of that. Never. It changes you. It makes you think you're the wolf man."

2

New Arrivals

Huey and his friend Jerry hung out together at Jerry's father's grocery store. Huey would help out on Saturdays, plucking feathers from chickens and doing other odd jobs. Because Jerry kept a piano and drum set at the store, the boys played music together there. One day when Huey passed by on his way home from school, Jerry told him that a gentleman playing a guitar had been in the store. "Sound like Gatemouth Brown," Jerry said. "I want you to meet him."

The man with the guitar was twenty-three-year-old Eddie Lee Jones, a blues singer and guitar player from Hollandale, Mississippi. Tall and slim, Jones took the stage name Guitar Slim. A crowd-thrilling dancer in his hometown, he'd previously been known as Limber-Leg Eddie. His singing experience included a church choir and a blues trio. Hoping to become a recording artist, the former cotton plantation worker arrived in New Orleans in 1950. He performed anyplace he could scratch up some money, including street corners. Veteran New Orleans singer, guitarist, and pianist Pleasant Joseph, professionally known as Cousin Joe, met Slim when the new arrival was playing for wine at the Savoy on Conti and Burgundy streets. "Nobody knew about this boy," Joseph said. "He was sitting in a booth, you know, and he had his guitar with him, a straight guitar, not electric."

Jerry told Huey he'd give him a call when Guitar Slim came by again. The call came one evening, and Huey ran over. He played a few things with Slim and their quickly profitable partnership began. "I'm going to high school, but I had more money in my pocket than the other kids because we played three clubs on the weekend, just me and Guitar Slim."

The pair was playing at the Hotel Foster on LaSalle Street when Huey's mother arrived in search of her teen son. "Huey doesn't have any business in here!" she protested. Slim countered, saying, "He in here with adults." Huey stayed, but when he got home that cold night he found the door locked. Because his parents had separated, he had somewhere else to stay. "I ran straight to my daddy's. It wasn't too far. I start staying by my daddy's house."

Guitar Slim would go looking for Huey at Walter L. Cohen High School. "A man out there and he looking for Huey!" a boy shouted one day when Slim arrived. Slim's appearance, including orange hair and pant legs of contrasting bright colors, tickled the students. They crowded the school's windows, laughing at the man outside who resembled a clown. But Slim had something serious on his mind. "Come on, boy," he told Huey. "The man at the Tiajuana want us to play on intermission."

Like the Dew Drop Café, Club Tiajuana on Saratoga Street was a major African American nightspot. A year away from high school graduation, Huey dropped out to perform with the flamboyant Slim. He didn't mind doing so. His reluctance to go to school sprang from his misspelling "Jehovah's Witness," his mother's religious affiliation, on a school information card. He'd written it as "Jehobah" rather than "Jehovah." The teacher's reaction to the card startled him. "Look at there!" she said angrily as she pointed to the card. "You can't even spell it!"

"From then on," Huey remembered, "like every five minutes, she say, 'You think you something?!' I was astounded. I didn't want to go back to school no more."

Guitar Slim and Huey got a second break at the Tiajuana when the venue's regular band—featuring singer-pianist Spider Bocage, later known as Eddie Bo—left town for an engagement in Mexico. Tiajuana owner Oscar Bolden asked Slim to fill in. The step up in billing led to the duo adding a drummer. Eddie Bo and his band stayed in Mexico longer than Bolden expected. By the time they returned, Slim and Huey had become their permanent seven-nights-a-week replacements. A Tiajuana comedian cracked jokes about young Huey's slight frame. "Huey's so skinny, you got to put two bricks in his pockets to keep him from flying away!" The pianist also was called "breath and britches."

Some members of Huey's earlier band, the Joy Jumpers, protested when they learned he was working with Guitar Slim. "That's our piano player!" "Well," Slim said, "y'all pay him then!" And after nightclub owner and promoter Melvin Cade hired Huey to accompany Mr. Google Eyes for a show in Biloxi, Mississippi, Google Eyes told Slim, "This is my piano player!" "Well," Slim repeated, "you pay him then!" Apparently Slim's contention that Huey should be paid was too strong to refute.

Huey, knowing how important a bass player is to a band, offset the Guitar Slim trio's lack of a bassist by playing deep left-handed piano patterns. "I put a bass player in our band with my left hand," he said. "So I had to do that with an octave. And I amplified it. But it was no specific plan, not that that's the way I would normally play. In fact, it limited me because I didn't play too much with it. And Professor Longhair also was playing a bass line, all the time." Huey also adapted to Slim's habit of not completing all twelve bars, or measures, of a song. Musicians called it "jumping time." Slim also added measures to songs. "Slim was going the wrong place and I went wrong with him," Huey explained. "The people didn't feel it because we were wrong together." Besides being musical partners, Slim and Huey were great friends. They were seen together so often that people called the pianist Slim's shadow. Huey's friend Earl King thought they were brothers.

In August 1950, Guitar Slim made his debut at New Orleans's top African American night spot, Frank Painia's Dew Drop Café. Some weeks later the *Louisiana Weekly* described him as a blues sensation and an exact copy of Clarence "Gatemouth" Brown. Painia held Slim over at the Dew Drop week after week.

Showman Guitar Slim performed with an unusually long cord that let him roam through the club, out the door, and into the street. "That's what people used to be amazed about," Huey said. "And he turned that thing up loud, and you heard it all down the block. And he played it behind his head, acting a fool. He was a *performer*." Slim even brought his guitar into an outhouse, wailing all the while. Other singer-guitarists followed Slim's lead in showmanship and amplified distortion. The list includes Jimi Hendrix, the brilliant improviser who detonated the electric guitar's sonic potential, became an international star during the psychedelic 1960s, and, like Slim, died young; Stevie Ray Vaughan, the fiery blues-rock star from Texas who took Slim's songs "The Things That I Used to Do" and "Letter to My Girlfriend" to that summit of concert venues, Carnegie Hall, in 1984; Frank Zappa, the leader of the irreverent 1960s and 1970s rock band the Mothers of Invention and a vastly imaginative musician and composer who cited Slim's "mangle-it-strangle-it attitude" as his "aesthetic guidepost"; and Buddy Guy, the Louisiana-born singer-guitarist who left Baton Rouge for Chicago in 1957, worked for years in the blues trenches, reached stardom in the 1990s, won four Grammy awards, and was inducted into the Rock and Roll Hall of Fame. "I wanted to be Guitar Slim," Guy said.

Huey met Doretha Ford at a Cohen High School Halloween dance. Though he was dating another girl, he and Doretha danced together that night. A teacher who couldn't help but notice them smiled. Doretha lived a block from Club Tiajuana. "Okay, I'm playing at the Tiajuana," Huey remembered. "Veronica, my girlfriend, was sitting at the piano stool on one side. Doretha came and sat on the other side. We end up seeing each other quite frequently."

Huey was a charming, funny young man, Doretha recalled. "He had a smile that said, 'I know a secret that I am not telling you.' When Huey was in school, he had this following—girls, girls, girls, and *more* girls. And he had a way with words. I told him he could make wrong sound right." His musical talent impressed her, too. "He played the piano at Cohen's talent show and the students went wild. I will always remember the first time I heard him play 'After Hours' [recorded by Erskine Hawkins and Lloyd Glenn]. I sat there in amazement watching him work the crowd. I left that night feeling very proud of him. Yes, that was our first date."

Coming home one evening, Huey spotted Doretha and her mother talking to his mother. He quickly turned around and left. Upon his return, his mother told him Doretha was pregnant. "I resented it because Doretha's mama had fashioned ribbons in her hair and she wore saddle Oxfords for shoes, like what little girls wear," he recalled. "She was probably the same age I was. It just looked a little deceitful." Huey's family pressured him to do the right thing, meaning, of course, marry Doretha. "Me, myself, I was terrified at the thought of leaving my lifestyle and getting married," he explained. He began to avoid Doretha. Eventually, a young lady in the neighborhood, Dorothy, persuaded Huey to soften his feelings toward Doretha. "You know that girl human, yeah," Dorothy admonished him, "but you don't say nothing to her?!" He began speaking to Doretha again, and by the time their daughter, Acquelyn, was born, they'd gotten a room together.

Both Huey and Guitar Slim auditioned for Imperial Records in May 1951. The nervous Huey sang one of the few songs he'd been taking the vocal lead on during his engagements with Slim. Imperial A&R man Dave Bartholomew quickly turned him down. "Well, maybe next time," he said. But Slim, already a crowd-pleasing front man, passed the audition. Huey and drummer Willie Nettles later joined him in Cosimo Matassa's recording studio. The trio cut four Slim originals, "Standing at the Station," "Crying in the Morning," "Bad Luck

Is on Me (Woman Troubles)," and "New Arrival." The latter two sides, released first and credited to Eddie Jones and His Playboys, reached a few jukeboxes but didn't become hits. Follow-up "Standing at the Station" and "Crying in the Morning," credited to Eddie "Guitar Slim" Jones, also failed to chart.

Slim had better luck in the performance arena. Percy Stovall, a blind but shrewd New Orleans agent and promoter, booked Slim and Huey on a circuit of small southern towns. They traveled in Stovall's black limousine, a vintage model that looked as if it had once belonged to an undertaker. Making the vehicle even more conspicuous, the promoter hooked a big yellow trailer behind it. The troupe drove to such nearby places as Gulfport and Biloxi, Mississippi, and Rayne and Gonzales, Louisiana. Traveling for the first time, Huey mailed postcards from each town to his relatives back in New Orleans. "We were just a hop and a skip from New Orleans, but it was just thrilling to be going different places," he said.

But traveling could be dangerous, and not only because the black musicians were motoring through the Jim Crow–era South. Driving east from New Orleans to a gig in Slidell, drummer Willie Nettles sat behind the wheel while Guitar Slim and Huey rode along. Slim spotted a car in the wrong lane rocketing toward them. "Hey, Nettles," he said. "Pull over on the side there and let him have this lane." Nettles refused: "Uh-uh!" "Get over, Nettles," Slim repeated. "No! He's supposed to be over there!" the drummer insisted. Huey, fearing a head-on collision, pleaded with Nettles, saying the other driver might actually want to kill himself. Slim finally put the lid on Nettles's potentially fatal pride. "If you don't get this car over there, I'm go' bust you a' side your head!" Nettles pulled over as the oncoming car sped past, never leaving the wrong lane.

H uey and Slim's Stovall-booked engagements took them to the same towns that Lloyd Price, Clarence "Gatemouth" Brown, Roy Brown, Smiley Lewis, and other black music stars played. Most every place they went Roy Brown had been the week before. The shows were big attractions, and the musicians playing them were grateful for the gigs. "You see all the cars out, like that's all the people have to do," Huey said. "The band members each received like $25 a night. That was good to us. We made seven nights, we got $175."

White policemen, Huey remembered, often confiscated the money black bands made at the packed dances. After lying in wait, the officers stopped musicians on their way out of town, charged them with bogus violations, and seized their money. The entertainers learned they could avoid such traps by sneaking through back streets and cotton fields.

During the Stovall troupe's road trips, Slim expressed his peculiar religious views. "See, that tree might be God," he speculated. One of the other musicians, a tenor sax player and college boy named Calvin Cage, impressed Stovall and the others with his philosophy. "Man created God," Cage espoused. "You see, humans need something to keep them in line. So they developed this concept about a god." Besides his atheism, Cage was noted for his large head, which inspired his bandmates to nickname him after cartoon character Elmer Fudd. Cage was odd in another way, too. Unlike the other musicians, he did not chase girls. "I'm saving myself for marriage," he explained.

Guitar Slim had a habit of naming musicians after their instruments. For instance, he'd say, "Oscar 'Drummer' Moore" and "Tenor Red." Some names didn't take, but others, such as Huey "Piano" Smith, stuck.

Touring was an eye-opener for Huey. Stopping in Nashville in 1952, the group played Grady's Supper Club, an establishment that offered patrons illegal gambling as well as entertainment. Rumor had it that Fats Domino, who played an extended engagement at Grady's in April 1952, lost $100,000 there. And it was at Grady's that Huey first saw homosexual couples in public. The sight of two men sitting at a table together, holding hands, astonished him. "Male couples and female couples, I mean *openly.* And more than that—you come downstairs and two policemen in uniform say, '*Hi* there.' We ain't never seen nothing, ever, nowhere before like that. I guess we were looking stupid, staring at them, so we looked the other way."

Little Eddie Lang, a diminutive sixteen-year-old singer-guitarist, also traveled with Stovall's group. Known as the Boy Wonder, Lang played the guitar just like B. B. King. Lang and Guitar Slim made a crowd-thrilling pair, Stovall said. "Business started coming, like pouring water from a pitcher. Everybody wanted to see that little boy and that man walking tables, walking the bars."

One of Lang's girlfriends became enraged at the Boy Wonder, perhaps about some sexual indiscretion, just as he was going on stage at Grady's. "Soon as you get down, I'm go' circumcise you!" she screamed. Stovall became furious with Lang, too, after the youngster bought himself a mouthful of gold teeth. "I can't book you like that!" Stovall yelled. "Got all that gold in your mouth like that now! You done messed up everything!"

In addition to performing in Nashville, Guitar Slim and his band recorded for Nashville-based independent label pioneer Jim Bulleit. Cofounded by the former Grand Ole Opry booking agent in late 1945, Bullet Records issued hillbilly and pop recordings as well as white and black gospel. Bullet's best sellers came in the late 1940s via rhythm-and-blues releases by versatile Nashville singer-pianist Cecil Gant and risqué jump-blues shouter Wynonie Harris. Guitar Slim's only release for Bulleit's J-B Records, a gloomy blues number called "Feelin' Sad" and the gospel-based "Certainly All," features Huey at the piano. Bulleit perhaps unwisely issued the disc under Slim's real name, Eddie Jones. Like Slim's earlier Imperial recordings, neither song caught on.

In Nashville, Huey met Richard Penniman, a singer and piano player from Macon, Georgia. They ran into each other another time in Florida. "He started singing, no music whatsoever," Huey remembered of this later meeting at a hotel bar in Pensacola. "I got goose-pimples on my arms." Huey couldn't wait to tell Johnny Vincent—the twenty-eight-year-old producer, artist, and repertoire man and roving southern goodwill ambassador for Art Rupe's Hollywood-based Specialty Records—about Penniman. But Vincent let the future star slip away. Three years later, Bumps Blackwell, also with Specialty, booked Penniman into J&M Recording Studios in New Orleans for sessions that would yield the singer's breakthrough hit. "But when Richard start to making them records, he was screaming and hollering," the disappointed Huey said.

Along with Guitar Slim, Huey Smith, and Little Eddie Lang, Stovall's talent pool included Dave Dixon, a singer who would later record for Savoy Records. During a show at the policemen's ball in Baton Rouge, Dixon got drunk and, oblivious to whomever might see, urinated in a flowerpot. His inebriated display didn't stop Stovall's entertainers from being booked at the policemen's ball the next year. In fact, attendance at the follow-up engagement doubled from the previous year. And once the musicians had played their full show for the night, Huey said, the crowd wanted more. "The people said, 'Where y'all going?' 'Well, we fixing to close down.' 'No! We came here to see the nigger pee in the flower pot!'"

It was the funniest request Stovall and the others had ever heard. Stovall, a nasal-toned stutterer, told Dixon he'd have to do an encore: "Dave, I believe you have to urinate in the flowerpot." Dixon hesitated. He wasn't drunk that year, so Stovall counseled and encouraged him. "Go get you something to drink then, because you go' have to do that before we leave here." And so Dixon urinated in the flowerpot again, inspiring screams of approval from the policemen and their wives. "That's what they came to see," Huey said, "and that came to be part of the show."

Teasingly, Stovall would muse out loud about firing Huey, whom he'd nicknamed Survivor, after a character played by Glenn Ford in the 1953 film *The Man from the Alamo*. The promoter suggested Allen Toussaint, another young New Orleans pianist, as a replacement. "We got to get rid of Survivor," Stovall said. "Ehh, what that boy name? Two Pennies?"

H uey and Earl King were among the young singers, songwriters, and musicians who gathered at Victor Augustine's little record and voodoo shop at 2019 Dryades Street. Augustine's place was part of a busy African American commercial district, located in the same block as Labadot's Meat Market, the Peoples Barber Shop, Lovelee Beauty Salon, and Dryades Cash Grocery. "Doc's place had candles, dream books, and dollars all over the floor," Huey said. "He believed in voodoo. Me, myself, I thought that was stupid, really. Doc never was engaging in nothing like that when we was there, but that was the basis of his place."

Augustine dubbed himself Doc the Mighty. He read palms and sold charms and dream books that supposedly contained lucky numbers for an illicit lottery popular nationwide among blacks. Augustine also owned a small label, Wonder Records, and acted as a talent scout for out-of-town record companies. Specialty Records owner Art Rupe—whose 1952 scouting trip to New Orleans yielded nineteen-year-old Lloyd Price's national crossover hit, "Lawdy Miss Clawdy"— considered Augustine an asset. "He's very friendly to us and will act as a good bird dog for you," Rupe wrote to his staff.

Augustine kept a worn piano and cold drinks in the back of his shop. Record companies knew about his little place and sent representatives there in search of songs and talent. Huey was a regular. "We be in Doc's all the time, banging on the piano back there with the curtain shut," he said. "We pass away time. We didn't go in the Dew Drop yet."

"Huey," Earl King recalled, "was a guy around there would play the piano for these people auditioning." Augustine invited Earl and guitarist John Davis to visit the shop after hearing them sing gospel on a street corner. "You boys ought to be singing the blues because you could make a lot of money," he advised.

The mutually musical Huey and Earl were born twelve days apart. Eddie Bo remembered seeing them together every day. "Those two were inseparable for so many years," the singer-pianist said. But when Huey, already working with Guitar Slim, first got entangled with Earl, he didn't know Earl was even interested in music. "Earl just was one of the boys on the street," he said. "Me, him, and Edgy looking for girls."

Sisters Efzelda and Herreast Johnson were among the girls who came to Augustine's shop, usually with their protective mother, Mattie. The sisters formed a vocal trio with a girl named Geraldine. "We would practice with Huey," recalled Herreast, the future wife of Donald Harrison Sr., big chief of the Guardians of the Flame Mardi Gras Indian tribe. "Huey helped us. He was still a teenager and very thin, but he always had a mature look about him. He was nice and, boy, those tiny fingers used to just fly on the piano. I mean he just had this rocking style."

Huey called Herreast "Hearse" for short. He, Earl, and their friend Edgy were at Zel and Herreast's home when Edgy begged their mother to let the girls go out with them. "Miss Mattie, we go' bring them home *early*," he pledged. Reaching into his back pocket, Edgy pulled out a handkerchief. A condom flew from the handkerchief, hit the floor, and spun like a tossed quarter. Everyone but Edgy saw it. The other young people laughed as he continued pleading with Miss Mattie. Despite the condom surprise, she let the boys take her girls out. "Their mama was a nice little lady," Huey remembered. "She really liked us."

Lee Magid, a visiting producer and scout for Herman Lubinsky's Newark, New Jersey–based label, Savoy, met Huey Smith and Earl King at Victor Augustine's shop. He produced recordings by both of them in June 1953. Magid and Savoy had a strong history in rhythm-and-blues, including hits by Johnny Otis and Little Esther Phillips. "Lee Magid came down to New Orleans to pick up some rhythm-and-blues acts," Earl remembered. "I went down there and they had a bunch of other writers trying to audition stuff. When any kind of record producer come to town, all the writers that got wind of it, they'd be down there with material." Magid particularly liked Earl's songs and singing. Savoy released Earl's "Have You Gone Crazy" and "Beggin' at Your Mercy" under the singer-guitarist's real name, Earl Johnson. The label also issued two raw, bluesy sides written and performed by Huey, "You Made Me Cry" and "You're Down with Me." A pet phrase—"I'm down wit' it and I can't quit it"—used by

Huey's friend Edgy inspired the latter song. While neither of the two nineteen-year-olds' Savoy records were hits, Huey overheard a neighbor in his apartment building singing "You Made Me Cry." She'd heard him playing the record in his room. Because he didn't like the sound of his voice on the record, he never told her that it was his voice and piano she'd heard.

Both Huey's and Earl's Savoy recordings are in the slow, mournful style typical of early 1950s rhythm-and-blues. Nonetheless, their songwriting was moving in a new direction. "People like Floyd Dixon, Little Willie Littlefield, the Charles Brown sound, almost everything had that particular flavor," Huey recalled. "So you either speed it up or slow it down. Me, myself, I start developing it. I start seeing what—and Earl King is familiar with this—we began to call patterns, a little different from the twelve-bar arrangement."

J unior partner of Guitar Slim though he was, it was Huey who, just as he'd brought Slim to Imperial Records in 1951, brought Slim to Victor Augustine's shop to meet Specialty Records' talent scout and producer Johnny Vincent. Slim was working on a new song at the time called "The Things That I Used to Do." The impressed Vincent booked Slim into J&M Recording Studios for an October 1953 session. Vincent hired Ray Charles Robinson for the session, bailing the twenty-three-year-old blind singer-pianist from Florida out of jail a few hours prior to entering the studio. "He got in some trouble and he called me," Vincent said of Robinson. "So I went down and put up $100 cash and he said he'd play on the session."

Later known simply as Ray Charles, this brilliant future star would soon help set the foundation for 1960s soul music. He'd arrived in New Orleans after working his way through Texas. "So we just sort of wandered down to New Orleans," he said, "just struggling, trying to survive, going anyplace anybody would hire us." Dew Drop owner Frank Painia paid Charles a few dollars to sit in with the band. New Orleans, Charles told the *Times-Picayune* in 1980, "was one of the very first cities that was good to me. I'm talking about the Dew Drop Inn and Frank Painia."

During Slim's J&M session, studio owner Cosimo Matassa recalled, Charles "kept the reins on Slim as best as he could, which, believe me, wasn't easy." Trumpeter Frank "Lefty" Mitchell, one of the session players, claimed Slim smoked three sticks of weed and drank a pint and a half of gin before his arrival and then more gin in the studio. Indeed, Slim often expressed his priorities to Huey. "There's whisky, there's women, and there's something t'eat."

Although Slim's tendency to jump meter precipitated a marathon session, "The Things That I Used to Do" finally got recorded. Huey wasn't there, but he heard a first-hand account of how it went. The musicians stayed in the studio, he said, "from morning to almost the next morning trying to record 'The Things That I Used to Do,' till [saxophonist] Lee Allen said, 'Yeah, that's it!' Slim was off a little bit then."

J&M was the same studio where Slim, Huey, and Willie Nettles had recorded four unsuccessful sides for Imperial Records two years earlier. Matassa worked as his own audio engineer in the compact space. Black rhythm-and-blues artists, including Fats Domino, who'd become a national recording star, were J&M regulars. Another New Orleanian, Roy Brown, cut the song many consider the first rock 'n' roll record, the mighty "Good Rockin' Tonight," at J&M in 1947. Matassa, besides providing a recording facility for the city's black artists, served as a guide for visiting record company people in search of talent. "They didn't have any idea who they were gonna record," he said. "I'd go to clubs with them and tell them about this guy or that guy, or they'd find somebody by talking to band members in the bar or lounge. The Dew Drop was the most active place, but there were a bunch of black clubs. People don't realize that black clubs in this town had big bands, chorus lines, comedians. Full-blown entertainment venues. Really great."

Frank Painia of the Dew Drop Café booked such national stars as Big Joe Turner, Clarence "Gatemouth" Brown, and Dinah Washington, and local entertainers, too. Murals on the back wall depicted the artists Painia loved the most, including Duke Ellington and Fats Waller. In addition to music stars, the venue featured shake dancers, snake girls, and female impersonators. The faux females could be attractive enough to fool even Painia. "Hmm," he gushed as one of them sashayed by, "where you been all my life?" "Whaaat?" the impersonator responded in a baritone voice. The shocked Painia jumped up and ran away. But Painia was no fool. Moving to New Orleans in the mid-1930s from Plaquemine in rural Iberville Parish, the entrepreneurial Painia had successively opened a barber shop, a restaurant, and, in 1945, a nightclub that would shape the music of New Orleans for more than two decades.

An opponent of the South's segregation laws, Painia famously was arrested at the Dew Drop in November 1952 along with white actor Zachary Scott. The police charged Painia with allowing whites in his establishment and permitting them to purchase "intoxicating liquor." Scott, on a national tour with Joan Bennett in the play *Bell, Book and Candle,* and the four other whites in his party, including the actor's wife, were booked with "disturbing the peace by congregating in a Negro saloon, being seated at tables in the place and mingling with Negro patrons and consuming alcoholic beverages." Scott told Municipal Judge Edwin Babylon that he'd visited the nightclub at 3 A.M. in search of talent for USO shows and had been unaware of the city's racial segregation laws. The judge dismissed the actor but warned him that "generally speaking, the colored people resent the encroachment of white people in their midst. It is not a good thing to go into those places, and when you do, go as a spectator, not as a drinker." Judge Babylon also dismissed Painia, adding the condition that henceforth he would need special police permission before admitting white patrons into his establishment.

The other members of Scott's party were acquitted, too, as was Frederick Mason, a twenty-three-year-old black patron. "Why didn't you get out of there?" the judge admonished Mason. "I hadn't seen him yet," the small, hunchbacked Mason answered. "Seen who?" Judge Babylon asked. "The actor," Mason said. "Well, boy, you can put this in your memoirs—you almost went to jail to see a great actor. Dismissed."

The Dew Drop Café got publicity in the *Louisiana Weekly* via ads containing the owner's photo as well as news stories about the venue and its performers. "A new show is on tap this week at Frank Painia's ultra swank Dew Drop supper club," the paper announced on May 30, 1953. The story described Painia as the genial, suave owner of the spot, which "is air-cooled and open twenty-four hours a day."

At the Dew Drop, Earl King reminisced enthusiastically, "I mean, you could see *everything.* And some of the greatest bands in the United States passed through there. If the stars come to play the Municipal Auditorium [the city's 6,000-seat concert venue], their last stop is the Dew Drop. Young entertainers would never get a chance to see these great folks, unless they went to the auditorium, but they could catch them in the Dew Drop for nothing because the stars liked to sit in and jam."

"All the cats played their gigs and then come to the Dew Drop," Eddie Bo enthused. "We jammed, enjoyed each other, learned from each other."

Along with Bo, Earl King, and many more, Huey was a member of New Orleans's extraordinary fraternity of young talent. "Back there in that time, whatever club, it was morning till night, and those were your friends," he said.

For a time, Huey, drummer Charles "Hungry" Williams, sax player Robert Parker (previously a member of Professor Longhair's Shuffling Hungarians band), and blind guitarist-bassist Billy Tate were the house band at Club Tiajuana seven nights a week. "I'd sing, Tate sang, every night," Huey said. "Johnny Adams ['I Won't Cry,' 'Release Me'], he came and sang a song or two. But we had to run Ernie K-Doe off the stage. He just stays up there. He didn't never get tired. We got tired of him. He couldn't sing. It wasn't pleasing at all. But he developed it, so he came out pretty good."

The cocky, resilient K-Doe—who'd later record for New Orleans–label Minit Records and get a national No. 1 pop and rhythm-and-blues hit in 1961 with "Mother-in-Law," written and produced by Allen Toussaint—learned a lot during Club Tiajuana's open-mike nights. He credited his eventual success to sharing stages at the Tiajuana, Dew Drop, and elsewhere with Huey, Earl, Little Richard, B. B. King, Bobby "Blue" Bland, James Brown, and Sam Cooke. "All these young mens, I've been on shows with them," K-Doe said fondly in 1998 at his Mother-in-Law Lounge. "So that's tuned me up like an automobile motor. You be around good people, some of that stuff go' rub off on you." Time in New Orleans also helped Ray Charles—who spent months in the city—and future star Little Richard find their voices. "New Orleans is, to me, the capital of music," Richard said. "That's where I met Earl King. He was a really great singer and guitar player and he influenced my style."

Despite being left out of Guitar Slim's Specialty Records session, Huey was making a name for himself. Earl Palmer, the drummer of choice in a city of great drummers, remembered Huey being well known when Professor Longhair—whose career resurrection in the 1970s preceded his secular canonization as piano saint of New Orleans—had fallen into obscurity. "Huey was the personification of New Orleans piano players," Palmer said. "People didn't know who Professor Longhair was then, but they knew where Huey was because Huey was Uptown. Clubwise, everything was Uptown."

When Huey, at home in Baton Rouge in 2002, read Palmer's praise, he reacted with customary humility. "Let Fess have his glory," he said. He told New Orleans radio station WSMB much the same years before. "They say, 'Yeah, we heard you was the father of this music around here.' I say, 'What music?' 'What we're playing.' I say, 'Well, that would be impossible because when I was a kid I listen at Professor Longhair. Maybe that's the man you talking about.'"

Guitar Slim's raggedly emotional "The Things That I Used to Do" debuted on *Billboard*'s rhythm-and-blues chart on January 16, 1954. It rose to No. 1, staying there fourteen weeks and earning a gold record award. Competing label Imperial exploited Slim's Specialty success by rereleasing the four recordings he'd made with Huey and Willie Nettles in 1951. Slim's sudden national success, however, meant the end of his partnership with Huey. Lloyd Lambert's band, picked to back the new blues star on tour, already had pianist Lawrence Cotton. Huey got left in New Orleans. "And I know it was against Slim's will," Huey said, "because he had a morbid fear to get on a stage without me, because he had what they used to call 'jumping time.' But I didn't hold him back. I said, 'Go ahead, Slim. Make it.'"

The *Louisiana Weekly* announced Slim's tour in its February 6, 1954, edition. "Guitar Slim, the idol of the South's blues colony, takes off this week to Texas and to California before heading to New York City's famed Apollo Theater for his national triumph." Huey's hopes for Slim became reality. Slim performed for sold-out crowds at Washington, D.C.'s Howard Theatre. His week-long engagement at the Apollo, bandleader Lambert said, outdrew Sammy Davis Jr. "That's how hot that record was," Lambert said. Of course, Harlem's Apollo was the apex of the nation's African American theaters. As Jack Schiffman, eldest son of Apollo director and co-owner Frank Schiffman, said in 1971: "On that narrow stage, in that dreary theater, on that grimy street, in that lousy neighborhood, in the world's cruelest city, are displayed as nowhere else the dazzling splendors of the Negro genius."

3

They Got Another Guitar Slim

uitar Slim left a guitar behind along with an amplifier that picked up radio station WWEZ. "Low, but we did hear it," Huey said. Huey also was left with a drummer and gigs to play, so he invited his friend Earl King to sing. "Earl, you want to make a gig?" "Make a gig?" Earl protested as much as asked. "Man, I don't know no songs," he added. "I'll show you songs," Huey replied. "They ain't no big deal." So Earl joined Huey's band for a regular engagement at the Moonlight Inn across the river in Algiers. Everything was cool for a few months, but then the club owner told Huey that his customers missed Slim's flashy guitar playing. "We like Earl over here, but we need somebody to play guitar," the owner explained. "See, these people used to that guitar but I can't afford to pay no extra for a guitar and Earl, too. We need somebody to sing and play guitar." "Well, we'll take care of that," Huey assured him.

Huey had learned a Clarence "Gatemouth" Brown song from Slim. "Slim used to sleep with his guitar," Huey said. "Like, when I was waiting for Slim to get out the bed and get dressed, I just picked up his guitar and played."

"Huey played a little guitar himself," Earl confirmed. "That's why he was able to tell me about the things that Slim did with the guitar."

Huey showed Earl what to play but found that Earl not only knew it already, it was easy for him. "So, I said, 'We're going over there to the Moonlight Inn, you're going to sing and you can put the guitar over the back of your head.' We did that and, man, people fell out! They said they had another Guitar Slim!"

Earl modeled himself after Guitar Slim, both as a performer and songwriter. "Guitar Slim was the performingest man I've ever seen," he marveled. "A lot of people didn't take Slim seriously, but I did. Slim gave me the idea to write lyrics from a psychological approach, saying things that people want to hear."

Huey also played one-nighters with New Orleans singer-guitarist Smiley Lewis, an Imperial Records artist who was a favorite of Imperial producer Dave

Bartholomew. A burley man with a big, brassy voice, Lewis would turn to his favorite pianist and say, "Come on, boy. Show them how the piano work!" When Lewis performed engagements that Dew Drop owner Frank Painia booked for him in surrounding towns, such as Covington and Raceland, Louisiana, and Moss Point, Mississippi, he insisted on bringing Huey along. "Naturally," Huey explained, "since Smiley liked my piano playing, wherever he go he want me, even if another band was there, due to the fact that he'd be wanting to sound as close to his records as possible."

A trilling piano intro and solo played by Huey became a signature part of Lewis's biggest hit, 1955's "I Hear You Knocking." Written by Bartholomew and Pearl King, the song reached No. 2 on the rhythm-and-blues chart, but a cover version by actress and singer Gale Storm stopped the Lewis original's rise in the pop charts, much to Bartholomew's disappointment. "Smiley wasn't going to make it because a white girl cut him out completely," the producer said. In the succeeding few years remakes by Fats Domino and Elvis Presley of songs previously recorded by Lewis would become vastly more successful than the Lewis originals. Regionally popular in 1954, "Blue Monday," a Bartholomew composition, was a No. 1 R&B hit and No. 5 pop hit for Domino in 1957. Presley's rendition of Lewis's 1956 rhythm-and-blues hit "One Night," another Bartholomew-King song, was a No. 4 pop hit and No. 10 R&B hit in late 1958. "We just couldn't get Smiley started," Bartholomew recalled. "His records would sell great all around New Orleans but we just couldn't break him nationally like everyone else."

Unlike the proudly unfaithful married men of New Orleans, married women with boyfriends were supposed to keep their infidelity quiet. Some "confusement," as they say in New Orleans, involving a married woman and Guitar Slim prompted Huey's mother to warn him that trouble was heading his way. "A man looking for you to kill you," Mrs. Smith said. "What man?" Huey asked. "His name James," she said. Huey protested. "I ain't got nothing to do with his wife! That's Slim." Later, Huey was standing outside of the Dew Drop Café when the man he'd been warned about, James Armstrong, arrived waving a pocketknife. People moved from the angry man's path, but Armstrong soon proved a tolerant husband. In an hour's time, Armstrong, his wife, Albertine (aka Slim's girlfriend), and Huey were drinking together at the same Dew Drop table. Armstrong explained his change of tone regarding his wife's relationship with Guitar Slim to Huey later at the couple's house. "See, ain't no sense in me hollering," he reasoned. "Because after she do whatever she doing out there, then she coming here. I go to hollering and then I ain't go' never see her no more."

Another time, Huey, a young man definitely not cavalier in the manner of Guitar Slim, did unintentionally get entangled with a married woman. He met her at the Dew Drop. While most of his girlfriends were more girls than women, this lady registered at the older end of his range. She talked Huey into going home with her to her apartment. "It had one way out," he recalled. "That morning, just before daylight—*knock-knock, knock-knock-knock.* 'It's me, baby! Warren.' *Knock-knock, knock-knock-knock.* Boy, boy, boy. After a while it wasn't no knocking no more. I got my shoes and my clothes and hit Canal Street. I didn't stop to wait for the bus. I ran all the way home." Huey was at Club Tiajuana later when he ran into a giggling Joe "Mr. Google Eyes" August. "Huey, a man looking for you to kill you! You were with his *wife!*" Hearing such disturbing news left Huey understandably frightened. His fear intensified when he saw the lady's husband enter the club. Fortunately, the man said nothing and gave no sign that he suspected the young musician had spent the night with his wife.

Hewitt!" Guitar Slim used to tell Huey, "one day I'm go' get a Pontiac station wagon like Gatemouth Brown!" Slim's popularity enabled him to get a car, which he soon crashed into a bulldozer parked near a tricky spot on Loyola Avenue. During his ensuing five- or six-day hospital stay, Huey acted as lookout for the sidelined Slim as he met up with his married girlfriend. More inconveniently, "The Things That I Used to Do" was hot, and the hospitalized Slim was booked to play a ton of dates. "The promoters in these places," Earl King remembered, "they was panicking, man, threatening to sue." Booking agent Painia solved his dilemma by sending an imposter, namely Earl, out as Slim. Photos of Earl, rather than Slim, were even printed on placards advertising the engagements.

Word about the ruse reached Slim. Earl, fresh from the tour, ran into the barely recovered real Slim at the Dew Drop Café. "Earl," Slim said, "I heard you went out there in my place. I better not hear anything you did to mess up my name!" "No-ooo," Earl swore, "everything went well." "They give you any money?" Slim asked. "Twenty-five dollars," Earl replied. The answer angered

Slim, so much so that he went to see Painia and raised righteous hell. "Y'all didn't pay Earl, so y'all gotta have some money for me!"

I n early 1954, Huey entered the studio with Earl King again for a Specialty Records session. Specialty artist and repertoire man Johnny Vincent liked Earl's song "A Mother's Love" because it sounded like Guitar Slim. The record became a Gulf Coast hit in 1954, but Earl later expressed low regard for his Specialty recordings. "Some of the stuff on Specialty, it was okay, for somebody just starting out," he said. "The only great thing about that was I had Huey Smith on most of my early things."

Vincent, though still producing sessions under the auspices of Specialty Records, began plotting the launch of his own label. "Johnny was putting half of Specialty's stuff in his briefcase," Huey said. "He put it out on Ace after Specialty paid for it." Vincent named his new record company after the Ace brand of combs. "I figured Ace would be first on everybody's bookkeeping list, and the first on the list to write checks to," Vincent said.

Officially, Art Rupe's firing of Vincent from Specialty was a money-saving move. Vincent claimed otherwise, saying Rupe balked at honoring their verbal agreement that he would receive royalties for Guitar Slim's "The Things That I Used to Do" as well as recordings by Sam Cooke and the Soul Stirrers, Wynonie Harris, John Lee Hooker, and Frankie Lee Sims. "Oh man, I had me some royalties coming," Vincent said. "That money was so big, that is why I got fired."

After being fired by Rupe and then hired and fired by the Atlanta-based Allstate Distributors, Vincent founded Ace Records, based in Jackson, Mississippi, in 1955. His extensive sales, distribution, promotion, production, and scouting experience meant that Vincent was poised for success.

Just as Vincent was behind the record that made Guitar Slim famous, he also helmed Earl King's first national hit, "Those Lonely, Lonely Nights." Lacking funds to book Cosimo Matassa's New Orleans studio, Vincent recorded "Lonely Nights" at Lillian McMurry's primitive, egg carton–covered Diamond Recording Studio in Jackson. "She'll let you use it for cheap," he told Earl and the New Orleans musicians he'd recruited for the two-hundred-mile trip. Huey played the studio's out-of-tune piano, which Earl and Joe Dyson's band tuned to. Unfortunately, Earl's guitar strings slipped during the session. "Johnny, that's outta tune," he complained. "That's not important," Vincent replied. The response may sound like indifference, but the Ace founder had his studio standards, derived directly from his former boss, Rupe. "I didn't care if the band was playing a wrong note on the thirteenth bar," Vincent explained. "I wanted the words to be clear and I wanted the voice to be above the beat." Earl hated his Ace debut and its out-of-tune instruments. "I liked to die when I heard it," he said. "But it sold."

A woeful blues number in the style of "The Things That I Used to Do," "Those Lonely, Lonely Nights" also was influenced by the heartbroken ballads Earl had heard in southwest Louisiana Cajun towns like Eunice and Opelousas. A blueprint for what would later be dubbed swamp pop, "Those Lonely, Lonely Nights" debuted on *Billboard*'s rhythm-and-blues chart on August 20, 1955. It peaked at an impressive No. 7. But the record also brought Huey the first of many disappointments he'd experience while working with Vincent. Hoping to capitalize on Fats Domino's fame, Vincent added the misleading "Featuring Fats on Piano" to the "Lonely Nights" label. "I want to be me," Huey lamented. "Talking about 'Little Fats.' Like they got two of them!"

"We couldn't wine and dine the disc jockeys the way the big boys did," Vincent rationalized. In addition to imposing the misleading credit, Vincent didn't pay McMurry for the studio time. During a subsequent phone conversation with Huey, he marveled at how persistent she was in seeking the money he owed her. "She still trying to get me to pay her!" he complained even as McMurry stood behind him.

Besides playing for Earl King's Specialty recordings and most of Earl's Ace recordings, Huey played for fellow New Orleans artists Lloyd Price, Smiley Lewis, Ernie K-Doe (during his stay with vocal group the Blue Diamonds), drummer Charles "Hungry" Williams (composing and playing for the 1956 Checker release "Mary Don't You Weep, Mary Don't You Moan"), blind bassist and guitarist Billy Tate, and others. When Imperial Records boss Lew Chudd heard Huey's uncanny recreation of the piano on Fats Domino's "The Fat Man" for Tate's 1955 release, "Single Life," Chudd assumed Domino had been at the piano. Furious, he reminded Dave Bartholomew that Domino was not to play for any recordings other than his own. "I thought I told you to keep Fats off that piano!" "No, that's not Fats," Bartholomew clarified. "That's a gentleman called Huey Smith." Chudd feared that Domino would diminish the commercial impact of his own recordings by sharing his distinctive piano touch with other artists.

Huey's piano isn't the only thing on "Single Life" that echoes "The Fat Man." Veteran New Orleans jazz and rhythm-and-blues acoustic bassist Frank Fields played for both Domino's 1950 hit and Tate's record. Fields was among the city's busiest session men, anchoring studio rhythm sections for Domino, Lloyd Price, Little Richard, and countless others. "You had to be real hard and groovy," he said.

Specialty Records producer Bumps Blackwell hired Huey for the flamboyant Little Richard's first New Orleans recording sessions, held at Cosimo Matassa's studio on September 13–14, 1955. The other players, according to Blackwell, included drummer Earl Palmer, saxophonists Alvin "Red" Tyler and Lee Allen, bassist Frank Fields, guitarists Justin Adams and Edgar Blanchard, and pianist James Booker. "All of them the best in New Orleans," Blackwell said. Huey played for many of the recordings, but Little Richard took the piano for "Tutti Frutti," a furious number that Richard had been doing on stage for years. Because the song's lyrics were too risqué for radio, Blackwell asked Dorothy La-Bostrie, a twenty-seven-year-old aspiring songwriter whose "I'm Just a Lonely Guy" had been recorded earlier that day, to clean up the lyrics. With only fifteen to twenty minutes of studio time left, LaBostrie arrived with the revisions. Blackwell put the new lyrics in front of Richard, who said he had no voice left to sing. "Richard," the producer insisted, "you've *got* to sing it."

There was no time to make an arrangement for "Tutti Frutti," so Blackwell let Richard play the piano himself. "It was impossible for the other piano players to learn it in the short time we had," the producer said. Blackwell later realized that Richard's wild piano was essential to the recording's success. "Tutti Frutti," the explosive final song to be recorded during his first Specialty sessions in New Orleans, made Little Richard a rock 'n' roll star. No one was more surprised than the singer. "I didn't go to New Orleans to record no 'Tutti Frutti,'" he said. "It never struck me as a song you'd *record.*"

The singer's forceful but rudimentary keyboard skills impressed neither Huey nor Edward Frank, a pianist who participated in subsequent Richard sessions in New Orleans. "I guess the thing that made 'Long Tall Sally' was the way he broke up the piano," Frank said. "They had to stop and get the tuner." "Richard jumped on the piano—*yung-a, yung-a, yung-a*—," Huey remembered. "And that went to selling. Okay, then I'm on somebody else's session. I'm going *yung-a, yung-a, yung-a,* too! Producers, A&R men, all of them—especially Johnny Vincent—they want what somebody else is selling. They want to copycat. I like to come creative, but they can't hear it till you come with it and let somebody else copycat you. Sometimes you got to follow to survive, but I prefer leading."

Earl King characterized Huey Smith in the mid-1950s as an encyclopedia of piano players, the entries including Albert Ammons, Amos Milburn, Little Willie Littlefield, Harry Van "Piano Man" Walls, Nat "King" Cole, Lloyd Glenn, Nellie Lutcher, and Charles Brown. "See, Huey listened at all these people," Earl said. "I didn't know anything about no piano players at all, because I only listened at guitar players, but Huey was telling me about these folks and how they function." At a session in Jackson, Mississippi, Earl recalled, "Huey said, 'Earl, I'm go' play an arpeggio on the intro of this song.* I'm go' put everybody in that arpeggio—a little piece of Little Willie Littlefield, a little Charles Brown, Van Walls.' And he did it. Oh, by the way, they got about three people I heard play Fats Domino's 'The Fat Man' to the letter. That's Huey Smith, Sugar Boy Crawford, and Allen Toussaint. Ain't nobody played the piano on 'The Fat Man' to the letter like that."

Adept at recreating the piano styles of others, Huey nevertheless developed a keyboard touch that was his alone. "Like Fats or Little Richard," Matassa said, "if you hear Huey play, nobody has to tell you it's him. He could do the national anthem and you could tell it was him. That's part of that star quality."

"You play what you feel," Huey said of his playing. "If something sounds good to you, you go try to do it. And you repeatedly play it. Then that becomes part of you. Like a person talking, the way they walk, they have a mannerism with everything they do. Like the amount of pressure you might put on the key, somebody else might have another pressure."

Following the regional success of "A Mother's Love," Earl King formed his own band and, in a reversal of fortune, hired Huey for his group. "And I was always gonna keep Huey," he said. "He played with me for a good while before something happened with him. I thought he was joking when he said he had the mumps or something. Then a guy brought another piano player on the gig with me one night in Alabama." Perturbed about the replacement pianist, Earl turned to saxophonist Robert "Catman" Caffrey and asked, "Do this guy

---

*The notes of a chord normally are produced simultaneously, but the notes of a chord executed as an arpeggio are played, or spread, one note after another.

know the music?" "Yeah, he play everything Huey play," Catman answered. The new pianist was Allen Toussaint, a seventeen-year-old from New Orleans who'd formed his first band at fourteen with blind guitar prodigy Snooks Eaglin.

"And right after that, Huey went to doing his own thing," Earl recalled. "I was glad for Huey when he went solo, but I was sorry he left my band. I always loved Huey because we had that kind of charisma together. Huey could always interpret where I was going, getting ready to go, or coming from, yeah."

4

Ace Recording Artist

I n early 1956, Ace Records president Johnny Vincent phoned Huey in New Orleans and invited him to sign with his fledgling record company. "Huey! Why don't you make a record?" Vincent asked. "Well, this will be fine," the twenty-two-year-old pianist and songwriter answered. Huey signed a contract with Vincent at his mother's residence as his friends Chris Kenner, Earl King, and a few others looked on. Even though Huey was legally an adult, Vincent sought to increase the contract's legitimacy by having the pianist's mother sign it, too. "Johnny said he wanted to make sure he had a good one," Huey recalled. "I believe that was the only real contract he ever had." That original contract with Vincent apparently is lost. Huey may well have signed only a recording contract that day, rather than contracts for both recording and songwriting. "Most of the recording artists didn't even write songs," he said later. "So we weren't really familiar with it, if there was any value to the writing of songs."

After the signing, Vincent rushed Huey into Matassa's studio, which had moved into a much larger space on Governor Nicholls Street in the lower French Quarter. He recorded the chant-filled "We Like Mambo" with musicians he was working with at the Dew Drop Café: bassist Roland "Cookie" Cook, drummer Oliver "Snow" Berry, and tenor sax man Robert "Catman" Caffrey. It was a nonunion nighttime session during which only "We Like Mambo" was recorded.

Prominent though Cook's vocals are on "We Like Mambo," everybody joined in. "Might be Cosmo, too," Huey said. "It don't make no difference. We're all saying the same thing. 'Weee like mambo. . . . ' If you fall in there, you're there. It ain't that you're *the singer*. It wasn't like that. Everybody who could open their mouth opened it. We appreciate that. Like somebody passing through there, the mechanic from across the street, stopped in to listen and he's staying to sing. He went home and told his family about it."

Some weeks after the session, Huey heard "We Like Mambo" on the radio for the first time. He was shocked when the deejay followed the song with the announcement, "That's Eddie Bo with 'We Like Mambo!'" Johnny Vincent, hoping to capitalize on Bo's local hit on the Apollo label, "I'm Wise," had pressed a previously unreleased Bo recording from Ace's vault, "I'm So Tired," on one side of an Ace single and Huey's "We Like Mambo" on the other. Both sides, however, listed Bo, who'd left Ace by then, as the artist. "Well, see," Vincent told Huey, "the printer made a mistake. She's go' correct it." Huey's fellow Ace act, Earl King, expressed his anger over his friend's lack of credit. "Johnny, man, what in the hell would you do that for?" "Eddie Bo had this other record out, and I figured he had a little more appeal than Huey," Vincent replied.

"Huey was really up the wall behind that," Earl remembered. "I don't blame him one iota. But Johnny liked pulling little deals and little scams."

Touring in the Northeast, Eddie Bo got requests for "We Like Mambo." "Sing your new song!" kids in Wilmington, Delaware, yelled. "What new song?" the puzzled Bo asked. He'd never heard "We Like Mambo." "So after I listened to it, I could do it," Bo remembered. "It was simple. But everybody knows Johnny Vincent. Huey didn't blame me." Huey's disappointment about "We Like Mambo," which Vincent designated as a B-side, swelled when that side of the record, not Bo's, became a local hit. "All day long, the disc jockeys were playing 'We Like Mambo,'" he said. "I'm passing the high school and the band and drum major are doing 'We Like Mambo.' But the problem with it, when they said 'We Like Mambo' on the air, they said, 'Here's Eddie Bo!'"

Billy Delle, future host of the long-running New Orleans radio show *Records from the Crypt*, was a member of a young group of music-loving friends who attended weekend shows featuring Bo, Joe Jones, Esquerita, Smiley Lewis, Shirley and Lee, and other local acts. Delle remembers "We Like Mambo" being a big local record. "The radio stations jumped on it," he said. "Eddie Bo was on everybody's playlist and his popularity at local gigs increased. But not only did Huey Smith get screwed by not having his composition released under his own name, Bo also got screwed. 'We Like Mambo' became Eddie's albatross. No matter how much cajoling, and we tried on numerous occasions, Bo wouldn't perform 'We Like Mambo.' I think he hated being associated with that song."

A subsequent Ace printing of "We Like Mambo" and "I'm So Tired" did credit "Huey Smith and Band" for "Mambo," but by then the damage was done.

Two celebratory recordings, "Little Liza Jane" and "Everybody's Whalin'," became Huey's first two-sided Ace release. They featured singers Dave Dixon and Issacher "Izzycoo" Gordon (a member of the great New Orleans vocal group the Spiders, and mentor to Aaron Neville), Lee Allen's melodiously swinging sax, Earl King's guitar, and Earl Palmer's rock-perfect drums. Huey had heard "Little Liza Jane," a southern standard since before the Civil War, sung by children in his neighborhood. "Just in the streets," he said. "So, actually, I considered it public domain, but every time somebody do' it, it sounds like what I was doing."

Huey titled "Little Liza Jane's" flipside "Blow Everybody Blow," but Vincent changed it to "Everybody's Whalin'," a title derived from a phrase musicians used to describe a hot band. Huey took offense. "I thought it was retarded to name a song after something not even mentioned in the lyrics!" He also disliked the record being credited to Huey Smith and the Rhythm Aces, a band that didn't exist. Vincent's title for "Everybody's Whalin'" came back to haunt Huey years later. Used as the title track for a foreign LP of his songs, the album's cover depicted a literal interpretation of "Everybody's Whalin'." "A bunch of people sticking, throwing harpoons in whales," Huey laughed. "That's sick! I said, 'Hey, they misunderstood what's going on here!'"

Despite his disagreements with Vincent, Huey came to regard the record company owner as a friend. And Vincent, a white Mississippian in the Jim Crow South, crossed racial lines in an effort to ingratiate himself with the black musicians who were the soul of his company. He socialized with them and adopted their slang and mannerisms, trying, Huey observed, to present himself as a hip cat. "I had a girlfriend, she called Johnny 'Swivel Hips'! And, like musicians talk, he'll hear them call the drums 'tubs' and then he'll say, 'Git your tubs.' And he would be intimate with you, where others may not be. He wants to ride around with you, where others won't. You go to their office, once they say whatever they gonna say, it's over. But Johnny would mingle like with you."

"I would go into every black club in every town and watch the bands," Vincent said. "I was the only white man in there."

Huey and Vincent would drive to the Desire housing project together to pick up Izzycoo Gordon, the mighty-voiced singer who appeared on "Little Liza Jane" and, credited as solo act Junior Gordon, recorded Huey's Latin-tinged "Blow Wind Blow" for Ace in 1956. "Johnny didn't want to ride in Izzycoo's sister's neighborhood by hisself," Huey said. "We were sitting in Johnny's car waiting for Izzycoo and we're eating mandarin oranges. He used to always have a bag of them when we go riding. But this particular day, Johnny said, 'Man, I was on my way down here and just as I got in town some cops pulled me over. They say, 'What you doing hanging around here? Open that trunk up.' I ask him, 'You got a warrant?' Man, he had my arm all in back of my head. And they brought me to jail! All I had in the trunk was some records and stuff like that!"

Vincent had a pet phrase that Huey's father used to say as well. "When I was in the Navy, if I'm washing dishes, you go' see yourself in that dish!" Vincent bragged. "Whatever I'm go' do, I'm go' do it good."

Now that Huey had recording artist credentials, he was credible as a supporting act for groups with major hits. "A recording in the charts, that's all you need from then on," he said. "That's what the agency needed to sell the backup band for Shirley and Lee. 'Little Liza Jane' was just getting a lot of local play around New Orleans, what they call regional sales, but everybody liked it." Huey joined New Orleans singing duo Shirley and Lee on the road as pianist. Headliners Shirley and Lee sang five numbers just before intermission and then returned shortly before the show's end. The band worked through the entire 9 P.M. to 1 A.M. show. "I have to play all night long with everybody," Huey said. "I'm so tired every night and, ooh, my back be hurting."

Shirley Goodman and Leonard Lee, both from the city's Seventh Ward, were high school students when they cut their first hit, "I'm Gone," at Matassa's studio in June 1952. The "Sweethearts of the Blues" followed that success with such teen-themed duets as "Shirley, Marry Me" and "Lee's Dream." The duo released their biggest hit, "Let the Good Times Roll," in 1956, just as Huey launched his recording career.

Married though Leonard was, he and Shirley were more than singing partners. "It wasn't no harmony when Leonard's wife was out there," Huey remembered. "Leonard sitting there, talking, with blood in his eyes. Yeah, fire. The show didn't go too good. He's mad with his lips all stuck out because he can't give no attention to Shirley." Huey and the other band members simply laughed at Lee's dilemma. Meanwhile, Shirley Goodman couldn't help but notice how popular her piano player was. "He had a lot of ladies in his room," she recalled. In general, Goodman was delighted with her young, talented, funny band of New Orleans musicians. Besides Huey, the lineup contained band leader and saxophonist Robert Caffrey, bassist Roland Cook, drummer Oliver Berry, and trumpeter Ike "Diz" Williams. "They took the road by storm," she said. "They were the best band." Older musicians gave Williams his "Diz" nickname because the twenty-four-year-old loved Dizzy Gillespie's be-bop jazz.

Shirley and Lee joined the fourteen-act lineup for disc jockey, rock 'n' roll impresario, and emcee Alan Freed's 1956 Christmas Jubilee at the Brooklyn Paramount Theatre. Topping the bill was Screamin' Jay Hawkins, who'd recently released "I Put a Spell on You," a spooky future rock 'n' roll classic and the genesis for the singer's horror film–inspired stage persona. Hawkins made his entrance by leaping from a coffin. He wore a vampire's cape and used a skull named Henry as a prop.

Diz Williams stood on the balcony by the Shirley and Lee band's dressing room and waved to the thousands of fans lined up on the street below. "Yeah, I'd go out there and clown," he said. "They had crowds all around the corner like, waiting to get to the next show. And the crowd be waving and carrying on." "They were blocks and blocks around," Huey confirmed. "They don't care who come out there on that balcony, they go to screaming. And Diz makes like he's the president giving a speech. He reaches his hand out and motions for his subjects to quiet down." Even though Williams enjoyed playing the role of rock 'n' roll star, he teased Catman Caffrey for playing the role of worldly New Yorker. When the group was in the city, the saxophonist made a big production of reading the *Wall Street Journal*, accenting his sophistication by smoking a cigar.

Ostentatious though Caffrey might have been, he gave Huey good advice. When Shirley and Lee played the Peacock in Atlanta, five hundred miles from New Orleans, he and Huey discussed the perils of Mardi Gras, their hometown's holiday of excess. After all, people got killed during Carnival. "See," Catman cautioned Huey, "like Carnival day, let me tell you something: I get me some beer and turn that television on and don't leave my house." "That was in 1956 Catman said that," Huey reflected decades later. "I reasoned on it and, do you know, ever since then I adopted that. I never go nowhere around New Orleans on that day. I just read the paper about them who's missing and things like that." Indeed, Carnival time produced such newspaper headlines as "2 Are Slain Amidst Mardi Gras Gaiety," "Mardi Gras 'Reveler' Is Fatally Shot," "2 Die in Mardi Gras Crash," and many more annual reports of Mardi Gras mayhem. Caffrey also offered his younger colleague counsel about avoiding the melees that erupted in clubs and dance halls. "Whenever the commotions come, don't never go to running with them people," the saxophonist said. "Take your time and see if you can see where it's at before you move and then go the other way."

Huey followed the advice. "Anyplace we were at when that started, I did like he said and, believe it or not, we didn't have no problem. Don't go to running, because you run right into it."

A large ad and accompanying story in the *Louisiana Weekly* announced Shirley and Lee's January 6, 1957, homecoming show at the Labor Union Hall on Bienville Street. The ad listed supporting acts Smiley Lewis, the Roland Cook Orchestra, and "Huey Smith singing 'Lil Liza Jane' and 'Everybody Whaling.'" Shirley and Lee, the newspaper reported, were returning to New Orleans following a tour of East Coast ballrooms, theaters, and auditoriums. "The youth warblers of song and rhythm are riding an unprecedented crest wave of popularity breaking every attendance record on the seaboard circuit." Admission was $1.50 at the door.

Huey was working with Shirley and Lee when a music-loving thirteen-year-old began hanging out with the band. Bass player Raymond Lewis made fun of the boy. "This young kid trying to be like a little man, trying to be hip," Lewis said. "He trying to follow us with his hand out for fifty cents." The boy was June "Curley" Moore, the same child who'd once stared through the Smith family's blinds watching Huey practice. Curley's mingling with musicians eventually led to his singing on stage with them.

Huey first saw the term "rock 'n' roll" in a 1954 issue of *Jet* magazine. He objected to it. "Well, how they get to naming it?" he asked. To begin with, musicians in his circle moved indiscriminately between blues, rhythm-and-blues, and jazz. "We played all that all the time, not that you go' call this 'this' and call that 'that.' It's *music*." Jump-blues shouters such as Cha Cha Hogan and Wynonie Harris, the latter a star of the genre who recorded sixteen Top 10 rhythm-and-blues hits for Cincinnati's King Records, inspired the rock 'n' roll tag. "They started calling *them* rock 'n' roll," Huey explained. "They the ones hollering, 'She walks right in, she walks right out, we go' *rock,* we go' *roll.*' I felt the terminology 'rock 'n' roll' musicians was insulting. What you mean, 'rock 'n' roll'? That's all you know?" Hogan's 1950 recording "My Walking Baby," released by Dallas's short-lived Star Talent Records, is a good example of blues-shouter lyrics. He repeats "She walks right in, she walks right out!" five times before shouting "She walk!" six times and continuing with "She wobble when she walk! She walks, she walks! She wobble when she walk! She walks, she walks! She wobble when she walk! She walks, she walks, she walks, she walks!"

Limited though Hogan's lyrics were, his refusal to be discriminated against at a New Jersey restaurant impressed Huey. The New Orleans–born singer spent much of his life outside of the South, in Detroit and later Las Vegas. "I remember it so good," Huey said, "because we hadn't seen Cha Cha in a long, long time. Me, Shirley, and Lee, sitting at a table in a little restaurant. A lady came and told us, 'You can't eat here.' Cha Cha, he jumped up from the table and ran three blocks. He come back with the police. We weren't in Mississippi, we were in New Jersey." When the police arrived, the restaurant denied telling Hogan and his fellow black entertainers to leave. Meanwhile, down in Louisiana, Act No. 579 of the Acts of the State of Louisiana 1956 regular legislative session prohibited "all interracial dancing, social functions, entertainments, athletic training, games, sports or contests and other such activities." The law further required separate white and black seating arrangements, sanitary facilities, and drinking water, designated by signs printed in bold letters.

Mac Rebennack, a round-faced, white teenager from the Third Ward who loved black music, began working for Ace Records in 1956. Thanks to his father's friendship with Cosimo Matassa and his own passion for music, the fifteen-year-old Rebennack was a familiar face at Matassa's studio. A fan of Huey's former bandmates, Earl King and Guitar Slim, Rebennack had studied guitar with Walter "Papoose" Nelson, guitarist with Fats Domino and Professor Longhair, as well as future Domino guitarist Roy Montrell. He reminded Huey of Clark Kent as played by George Reeves in the 1950s television series *Adventures of Superman,* and Jerry Mathers, the child actor who starred in the sitcom *Leave It to Beaver.*

Despite his youth, Rebennack became a producer, songwriter, recording session guitarist, and artist and repertoire man for Ace. Late in the 1960s, with the help of producer, arranger, and jazz musician Harold Battiste, Rebennack reinvented himself as the mystical New Orleans character Dr. John the Night Tripper. Despite being a reluctant front man, Rebennack, with his growling vocals and Crescent City–schooled keyboard, earned a Top 10 hit in 1973 with "Right Place Wrong Time." He'd go on to win Grammy awards in the 1980s, 1990s, and 2000s, tour incessantly, record prolifically, and be inducted into the Rock and Roll Hall of Fame in 2011. Huey was a major influence on Rebennack. "It's like so many sessions I played guitar, Huey was playing piano," he said. "I'm sitting there and Papoose is talking with me, say, 'Watch the piano player. Don't just listen at him, watch him. He might do something. Look at his left hand.' Well, I watched Huey's left hand. And people, a lot of other piano players, Edward Frank, James Booker, all told me, 'Hey, you got a lazy left hand, like Huey Smith.' And, I mean, that's *my* version of Huey. And Huey's left hand ain't lazy! Mine was, though, because when I think of Huey that's how it comes out of me. Coming up, he made that kind of impression on us as piano players. Hey, it's a lot of him in all of 'em. Huey is a major part of the whole thing."

Huey was a generous studio musician. He also encouraged Rebennack to etch a distinctive mark on the sessions he played. "Listen to what Huey did on Bobby Marchan's 'Chickee Wah-Wah,' what he did on 'Blow Wind Blow' for Izzycoo [Gordon]," Rebennack said. "I'm not taking nothing away from the artists, no, but what Huey did, his thing, he made a picture that made those records special."

In the mid-1950s, Huey's songwriting was blooming, and according to Earl King, he had an uncanny perception for music trends. "Doc, he always knew where things were going," Earl said. He was a natural arranger, too. "Huey could recite to horn players the progressions he had in his head," Earl said. "I thought, for to carry that around in your head for months, he had to be a brilliant person. Everything he did, it come out of Huey's head. Yeah, that's how he was, and I love him for that."

"Most of the things, I write them in my mind," Huey confirmed. "When I get to the studio, I just think about what I have in mind and put it together. Anybody in the recording studio, I'm go' tell them what to play. So, when I'm doing 'Little Liza Jane,' I tell Lee Allen to blow 'Humoresque' [the Antonin Dvořák classical piece that big band leader Tommy Dorsey recorded swing style]. Our music teacher come up with 'Humoresque' when I was in about sixth grade. I gave Lee Allen a solo and that came to be a standard part of the song. We didn't rehearse it. It might have been the first take. No, it couldn't have been the first take, but it wasn't a problem. And Earl King is playing guitar. I told him 'bluegrass music.' That's the session."

Huey tailored parts with specific musicians in mind, Rebennack added. "He made something different according to the guys that was in that particular band on that particular gig. That's a magical thing. And he had Lee Allen play the melody to 'Humoresque,' which was so like the Dixieland bands did but hipper because it was Lee playing, not no bunch of Dixieland front men. And Huey was catching the real second line on 'Little Liza Jane.' Of course, he had the right cats doing it, but he had that instinct for getting it. And with Dave Dixon and Izzycoo singing on it, man, he couldn't get no better."

Drummer Earl Palmer played the session that produced "Little Liza Jane" and flipside "Everybody's Whalin'," which features hot solos from the drums, piano, and tenor sax. "I told Earl, 'Fill in the breaks.' The same thing with Lee Allen. And I fill mine's in. So we know what we're doing. That's how most of the songs were made."

Palmer's other 1956 sessions included Fats Domino's "When My Dreamboat Comes Home," Charles Brown's "Merry Christmas Baby," Shirley and Lee's "Let the Good Times Roll," Little Richard's "Long Tall Sally" and "Slippin' and Slidin' (Peepin' and Hidin')," as well as recordings by Amos Milburn and Sam Cooke. "If you go' get the best, you get Earl," Huey said. "He was the drummer for the city. And you better be there on the beat, because Earl go' be there." Palmer credited his great sense of time to having been a tap dancer. He danced for tips on Bourbon Street at four or five years old. "Being a tap dancer, you're drumming, syncopation wise," he said. "And I knew the tunes before I played any drums, knew where the bridge was and if there was an elongated chorus or a couple of extra bars. I came by all those things as a dancer."

Busy performing R&B shows with Dave Bartholomew's band and jazz gigs with singer-bassist Earl Williams, Palmer seldom worked with Huey. "But I knew him and loved him. I don't know anybody that didn't love Huey, man. He's always been an introvert, and a lot of people thinking introverted people are stuck up. He wasn't stuck up. If anything, he was shy, but a wonderful person, man, because he was the same person all the time. He never got a swelled head. He didn't write volumes about whatever he created. He left it to your judgment. And what I found about Huey's material is that he never tried to fool anybody or do anything that would be complicated for the listener, be he a musician or not. You couldn't help but like that."

I n 1956, a twenty-one-year-old white singer from Memphis with a movie star face made to melt girls' hearts burst into mainstream American consciousness. Elvis Presley, a lover of white gospel and country music and a student of the black rhythm-and-blues of Ray Charles, Willie Mae "Big Mama" Thornton, Big Joe Turner, and Arthur "Big Boy" Crudup, marched across the South igniting mobs of screaming girls from Virginia to west Texas. When Sun Records boss Sam Phillips sold the singer's contract to major-label RCA, Presley's ascent to national stardom was inevitable. But Huey was not impressed with the teen idol. "Somebody played this 'Don't you step on my blue suede shoes.' I laughed at that. I say, 'You hear this? *Ooh*, this is horrible!' You know, it's marketing somebody. Almost like an election." As for Presley's massively popular remake of Big Mama Thornton's 1953 rhythm-and-blues hit "Hound Dog," Huey said, "he was just singing what she said, but it didn't have none of the flavor. But people bought it because it was *him* singing it, not because of how it sounds. Now, Elvis is better than a lot, but I never saw nothing unique. Matter of fact, I could really count the singers on my fingers that I recognize have something unique. I start off with Larry Darnell, James Brown, Ray Charles, Joe Turner. Oh, another name to put there, too, Sam Cooke. And you may as well put Clyde McPhatter with Billy Ward and the Dominos. Some, it was a power with their voice. Like Guitar Slim, it mostly was derived from his power and his conviction, but he was lacking in musical skill, really."

Huey's black musician peers in New Orleans were oblivious to Presley. "They didn't know he existed," he said. "Like they say some congressman said somebody wrote to him and said, 'If Elvis go' to the Army, would he have to cut his hair?' And the congressman said, 'Who is Elvis?' His people told him he better not let them hear him say that, 'Who is Elvis?!' But the congressman didn't know. We didn't know neither!"

5

Rocking Pneumonia

n early 1957, Huey recorded the song with which he's most identified. Guitarist Earl King, saxophonists Lee Allen and Alvin "Red" Tyler, drummer Charles "Hungry" Williams, and bassist Frank Fields joined him along with singers Sidney Rayfield (Huey's barber) and eighteen-year-old "Scarface" John Williams. An infectious example of pre-funk, "Rocking Pneumonia and the Boogie Woogie Flu" opens with a rippling, often imitated piano riff in Huey's right hand, immediately followed by repeating piano bass notes that let everybody know the party has started.

> I wanna jump but I'm afraid I'll fall.
> I wanna holler but the joint's too small.
> Young man rhythm's got a hold on me, too,
> I got a rocking pneumonia and a boogie woogie flu.

Existing songs, everyday phrases, and an off-color joke are among the inspirations for the "Rocking Pneumonia" lyrics. "When I was a kid a gentleman used to tell me dirty jokes," Huey said before repeating the lines and audibly bleeping the bad words. "'I got the tuberculosis and the Germany flu. I gotta stoppa in my *beep* and I can't *beep-beep*.'" Huey had also heard Chuck Berry sing "I got the rocking pneumonia, I need a shot of rhythm-and-blues" in the singer-guitarist's 1956 pop and rhythm-and-blues hit "Roll Over Beethoven." "So, I got the rocking pneumonia and the boogie woogie flu," Huey explained. And "Old Man River," from the musical *Show Boat*, became "young man rhythm." He based another line on something local singer and emcee Bobby Marchan overheard in a club. Bobby told him that a homosexual sitting at a table said, "I wanna holla but the joint's too small!" "Ooh, Bobby," Huey responded, "now you *know* I had nothing like that on my mind."

49

During the "Rocking Pneumonia" session, Huey kept moving away from the microphone even though the engineer repeatedly told him to move closer to it. Not caring for the sound of his own voice, Huey instructed John Williams to move nearer to the mic. "Get in closer, John," he said. "I'm trying to get a hit out of this."

"Rocking Pneumonia" and countless more New Orleans recordings of the late 1950s feature an extraordinary musician who, following Earl Palmer's move to Los Angeles in February 1957, became the studio drummer of choice in New Orleans. One year younger than Huey, the twenty-two-year-old, left-handed Charles "Hungry" Williams had worked as Fats Domino's valet in the early 1950s. He came to idolize Domino's drummer, Cornelius "Tenoo" Coleman, and practiced on Coleman's drums on the sly. After a stint as a poker dealer on Rampart Street, Williams began sitting in with the Club Tiajuana house band, which included Huey, Robert Parker, and Billy Tate. He soon became the group's regular drummer. Also during those Tiajuana days, Williams engaged in percussion contests with Ricardo Lopez, a Cuban expat who played congas and bongos. Williams's innovative, multilayered drumming evolved from a gumbo of influences, including Latin rhythms, marches, country and western music, and the drumming he'd heard as a teenager in a spiritual church. He emphasized the snare, used very little cymbals, and played a double beat on the bass drum. Williams named his bass-drum technique "double-clutchin'." "I'd take all this and hook it up and make a jambalaya out of it, and it'd come out like this funky thing," Williams said. Fats Domino was among the recording artists using the in-demand Williams. "Before I knew it, man, they weren't using anybody else," the drummer said. "Sometimes, man, I was in the studio six and seven days a week."

It was Huey, Williams said, who named him "Hungry." "I'd order a double-order every time I'd eat. I'd have a plate of beans stacked that high, beans and rice. I'd be walking around looking like a Baptist mule." It was the Dew Drop Café cook, Huey recalled, who noticed Williams's habit of ordering double portions and subsequently described the drummer as "hungry." Billy Tate and other musicians followed the cook's lead, and Charles Williams became Hungry Williams.

The musicians' union slapped fines on the "Rocking Pneumonia" session players for working nonunion. "I got fined five hundred bucks," Earl King complained. "The only guy didn't get fined was the guy who turned union evidence." Despite Earl's dislike for the musicians' union, union sessions paid better than the cut-rate clandestine sessions Johnny Vincent booked. "Say, like Johnny called a union session," Huey explained. "He pays the union and the musicians go to the union office and get their checks. The bandleader got $82 and the sidemen got $41. That was the union scale for recording sessions. But Johnny started not letting the union know. It would be basically four hours. The musicians stay there half the day and Johnny gave them $25 apiece. They needed the money and they would do it." All the while, New Orleans musicians, singers, and songwriters, including saxophonist Alvin "Red" Tyler, never imagined they were making an enduring contribution to the city's already rich musical legacy and American music in general. "We didn't know that it was gonna be big hits," Tyler said. "We were just having fun, getting a few bucks. It won't no big thing."

On tour with Shirley and Lee, Huey was at the Apollo Theater in Harlem when he learned during a phone call home that "Rocking Pneumonia and the Boogie Woogie Flu" was taking off. After Shirley and Lee's agency offered to book rising star Huey, he decided to form his own group. He used the classy early rhythm-and-blues vocal group Billy Ward and His Dominoes as his model. Ward and Huey were both songwriters with an ear for talent who hired singers to work under their banner. Ward's Dominoes included future solo stars Clyde McPhatter and Jackie Wilson. "Like Little Esther and Johnny Otis," Huey said of his concept for a group. "She was singing, but that was Johnny Otis's record, Johnny Otis's shows. So I'm going to have Huey Smith and the Clowns."

He invited twenty-seven-year-old Bobby Marchan, a natural entertainer with a piercing voice and crowd-thrilling stage presence, to join his new group. A native of Youngstown, Ohio, Bobby arrived in New Orleans circa 1954 leading a troupe of female impersonators called the Powder Box Revue. The group earned an extended engagement at Club Tiajuana. "They stayed week after week, so they almost lived there," Huey remembered. Huey's oldest sister, Oddress, was among the many young women who swooned over Bobby. "Woo," she gushed, "Bobby is some cute!" Years before "Rocking Pneumonia" and the formation of the Clowns, Huey tried to use Bobby's popularity for a purpose other than music. "When I first met Bobby, when he came to the Tiajuana, some sisters were living across the street," he said. "I wanted to take one of them out. Her sister told me, 'Well, you tell Bobby to take me out and we'll all go out together.' I told Bobby. He said, 'No, no!' I said, 'Please, Bobby, go out with her.' He said, 'Let me tell you something. See, when I was born my mother wanted a girl. I'm sorry, but you tell her all she can do for me is get her *brother*!'"

Marchan's relationship with Ace Records began in 1955 with a blues single released under a pseudonym, Bobby Fields, because he still was contracted to Aladdin Records. Session players Huey, Hungry Williams, Frank Fields, Edgar Blanchard, Lee Allen, and Robert Parker backed Bobby for "Helping Hand" and "Pity Poor Me." Huey composed Bobby's superior follow-up, "Chickee Wah-Wah," and recorded it with him, too. It's a comic, rocking number in which a reluctant young man wails about being confronted by a sexually aggressive female.

> I didn't know what it was all about,
> so I stood right back and began to shout,
> "Chickee Waaaah . . ."

A story in the March 30, 1957, edition of the *Chicago Defender*, datelined New Orleans, reported that Bob Astor of New York's Gale booking agency witnessed Bobby's "torrid" rendition of "Chickee Wah-Wah" during a visit to the Dew Drop. The Gale agency leased the song from Johnny Vincent and re-released it through Gale Records. The agency began booking Bobby, too, including a high-profile spot on Alan Freed's Easter show at the Brooklyn Paramount Theatre. Just two days before Astor caught his act, the *Defender* reported, Bobby, thinking he'd never make it as a singer, had told his associates that he was ready to quit show business and become a playground supervisor.

"That's what Bobby made and it was half-way hitting," Huey recalled of "Chickee Wah-Wah." "That's why he was in the Apollo as a single artist. And I know Bobby was a good showman. I've seen him turn around to the audience, make one [butt] cheek tremble and then the other. It makes the house come down. Well, that's where the clowning aspect comes from. With the hit record, 'Rocking Pneumonia,' and Bobby on the front line with the group, we were going to be successful. Bobby was aware of that, too."

"I was on the show and Huey Smith was the piano player for Shirley and Lee," Bobby recalled. "So Huey said, 'Bobby, I ain't making no money here.' I said, 'Well, I'm doing real good off the record you wrote for me.' He said, 'Yeah, but *I* ain't making no money. Let's go back to New Orleans and see if we can't put a group together.' And that's what we did."

Huey gave Shirley Goodman two weeks' notice. She paid him $100 for the two uniform jackets he wore on stage with the band. She also balled a $50 bill up and pressed it into his hand. Huey's replacement, Allen Toussaint, dropped out of New Orleans's Booker T. Washington High School to join the tour. Huey and Bobby caught a train home from Baltimore.

Road manager Billy Diamond—who'd been Fats Domino's road manager till the star's drinking, tardiness, and missed shows helped ignite riots that led Diamond to fear for his life—and others in Shirley and Lee's troupe doubted that Huey would really form his own group. "He was so quiet, we didn't think he was gonna do it," Diamond said. But upon returning to New Orleans, Huey recruited "Scarface" John Williams and Sidney Rayfield, the singers with whom he'd recorded "Rocking Pneumonia," to join him and Bobby in the new group. Huey Smith and the Clowns made their debut just outside of New Orleans at a small club in the Jefferson Parish community of Shrewsbury. "They made placards of some old picture they had of me looking like Ed Sullivan," Huey said with a laugh. The fledgling Clowns performed Huey's songs as well as material by other groups, such as the Coasters' "Searchin'" and "Young Blood." During the latter song, Roosevelt Wright, a tall young man in the audience who frequented Club Tiajuana, filled in the bass vocal part. "He was deeper than the Coasters' bass," Huey marveled. "The people were screaming. So I say, 'Hey, Bobby, get him.' From then on, Roosevelt was in the group."

Huey "Piano" Smith and his Clowns, featuring Bobby Marchan, performed Sunday, June 9, 1957, at New Orleans's Labor Union Hall, a venue that played host to such national stars as Ray Charles and Sam Cooke. Admission was $1.50 at the door. Professor Longhair was the opening act. The following Sunday, Dew Drop Café owner Frank Painia booked a show billed as Huey Smith and His Orchestra at the Sans Souci Ballroom.

On June 17, 1957, *Billboard* featured "Rocking Pneumonia and the Boogie Woogie Flu" in its "This Week's R&B Best Buys" column. The record's A-side, identified on the label as Part 1, features vocals, while the B-side, Part 2, is mostly instrumental. "Smith chalks up a strong selling job on a medium-beat blues," the review states. "Part one is a low-down vocal with a gutbucket piano and baritone sax moaning in the background." The magazine spotlighted "Rocking Pneumonia" again in its July 8 edition. "The platter heads the list on the New Orleans best-selling chart and it is a very strong southern favorite. It also has caught on in the other top markets and figures to be a big one." *Billboard*'s "R&B Territorial Best Sellers" Top 5 for New Orleans listed "Rocking Pneumonia" above Larry Williams's "Short Fat Fannie," Fats Domino's "Valley of Tears," Chuck Willis's "C. C. Rider," and the Coasters' "Searchin'."

"Rocking Pneumonia" debuted on *Billboard*'s rhythm-and-blues chart on July 15, 1957. Johnny Vincent pumped up the publicity in the trade magazines:

> The hottest R&B, pop, & rock-a-billy record of 1957. "A Rockin' Pneumonia and the Boogie Woogie Flu" by Huey Smith and his Clowns. 10,000 sold in 8 days in New Orleans—7000 in Philla.—6000 in Memphis—and SPREADING everywhere.

On an oppressively hot Louisiana summer day, Huey and Sidney Rayfield drove to Lincoln Beach, the carnival-like amusement park for blacks on Lake Pontchartrain. They heard "Rocking Pneumonia" playing everywhere, over and over again. "It's hitting, taking off, and that's all they played," Huey said. "You get tired of anything, but we didn't get tired of 'Rocking Pneumonia.' And then when we left Lincoln Beach, the first place we passed we heard it again. And then we heard it on the radio while we're riding. Yeah, that's all they played all day long. That's how we know we was in."

Two "Rocking Pneumonia" covers were swiftly cut—one by veteran West Coast rhythm-and-blues star Roy Milton and his wife, Lake Charles, Louisiana, native Mickey Champion, for Cincinnati's King Records, and another by New Orleans's own Larry Williams (with Art Neville) for Johnny Vincent's former employer, Specialty Records—but the Huey and the Clowns original became *the* hit. Peaking at No. 5 on *Billboard*'s rhythm-and-blues chart and No. 52 on the pop chart, "Rocking Pneumonia" meant Ace Records was in, too. Vincent's southern independent would become one of the most commercially potent New Orleans–linked labels.

Huey was a newly risen recording star when he and the Clowns performed on August 4, 1957, in a multi-act show starring Roy Hamilton at New Orleans's Municipal Auditorium. It was the first time Huey's mother saw her suddenly famous son perform with his group. Bobby Marchan recalled: "I remember we played with Roy Hamilton on that great big show. So we had tuxedos cut down to Bermuda shorts, and we came on, our hometown, New Orleans, at the Municipal Auditorium with black tuxedos, Bermuda shorts suits on. It tore the house down." In addition to Hamilton—a 1950s star who sang his rhythm-and-blues chart hits "You'll Never Walk Alone," "Ebb Tide," and "Unchained Melody" with an elegant mix of classical technique and gospel conviction—the performance featured Annie Laurie, the Spaniels, Johnny and Joe, Screamin' Jay

Hawkins, Huey Smith and the Clowns, the separately billed Bobby Marchan, Donnie Elbert, and Ella Johnson and her bandleader brother Buddy Johnson with his big band.

The New York–based Hamilton was touring the segregated South with a white music director. A Municipal Auditorium official, in accordance with Louisiana law, forbade conductor-pianist Graham Forbes from joining Hamilton and the band on stage during the night's Negroes-only late show. Forbes, a white casualty of Jim Crow, conducted the band from behind the auditorium curtains. His distance from the musicians and their obstructed view of him, the *Louisiana Weekly* reported in a front-page story, hindered Hamilton's performance.

Regardless of the era's segregation drama, the happy-go-lucky Clowns played on stage and off. "We were always clowning," Bobby said. "We were the Clowns." "Like, we just used to hang out all day long in the Dew Drop," Huey said. "And the Clowns be doing the same jokes, just like when we get up there on stage."

"Rocking Pneumonia" appeared in what may be rock 'n' roll's greatest year. In addition to continuous hits from white teen idols Elvis Presley and Pat Boone, 1957 saw the debuts of Fats Domino's "I'm Walkin'," Lloyd Price's "Just Because," Jerry Lee Lewis's "Whole Lot of Shakin' Going On" and "Great Balls of Fire" (all of the latter three artists from Louisiana), Chuck Berry's "Rock & Roll Music," Little Richard's "Lucille" and "Jenny, Jenny," and Buddy Holly's "Peggy Sue."

Despite the breakout success of "Rocking Pneumonia," Johnny Vincent didn't pay Huey—the artist and composer who put Ace on the national map—properly documented royalties for his recordings and songwriting. Being a rare white man in the Deep South who socialized freely with blacks didn't translate to Vincent accurately compensating them for their musical labors.

S. J. Montalbano, founder of Montel Records, the Baton Rouge label that would release Dale and Grace's No. 1 pop hit, "I'm Leaving It Up to You," in late 1963, learned a lot from Vincent. Like Vincent and Cosimo Matassa, Montalbano was a young southerner of Italian heritage who loved music. "Cosmo and Johnny was my mentors," he said. "And Johnny was very big. He was shrewd and he knew a lot of important people in the business." But Montalbano disliked Vincent's modus operandi. "I didn't appreciate the way Johnny treated his artists. Huey was a good friend of mine and I know he got royally done. I mean he didn't get one-fiftieth of what he deserved. And that's also a study in itself of that era."

Montalbano and Vincent were at Cosimo's recording studio on Governor Nicholls Street, a lower French Quarter spot where musicians and music business people hung out, when Vincent told his protégé that Huey was coming by. "So before we go over and listen to this other band, I gotta give Huey his royalties," Vincent said. "Oh yeah, that's right," Montalbano said, "he's got 'Rocking Pneumonia'! How much he got coming?" "I'm a' give him that station wagon they been using," Vincent said as he pulled the title from his coat pocket. "I put it in his name."

"That's it?" Montalbano asked. "Oh, Johnny, man, you go' give the business a bad name."

When Huey arrived, Vincent handed him the station wagon's title in the studio driveway. "Huey, this is your royalties," he said. Puffing a big cigar, Vincent walked away with Montalbano. "Johnny," Montalbano whispered, "I'm embarrassed."

"Johnny didn't know anything about music," Huey recalled. "Really. Johnny had to look around to see the reaction of something to come to a conclusion. He looked at Red Tyler, especially, to see if he was moving to the beat. Then he knows something sounds good. But Johnny, he can't clap in time, nowhere around the beat. He's just not there, that's all, and you never heard him attempt a note. Never." "Vincent," Earl King agreed, "never came up with no ideas about nothing."

Yet Vincent knew what he wanted. "The most important thing about a record is not the artist, it's the sound," he said. "I wanted to make sure there was a beat on my records. I figured if you could dance or sing along, that was important. I tried to get that out of my musicians." "Johnny had a good ear for saleable products," Earl admitted. "That's where Johnny ends. He would not have put a lyric together if you gave him a million dollars. He don't know nothing about that."

6

Rockin' and Drivin'

With a major rhythm-and-blues hit to his credit, Huey and his Clowns toured on the northeastern black theater circuit, including the Apollo in Harlem, the Howard in Washington, D.C., the Royal in Baltimore, and the Uptown in Philadelphia. The group also played college fraternity gigs in the South and Northeast. Performing provided much of Huey's income because he couldn't depend on documented royalty payments from Johnny Vincent for records and songwriting. By December 1957, the station wagon Huey and the Clowns traveled in had logged more than ninety thousand miles. "We was on the road, back and forth to New York, Washington, New York, Carolina, Georgia," he said.

Before one of the Clowns' early out-of-town trips, Huey realized he couldn't afford to pay everyone. One performer too heavy, he cut singer James Black from the lineup. The decision left Black's friend and fellow vocalist, "Scarface" John Williams, livid. "Black can't go, I ain't go' go!" Williams said. But just a few blocks into the troupe's drive out of town, there was Black, waving the entourage down from a street corner. "I'll go in John's place!" he yelled. Bobby Marchan was all for picking Black up, but Huey wouldn't have it. "No, Bobby, I can't do that," he said. "I wouldn't do John that. How he go' feel knowing that Black took his place like that?"

Williams, the dominant voice on "Rocking Pneumonia," was the adopted son and only child of Della Gatlin Williams. Della, a guitar-playing gospel singer and French Quarter street performer, doted on her son and encouraged him to pursue music above all else. When John did travel with the Clowns, Huey remembered, "His mama would send him red beans in a jar, with no meat, because that's how he enjoyed it. No meat in them, not that it wasn't cooked with meat. So John waited every time we got somewhere for his red beans, coming in the mail at the hotel."

John got his nickname from the long scar that ran from his eye to his chin. The scar proved useful one night when a promoter came up short with the group's money. Bobby Marchan handled such business, but his insistence on payment wasn't the reason the promoter finally surrendered the money. "I'm go' pay you now," the promoter said, "because, see, first of all, my boys scared of y'all boys, especially that one with the scar on his face!" But John didn't get the scar in a street fight. Like bass singer Roosevelt Wright, he was a mild-mannered young man. The scar was the consequence of being hit by a car when he was a small boy and the wound's stitches being prematurely removed.

John's wife, Mary, joined the Clowns during a road trip to Mobile and Phenix City, Alabama. She enjoyed neither the trip nor the way Bobby dominated the group. "Bobby Marchan wanted to run everything and be the main show person at all times," she said. "Huey just let him have his way. And that's the only time I ever went on the road with them. We had to stay in a fleabag hotel. Bedbugs was biting us. I was done with that."

The first thing Huey bought after "Rocking Pneumonia" became a hit was a marriage license. Confident that he was past scuffling for $8 a week in rent money, the hit recording artist and in-demand performer felt secure enough to marry Doretha Ford, mother of his children. He also wanted his and Doretha's oldest child, Acquelyn, to have the surname Smith. Getting married, a lady at the vital statistics office in New Orleans said, would take care of that. Doretha traveled with the touring Clowns to Ohio, where Huey and Bobby Marchan bought a marriage license. The Clowns attended the couple's fifteen-minute church wedding.

"Life with Huey was like living in a three-ring circus," Doretha remembered. "One laugh after another, all the time, and everybody there was a star."

Married or not, Huey and his peers had girlfriends. He'd later regret being unfaithful, but at the time men in New Orleans were thought to be strange if they didn't have girlfriends. They also competed to see who could be the most successful with females. According to Earl King, Huey was extremely success-ful. "Huey, he never missed," Earl said. One of Huey's dates drew a harsh reac-tion from Earl's friend and former gospel-music partner, John Davis. As Huey and the young lady were leaving the Gladstone Hotel in New Orleans, Davis, standing next to Earl, expressed his disapproval of Huey's relationship with

Doris, a dwarf. "Don't you never speak to me no more long as you live!" Davis proclaimed self-righteously. Huey attributes Davis's negative reaction to prejudice. "The reason John said that is because my date was three-and-a-half-feet tall," Huey said. "But Doris was very nice and lovely. As matter of fact, she was important to me." The open-minded Earl took no offense. "Earl was liberal," Huey explained.

Touring with Shirley and Lee in 1956, Huey double-dated in New York with bass player Roland Cook. His date showed up at the theater again in late 1957 when Huey returned with the Clowns as part of the Roy Hamilton Show featuring Jackie Wilson. "I want to give you a picture of my little boy," the young woman told him. "Oh, yeah, that's nice," Huey said as he looked at the photo. "*Our* little boy," she added.

On-the-road romances precipitated some close calls. During one trip, Maryland police stopped bandleader Buddy Johnson's bus because of a paternity matter, but Huey was traveling in his group's station wagon rather than the bus. Another time, Clowns driver Rudy Ray Moore said, some angry men stopped the Clowns' vehicle between Baltimore and Washington, D.C., and mistook Bobby Marchan for Huey. "Some fella was running Huey down," Moore said. "They knew Huey was in the wagon, but Huey knew he was getting looked for and he split. So, these boys pulled Bobby out of the car. Bobby says, 'I ain't had nothing to do with your sister! Furthermore, I don't want your sister! If anything, I'll take you!' The boys got tickled and told us to go ahead on."

Bass singer Roosevelt Wright could be counted on to show up for gigs and rehearsals *and* keep a secret. When Huey and Roosevelt double-dated, they assumed aliases. "Like when we go out, I'm Charles and Roosevelt is my boy, Frank," Huey said. "You're not telling your real name." Roosevelt had many girlfriends, but they weren't necessarily top notch. "Bobby Marchan strutted through there," Huey remembered, "talking about the girl with Roosevelt. And Roosevelt was talking about her, too. Bobby said, 'Look, Miss Roosevelt. You're not exactly a bargain yourself!'"

A double date that Huey and singer and body-and-fender man Lee Dorsey ("Ya Ya," "Working in the Coal Mine," "Ride Your Pony") had in New Orleans with two young ladies from New York landed Huey in jail for a few days. During the date, Dorsey told Huey that the girl he was with wasn't being cooperative. In fact, she turned her eyes and smile toward Huey. "Like I told you, I wasn't no angel," Huey admitted later of his past life. "So I told this girl I had just been with to go ahead on home, that me and the other one, we're going somewhere else. So her and I went in the graveyard on Loyola Avenue."

Apparently Huey's original date got jealous. She called the police and told them Huey forced the other woman to go with him. The police assumed rape. Their scenario was undercut when an officer observed the alleged rape victim kissing Huey good-night as she exited his car. Meanwhile, attorney Charles Levy Jr. told Huey to lay low. Instead of doing as Levy asked, he phoned the police and told them that he was at his auntie's house. Levy got angry. "I thought I told you to stay away till Monday!" the lawyer said. "I can't find no judge over no weekend!" Huey ended up spending the weekend in a cell with a notorious outlaw known as "The Man with the Big Gun." The bandit had robbed so many places that he'd achieved Robin Hood status in New Orleans. During their jailhouse conversation, the famous stick-up man told Huey that he'd never actually hurt anyone. After Levy arranged for Huey's bond, Frank Painia, one of the Man with the Big Gun's victims, bought the two young ladies tickets back to New York.

E rdine Hall, a copper-toned young woman of African, Spanish, and American Indian descent who'd been singing as long as she could remember, worked as a barmaid at the Dew Drop. A natural clown and fan of comic Jerry Lewis, she took the name Gerri. "Pretty as a speckled pup," said John Williams, a photographer who accompanied celebrity disc jockey Larry McKinley to clubs. "She looked like a Mexican girl, and wild like an Indian," Williams added.

Gerri was working in the Dew Drop when a record playing on the jukebox struck her as special. She asked Painia what the title was. He looked for it in the box and found a record with a white label called "Everybody's Whalin'." No artist was listed. Whoever it was, Gerri thought it was the best record in the box. Of course, "Everybody's Whalin'" was a Huey Smith record.

Gerri was part of a Dew Drop scene that included dozens of gifted performers. "We were all there, coming and going, people in the Dew Drop," she reflected. "And I was always singing and dancing by myself." Working one night at the bar, Gerri saw Huey and Bobby Marchan come in. Gerri waited on the local stars as they sat and talked at the bar. "Say, Bobby, how about Gerri?" Huey asked. "I got her, yeah," Bobby replied. The two of them left, but Bobby returned about 11 P.M. "Gerri, come here," he said. "We need a girl to go on this gig." "Oh? What gig?" she asked. "Come on and go to work with us," Bobby said. "Where you going?" she asked. "Atlanta." "Who I'm going with?" "Huey Smith and the Clowns." "Yes, indeed!" "Go get your things, Miss Gerri." The new Clown cleared out her upstairs room at the Dew Drop hotel, took her things to her sister's place, and hit the road running with the Clowns. Replacing Sidney Ray-field, she became the first female Clown. "It could have been a boy, but we desired Gerri," Huey said of adding her to the group. "She's good. She's gorgeous. What else you need to know?"

O n the road with the Clowns, the spotlight-loving Bobby Marchan was in his glory. "Made plenty of money," he said. "Ate good food and just had a stomp-down-party good time. . . . I was the road manager for the group and everything! I handled all the business, period." "Bobby took care of the chauffeurs and the band *and* the Clowns. I guess he was the boss," Huey said and laughed. Bobby also rehearsed the fifteen- and sixteen-piece bands at the theaters where the Clowns performed. "They go' play it right because Bobby showed them how," Huey said. And on the band's days off Bobby contacted promoters. The only thing they cared about was whether or not Huey and the Clowns were in the *Billboard* and *Cash Box* charts. When those promoters showed reluctance in paying for performances, Huey played good cop to Bobby's bad cop. "At a night-club," Huey explained, "if the promoter's not acting right, well, me and him are laughing and talking; but I already told Bobby the promoter's not acting right. Bobby go' come and cuss him out. That's Bobby's job, but I'm go' laugh and wave at them from across the room, yeah."

The rest of the entourage knew nothing of Huey and Bobby's business dealings. While Bobby happily handled the money, Gerri Hall and Roosevelt Wright were having dinner or drinks. Eugene Harris would be walking up and down the street "meddling everybody," as Gerri put it. "Eugene liked to meddle people, he liked to talk to them," she said. Eugene, a former valet for singer Donnie Elbert ("What Can I Do") who later performed acrobatics on stage with John Williams, did not impress Huey. "Eugene didn't have no type of a voice, but he could dance pretty good," he said. "So Bobby gave him a try." But after Eugene complimented Huey's wife, Doretha, suggestively, Bobby took note. "I see you not go' be with us long," he told Eugene. Bobby respected Huey, to the point of insisting that the troupe's singers and musicians address him as Mr. Smith.

As for Eugene, there was more to his name than Eugene, something the rest of the group never knew until he married the sister of New Orleans jazz pianist Ellis Marsalis (father of future jazz musicians Wynton, Branford, Delfeayo, and Jason Marsalis). The minister revealed Harris's full name during the wedding ceremony. "Do you, Francis Eugene Harris, take Yvette. . . ." Upon hearing "Francis," Bobby burst out of laughing. "I didn't know his name was Francis!" the tickled, high-pitched Bobby remarked. "Ooh, *Francis.*" "O-o-oh, Francis!" Roosevelt Wright repeated in his booming bass tones. And everyone started laughing. Francis Eugene and Yvette subsequently made touring with the Clowns their honeymoon. "But he just treated her so bad," Huey remembered. After returning to Louisiana, Eugene and Yvette lived at her father's hotel just outside of Orleans Parish, the Marsalis Mansion. He bragged about his plans to take control of the hotel and fire his own father-in-law, Ellis Marsalis Sr.

The openly homosexual Bobby Marchan delighted in calling men "miss." He feminized men's names so often that Huey caught himself doing the same while speaking to Drifters founder and subsequent solo star Clyde McPhatter. "Bobby had told me what time to come call him from a card game, because he wins all the time," Huey recalled. "I called Bobby and Clyde McPhatter opened the door. Then I say, 'Clydie Mae, is Bobby in there?' Maybe Clyde McPhatter didn't hear me. He didn't say anything. But Bobby got me calling the man Clydie Mae! So, we just got used to him calling everybody 'Miss,' because he really didn't mean no harm."

It was Bobby, though, who took offense when Johnny Vincent asked if he and Huey were lovers. He didn't even let Vincent finish the question. "Don't you never say nothing like that long as you live! I respect Huey. On top of that, I respect his wife, too!" Bobby's quick rebuke knocked the smiles off the faces of Vincent and Joe Caronna, his partner in Record Sales, Inc., a distribution business in New Orleans.

Bobby didn't hide his past from Huey and the Clowns. He told them he'd worked as a prostitute in an area with a heavy military presence. Posing as a female, Bobby never got caught pretending to be a woman.

Even in the repressive 1950s, Bobby claimed he could always spot a fellow gay man. He'd point them out to Huey and the rest of the troupe. They included policemen on the beat in Nashville, a city Bobby knew well. "Them homosexuals, yeah!" Bobby said of some officers. "And," Huey remembered, "if the police open their mouths, you know it! They'd say, 'Hi, Miss Thang.' Bobby told us, 'Yeah, but they good police, too!' And somebody said they were extra strong, like mules."

S ometimes Huey and the Clowns traveled in the station wagon Johnny Vincent provided, dubbed the Rocking Pneumonia. Other times they shared a bus with fellow entertainers, including rock 'n' roll star Bo Diddley. Huey enjoyed hearing Diddley mock the lead character in the controversial television comedy series *Amos 'n Andy*. Featuring an all-black cast led by Tim Moore as the always scheming George "Kingfish" Stevens, the series riled the NAACP throughout the civil rights era because of its portrayal of African Americans and its dialogue filled with mispronunciations and incorrect grammar. "When Bo Diddley talked to you, he talked only in the tone of Kingfish," Huey said of the bus rides. "All day long, sounding just like Kingfish. You wouldn't know it wasn't the Kingfish!"

Huey acted as private banker for another traveling companion, blues star Jimmy Reed ("Big Boss Man," "Honest I Do"). Reed wasn't allowed to carry money on the road because he'd spend it on liquor. He got around the ban by getting interest-free loans from Huey, which he always repaid. "In Canada you had to have a card to buy liquor," Huey said. "Jimmy Reed had a card for every town over there." Reed was a jokester and a troublemaker. After the bus driver told the tour's promoter that he was misbehaving, the blues man positioned himself at the front of the bus. Playing the part of a grandstanding prosecutor, he addressed his fellow entertainers as if they were the jury. Reed turned and pointed his accusing finger at the driver. "You! Don, the bus driver," Reed snarled, "had the nerve to call my boss man! Talking about, 'Jimmy Reed disturbing the people on the bus.' Got the nerve enough to do somebody like that!"

Traveling as often as they did, the Clowns often witnessed auto accidents in the era before seatbelts, air bags, and interstates. "We traveled all up and down the highway, wrecks behind wrecks, turning over, upside down, all kind of ways," Huey said. "The band members, they'd holler, 'Oh, Lord!' I'd say, 'Oh, Jehovah.'" Driving in two vehicles on the way to St. Petersburg, Florida, in 1958, Huey and band members James Rivers, Raymond Lewis, Jessie Hill, and Robert Parker led the way in their station wagon while the singers and dancers who performed as the Clowns followed in a second car. At the small town of Perry, the troupe encountered a hazardous combination of roadway construction and a truck loaded with live chickens. As Parker recalled it, "my back tire went off the shoulder because they was putting down new gravel and stuff. When the tire went off the road, we was loaded down. That back tire dropped two feet or three off the side. The whole wagon just flipped over in the ditch." "A woman tried to miss a chicken," Huey said. "She's trying to miss him, but we end up in bad shape. I know we turned over. And chickens all over the place, all over the ground."

In the minutes after the accident, Hill took off running down the highway. "He's in the middle of the highway," Huey said, "with his head up in the air, like he had just lost track of everything. Somebody had to drive to catch him, and then he came to his senses."

The nineteen-year-old Rivers was badly hurt. "Rivers was sitting in the back by the drums," Parker said. "I think one of the drum legs caught him behind his ear in the back of his neck." "A couple of guys were shook up, but nothing like what I had," Rivers said. "I still got a scar right over my ear. That last lick hit the side of my head." Segregation being strong in the South then, Rivers got patched and sewn in an emergency room and then shipped two hundred miles to a hospital in St. Petersburg. "Blacks not only couldn't be hospitalized in Perry, them people hardly had seen any blacks," he said.

Huey phoned Johnny Vincent in Jackson, Mississippi, but the record company boss was out. Someone in the Ace office told him that Vincent had gone to see if his insurance on Huey was paid up. "Johnny was looking for me to kick off," the amused Huey recalled. "Back there then, $50,000 key-man insurance was a lot of money."

Rivers spent about a week in a St. Petersburg hospital before catching a train to New Orleans, where he continued his medical care. Ace Records paid the bills, Parker said. "He really took care of the man. He didn't throw him away and we didn't forget him either. Because it just was a freak accident. We wasn't drinking or nothing like that. We were just trying to make it to the next gig. And we happened to go down this particular highway and they was fixing it. Somebody coulda got killed, you know."

Accidents were a common occurrence, Huey said. "I had been in a million of them. Sometime you don't feel anything." He didn't think he'd been hurt in the Florida accident, but the pain started later, including headaches and debilitating spinal pain. He took five headache tablets at a time and rubbed ointment on his back. "I'm putting it on all day long. Every once in a while I can't even walk."

7

Don't You Just Know It

Bobby Marchan and Clowns driver Rudy Ray Moore, who later found fame as the foulmouthed underground comic Dolemite, were old friends from their native Ohio. Moore joined Huey, Bobby, and the Clowns during a stop in Cleveland. "They had a Plymouth station wagon with no heater in it, in the hard winter time," Moore said. "They asked me to go on the road with them because nobody in the band had a driver's license."

Moore's pet phrase, "Don't you just know it," inspired the biggest hit by Huey Smith and the Clowns. During a drive home to New Orleans from the Carolinas, the alarmed Huey asked Moore why he was driving so fast. "Because I don't like up here," Moore said, referring to a stretch of elevated roadway. "Well," Huey reasoned, "why don't you slow down? If we get a blowout, we'll still be up here." "Don't you just know it!" Moore responded.

"Like we're riding along," Huey said of Moore's constant use of the phrase, "after everything we'd say, he'd say, 'Don't you just know it!'" "Every time we would go somewhere," Bobby recounted, "and Huey said, 'Boy, that sure is a nice-looking girl,' Rudy Ray Moore would say, 'Don't you just know it!' And he kept on saying that, till Huey got 'round to writing the record."

The comic, high-spirited "Don't You Just Know It" features vocals by Bobby, Gerri Hall, Roosevelt Wright, and Huey plus the distinctive polyrhythmic drumming of Charles "Hungry" Williams. The song's joyful call-and-response chorus is, like so many of Huey's songs, infectious: "Ha, ha, ha, ha! *Ha, ha, ha, ha!* Hey-ey, oh! *Hey-ey, oh!* Gooba-gooba-gooba-gooba. *Gooba-gooba-gooba-gooba.* Ha, ha, ha, ha! *Ha, ha, ha, ha!* Hey-ey, oh! *Hey-ey, oh!*"

Billboard made "Don't You Just Know It" and flipside "High Blood Pressure" one of its R&B spotlight reviews in the January 27, 1958, issue. "The cat goes in for off-beat titles," the anonymous reviewer observes. "He sells 'High Blood Pressure' with the appeal that made 'Rocking Pneumonia' a big one. . . . 'Don't

You (Just Know It)' is a novelty-blues that also delivers with a money sound." Below the review, Johnny Vincent's ad claimed 120,000 copies had been shipped in the record's first ten days, adding that both sides had been covered but no imitation can match "the original with the beat, as only Huey can give you!"

"'Don't You Just Know It,'" Bobby recalled, "took off so fast it *scared* Johnny Vincent!" Ace being a small southern independent, Vincent had reason to worry. ABC-Paramount Records, home to New Orleans singing star Lloyd Price, was one of many labels coveting the looming hit. Vincent traveled to Philadelphia for a meeting with ABC-Paramount president Sam Clark, who offered $25,000 for the record. If Vincent didn't sell, Clark promised, Price would cover the song and bury the Ace original. Vincent asked for a minute to consider the offer. He promptly phoned Buster Williams's record-pressing plant in Memphis. Williams asked, "Do you want to be in the record business, son?" "Yes, sir!" Vincent said. Williams pledged to press all the records Ace needed and give Vincent unlimited credit. The still-worried Ace president then went to see Dick Clark, the all-American, genial, low-key but vastly influential host of the ABC television network's Philadelphia-based teen dance show, *American Bandstand.* "I told him, 'Mr. Clark, if Lloyd Price covers our record, we won't have a chance.' He said, 'Now, don't you worry about a thing. If you got it in the grooves and I like your record, I'm going to play it.'" Clark did play "Don't You Just Know It" on *Bandstand.* "We sold about 800,000 copies real quick," Vincent said. *Billboard* reported Vincent's rejection of the $25,000 bid, adding it was among the highest offers yet for a master recording and that the many bidders for the master included the ABC-Paramount, Cameo, and Mercury labels. "I don't need to sell masters to make money," Vincent told *Billboard.* "I make out pretty well selling records."

On March 15, 1958, Huey Smith and the Clowns appeared on Clark's other ABC show, the New York–based *Dick Clark Saturday Night Show.* In front of an audience of standing kids who sang along, Huey, Bobby Marchan, Roosevelt Wright, and Eugene Harris lip-synced and danced to "Don't You Just Know It." On stage with no piano in sight, Huey conducted his three Clowns and lip-synced Bobby's lead vocals while Bobby took the absent Gerri Hall's part. The night's other guests included Andy Williams and Frankie Avalon. The group also made local television appearances in various cities, including Washington and Baltimore.

"Don't You Just Know It" debuted on the *Billboard* Top 40 singles chart on March 31. Huey and the Clowns made a second national television appearance on April 18 on *American Bandstand*. An audience as large as 20 million, mostly teen viewers, watched the program every weekday afternoon. During Clark's interview with the group, the girls in the studio audience shrieked when Roosevelt Wright told Clark his name in rumbling bass tones. "I mean they screamed," Huey marveled.

"Don't You Just Know It" reached No. 9 on *Billboard*'s Top 40 and No. 4 on the magazine's rhythm-and-blues chart. Reflecting Bobby Marchan's new prosperity, *Jet* magazine reported in its June 19, 1958, issue that the singer bought a $15,000 house in Youngstown, Ohio, for his mother. She refused to use the home's electric washing machine, the story added, preferring the wooden tub that had been in the family for fifty years.

Huey and his wife, Doretha, moved their growing family—eventually to include Acquelyn, Sherilyn, Huey Jr., Huerilyn, and Hugh "Baby"—to a house in the new Pontchartrain Park subdivision. Dredged from swampland and nearby Lake Pontchartrain, Pontchartrain Park was among the first New Orleans developments designed for middle- and higher-income blacks. It included parkland, playgrounds, lagoons, and an eighteen-hole golf course. When Huey went to see the house on Congress Avenue, Johnny Vincent showed up and handed the real estate agent a check for $4,000. "That's the highest money I ever got from Johnny in my life," Huey remembered.

Happy though Earl King was about his former bandmate's chart success, he regretted that Huey's piano had receded into the mix. "Most of the people that was recording during the '50s in New Orleans, Huey was playing a lot of piano for them on many sessions," Earl said. "He was the top R&B pianist in New Orleans. He played a lot more piano on those sessions than he played with Huey Smith and the Clowns. He fell into a niche that really diminished the piano playing that he really could do."

Even while "Don't You Just Know It" was high on the charts, Johnny Vincent bought a large *Billboard* ad to publicize a new single, "I Think You're Jivin' Me" and "Little Chickie Wah Wah," credited to Huey and Jerry, the Jerry being Gerri Hall. The single was the debut release from Vincent's new label, Vin. The ad contains a message of gratitude to disc jockeys, attributed to Huey. "Thanks for 'Don't You Just Know It.' Wish I could see each and every one of you personally."

Although it was "Don't You Just Know It" that became a hit, Vincent likely squandered the B-side, "High Blood Pressure." A-side worthy, it is a personal favorite of its composer. Huey liked it so much that he'd stay up all night, playing the record over and over again, much as he'd loved hearing Hank Williams's "Lovesick Blues" playing through the night on South Robertson Street almost a decade before. "That was when they had that 45 rpm record with a hole in it," he said. "And the best part is when Roosevelt says [*lowering his voice*], 'All because of you.' I said, 'This is a hit here.' Whenever you play something and you can imagine how it will be in the ear of those who're listening to it, well, you know you got a hit."

"High Blood Pressure," like "Rocking Pneumonia and the Boogie Woogie Flu" before it, is one of Huey's numerous ailment songs. "We don't want to forget Little Willie John had 'Fever' all over the United States," the songwriter explained. "That was one before mine's, so it opened the door for whatever I want to come with. So I'm going to do some more of these, what people like. So I got to be sick!" "High Blood Pressure" also contains the rolling, trilling piano solo Huey previously played for Smiley Lewis's "I Hear You Knocking" and Earl King's "Those Lonely, Lonely Nights." "The thing he did on 'High Blood Pressure,'" Dr. John said, "it's just three little notes, but the note he puts in the middle of it, it's a Huey Smith signature. That very lick is one thing that Allen [Toussaint] used in Chris Kenner's 'Something You Got.' It was used a million other ways, by me, everybody else, but it originally came from Huey."

The follow-up release to "Don't You Just Know it" featured "Havin a Good Time," a raucous party song with Bobby Marchan's lead vocals, and "We Like Birdland," a remake of the original, falsely credited "We Like Mambo." "Birdland's" half-sung, half-chanted lyrics and dramatic piano riff made it a favorite at the Clowns' shows. Huey recorded the "Birdland" music with his road band, including tenor saxophonists Robert Parker and James Rivers, baritone saxophonist Walter Kimble, and bassist Raymond Lewis, at Cosimo Matassa's New Orleans studio. He took the unfinished tape with him to New York City, where Huey Smith and the Clowns were booked at the Apollo Theater in May 1958. Also on the Apollo bill were the Bobbettes, the five girls from Harlem who'd leapt from amateur nights at the Apollo to a No. 6 pop and No. 1 rhythm-and-blues hit, 1957's teacher-inspired "Mr. Lee."

Huey booked a studio in New York to record the vocals for "We Like Birdland." He invited the Bobbettes to come to the session. "And everybody just joined in," he said. "'Sha-ba-do-da, sha-ba-do-day.' It was a real party. Even the engineer was hollering and singing."

In addition to writing song lyrics featuring phrases he overheard, Huey developed characters who appeared in multiple songs. Chickee Wah-Wah debuted in 1957 in the Huey-penned Bobby Marchan single of the same name. She reappeared in 1958's Huey and Jerry single "Little Chickie Wah Wah." Liza Jane appears in 1956's "Little Liza Jane," 1957's "Just a Lonely Clown," and 1961's "More Girls." "I like to use the same characters again," Huey said. "I get to know them. Like you see Elmer Fudd on TV in different things. Little Chickie Wah Wah was getting to be a person like Liza Jane."

Mac Rebennack loved to watch Huey write songs. "He took his time. He'd start with something and just keep working on it. Mighta been a bass line with his left hand and a chord thing. And then he slowly put a little melody thing, even humming it to hisself. And he was so relaxed about it. He be sitting there with these four or five cats, Earl, Dave Dixon, Izzycoo, or whoever, and he's just doing something in spite of whatever else we doing. He could concentrate on that and never ever said a word, like, 'Will y'all be quiet?' He always had that thing and it was so relaxed that we be forgetting sometimes he's writing the song. Huey's just a warm cat, make you feel comfortable in the studio."

Rebennack learned much about writing from Huey. "Anyone," Huey told the young guitarist, "who can talk, can write a song. So whatever you got to say, play good music and say it. You just put it where you need to say it." "One of the things that I learned from Huey," Rebennack said, "if you don't have a song that's got some kind of simple melody people can hum, sing with and roll with, it's like, what do you got?" To help Rebennack learn to write verses, Huey gave his protégé a book of poems for children. "And if I didn't have a melody," Rebennack said, "he said to go listen to children on the street. . . . Huey gave me a path to follow that was beautiful. He started me to where I was able to get songs recorded. It changed my life."

The *Times-Picayune* published a profile of the then eighteen-year-old Rebennack in a 1959 issue of its Sunday magazine, *Dixie Roto*. He'd written four hundred compositions by then, the story reported, sixty-seven of which had been recorded in the past fourteen months. "Rock 'n' roll is the only thing that is selling now," Rebennack explained. "But some day I'd like to be able to market *my other stuff*—blues, spirituals, ballads. I'd like to write something as good as 'September Song' and as popular as 'Stardust.'"

The rhythm-and-blues emanating from New Orleans wasn't only influencing locals like Rebennack. Eighteen-year-old Levon Helm, a cotton farmer's son and drummer from Arkansas who'd recently been hired by rockabilly singer Ronnie Hawkins, knew Crescent City music well. "Huey 'Piano' Smith and the Clowns, those records were real big all through the Delta," Helm said. "All the New Orleans music was on the radio and available, and was my cup of tea right from the very front." A thousand miles northward, fifteen-year-old Canadian Robbie Robertson, Helm's future bandmate in Hawkins's band, the Hawks, and, later, in one of the great groups of the 1960s and 1970s, The Band, also immersed himself in the music of the American South. A neighborhood band called Little Caesar and the Consuls was the most significant of Robertson's early collaborations. The Consuls specialized in performing New Orleans songs, such as Fats Domino's "Blue Monday," Lloyd Price's "Stagger Lee," and Huey "Piano" Smith's "Don't You Know Yockomo." Robertson opened his keynote address at 2002's South by Southwest Music and Media Conference in Austin by saying his career began with a Huey "Piano" Smith and the Clowns wannabe band.

8

Clowns on Stage

Concurrent with the chart rise of "Don't You Just Know It," Huey Smith and the Clowns' personal appearances included Irvin Feld's rock 'n' roll package show, "The Biggest Show of Stars for 58." Writing for *Billboard*, June Bundy reviewed the show's April 13 stop at the Arena in New Haven, Connecticut. Her account highlights Frankie Avalon's performance in a concert including Paul Anka, Sam Cooke, Clyde McPhatter, LaVern Baker, Jimmy Reed, Jackie Wilson, George Hamilton IV, and the Royal Teens. "The handsome young warbler may very well be the successor to Elvis Presley," Bundy wrote of Avalon. Her review also mentions that Feld, in an effort to prevent riots, "wisely advised his acts to play down suggestive gestures and material." Nevertheless, Bundy describes Huey Smith and the Clowns and the Silhouettes as "the most entertaining frantic-type acts on the bill."

Huey and the Clowns were especially popular at colleges. Performing in a massive indoor facility at Princeton University, the group was one of a half-dozen acts, including jazz giant Lionel Hampton and his big band. Huey turned his electric piano up loud, in imitation of Bo Diddley's thundering electric guitar. "We had to get their attention," he explained. "If we playing 'We Like Birdland,' well, they coming over here and see." Come they did, so much so that Gerri Hall couldn't believe her eyes. "You mean to tell me," she asked the other Clowns, "with all these classical people in here, all these great folks, people go' come and watch the Clowns?" "Look at that, Miss Gerri," the likewise astonished Roosevelt Wright said. The response delighted Bobby Marchan. "They coming from everywhere!" he said. "Yes, Miss Gerri! We're the Clowns and we're great!"

"We do 'Don't You Just Know It,'" Huey recalled, "the whole place singing 'Don't you just know it!' Everybody 'ha, ha, ha, ha. Ey, ey-oh.' And Lionel Hampton and them just ain't playing. They wait till the people come back to listen at them. That whole area looked like it was just watching us. Not to boast or nothing like that. Maybe not. Maybe it just looked like that to me." But Gerri doesn't doubt her memory of a great day in Clowns history. "They was all by us!" she said with pride. "We was over there carrying on terrible on the stage. People just come easy. They want to see us Clowns."

Just as they'd done at Princeton, Huey and the Clowns stole shows in theaters, too. Rudy Ray Moore taunted the upstaged acts. "Man, y'all got up there and peeved," he told them. And when it became obvious that the Clowns had stolen a show, Huey said, "somebody had to talk to whoever was supposed to be the star, because we had to close the show." "My act went over big wherever I went because I'd make it go over big!" Bobby said. "We used to do all kind of songs, make dance steps and things and make people laugh and whatnot and just upset every show we go on."

"Bobby was the act," saxophonist James Rivers remembered. "Oh, yeah, Bobby could put on a show. And the Clowns had their little act together, steps and different things they would do, and different uniforms that had all that glittering, metallic stuff."

Natural entertainers though all of the Clowns were, Bobby's fierce competitive streak was something the other members of the group didn't share. He aimed to steal every multi-act show the group was on. "Bobby viewed it like, 'We go' beat them at whatever they doing!'" Huey said.

The Clowns' stage prowess sparked a brawl following a show at Baltimore's Royal Theatre. Comedian Stu Gilliam was out to get Bobby, but he found Huey first in the club of the hotel where the entertainers were staying. "If you open your mouth, I'm go' punch you!" Gilliam promised. Huey, hoping to get the upper hand, threw the first punch. "I laid him down," he said. "That's what you got to do. If I don't get no more than that, well, I got that one, and that took care of everything."

The Clowns' allies in the fight included fellow New Orleanian Ernie K-Doe. The opposition included Screamin' Jay Hawkins. Another New Orleans performer, singer-pianist Clarence "Frogman" Henry ("Ain't Got No Home," "I Don't Know Why But I Do"), watched from the sidelines with Baton Rouge blues man Slim Harpo ("Baby Scratch My Back," "I'm a King Bee"). "I stayed out of it," Henry recalled with a chuckle. "We were just looking, you know. It was a rough fight. But Stuart Gilliam was in it, him and Bobby Marchan and all of them." After the ruckus, Huey paid the jail fine for a big, tough fellow named Williams, who proved extremely grateful to his benefactor. Huey couldn't take off his coat without Williams grabbing it for him. Bobby noticed the gratitude, too. "He go' follow you everywhere you go," Bobby told Huey. "He think he owe you."

Despite the post-show rumble in Baltimore, the show itself was a big hit, Henry said. "The people in Baltimore, if they didn't like you, they'd throw a wine bottle at you. There wasn't no wine bottles at that show."

At the Apollo Theater in New York, the simple presence of Huey Smith and the Clowns from New Orleans made veteran actor and comedian Mantan Moreland wary. A native of Monroe, Louisiana, Moreland had enjoyed a career stretching from the circus to vaudeville to Hollywood. Reflecting portrayals of blacks in movies through the 1940s, the funny-faced comic often played a nervous train conductor or a manservant. He's best known as Charlie Chan's chauffeur, Birmingham Brown.

"See them boys there," Moreland said as he pointed to the Clowns backstage at the Apollo. "I'm scared of them." And whenever Moreland got a drink, he made sure none of the Clowns had been near it. "Where you got this drink from?" he'd ask. "Ruben [the bartender]," the waiter answered. "Okay, then," Moreland said, "because I thought you might have got it from them boys there. They from New Orleans." "What that got to do with it?" the waiter asked. "You know," Moreland explained, "they have that voodoo stuff down there. They give you that stuff and you get the June-bug leg." "Well, I got this from Ruben," the waiter said again. "Okay. Where Ruben from?" "From the Bronx." "Okay. Say— you sure Ruben didn't move from New Orleans to the Bronx?!"

Regardless of his purported fear of New Orleans voodoo, Moreland offstage was nothing like the frightened, bug-eyed clown he played on screen. Huey found him to be a conservative fellow and very nice company. "He didn't act stupid like he did in the movies," Huey said. "Like, one time, Charlie Chan told him to go in a room and he was scared. So Charlie Chan said, 'What's the matter? Are you yellow?' 'Mr. Chan, you color-blind?!'"

The musicians' union representative at the Apollo gave Huey and the Clowns some advice. "Let me tell y'all how to get them girls," he said. "You write them a letter and, soon as you come back here, they looking for you. And don't be drinking that stuff. Your eyes get all red." Roosevelt Wright took offense at the latter remark. "He said that looking right at me!" Yes, the bass singer's eyes were red, but not from drinking. They were naturally bloodshot.

Back home in New Orleans, Gerri Hall, Roosevelt Wright, and Huey's other singers and dancers became members of an extended family. "All our people stayed together and kept each other a long time," Gerri said. "Huey carried a group of people that come to him. Earl King have a group that clings to him. Allen Toussaint have a group that cling to him. And I'm not talking about one or two people. They have a tribe. Twenty, thirty, forty people. And one bunch didn't fool with the other bunch."

Offstage, the Clowns weren't pretentious like other entertainers. Other groups, Gerri said, "had this dignified attitude. When they in a group they all know they better than everybody else. But we weren't. We mixed right in with the people!"

While the Coasters, one of Atlantic Records' top acts, were known as the clown princes of rock 'n' roll, Huey Smith's Clowns earned their name as well. "Each individual was at liberty to decide what he would do to act foolish," Huey explained. "That's what tickled the people so much. We had the songs down so each member of the group would break out and go to clowning." "Look," Gerri Hall said, "one time we had blond hair, red hair, and black hair. Another time I had on a man's suit. Mardi Gras. I think we were in Mobile. I had on a suit and a tie, Bobby had on a dress, and Bobby had Eugene Harris in a suit with a woman's blouse and a woman's hat." But Roosevelt Wright balked at wearing a costume. "I'm not putting all that shit on me!" he exclaimed. "That's all right, Roosevelt," Bobby said, "you don't have to do it."

"Being with the Clowns," Bobby reflected decades later, "being lead singer and choreographer, I mean it made you feel real great. . . . We did a whole lot of things that normal groups wouldn't do. It'll make people laugh." "I knew how to dance, Eugene knew how to dance," Gerri said. "Roosevelt would make a couple of little steps, do a little snap and turn and make everybody laugh. Bobby, he liked to do his little shake and make his butt bounce. It tickled everybody to death. And, see, once we get it all done, then we all come back in and do the tunes again. It always jelled. The people loved it."

Locally and regionally, Jim Russell—a New Orleans promoter and disc jockey manager who'd been a disc jockey himself in Canton, Ohio, and a promoter in Akron with pioneer rock 'n' roll radio personality Alan Freed—remembers Huey's group being second in popularity only to Fats Domino. Russell booked the Clowns often at Tulane University in New Orleans and at Louisiana State University in Baton Rouge. The students, Russell said in 2001 at his Jim Russell Records store in New Orleans, "really liked his act. I figured, and so did Huey, he was worth much more than just an ordinary band. Even Dave Bartholomew, I booked him in 1956 for a hundred bucks, him and his whole band. Okay, so when I booked Huey it was usually around $350 for him and the group. It was a tremendous show because everyone was a performer. And he had some good tunes, man, and they weren't just tunes, it was like Mardi Gras tunes. Exciting. They danced the hell out of it. Bobby Marchan inspired the whole band. And Huey, he was meticulous. He wanted everything to go down just right."

The fraternities the Clowns played in the South were always white, as were most of the group's other audiences. "Really, we didn't know nothing about playing for blacks," Huey said. "One time we played a colored club, we went in there and Bobby say, 'You saw them looking at us like this?' [Sitting, staring and pouting with their arms folded.] Really, that's how it was. They wasn't moved by 'Don't You Just Know It' or 'Little Liza Jane' and stuff like that. 'High Blood Pressure,' they got a little out of that. Other than that they was wondering when we was leaving!"

Though Huey and his mother had their differences when he was growing up, Mrs. Smith's newly prosperous son bought a beautiful pocketbook for her and slipped a surprise inside. Mrs. Smith found the $100 bill while she was attending a Jehovah's Witnesses convention in New York. The money was a blessing because Mrs. Smith had begun wondering if she could afford the hotel bill. "She prayed," Huey said, "and found assistance to sustain them, her and my little sister, up there by means of that hundred-dollar bill. She said, 'Huey, I thanked Jehovah because we was running very short.'"

Back in New Orleans, Huey's mother learned that people were confused about her son's identity. She got angry when a lady in a beauty parlor said, "Huey Smith is a big fat sissy." "Wait a minute," Mrs. Smith countered. "Huey Smith is my son. First of all, he's not fat. And I know he'll never be a sissy!" The woman who called Huey a sissy had mistaken him for the Clowns' front man, Bobby Marchan. "We went out so much without Huey Smith," Bobby recalled in a characteristic rush of words, "they thought I was Huey Smith, because I was doing all the lead singing."

Adding to confusion about who was Huey, the extraordinarily talented, eclectic, and eccentric James Booker played piano for the Clowns after Huey grew both weary and wary of the road. "Me and that highway didn't get along too good," Huey explained. "I'd been upside down too many times for that. Believe it or not, I got on a plane with storms and things, no hesitating." The eighteen-year-old Booker had studied classical piano and had been mentored by the similarly versatile New Orleans piano great Tuts Washington. At fourteen, the piano prodigy made his first record, "Doing the Hambone," for Imperial Records. "When Huey didn't come out," James Rivers remembered, "then there was Booker, because Booker could play all of Huey's stuff that people hear on the record. Booker not only could play Huey Smith, Booker could play everybody else, too. Man, after some gigs we'd go on a jam session and Booker would be cleaning cats out left and right." "Little James Booker played piano exactly like Huey Smith did," Bobby said. "And our group and act was so sensational that people never questioned it at all."

Unfortunately, Booker's ego was as big as his talent. Bobby phoned Huey from the road with a distress call. "Oh, Booker!" he complained. "I'm in here playing cards and everybody sitting around. Booker strutted through the door like Bette Davis! He says, 'You say you go' call Huey and tell him I'm fired? Don't call him and tell him I'm fired. See, the people think I'm Huey. Tell him I want a raise—because you needs me!' And he strutted on out the door." Another time the unhappy Booker stared at Bobby and lamented: "You got curls in your hair. I ain't got none. I ain't going on." "Well, I'll be doggone," the astonished Bobby reacted. Rather than do a Huey "Piano" Smith and the Clowns show without a piano player, Bobby curled Little Booker's hair himself. Afterward, the sight of Booker shaking his new curls as he played piano cracked Bobby up.

Huey did come out and play now and then, saxophonist James Rivers said. "Certain gigs he'd want to be on. But all Huey would do was just stand up and play the piano. You wouldn't even know he was Huey Smith. He would be almost like one of us in the band. And Huey was shy. He's not one of them guys, 'Well, yeah, I'm Huey! That's my record!' He didn't do that. But when he played he'd wear his pretty stuff and bow tie."

"No matter what people saw of Huey," Dr. John said, "they didn't see all of him because he wasn't the kind of guy to stick it up front."

Just as Rivers said, Huey preferred to stand at the piano when he performed. "It was comfortable," he explained. "It got to be a habit like, especially with the electric piano. I didn't just play it, I beat it." And playfulness of the kind heard in Huey's lyrics emerged at fraternity parties through surprise encores of "We Like Birdland." "Because I do it all night," he recalled. "The people think the show's over, they're sitting down out there—I come back and play dun-dun, dun-dun-

dun-dun! And they come back. And then they think it's over again because we start talking—and I slip back to the piano and do it again!"

"We had a time on the stage with that!" Gerri said of "Birdland." "They love that. Them white folks, they white but they know how to really do it!" "They're pouring beer over each other's heads," Huey added. "They're pouring beer over us, too. We be slipping all over the floor. And Billy [Brooks, another one of the Clowns] on the floor splitting his pants and people see his red-and-white drawers. The people died laughing. They thought that was part of the show, but it just happened. Then we really started doing it in the show, though." "Oh, yeah," Gerri said, "in those days, you just have a ball. Whenever everybody got together, the Clowns, they used to really be the Clowns. Go off. For many nights, many days."

But the happy, even riotous performances were affecting Huey's hearing. He often performed next to the drummer, and the cymbals left his one good ear ringing.

O n July 15, 1959, Jamaica's *Daily Gleaner* newspaper announced the upcoming "Rock Jamaica Rock" show. Huey "Piano" Smith headlined a roster of Louisiana talent, featuring in descending order the Clowns, Bobby Marchan, Professor Longhair, and the Baton Rouge–based backing band Earl Davis and the Upsetters. "'Rock-Jamaica-Rock' is the second of the popular summer shows scheduled for Jamaica," the *Gleaner* reported. "The first, Lloyd Price's Stagger Lee Show, was one of the year's big smashes, and Huey Smith, aware of this, has packaged his show with outstanding performers who can deliver a 'Sock-O' job with plenty of punch."

New Orleans rhythm-and-blues was a major influence on the island's ska music and such future Jamaican reggae stars as Bob Marley, his bandmates in the Wailers, Peter Tosh and Neville "Bunny" Livingston, and James Chambers, a singer-songwriter who took the stage name Jimmy Cliff to perform Fats Domino songs at talent contests. Still in his teens, Cliff recorded Jamaican hits before going international with such crossover successes as "Wonderful World, Beautiful People" and starring in the music-rich, semiautobiographical film *The Harder They Come*. Unable to afford records, young Jamaicans listened by night to New Orleans and Florida radio stations that played the American hits of Ray Charles and Sam Cooke and New Orleans acts Fats Domino, Smiley Lewis, Lloyd Price, and Huey Smith: "Smiley Lewis, Professor Longhair, all the jazz people," Cliff recalled. "How ska emerged," said Chris Blackwell, a London native who grew up in Jamaica and founded the internationally successful Island Records in 1959 at twenty-two, "was through the Jamaican attempt to play the grooves of New Orleans R&B."

A July 30, 1959, *Daily Gleaner* ad announced the postponement of "Rock Jamaica Rock" starring Huey Smith, "Owing to the PUBLIC PREOCCUPATION with the GENERAL ELECTIONS." Without Huey, road manager Billy Diamond later brought a Shirley and Lee show (with bassist Roland Cook impersonating the ill Leonard Lee) to Kingston and Montego Bay. Whatever preoccupation the Jamaican public may have had with the island's elections, Huey Smith and the Clowns' Jamaican engagements were, in reality, scrapped to meet domestic demand for the group. "Instead of me going with Shirley and Lee to Jamaica and California and them different places, I'm sentenced to the same old fraternity rooms in Carolina, Virginia, New Jersey," Huey said.

Huey's friend and fellow songwriter and recording artist Chris Kenner as well as Clowns driver and road manager Ike Favorite told Huey that booking agent Frank Sands and the New York City–based Circle Artists Corp. were charging fraternities five times the sum written on his performance contracts. "They got $5,000 from rich people at them colleges," Huey said. "That's why they kept sending us to every fraternity, all around that circuit. We almost felt like we'd be strangers if we go to a nightclub. We didn't have that experience."

The Clowns also played informal engagements at colleges. Students at elite schools financed private concerts by pooling $100 apiece. "They want you to just come to their dorm and play a little for them and party with them," Huey remembered. "That was on the side. They have houses in the woods and things. We'd be there all the week doing that, just us and my piano. Yeah, we made more money like that, just hanging around."

Playing fraternities and theaters, Huey and the Clowns naturally were surrounded by alcohol. Huey drank to loosen himself up for the show. "Me being a type of a shy individual, I would drink," he said. "But I'm playing fraternities, and I got Huey Smith and the Clowns, so you have to halfway be the life of the party. Now, the place where I played the piano with my feet, that's when I drank the whole pint. And I had my foot up there, playing with my toes. I used drink as a crutch to do stupid things I might not normally do. . . . Did I get tore down? Yeah, but it wasn't a problem, because Monday I didn't fool with it. The problem's when somebody can't stop drinking." Even when Huey drank, Earl King said, he stayed cool. "He was a party person, but a laid-back party person." Contrary to the Clowns' festive image, Dave Bartholomew, the creative light behind Fats Domino, remembers Huey being the quietest young man around. "Nothing rowdy about him," Bartholomew said. "Just a soft-spoken gentleman with an awful lot of talent. He was such a nice man he was actually a friend of Johnny Vincent! I don't know if Johnny was a friend to him. Huey could have been working for anyone because he had so much talent. But if something was going wrong, you wouldn't never know it from Huey. The man was always just such a quiet person. Actually, he could be a priest!"

9

Sea Cruise

ollowing the Top 10 success of "Don't You Just Know It," Huey Smith and the Clowns' next spotlight review in *Billboard* did not appear until November 10, 1958, nearly ten months later. Gerri Hall, Huey, and anonymous female session vocalists sang the up-tempo "Don't You Know Yockomo." Bobby Marchan led flipside "Well I'll Be John Brown," one of Huey's comic ensemble numbers. *Billboard,* alongside reviews of new records by the Platters, the Big Bopper, and LaVern Baker, judged "Yockomo" an earthy rocker performed with verve and "John Brown" a "strong prospect for R&B coin."

"Yockomo" opens with a guitar intro played by Earl King. It features Huey's signature piano trills, high-spirited call-and-response vocals, and lyrics including the New Orleans Mardi Gras Indians' phrase "Two-way pock-a-way." "Well I'll Be John Brown" is another example of Huey crafting a song from various sources. The song takes its name from a phrase inspired by abolitionist guerrilla fighter John Brown. The leader of a raid on the federal arsenal at Harpers Ferry, Virginia, in 1859, Brown was caught and hanged. The Civil War–era "John Brown's Body," a variation on "The Battle Hymn of the Republic," became a popular marching song among regiments of the Union Army. "John Brown was a slave liberator," Huey explained. "We sang about him in grammar school. . . . We know 'John Brown's Body,' and people say, 'I'll be John Brown.' Well, I use slangs and things like that. . . . When you put the music with words and things together, the songs just make themselves. And after you listen at it, it says something its own self, that you hadn't planned."

Huey enjoyed his work but, more importantly, saw songwriting as a practical discipline. "A song, it doesn't really reflect the artist," he said. "Like a painter, he paints something for the audience to appreciate, not for himself."

In *Billboard*'s first issue of 1959, "Yockomo" led the week's fifteen new arrivals on the Hot 100, debuting at No. 71. The issue also listed two earlier Ace

Records releases, "Don't You Just Know It" and Jimmy Clanton's "Just a Dream," among 1958's million-sellers.

"Don't You Know Yockomo" peaked at No. 56, far short of the Top 10 rank for "Don't You Just Know It." But another song written and recorded by Huey, and released by Ace immediately after "Yockomo," would become a major hit. "Sea Cruise," like so many New Orleans hits, was recorded at Cosimo Matassa's studio. "One afternoon I went in the studio with every note in my head outlined for every instrument in my road band," Huey remembered. Of course, he played the song's rolling piano part himself. Huey and Gerri Hall shared a piano stool when they sang the song's playful lyrics into a single microphone. "Sea Cruise" opens with a bell and booming horn. "I used the sound effect of a boat blowing its horn and, man, I tell you, the horn of the boat made me feel as though I really was on a cruise. I could not wait to get before the public leading my group doing 'Sea Cruise.'"

James Booker, who'd been hanging out at Matassa's studio, joined Huey at the piano for "Loberta," the song that became the "Sea Cruise" flipside. "Booker was at one end and I was on the other end," Huey said. "I ain't go' say, 'No, you ain't go' sit here, too.' It's not the Army. We're having fun, that's all. Whatever we go to do, just do it and see how it comes out." That open-minded approach applied to lead vocals, too. "Some things, like 'Beatnik Blues,' 'Genevieve,' I figure John [Williams] can do better than Bobby," Huey said. "But it wasn't no squabble about none of it. A lot of times it's whoever's around. Yeah, he was somewhere, he rehearsed it, he got it down pretty good." Bobby Marchan sang lead for "Loberta," doing a knockout job of it. Like the earlier "Little Liza Jane," Huey based "Loberta"—pronounced Loo-berta—on lines he'd heard children in his neighborhood singing. He placed a twelve-bar blues bass line beneath the lyrics.

> Loberta, Loberta, won't tell me where you slept last night.
> Your clothes all ranky, musta slept with a hermaphrodite.

"They just make that up," he said. "Like, 'Hey, little girl with your nose all snotty, don't know nothing, whyn't you ask somebody?' Them type of things. That was like the little boys sitting out on the porch and they want to be vulgar. They bad. 'Loberta' was a street song, really. It was really vulgar, the whole thing. I used those phrases but I cleaned them up."

Huey's creativity in the studio also included experimentation with instruments. "On all Huey's old recordings," guitarist Earl King told music historian Tad Jones in the 1970s, "you hear something you think is congas or bongos. That's the guitar on there. That's me." "Huey," Dr. John confirmed, "would tell you stuff like, 'Make your guitar sound like a bongo.' He'd hear different things, let you know what it was and get it out of you real hiply. I loved that about Huey. And a lot of it worked. We tried things with the electric keyboard early on. Huey always had this idea that it should sound like a guitar, but it was Huey's version of what a guitar thing might be. And then he'd add organ and a piano. So you got three keyboards, whether it was Huey and Booker or overdub, way before Phil Spector or whoever was doing that crap later. And Robert Parker, James Rivers, all them cats was coming up around Huey. He made them sound like they been old-time pros. And he had that little band, whether it was Catman [Caffrey] and Diz [Williams], all with them kind of guys. And they sound just as good as the regulation studio band, but in a different way. Huey wasn't one of them cats that went for the regulation anything."

J ust as Huey knew "High Blood Pressure" was a great record, he knew that "Sea Cruise," with its contagious groove, sparkling lyrics, and driving horn chart, was destined for success.

> Old man rhythm gets in my shoes,
> No use to sittin' and singing the blues.
> So be my guest, you got nothing to lose.
> Won't you let me take you on a sea cruise?

"I was always able to tell a hit before it came out. Evidently, someone else also could tell." That someone was Joe Caronna. A hard-drinking, heavy-smoking Italian, Caronna liked to brag about his heart condition. "I got half a fucking heart!" he boasted. Johnny Vincent's partner in the New Orleans–based record distribution business, Record Sales, Inc., Caronna had moved into artist management. He told Huey the day after "Sea Cruise" was recorded that Frank Guzzo, a young white singer from nearby Gretna, would cut a new vocal track for the song. Caronna believed that this big-voiced eighteen-year-old, a performer since childhood, would be America's next teen idol. "Johnny Vincent agreed that if you can sell a million on this record, Frankie can sell ten million," he told Huey. The song's creator begged Caronna not to take "Sea Cruise" from him, but the die was cast. "That's the way it's gonna be, and there ain't nothing you can do about it," Caronna said.

"I was crying as he said that," Huey remembered. "I had been drinking a little bit. It hurt me to my heart when he told me he was taking that. Cosmo let him listen at it. They went in Cosmo's studio late at night, behind closed doors. We had never heard of no Frankie Ford. Joe Caronna substituted that voice in there, him and Cosmo, and sent that thing up to the pressing plant. Johnny Vincent had never even heard my 'Sea Cruise.' He was in Jackson, Mississippi. But Johnny went along with it, all right." On the "Sea Cruise" record label, Guzzo's stage name, Frankie Ford, appears in large letters while "Huey 'Piano' Smith and Orch." appears in tiny letters below.

Billboard's December 22, 1958, issue predicted success for "Sea Cruise." The magazine placed the Frankie Ford–credited "Sea Cruise" and "Roberta," formerly known as "Loberta," among its "spotlight winners." "'Sea Cruise,'" the review states, "is a rocking blues on which the artist is backed by a driving, colorful arrangement. 'Roberta' is also a blues that gets an authentic shout."

James Rivers, the young saxophonist who'd been so badly hurt in the automobile accident that Huey and his band experienced in Florida, had been thrilled to be on the "Sea Cruise" session. "We were just so happy to get in the studio," he said. "I used to like to say, 'Oh, I'm on that record. That's me playing, right there.'" After the "Sea Cruise" session, Rivers assumed Bobby Marchan would add his vocals to the music later. "Bobby wasn't there when we did the session, but he was singing with the band at that time," Rivers said. "Man, about a month later, I'm hearing 'Sea Cruise' [on the radio]. I say, 'That's not Bobby Marchan!' We was shocked when we was coming down the road hearing something that we had put the music behind and the disc jockey said, 'That was Frankie Ford!' We say, 'Frankie Ford? Who the hell is that?!' Man, we didn't even know no Frankie Ford. Huey wrote the song and, of course, he wrote it for Huey Smith and the Clowns."

Saxophonist Robert Parker, another of the "Sea Cruise" and "Roberta" session musicians, was shocked, too. "The business part of it, I don't know whether they took the song or what," Parker said. "I do know Frankie Ford is getting all the credit for it."

"A lot of heavy-duty stuff went on," Dr. John said. "I mean, that whole scene with Johnny and Joe Caronna, and him just taking the 'Sea Cruise,' Huey's big follow-up to 'Don't You Just Know It,' it's so crazy. Look, Joe Caronna, Johnny Vincent, naw. It's like no respect for Huey. It's like here was the guy making 'em all the money they made and what do they do? Listen, it had to have shattered a lot of stuff in Huey, in anybody." Despite the financial disappointments and social hardships Huey and his Clowns faced, Dr. John added, they didn't lose sight of the job at hand. "They had a good time making the people have a good time, no matter what they went through to get to do that. If you go down the line of what wasn't cool, by the time you got to what was cool, it was *them*."

Huey's faith in "Sea Cruise" proved correct. The song debuted on the *Billboard* Top 40 pop singles chart on March 9, 1959, peaked at No. 14, and stayed on the chart for twelve weeks. "Sea Cruise" got even higher on the rhythm-and-blues chart, peaking at No. 7. A Crescent City classic, the song has been heard in commercials and movies through succeeding decades. Fiery flipside "Roberta" was popular, too, and, like B-side "High Blood Pressure" before it, was worthy of being an A-side.

Huey's and Frankie Ford's versions of events surrounding "Sea Cruise" and "Loberta" are as different as black and white. Huey read Ford's multiple explanations for the switch in a succession of interviews through the years. "Of course," Ford said, "'Sea Cruise' was cut to be the follow-up to 'Don't You Just Know It,' the Huey 'Piano' Smith song. And then when they heard me, and Huey didn't need a song at that time, they put it out on me. . . . Huey taught it to me. Somewhere I have the original chart with his handwritten remarks."

"That's stupid," Huey countered. "Well, why didn't I write the words to the other side down, 'Loberta'? See, that's proof of it. You're singing the wrong words. We, the background voices, still singing 'Loo-berta.' You hollering, 'Roberta!' Roberta is a white girl's name. *Loo*-berta was a black gal. Believe it or not, I don't even write. I scribble, I scratch. I never wrote nothing. And you claim you was a member of the Clowns. You just now realize that that was against the law?* You are white, aren't you? How could you have been a member of the Clowns? Let's tell it like it is."

Vincent had an obvious reason for allowing the switch: Hits by white singers who appealed to white teenagers typically out-sold records by black artists.

---

*Louisiana law forbade blacks and whites from congregating in public places.

"When we realized the teenyboppers were going crazy over Elvis, Frankie Avalon and Fabian, we decided we were gonna get some of that market, too," Vincent said. "We were trying to git the white crowd." Ford, perhaps in less guarded moments, admitted as much. "Then when I cut 'Sea Cruise,' at the time—and you look at history, it'll tell you—white records were selling a lot more than black records."

"See," Bobby Marchan pointed out, "Johnny Vincent was out for making plenty of money and he thought we didn't know no better down here. He would go into Cosmo's studio and him and Cos would have a cup of coffee and they come out with a hit."

An interview with Johnny Vincent about his successful southern indie label appeared in Ren Grevatt's "On the Beat" column in the May 4, 1959, issue of *Billboard*. The column notes that hit records weren't coming only from major cities, but from throughout the country, including such remote spots as Jackson, Mississippi. "I've always been hipped to the record business," Vincent told Grevatt. The Ace president also mentioned the label's breakout hit of 1957, "Rocking Pneumonia and the Boogie Woogie Flu," and his initial lack of confidence in the young man who created it. "Huey would play for the singers on the recording dates but he wanted to make a record himself. I didn't think he had a chance but we finally made one. It was called 'Rocking Pneumonia.'"

After "Sea Cruise" had made Frankie Ford a star, he needed to look the part. Ford got a makeover, including a visit to a New York dentist to fix gaps in his teeth and a $600 shopping spree for new clothes. Huey coordinated the most dramatic alteration—straightening Ford's kinky hair. "Huey," Johnny Vincent said, "yo' hair look more like Elvis Presley than Frankie's. Bring Frankie down on Rampart Street where you get yo' hair fixed. See if they can help Frankie out." Huey took Ford to a musically inclined, whistling barber, Kelly, operator of one of the first process shops in New Orleans. Ford's natural hair resembled that of future president Bill Clinton's, Huey recalled, "but not that good. He was nappy, very nappy. So they gassed Frankie up, just like me!" After Ford's straightening, Huey and Earl King took him out for sandwiches. They told the new American idol how good he looked.

"Well," Ford remembered in horror of that day, "my hair did not turn red, it turned fuchsia. I was in bed for three days with fever from the lye and everything.

I was lucky not to lose it. So, it was so funny, because Huey was so laid back. He said, 'Well, we ain't never done a white boy's hair before, but we want to try.'"

"Sea Cruise" and "Roberta" launched Ford into the ranks of Fabian, Frankie Avalon, and Johnny Vincent's first teen idol, Jimmy Clanton. Vincent told Huey he should write songs for Ford. "See, you go' make a million dollars writing," he promised. "You got all that other money coming, what you got already on the other stuff, so you'll be rich." "If you can't beat them, join them," Huey reasoned. "You took mine's first and so now you're a big star. So I take Frankie under my wing. I'm teaching him 'Alimony.' He didn't steal it. But Johnny never paid me for that song or none of the rest neither. And they didn't pay me for the writing or bringing Frankie to the barber. I had to use my own gas to get him down there!"

The twenty-five-year-old Huey also taught veteran rhythm-and-blues acts Charles Brown and Amos Milburn a song he'd initially written for himself, the fervently rocking, characteristically comic "Educated Fool." "It was very nice to be in their company," he said of his elder peers. Ace released the collaboration as a Brown and Milburn duet in 1959. Friends and traveling companions, singer-pianists Brown and Milburn played many Gulf Coast engagements together in late 1958 and early 1959, including an extended stay at New Orleans's Club High Hat with headliner Roy Brown and multiple weekends at the Dew Drop Café.

The original "Educated Fool" vocal track, recorded in November 1956, featured New Orleans singer Danny White. Huey also cast White in the slyly romantic "Let's Play" and driving rocker "Too Late." He knew White from the Dew Drop and brought him to Johnny Vincent. "I thought he was a good singer, but Johnny never did anything with him." Ace Records didn't release the potent material White and Huey recorded together. "I thought it could really be, but they sit on it all them years." White eventually confirmed Huey's belief in his talent. "Kiss Tomorrow Goodbye," the singer's heartrending debut for the New Orleans–based Frisco Records, became the city's No. 1 record in 1963. It remains a Gulf Coast favorite.

The excessive behavior of Huey's former partner Guitar Slim astonished even his New Orleans peers. Vocal group the Spiders ("I Didn't Want to Do It," "Witchcraft"), featuring brothers Chick and Chuck Carbo, encountered Slim at a party in New York City after an Apollo Theater show. "They used to have the little sample bottles of wine," Chuck Carbo recalled. "Slim said, 'I'll buy the whole box.' And he stood there with it, opening each bottle, just pouring it down, one right behind the other. That's the type of dude he was."

Slim began having difficulty breathing in 1958. During an East Coast tour the next year a doctor in Rochester, New York, told the blues star to stop drinking. The troupe moved on to New York City the next day. Slim was weak when he and the band checked into the Cecil Hotel. He collapsed in the elevator. Two band members, thinking Slim was simply drunk, carried him to his room. He could not be revived. Eddie "Guitar Slim" Jones died February 7, 1959. He was thirty-two.

Lawrence Cotton, the pianist who'd backed Slim in Lloyd Lambert's band from the singer-guitarist's early days of stardom, had quit the band a few months before. Slim's demise didn't surprise him. "He didn't take care of himself," Cotton said. "He drank so much that he had the DTs. Some nights he'd come off the stage ringing wet and go straight into freezing weather. Lloyd told me he was driving around New York in the winter with no heater in his car right before Slim died. But, you know, if Slim was alive today, he would be bigger than that guy that had 'Boom, Boom, Boom' [John Lee Hooker] or any of those other blues guys."

Manager Hosea Hill shipped Slim's body by train to the small southeastern Louisiana town of Thibodaux, the singer-guitarist's final residence. Slim and Albertine Armstrong's son, seven-year-old Rodney Armstrong, who'd later be known as the singing, guitar-playing Guitar Slim Jr., attended the service. "At my daddy's funeral, somebody said, 'Aw, Guitar Slim, he ain't had no family.' Somebody else said, 'Yeah, he do! He got two sons. One of 'em here now!' So they come got me and put me on the pulpit in the church. I looked at my daddy in the coffin. He had a smile on his face."

Back in Hollandale, Mississippi, Sarah Bowdre—mother of Slim's second wife, Daisy, and grandmother of the couple's daughters, Annie Lee and Sarah May—was sorry to see him go. The famous blues man had stayed in touch with his family in Hollandale after Daisy's death in 1952. "Lord, have mercy, that was a good man," his mother-in-law said.

The year of Slim's death, Huey was playing an extended engagement at Keesler Air Force Base in Biloxi, Mississippi, with Fats Domino's singing, trumpet-playing first cousin, Freddie Domino. Professor Longhair was there, too. As usual, the future New Orleans piano legend was scuffling. His sleeping accommodations consisted of a cot in a tiny room. Given his tight money, Longhair grew annoyed when his drummer, Charles "Honey Boy" Otis, showed no interest in a well-off, local young lady. "*Hooney* Boy talking about she don't appeal to him," he complained to Huey. "Like we living on scraps, trying to make ends meet, but this girl got this nice big automobile and a pocket full of money and *Hooney* Boy around here talking about, 'She don't appeal to me.' I said, 'She don't appeal to you? Make her appeal!'"

Longhair confided to Huey that another young lady had expressed admiration for the old professor: "That girl over there told me she likes my eyes." But the 41-year-old musician figured she was just joking. "She really must have told him that, though," Huey said. "Well, it was pretty dark in there. But Fess figured he wasn't really attractive. He was astounded hisself!"

B obby Marchan, away from the Clowns doing his female impersonator act in the Midwest, was getting a great reaction to his rendition of Big Jay Mc-Neely and Little Sonny Warner's 1959 hit, "There Is Something on Your Mind." Bobby decided he should re-record the song, which he'd spiced up with a jealousy-fueled recitation of the kind that helped make Larry Darnell's Dew Drop Café favorite, "I'll Get Along Somehow," a national hit in 1949.

Bobby gave Ace Records the first shot at the remake, but Johnny Vincent, saying it had already been a hit for McNeely and Little Sonny, rejected the idea. Bobby also asked Huey about re-recording the song. "Huey just said, 'It's not my record company. There's nothing I can do.' . . . So I told Johnny, 'Since you ain't record it, I'm going somewhere and get it recorded. You'll be sorry.' And he was."

The determined Bobby sent a tape of himself performing "There Is Something on Your Mind" to Bobby Robinson in New York City. Robinson, the owner of the Harlem-based Fire and Fury labels, had recently released Wilbert Harrison's No. 1 pop and rhythm-and-blues hit, "Kansas City." Robinson first heard Bobby's take on "There Is Something on Your Mind" during a party at his home. "Somebody made a mistake and put that on," Bobby told interviewer Ben Sandmel at the New Orleans Jazz and Heritage Festival in 1998. "And the room got quiet. Bobby Robinson said, 'Who's that?'" Upon learning the singer's identity, Robinson phoned Bobby and asked if they could meet in a few days in Chicago at Universal Studios, where Robinson had recently recorded Elmore James's soon-to-be blues hit "The Sky Is Crying." "I just sent you a dub!" Bobby protested, thinking the version he'd already recorded was worthy of release. "We go' do the real thing now," Robinson responded.

"It was so different that I really thought it could be a hit," Robinson said in 1992 of Bobby's demo. He sent Bobby plane fare to Chicago, but the nonflying singer took a bus instead. He re-recorded "There Is Something on Your Mind" with a five-piece band organized by the veteran Chicago session guitarist Lefty Bates, and featuring local musicians as well as New Orleans saxophonist Alvin "Red" Tyler.

"We cut the record like Friday and went back to New York," the ever-effusive Bobby told Sandmel. "Monday they had a call for five thousand records for 'Something on Your Mind.' We knew it was a smash right off the bat!"

Robinson wisely issued the entirety of Bobby's version of the song, dividing the performance onto two sides of a 45 rpm single. "I decided to start part two where Bobby begins his monologue," Robinson said. "That was really one of the first raps, you know! Naturally, the disc jockeys started playing part one first, but soon people began requesting part two, which really gave the record a second lease on life. And it ended up a smash!"

In the wake of Huey's "Sea Cruise" disaster, Bobby became a solo star. In the summer of 1960, his passionate and funny rendition of "There Is Something on Your Mind" went to No. 1 on the rhythm-and-blues chart and No. 31 on the pop chart. "I did the record by myself and then I got booked to do a solo tour for a thousand dollars a night. That was the funniest thing that happened to me while I was with the Clowns."

Bobby was just one member of Huey's ever-changing singing groups and bands to go solo. Drummer Jessie Hill's "Ooh Poo Pah Doo," an irresistible slice of New Orleans nonsense inspired by bassist Raymond Lewis's pet phrase about girls, "I created a disturbance in her mind," became a No. 3 rhythm-and-blues hit and No. 28 pop hit in the summer of 1960. Robert Parker ("Barefootin'"), James Booker ("Gonzo"), Raymond Lewis ("I'm Gonna Put Some Hurt on You"), John Williams, Gerri Hall, Curley Moore ("Soul Train"), Jesse Thomas, and James Rivers were among the other Clowns alumni who pursued solo careers on stage and in the studio.

The Money's Funny

n 1957, performance rights organization Broadcast Music, Inc. (BMI) began distributing songwriter royalties to Huey for radio and television broadcasts, jukebox play, and live performances of his compositions. Johnny Vincent, however, didn't pay properly documented royalties to artists and songwriters. Huey claims to have never received a royalty statement from Vincent. Without these statements, which break down sources of income, artists and writers had no way of knowing if they were being paid fairly.

Vincent started artists on Ace and his other labels at a 1 percent royalty rate per record sold. The 1 percent was based on 90 percent of a record's list price. The reduction from 100 to 90 percent was an industry-wide record company charge for assumed breakage of vinyl discs during shipping and handling. In his later years, Vincent cited a 3 percent royalty rate during a discussion of Earl's 1955 rhythm-and-blues hit "Those Lonely, Lonely Nights." If Vincent paid Huey a 3 percent royalty rate for his 1958 Top 10 pop and R&B hit, "Don't You Just Know It," and if, as *Billboard* magazine reported, the record sold 1 million copies, Huey's royalties based upon 3 percent of 90 percent of the then recently increased list price of 98 cents per record sold would be $26,000. By contrast, the total list-price receipts from sales of 1 million copies would be $980,000.

Of course, Vincent had expenses. He bought studio time. He paid musicians and singers for session work, at union scale or less for nonunion sessions. Vincent claimed the total cost for recording a session in the mid to late 1950s could be $1,000 to $1,200. He also paid record manufacturing and distribution costs. His record promotion expenses included display ads in *Billboard* and *Cashbox*. A congressional committee also cited Ace as a record company that engaged in payola. Meanwhile, most of the recordings released by Vincent's various labels, and labels in general, were not profitable hits.

Royalty rates for recording artists in the 1950s being so low, the multiple sources of royalty income were important for songwriters, especially if interest in a song continued through the years. Normally, composers and publishers share a 50–50 split from the income produced by licenses granted to record companies, known as mechanical licenses. Composers and publishers also receive a 50–50 share of licensing fees for music used in movies, television, and, more recently, video games and DVDs. These are called synchronization licenses. Composers and publishers collect another 50–50 share from performance royalties collected by performance rights organizations such as BMI and ASCAP (American Society of Composers, Authors and Publishers). On top of Vincent not paying royalties from his publishing side of the business, he reduced Huey's BMI songwriter's income by 50 percent whenever he claimed to have cowritten a song. The latter practice, common at the time, bestowed royalties on music executives, producers, disc jockeys, and others who had nothing to do with songwriting.

Despite Vincent's apparent shortcomings as a record company owner and music publisher, Huey thinks fondly of Vincent. "Just because Johnny's trying to put the dollars in his pocket, that has nothing to do with it," Huey reflected. "Like, you be around them, you know them, and you're sorry they're like that. Me, myself, I think being a racist was more Johnny's problem than anything else, but he was fighting to not be one."

When Huey noticed whites moving out of a New Orleans neighborhood, he phoned Vincent in Jackson with an idea. Inspired by photos he'd seen of Berry Gordy's Motown Records studio and offices in Detroit—the company's headquarters was a simple, two-story frame house dubbed Hitsville U.S.A.—Huey envisioned recording studios in the changing New Orleans neighborhood. "The whites were moving out of there, 'For Sale' signs," he recalled. "A lot of them were emotional about it. They might of hadn't planned to move. But I was telling Johnny, 'Look, you buy this up and we'll be in business.' But he misunderstood. He thought I was marking up a victory for blacks. Before I told him that, I didn't worry about my royalty statement. He would send some money, a $100 or so. But after that I didn't never get nothing no more from him. So I figured it was that conversation."

Earl King defected to Imperial Records in 1960. "The first time I ever collect royalties was when I quit Ace and went with Imperial," he said. Dr. John, too, recalls Vincent habitually not paying musicians. "It was like this guy had plots in his head about not paying for anything from the beginning till the end. . . . Hey, you'd think one of us had a' had sense to say, 'Well, Johnny's beating us.' But no, it was like we wanted to play music and we were trying to make a living." Vincent claimed he compensated Huey, Earl King, and other Ace artists generously. "Every artist thinks their record sells a million," he complained. "Earl used to think that 'Lonely, Lonely Nights' sold five million records. We didn't sell but 60,000. At three cents a record it wouldn't have been but $1,800. What the hell did I have to beat him out of? I bought Earl a damn down payment on a damn car. I bought him his whole damn wardrobe. Every week we sent him a check for three and four hundred dollars. What the hell did we have to beat him for? He owed the company. . . . Like I told you, Earl, he'd still be washing dishes!"

Vincent and Huey argued about money often. "Now," Vincent would say, "see, you part of the company. This ain't just me, this yo' company. I'm getting all this for you. See, you go' have you a lot of money now." But when he needed money, Huey said, Vincent gave him excuses instead. "Let me get with the bookkeeper, see what I can get you. You go' get a statement. But we ain't doing too good. See, your sessions was so high. See, this Cosmo, he really hit me hard this time for studio time and the musicians and things like that. So I got to pay Cos something, and Jimmy [Clanton] is calling me now, too. I'm go' see if I can—what you need?" One argument between the two men arose over the washing machine Huey wanted for his growing family. "What y'all go' do with a washing machine?" Vincent asked, characterizing the common household appliance as a luxury item. The angry Huey struck back, saying, "Your wife got a maid putting your clothes in your washing machine!"

Vincent had a brother named Salvador who answered the phone at Ace. Many musicians thought Salvador was simply Johnny avoiding their calls. "Maybe Salvador did answer the phone," Huey speculated, "but he sounds so close to Johnny. Bobby and them saying, 'Yeah, yeah, Johnny there! Talking about this his *brother*, Salvador. Like we don't know Johnny's voice!'"

Blind bass player and guitarist Billy Tate shared his take on the way record companies operate. "See, they got people to talk to you," Tate told Huey. "Say, you call the company. I don't care who you are, but say you Huey Smith. 'Hey, Huey baby, what's going on?' 'Well, look, I didn't get my statement today.' 'Well, like, baby, it's go' be on the way.' And yet that man talking don't know you from Adam! But his job is to talk to you. And the next one who calls, he's go' tell them the same thing. All he do is talk and you ain't went nowhere. He say, 'Oh,

I didn't get back wit' you? Oh, man, I been tied all up.' When he finishes talking to you, you'll probably quit calling!"

Vincent's former boss, Art Rupe, the disciplined owner of Specialty Records, believed that a successful record company provided ample profit for both the company and the artist. "I was scrupulous in paying the royalties, not only accurately, but in a timely manner," Rupe claimed. "As far as the other companies are concerned, it's unfortunate. A lot of the people in the industry weren't very well educated." As for one-time Specialty employee Vincent, Rupe said, "He's a hell of a promoter. He has a vivid imagination."

One of Vincent's white teen idols, a handsome teenager from Baton Rouge named Jimmy Clanton, got a huge hit with a self-penned ballad inspired by his first heartbreak, "Just a Dream." Boosted by an appearance on Dick Clark's *American Bandstand*, the record sold a million copies. Clanton didn't lack appreciation in his hometown. City officials declared a November day in 1958 Jimmy Clanton Day. At Memorial Stadium, the singer was showered with state and local honors, and Vincent presented a gold record to him.

Huey was at Cosimo Matassa's French Quarter studio one day when Matassa complained about a Cadillac blocking his driveway. "Somebody's got a car in the driveway. Move it!" "Oh, that's Jimmy Clanton's Cadillac," someone in the studio said. "I don't care if it's Peter Pan!" Matassa said. "Get it out of my driveway!"

"'Just a Dream' just come out and Jimmy Clanton is there with a Cadillac," Huey remembered. "Well, that come from Johnny. But I'm walking. What I had probably was in the shop. But I ain't looking at what nobody else got. That's his business."

Following Elvis Presley's lead, Clanton got in the movies, appearing with Alan Freed and Chuck Berry in 1959's *Go, Johnny, Go*. All the while, Vincent was making more money than he knew what to do with. According to historian Donald Mabry, Vincent hid hundreds of thousands of dollars in his Jackson office because he feared it would be stolen, lost in a fire, or get him in trouble with the IRS. Heeding his accountant's advice, Vincent formally established Ace Recording Company, Inc., in June 1958, and Ace Publishing Company, Inc., in March 1959. He also owned Vin Records and the distribution company Record Sales, Inc.

Huey and Earl King weren't the only ones unhappy with Vincent. When Joe Caronna asked Huey to go with him and Frankie Ford to a lawyer's office, Huey assumed Vincent wasn't paying Ford either. "Huey, Johnny's not giving you yo' money," Caronna said. "So we go' sue Johnny." The three of them gave a lawyer much information. "Now he go' pay you, Huey, for using all yo' stuff," Caronna promised. But three or four months later, Caronna opened a nightclub on Claiborne Avenue. The matter of the royalties didn't come up again. "That nightclub had to come from Johnny," Huey surmised. "Joe Caronna and Johnny were tight again. But nothing never for me. Never heard of it."

Herb Holiday, a New Orleans disc jockey who worked with Huey and the Clowns and managed Edgar "Big Boy" Myles, believed that Vincent cheated Myles as well. Myles recorded a great cover version of Gary "U.S." Bonds's 1960 hit, "New Orleans," for Ace Records. "I had to fight for some royalties that Big Boy had coming at the time we were doing business with Johnny," Holiday said. "Everybody was having the same problem with the guy. He had a bad reputation."

Jimmy Clanton, too, eventually grew unhappy with Ace Records. His 1962 comeback hit, "Venus in Blue Jeans," sold more than four hundred thousand copies, but he never received anything from it. Clanton maintained that Ace withheld $32,000 in "Venus" royalties because his 1960 double album, *Jimmy's Happy, Jimmy's Blue*, flopped, leaving thirty-five thousand albums unsold. Ironically, Vincent was able to charge Clanton for the loss after he re-signed with Ace. "This broke my back and it broke my heart," the singer said. "It kind of killed everything I felt, not necessarily for Johnny Vincent, but for the structure of Ace Records."

Even while Huey and Frankie Ford were still with Ace, they moonlighted for a small New Orleans record company formed by Ford and Joe Caronna. The Spinett label released nine singles, including the Louisiana State University football homage "Chinese Bandits." A regional hit, it is credited to the fictitious Cheer Leaders.

"We all used different names," Ford explained. "And there were a lot of midnight sessions, believe me. They were closed sessions, renegade sessions. . . . They were all parties." The Spinett label, for instance, attributed Huey's "Lumumba" and "Angola" to Snuffy Smith.

Huey named "Angola," a hard-driving instrumental, after the infamous Louisiana State Penitentiary, an eight-thousand-acre prison farm in East Feliciana Parish. The name dates from the prison's plantation years, when many of the slaves there originated from Angola in southern Africa. Patrice Lumumba, the charismatic prime minister of the newly independent Congo, inspired "Angola's" rumba-tinged flipside, "Lumumba." The African revolutionary's rise to power in 1960 made headlines in the United States. "Lumumba, Lumumba, that's the latest news," Huey sings. "Somebody's got to go out the Congo, the U.N.'s got the blues." "Lumumba then was an up-and-coming threat," Huey said. "So I know where he was going. If I see a little boy run into an alley full of glass, he's going to get cut feet."

Shortly after the song was released, a power struggle erupted between the Congo's anticolonial prime minister and Belgian-backed president Joseph Kasa-vubu. In succeeding months Lumumba was jailed, nearly lynched by Congolese soldiers, beaten in front of television cameras, and on January 16, 1961, secretly executed. The following day, a senior Belgian policeman and his companion ex-humed Lumumba's body and the bodies of his two slain comrades from shallow graves. They butchered the bodies, dissolved the pieces in acid, and, fulfilling orders to make the victims disappear, burned what remained.

Even before "Lumumba," Huey wrote and recorded another song inspired by current events, "Rockin' Behind the Iron Curtain." In this irreverent Cold War–era romp, released by Ace in 1959 as a Bobby Marchan and the Clowns single, Bobby and bass vocalist Roosevelt Wright sing about the citizens of Communist-ruled China and Eastern Europe secretly rockin', swingin', and jumpin' to forbid-den American rock 'n' roll. "Hey, comrade," Bobby says sarcastically in a spoken aside, "pull down the shades. Here comes *the man*."

"Everybody was talking about the Sputniks and people were worried about going to war with the Russians," Marchan told music journalist Jeff Hannusch in 1998, nearly a decade after the collapse of Communism in Eastern Europe.

G erri Hall, in addition to singing, worked as a stock clerk next door to Rec-ord Sales, Inc., Vincent and Joe Caronna's distribution business in New Or-leans's warehouse district. It was there that she put Caronna on the spot. "Joe Caronna was my boy," Gerri recalled. "I whispered to him, 'Whyn't you give Huey his money?' Joe said, 'Oh, man! Why you wanna ask me that? Now you go' have me fighting with Johnny Vincent!' I said, 'Well, why you go' fight with Johnny? Y'all *owe* Huey the money.' 'You go' get some of it?' 'No!' 'Well, leave it alone!' And Joe run me out the office!"

T he payola scandal of 1959 and 1960 rocked the music industry, bringing down one of the most powerful men in music, disc jockey and television host Alan Freed. *American Bandstand* host Dick Clark came under fire, too.

He was called to testify during congressional hearings on payola, the record company practice of rewarding disc jockeys for radio airplay with cash and gifts. During its investigation, the Special Subcommittee on Legislative Oversight of the House Committee on Interstate and Foreign Commerce cited Johnny Vincent's Ace Records among the labels that practiced payola. Vincent claimed to have given private testimony at payola hearings in Washington, D.C. He refused to name Clark as a payola recipient. "They said, 'Now, here is what we want you to do,'" he remembered. "'We want you to stick this guy.' I said, 'You can't stick that guy. You might stick some other guy but this is one straight guy.' I said, 'He may have guys around him phoning you and asking you for these songs, but they are trying to get some of the meat off the bones for themselves. . . . Y'all got the wrong guy. That son of a bitch does everything in the world for poor people and the kids love him.'" The payola scandal ended Freed's career, but Clark, at the insistence of ABC-TV, divested himself of his lucrative music-related businesses prior to his April 1960 testimony to the House subcommittee. The sell-off cost him millions, but with the congressional heat off, Clark proceeded to build a television-based media empire during the succeeding decades.

Huey heard that Vincent had been telling disc jockeys: "Hey, chief, I'm gonna send you this tie. It's made out for you," and, "I got this suit I'm go' send you," and, "I'm go' send you a little check in the mail."

"We didn't ask Johnny for nothing like that," a disc jockey told Huey. "It's like he wanted to make a fool out of us! We were just playing the records because we like them. And other people tell us he's doing the same thing with them."

"Many disc jockeys," Huey said of that time, "were telling me they ain't go' play nothing for Johnny, they don't care how good it is. They said, 'Excuse me. We're not playing nothing by Huey Smith neither.' And whatever new label Johnny come up with, they're not go' play it."

L ess than a year after Huey's Top 10 national pop hit "Don't You Just Know It," a new publicity photo of him appeared in the January 10, 1959, edition of the *Louisiana Weekly*. His downbeat expression in the photo may well reflect the financial and artistic disappointments he'd endured in 1958. The beaming smile in his "Rocking Pneumonia" headshot was as thoroughly erased as his "Sea Cruise" vocals.

Having signed with Ace in 1956, Huey figured his three years with Vincent were up in 1959. He sought greener pastures at Imperial Records, home to teen idol Ricky Nelson and New Orleans's most successful music star, Fats Domino. Tired of not getting paid as he thought he should, Huey went to talk with Dave Bartholomew at Imperial. "Dave was telling me, 'Now, you fixing to go with this record company. Now, look, ask them for some money—no, I forgot I'm talking to you. You go' ask!'"

Imperial released four singles by Huey and the Clowns in 1961, including "More Girls" and its Gerri Hall–inspired flipside, "Sassy Sara."

"Huey started playing 'Sassy Sara' and it just come out," Gerri remembered. "He could write for me. He could write for all of us who worked for him. Look, they used to give me a bad time, because I *was* Sassy Sara. I was flip-mouthed. I always had something to say and I always could tell you off, too, yeah."

"Sassy Sara's" call and response flipside, "More Girls," reflected the womanizing lifestyle typical of New Orleans musicians:

> On Fridays, there's Mary Ann. On Saturdays, there's Sweet Loraine.
> On Sundays, there's Liza Jane. Then I go making my round again.

Among his Imperial recordings, Huey especially likes "More Girls." "It just never got airplay," he said.

Gerri Hall also inspired "Psycho" and "Snag-a-Tooth Jeanie." The latter song's comic, rhyming verses, spoken by Huey, and its ensemble-sung choruses anticipated rap by about twenty years:

> She got eight fingers, she got two thumbs.
> She ain't got no teeth, just gums.
> In her hometown, really, they had some fun,
> A beauty contest, and ain't nobody won.

Huey didn't much care for "Snag-a-Tooth Jeanie." "We didn't even think about listening to that back then," he said years later, during an era when rap and hip-hop dominated the music charts. "But different things appeal to the kids now. Mostly, instead of the music and how it sounds, they listen to what you're saying. But I have never understood one rap record yet. Not one sentence!"

Enjoy making records though Huey did, he took the process seriously. "Huey was always maestro," Gerri Hall said. "He didn't play no games with us. He was always boss, yeah." "It's not at a party," Huey said. "You're making a living. It wasn't about having fun, but, say, if you have fun while you working, well, you doing good." "All the Huey Smith sessions were very, very happy," saxophonist Alvin "Red" Tyler said. "I think all of us were making enough money and I imagine we thought that this would never end."

As far as Imperial Records and Cosimo Matassa were concerned, Fats Domino was always top dog in New Orleans. Whenever he was ready to work, others were shown the studio door. As Huey recalled: "Like we got a session scheduled with Cosmo. I'm fixing to cut some things, but somebody must have called Cosmo about recording with Fats. We're scheduled there at 11:30, whatever it was. So it's twenty after eleven and Cos come in and say: 'Ah, Lew Chudd just called. He wants me to do this thing on Fats Domino. If it makes anybody feel better, I'll say I'm sorry.'"

The memory of Matassa's offer to apologize got Huey laughing. "Get out of here. I don't care nothing about your appointment. Cosmo the man and he knows where his bread is coming from. Fats Domino hit. So ain't nothing you could do about it. Like a man got a dance hall here and you got Ernie K-Doe and then somebody says, 'Well, look, the Beatles coming through here that night.' Later for K-Doe!"

"Fats," Matassa reasoned many years later, "had to have priority for all kinds of reasons. First, his personality is kind of laid back, so, if he agrees to come in the studio, you don't want to miss that opportunity." Domino knew very well how important he was. "I could go in the studio and tell Dave what I want done, tell the studio the way I want to be recorded and tell the record company like I wanted it out." Domino, accompanied by his valet and chauffeur, often made a kingly entrance into the studio. He once intentionally annoyed other musicians by placing an IRS refund check for $95,000 on his piano. He might also miss sessions, leaving Bartholomew, Matassa, and the musicians waiting. "To tell you the truth, he was a pain in the ass to record," Matassa said. "Not because he was a nasty guy about anything, but right in the middle of a take he'd say, 'How do I sound?' Pretty bad, especially if it's the first good take of the thing you had."

The mansion Domino and his family moved into in April 1960 evidenced his success. The $200,000-plus home's luxurious appointments included a $35,000 porcelain tile roof, drapes costing $30,000, murals, Japanese- and Italian-themed furnishings, a twenty-four-foot-high ceiling, a twelve-foot fireplace topped by a ten-foot Italian mosaic green hood accented with fourteen-karat gold, and an intercom system. Domino also installed a white Steinway concert grand piano in a glass-paneled music room finished with pink carpet and red and white silk drapery from Hong Kong. The *Louisiana Weekly*'s Elgin Hychew reported that twelve hundred people, both black and white, toured the home after he'd featured it in his "Dig Me!" column. When a woman asked Domino if she'd arrived on the day for black tours, the singer good-humoredly replied, "Why, of course. It's the day for anybody."

While the Dominos prepared to occupy their grand new residence, New Orleans Police Department narcotics officers arrested Professor Longhair as he stepped on stage at the San Jacinto Club to play a Mardi Gras day dance. The brilliantly original pianist and singer responsible for the already classic Carnival anthem "Mardi Gras in New Orleans" spent most of Fat Tuesday, 1960, and a few days more, in jail. Nabbed for buying marijuana from an undercover police officer, Longhair couldn't afford the $2,500 bond. Through most of his life, in fact, he was unable to support his family through music alone. He boxed, worked as a cook, earned much of his income as a card-playing gambler, and, ironically for such an influential, revered-in-death artist, swept the floor at the One-Stop Record Shop on South Rampart Street. "Really, no, I wasn't making a living off of the music," he said. "It was just a help. Other than sessions, I would play gigs sometimes with different fellows. Then after the gigs if there wasn't no gigs, well, I know where my spot was, and that was right back on the corner with those cards."

In addition to recordings by Fats Domino and Huey Smith, Imperial Records' early 1960s artists from New Orleans included Smiley Lewis, the Spiders, guitar prodigy Snooks Eaglin, singer-saxophonist Robert Parker, Wardell (Quezergue) and the Sultans, and Shirley and Lee. Like Earl King, Ace act Frankie Ford also moved to Lew Chudd's Los Angeles–based Imperial. Huey played piano for Ford's 1960 Imperial cover of Joe Jones's novelty record "You Talk Too Much." Originally released by local label Ric Records, the song's rising popularity prompted a suit by Jones's former label, Roulette Records in New York. A court-ordered halt to the record's sales presented the perfect opportunity for Ford and Imperial to cover "You Talk Too Much." In the purest sense of the term, Ford and producer Dave Bartholomew hoped to cover Jones's version up with their own.

"A cover," Huey explained, "would be if you do it at the time that a song is originally out by someone else. But instead of their hitting, yours go' be hitting, because they can't get theirs distributed and you're going to cover them. That's what we tried to do with 'You Talk Too Much.'" As perfect a copy as Imperial's cover is, it was Jones's version, this time released by Roulette—a label founded by Morris Levy, a powerful music-business figure and owner of the famous New York City jazz club Birdland—that reached No. 3 on the *Billboard* pop singles chart.

Huey's ex-bandmate Earl King found Imperial a big improvement over Ace, creatively and financially. There he worked with producer Dave Bartholomew, arranger-conductor Wardell Quezergue (whose decades of studio credits include Professor Longhair's "Big Chief," the Dixie Cups' "Chapel of Love," Robert Parker's "Barefootin'," and King Floyd's "Groove Me"), and session players such as singer-pianists James Booker and Wilson "Willie Tee" Turbinton and drummer Bob French and his bass-playing brother, George. Earl recorded two proto-funk New Orleans classics during his two years at Imperial, "Trick Bag" and a song subsequently recorded by future guitar stars Jimi Hendrix and Stevie Ray Vaughan, "Come On," aka "Let the Good Times Roll."

"Dave Bartholomew gave me the liberty to do anything I wanted to do on Imperial," Earl said. "And by him being a songwriter hisself, a great musician, arranger, and producer, he understood where I was coming from. I heard a lot of bad things people say about Dave, but I never experienced none of that with him. He showed me the direction that I can really go. If somebody gives you the space, you can do what you need to do." Given the conditions Huey and Earl experienced working at Ace, it's a wonder they cut the classic records they did. "I think about Huey and us trying to get things together," Earl mused, "and people squawking about $25 an hour in the studio and rushing you out."

Earl experienced another artistically friendly atmosphere when he briefly worked at Berry Gordy's 1960s hit factory, Motown Records. Earl joined the delegation of New Orleans talent that traveled to Detroit in August 1963. The troupe included singers Johnny Adams, Chris Kenner, Esquerita, singer–music businessman Joe Jones, arranger Wardell Quezergue, singer-pianist-songwriter Reggie Hall (Fats Domino's brother-in-law), drummer Smokey Johnson, and bassist George French. Although a Motown–New Orleans alliance never materialized, Gordy's operation impressed Earl. "When you get to places like Motown, man, it's so easy," he said. "What you didn't get today, you go back and do it tomorrow. It was like a songwriter's or singer's or musician's dream come true."

11

Pop-Eye

Going by Cosimo Matassa's studio one day, Huey found his Clowns Curley Moore, Billy Brooks, and Gerri Hall adding vocals to an instrumental track he'd recorded some years before. "What y'all doing with my song?" he asked. The track originally accompanied Gerri's vocals for "It Was a Thrill," which he'd written for her to sing. Cliff and Ed Thomas—white brothers from Jackson, Mississippi, who'd released recordings through Sam Phillips's Phillips International Records in the late 1950s and a single via Ace in 1961—wrote new lyrics and a new melody for Huey's existing music. The Thomas brothers also whistled for the new vocal tracks. Joe Caronna, the instigator of it all, hoped to use the resulting composite recording, dubbed "Pop-Eye," to capitalize on a local dance craze, the Popeye, already the inspiration for records by Eddie Bo and Ernie K-Doe.

"Joe Caronna," Huey recollected, "however he seduced Gerri to go in there and use her track for to do something else, they were going to alter her song. Maybe a Popeye by her, Gerri Hall, and them two white ones, who wanted to get a Popeye out. They were trying to erase the Eddie Bo and K-Doe Popeye things. So then I started in there with them, writing it, too, and then I did it with them."

> Down in New Orleans where it
> Got its start,
> Everybody's doing it from
> Dawn to dark.
> So let's do it,
> Popeye the sailor man.

Just before the riotously fun record begins its fadeout, Billy Brooks shouts, "Ah, Gerri! You're looking good!" "Yes," Gerri later recalled, "we did the Popeye over

101

the whole studio. Boy, we were singing the Popeye like we was in a parade, yeah. Cosmo say, 'They crazy!'"

In January 1962, *Billboard* reported that the Popeye dance had eclipsed the Twist in New Orleans. Just before Mardi Gras, the story continued, Huey Smith and the Clowns' "Pop-Eye" had become a breakout local record. New Orleans record stores also were getting requests for Bo's "Check Mr. Popeye" on Ric Records and K-Doe's "Popeye Joe" on Minit. Both of the latter labels were New Orleans based.

The February 3, 1962, edition of *Cash Box* listed the Clowns' "Pop-Eye" among the top three sellers at Philadelphia's Flying distributorship. A page-one *Billboard* story that same week reported Popeye records breaking in multiple markets. In succeeding weeks, sales in Milwaukee, Baltimore, and Detroit were particularly strong. Based on the Clowns' pop chart–climbing "Pop-Eye," *Billboard* printed a large house ad in its March 3, 1962, issue bragging about the magazine's ability to pick a hit.

Wardell Quezergue released yet another Popeye record, "The Original Popeye," credited to Wardell and the Sultans. Despite the Popeye dance's New Orleans origin, the South Philadelphia–based Chubby Checker recorded the most popular Popeye record. A national star since his cover of Hank Ballard and the Midnighters' "The Twist" became a No. 1 pop hit in 1960, Checker rode "Popeye (The Hitchhiker)" to the No. 10 pop and No. 13 rhythm-and-blues spots in *Billboard*. The following year Checker's high-spirited, Latin-tinged remake of Huey Smith and the Clowns' "We Like Birdland" reached the Top 20 of *Billboard*'s pop and rhythm-and-blues charts.

Ace issued its "Pop-Eye" as a Huey Smith and the Clowns single, even though Huey had not re-signed with Vincent's label and had no intention of doing so. "Joe Caronna again," Huey sighed. "When Joe sent 'Pop-Eye' off, I'm with Imperial Records, but he sends it off as Huey Smith on Ace. I guess he was trying to make up for the 'Sea Cruise.' So Joe came back, talking about, 'Johnny was mad with me because I put it out by Huey Smith! Johnny told me he didn't want me to put nothing out by you.' But it went in the charts somewhere, so we got us some gigs. We went straight to the Apollo with it to headline, me, Billy, and Curley."

The popularity of "Pop-Eye"—it reached No. 51 on *Billboard*'s pop chart in April 1962—became an unexpected mixed blessing for Huey. Imperial threatened to sue both him and Vincent. "Like I had went back to Johnny," Huey said. "So then Johnny came up with a forged contract and told Imperial I signed with him. Well, Imperial didn't record me no more."

"Pop-Eye" may not have been the only reason Imperial dropped Huey. Imperial's table may not have been big enough for its long-time star, Fats Domino, and Huey, too. Or at least that's what Huey heard from someone familiar with the situation. "Fats put pressure on them to cut you loose," he was told. "He don't want you on Imperial. They weren't worried about the 'Pop-Eye.' Fats didn't want Imperial giving no attention to you." Glancing back through the years, Huey pondered what the man said. "I understood what he was talking about. Like I know that 'More Girls,' which I liked, it came out and it just lay flat. The man said Fats told them, 'Step on it, hold it down.' Like Fats figured that's competition. Well, they needed a moneymaker, so they listened at that. And Fats was that type of individual. He wanted everything centered around just him. There were people who were like that. Not many, but some, and Fats was one."

Imperial Records owner Lew Chudd said Domino was especially jealous of the label's white teen idol, Ricky Nelson. "He thought the label should be one-track—Fats Domino. He didn't even appreciate Dave [Bartholomew]." Dave Bartholomew heard from a major record distributor that his connection to Domino coupled with his A&R position with Imperial kept his own records from being promoted. "Well, everybody's crazy about your personal records," the distributor told Bartholomew. But Chudd, Bartholomew reflected, "didn't want that being. I was young. I would have liked to have gotten a hit record. But the man upstairs made it so that I was a producer. My success came from that. I didn't get millions, but I raised my family working for Imperial."

Though Huey did not enjoy traveling, he continued performing out-of-town gigs in the early 1960s, a time when it was still risky to be a touring black musician in the South. Besides fraternity parties, auditoriums, theaters, and clubs, black performers were often booked into jails. After Huey returned to the national charts in 1962 with "Pop-Eye," he arrived for a fraternity gig in Athens, Georgia, only to be arrested for not showing up for a previous engagement at the same fraternity. Suddenly he realized why he'd been hearing about impostor Huey Smith and the Clowns groups being arrested. "A lot of people were saying, 'Man, people are out there looking for y'all!' And the people at this fraternity were looking for me. They had a charge of cheating and swindling. They had sent an agency a deposit, but I didn't make it."

Huey had missed the earlier Athens fraternity show because his group's driver, a trumpet player who called himself Little Louis Armstrong, never made it to the Dew Drop Café to pick the group up for the trip. Armstrong later gave guitarist Billy Tate his excuse. "Tate, I didn't tell your boy this, because he probably not go' believe me, but, you know, when I was on my way, I went to pass a red light and the police hauled me off to jail!" "Well, you right, Louis," Tate snapped back. "Don't tell Huey that, because I don't believe you neither!"

Armstrong's negligence landed Huey in the county jail. Clowns driver and road manager Ike Favorite found a lawyer who, by Huey's estimation, was ninety-nine years old. Feeble though the attorney was, the old gentleman waved his walking stick and spouted a passionate, albeit wobbling, plea for his client. "Ay-ay-ay, they're try-ay-ay-ing to railroad this boy-oy-oy!"

The officer who escorted Huey to a communal cell asked him if he had a knife. "Oh, no sir," Huey replied. "Well, here, you better take this then," the officer said, handing the unarmed musician a small knife. "Okay, thank you," Huey replied. And just in case the knife wasn't protection enough, Huey noticed a big stick under his bunk. Meanwhile, his cellmates listened to transistor radios through the night, paying special attention to newscasts. "It's coming on!" one prisoner announced. "They talking about—that boy there now! Huey 'Piano' Smith. They say 'a charge of cheating and swindling.' Say, yeah, he at the county jail. Now they talking about that girl. Say she went up on that hill. They talking about Mary Lou!" "Is she dead?" another prisoner asked. "I don't know," came the answer, "but they do say she is 'fatally stabbed.'"

Word got around the jail that poor Mary Lou was indeed dead. "You know," one inmate said, "I done told Mary Lou not to go up on that hill." "Yeah," another said, "see, I'm the one was supposed to kill her!"

Despite the violent talk, Huey never needed the knife that the thoughtful officer had provided. He and his cellmates got along fine. "They were nice," he remembered fondly. "I talked to them a good little while that day."

John Williams, James Black, and Eugene Harris had left Huey Smith and the Clowns by the early 1960s to organize the Clowns-styled Tick Tocks. "They came out with a record," Huey said. "'Tick-tock goes the clock, when I'm with my baby, we never stop.' It didn't go nowhere." Deacon John Moore, a guitarist who worked with Huey and the Clowns at the College Inn in Thibodaux during the "Pop-Eye" era, also gigged with Dew Drop Café regulars the Tick Tocks. "The Tick Tocks did all the Clowns songs and some Coasters songs,"

Moore said. "They were like a show group. They had crazy antics and a lot of good choreography, a lot of tumble sets and splits. They would come out in costumes. Some would be dressed as women. They would do that song Bobby Marchan revitalized, 'There Is Something on Your Mind,' with the rap part in it. They'd sing the 'doo-doo, doo-doo' on the end and Eugene would take out a roll of toilet paper and he'd wipe his ass the moment he said 'doo-doo, doo-doo.' Bring the house down every night."

12

Christmas Blues

Seeing an opportunity for holiday season radio play and gigs, Huey assembled a large group of singers and musicians to record a Christmas album at a new studio on Magazine Street. "All of us knew a seasonal record could play every year," he remembered. "Bing Crosby. Yeah, we already hear, 'I'm dreaming of a white Christmas. . . .' Every year, the same thing. Well, we can have this ready for the next Christmas, so we'll be working all over the country when it comes out."

The vocal cast for 1962's *'Twas the Night before Christmas* album includes Huey; Jesse Thomas; Pearl Edwards; Johnny Meyers, a member of the New Orleans vocal group the Moonbeams (he also worked as a chef at the African American–owned Dooky Chase Restaurant); Curley Moore; and three female session singers whose names are lost to time. The songs came together like spontaneous combustion. "So I started putting the melodies into my mind, how it would go," Huey recalled. "'I want to make it up to you, baby, standing under the mistletoe.' That's how that goes, and the horns go like this. So that, this, that, that. Just go to do it and it's like it makes itself."

The album's title song features Jesse Thomas soul-shouting about a boogie-woogie Santa Claus and Huey rapping the classic Christmas poem, "'Twas the Night before Christmas." Following Mabel Scott's "Boogie Woogie Santa Claus" (a 1948 rhythm-and-blues hit that white pop star Patti Page covered) and jazz vocalist Babs Gonzales's hipster holiday number, "Be-Bop Santa Claus," the Clowns added a particularly hip and festive twist to "'Twas the Night before Christmas."

Taking its cue from the Drifters' doo-wop rendition of "White Christmas," the album's elaborate "White Christmas Blues" features Johnny Meyers singing sweet, high tenor and Huey rapping about having a blue Christmas. Another song, "Happy New Year," fits new lyrics to the 1956 Ace single "Little Liza Jane" and replaces "Liza's" sax solo based on Dvořák's "Humoresque" with singers and a horn section performing "Auld Lang Syne." "Almost Time for Christmas" recasts "We Like Mambo"/"We Like Birdland." "Doing the Santa Claus" contains more soul-shouting from Jesse and sly vocal asides from session guitarist Mac Rebennack. The high-spirited "All I Want for Christmas," based on the same music track as "Doing the Santa Claus," cites dance crazes the Twist, the Hully Gully, and the Popeye. "Santa won't you bring my Popeye record today!" the group sings. There's also a swinging take on the normally serene "Silent Night."

Billboard's December 15, 1962, review of *'Twas the Night before Christmas* listed it at the top of its "strong sales potential" column. The anonymous reviewer describes the album as a happy collection of rock tunes that's not the usual Christmas fare.

Touring in late 1962, Huey and Clowns Curley Moore, Jesse Thomas, and Johnny Meyers were in Charlotte, North Carolina, for a show with Maurice Williams and the Zodiacs ("Stay"). They were watching television in their hotel room when a local teen dance show played "Silent Night" from their new Christmas album. Johnny Vincent hadn't even told them that the album was out. "Hey!" Huey said as he sat on the hotel floor. "We're in if this record go' to playing around here. It'll be unending where we'll be playing at." But the program's host cut the song short. "They should be ashamed of themselves!" he proclaimed. "Mocking Christmas! This is a disgrace! Let me show y'all what we do with this." He smashed the album and threw it in a trash can. The host's violent objection to their high-spirited take on "Silent Night" shocked Huey and the Clowns.

"Our 'Silent Night' was sacrilegious in his opinion," Huey said. "Other words, 'Silent Night' is supposed to be sad, not up like we did it."

Clowns driver and road manager Ike Favorite reacted by phoning the television station. "Huey Smith is in town and we just saw what you did," Ike said over the phone. "You'll be hearing from our lawyer!" "Well," Jesse Thomas recalled, "*boom, boom, boom*, the TV people were in shock then. They just hold up. They didn't say anything else."

Even New Orleans reacted negatively to Huey and the Clowns' Christmas album. One angry fellow told Huey's mother, "Huey Smith'll do anything for money!" Johnny Vincent told him the record had been banned and that Ace was pulling it off the market. "We were before our time," Huey mused. "It's like when I named an instrumental we recorded 'Funky.' Melvin Lastie took the [trumpet] lead. Melvin said, '*Ooh, that's funky.*' I said, 'That's going to be the name of it.' Then Johnny took the tape and said, 'No, we ain't go' put that out! You can't say

'Funky' on no record!' But today that's all you hear. Everything is funky." Huey reminded Vincent about the Christmas album controversy many years later. "Huey, I believe you was before yo' time," Vincent said.

Some altercations occurred among touring members of the Clowns. In Washington, D.C., Huey and his girlfriend, Barbara,* were having sandwiches at the Dunbar Hotel when Curley Moore appeared before them with a swollen eye. "Billy [Brooks] jumped on me!" Curley told his boss. Huey went upstairs and found Billy with a bleeding mouth. "Hey, Billy," the serious Huey said. "Did I tell you to never fool with the members?" Although Billy was a big, tough guy, Huey ended up punching him. Curley tumbled in, too, smashing a pitcher over Billy's head. Blood splashed around the room and the suddenly sorrowful Billy found himself sprawled over the floor. "Ooh, mama," he moaned. The hotel charged Huey for the damages. "That's Billy," Huey reminisced. "Yeah, he had trouble."

Big and tall Clowns driver Jimmy Cole once complained to Huey that Curley Moore was trying to manipulate him into beating Billy up. "Say, boss man," Jimmy said. "Curley come telling me, 'Billy go' try you, yeah.' Curley's trying to get me to whip Billy's ass for him!" Meanwhile, Jimmy wasn't above being manipulative himself. "Say, boss man," he'd say. "Man, your hair looks just like it's supposed to look! Them white gals was peeing on theirselves tonight! Got a few dollars?"

When Huey and the performers he hired to sing and dance traveled to shows, promoters often provided a band for them. "Just me on the piano, Bobby, and whoever else, we would go sing," he recalled. "We don't know the band, but it wasn't no problem at all. We worked with, ooh, goo-gobs of bands. Sometimes with three pieces and they're just as good as the ten-piece bands. I had Illinois Jacquet [the tenor sax star] on one of them. Yeah, Palisades Park."

Performing with pickup bands usually worked fine, but doing so became impossible at one radio station–sponsored dance in the north Louisiana city of Monroe. The band hired to back the black performers was white. Louisiana's segregation laws dictated that Huey and his group could not share a stage

---

*A previously unreleased song entitled "Barbara," recorded in Washington, D.C., appears on the 1999 British compilation CD *That'll Get It (Even More of the Best)*.

with white musicians. That meant that he and the Clowns, which still included Bobby Marchan at the time, would have to perform without a band. "That was a little awkward to do, but after the dance I was feeling good," Huey said. "But then the proprietor came in with about eight state policemen, about eight-feet-tall each. He said, 'Huey, you supposed to pick up $800 tonight. I'm go' give you $300. Would you accept that?' I just looked at the proprietor and the eight policemen. I ain't crazy. Everything was obvious. I said, 'Well, thank you.' And I fell out laughing. And then Bobby start laughing and the police start laughing. The proprietor is laughing, too. Then the police are hugging me, escorting me to the car and the city limits. So we got the $300 and we left town laughing. They wasn't go' get no problems. You know, you have to keep your cool sometimes."

In that same Louisiana city in April 1963, state police officers stopped New Orleans singer-pianist James "Sugar Boy" Crawford and his band, the Cane Cutters (including guitarist Smiley Lewis), and singers, the Sugar Lumps, as they entered the city. (Crawford had famously combined two Mardi Gras Indian chants, "Iko Iko" and "Jock-A-Mo," to create the classic 1954 Carnival record "Jock-A-Mo.") The police "made Sugar Boy get out of the car," singer Linda De-Gruy recalled. "When he reached into his pocket for his driver's license, the man hit him with a billy club in the head and blood gushed out. . . . When they finished with Sugar Boy, he was laying on the ground, bleeding half to death." The unconscious Crawford was taken to jail instead of a hospital. He remained imprisoned for days. The beating caused a blood clot that required surgery in Monroe. Following a second operation several weeks later at Charity Hospital in New Orleans, Crawford began having seizures. He needed medication for the seizures for the rest of his life. "The police stopped me and said I was speeding and drunk," Crawford recalled. "I wasn't doing either. Then they hit me in my head and I was paralyzed." For a time Huey thought Crawford had died. Crawford's his recovery was long. "I had a brain injury, and it took me two years to come back," he said. "I had to learn how to walk, talk, play the piano, everything." Knowing his abilities were diminished, Crawford left the music business. "I looked for other things to do with my life."

Huey's group received a warning about one venue because the white patrons there had an especially bad reputation. "Let me tell y'all something," a concerned person told the group. "Don't be talking to them white gals, no. See, them people out there are white niggers. When they get drunk, them some crazy niggers! So leave them white gals alone now."

"White niggers is bad," Gerri Hall remembered later during a visit with Huey in Baton Rouge. "Worse than Indians," Huey said, adding, "Gerri, did you know Joe Caronna was one of them Indians? Give him a drink, you'd know then." "Wild as a chicken!" Gerri agreed. "Mac Rebennack," she continued, "Joe Caronna, Roland Stone, all of them, they white, Indian, Italian, and Jewish! All of that is in that bunch—but they all niggers. Believe it!"

Yet even in the dangerously racist South, Huey dared to travel from Mississippi to Virginia with a young white woman. "Wanda, somebody Curley introduced me to from the French Quarter," he said. "Like we're in the Dew Drop and somebody came and said, 'I got a lot of friends that's colored!' Wanda said, 'We don't talk like that in here!'"

The perils for black musicians on the road could have as much to do with greed and corruption as race. Curley Moore was sent to jail in the Carolinas for a traffic violation. If the troupe didn't pay his fine in a day's time, he'd be sentenced to a prison farm. The police made the situation very clear. "I don't care how much money you got after that, he go' be digging potatoes!" one of them pledged. During another police stop some members of Huey's party dared to mock the arresting officers. "I wouldn't call an officer of the law that!" one of them said as he and the others unsnapped their guns. "That's how it was," Huey reflected. "But we knew how to cool it down."

Following Bobby Marchan's departure from the Clowns in 1959, Curley and Jesse Thomas stepped into the group's front line. Jesse kept an eye on the mischievous Curley. "He was young and wild," Jesse explained. "Curley did things without realizing how dangerous they were, till it's too late. And he liked to mess with everybody's head. See, sometimes when you mess with people's heads, you get into trouble." Curley, for instance, courted trouble as he stood backstage watching Esther Phillips, the singer who'd recovered from heroin addiction and returned to the charts in 1962 with the No. 1 song "Release Me." Unbeknownst to Curley, he was standing next to Phillips's boyfriend, an off-duty policeman. "*Ooh*, look at the lips on that bitch!" Curley gushed out loud. Ike Favorite reported Curley's poorly timed comment to Huey. "You got to tell Curley to watch his mouth!" Ike warned.

At a show in Richmond, Virginia, Curley set his eyes on a member of the girl group the Shirelles ("Soldier Boy," "Baby It's You"). He followed her everywhere—so much so, Huey recalled, "that girl couldn't breathe for Curley!" Back in New Orleans, Huey would let Curley borrow his car. He always returned it, but the vehicle might be missing a fender or two. And then there was the time Curley and the like-minded Billy Brooks helped turn a Clowns recording session in Jackson, Mississippi, into quite another kind of gathering. "They had about five white musicians," Huey recalled. "Nobody was black but me, Billy and Curley. The studio was airtight. So Curley or Billy, one of them, passed gas." Not missing a beat, the white musicians threw their gauntlet down. "You in our ballgame now!" one of them boasted. "Yeah," Huey said of the ensuing whites vs. blacks farting contest, "they were laughing and rolling on the floor. . . . I said, 'I can't do no session in here!'"

Curley prompted a lockdown at a hotel in the Carolinas when the establishment's manager spotted him on a street corner singing the Ernie K-Doe song "A Certain Girl." "No girls!" the wary manager said after canceling his planned weekend off. "He go' sing them girls right back here and they go' close me down. That's what you fixing to do!"

Traveling musicians from party capital New Orleans brought their hometown revelry with them, Gerri Hall said. "Clowning and going up and down and having a good time through the whole hotel. Like one of us come in from Chicago and somebody else'll come down from New York and we meet them in Washington, D.C. The whole hotel be *ours*. You can find us on every floor in the place! And you can hear us! We're noisy." But as wild as rhythm-and-blues and rock 'n' roll acts were, Huey heard that their road antics were modest next to those of gospel, or spiritual, groups. "Y'all thought y'all bad!" a hotel manager said. "Them religious groups, when they come here, they be all up and down them steps. Neked! All of them! The preacher, too! Y'all just *think* y'all bad."

At home in New Orleans, Huey and his mother, by now a longtime Jehovah's Witness, discussed the system by which humans govern themselves on Earth. "Well," Huey suggested, "suppose a good man got elected, got in office." "He could," Mrs. Smith conceded, "but then they gonna kill him." Jehovah, or God, is the only legitimate government in the Witnesses' view. Shortly thereafter, Huey and his three-year-old-son, Hugh "Baby," were tossing a football in their yard when the news of Friday, November 22, 1963, broke. President John F. Kennedy had been assassinated in Dallas. In the months before his death, Kennedy had set the landmark Civil Rights Act of 1964 in motion during a televised speech to the nation. "One hundred years of delay have passed since President Lincoln freed the slaves, yet their heirs, their grandsons, are not fully free," he said in a June speech. In September, against the strident opposition of Alabama governor George C. Wallace, Kennedy had federalized the Alabama National Guard for the purpose of integrating the state's public schools. Also in September, Kennedy had launched a campaign to raise $50 million from private sources for black colleges.

New Orleans's African American newspaper, the *Louisiana Weekly*, eulogized the slain president in a front-page editorial. "There is no doubt whatsoever that the Deep South's hatred of President Kennedy was based primarily upon his stand on civil rights. . . . John Fitzgerald Kennedy, our symbol of hope, was a martyr to freedom."

Huey performing with the Clowns at Tipitina's, 1979.

Photograph by Michael P. Smith, © The Historic New Orleans Collection, 2007.0103.1.801, Negative 5A

Huey and the Clowns at Tipitina's, 1979. *From left:* Curley Moore, Roosevelt Wright, Margrette Smith, Gerri Hall, Bobby Marchan in white jacket, Huey at piano. In the background behind Marchan is Greg Arthur, bass player for the back-up band Skor.

Photograph by Michael P. Smith, © The Historic New Orleans Collection,
2007.0103.1.801, Negative 6A

"Scarface" John Williams, the original lead vocalist for "Rocking Pneumonia and the Boogie Woogie Flu."

Photo courtesy of Deborah Williams

Earliest known photo of Eddie Jones, aka Guitar Slim.

Courtesy Tad Jones Collection, Hogan Jazz Archive, Tulane University

Eddie King, 1975.

Photo courtesy of Jim Scheurich

Malcolm "Mac" Rebennack, playing guitar at his home on S. Jefferson Davis Parkway in New Orleans, 1959.

Times-Picayune/Landov

Frankie Ford signing autographs at a teenage dance benefit at the VFW hall
in Gretna, Louisiana, August 28, 1959.

Times-Picayune/Landov

Huey holding the Jehovah's Witness publication the *Watchtower*, 1973.
Courtesy Tad Jones Collection, Hogan Jazz Archive, Tulane University

Huey with former Clown Gerri Hall, September 2000.

Photo by author

13

Pitter Patting

n Great Britain, in the hours before the American president was killed, fans of the Beatles besieged record stores. The occasion was the release of *With the Beatles*, the young Liverpool group's second album. Beatlemania soon reached America. The gloom that hovered over the country in the months that followed the Kennedy assassination is said to have lifted when the Beatles appeared on the *Ed Sullivan Show* on February 9, 1964. A record-breaking audience of 73 million watched the mop-topped foursome's American television debut, broadcast live from New York City that Sunday night. In the Beatles' wake, more young British music acts entered the American charts, beginning with the Dave Clark Five and continuing with Billy J. Kramer and another Liverpool group, Gerry and the Pacemakers. The parade of shaggy British invaders continued with Peter and Gordon, the Animals, the Kinks, the Rolling Stones, Herman's Hermits, and Manfred Mann. All of them released their first American hits in 1964, a year when British acts accounted for nearly one-third of the top ten U.S. singles.

Ironically, the guitar-playing English lads usurped the American rhythm-and-blues and rock 'n' roll acts they emulated. Suddenly, in New York, Los Angeles, Chicago, and even New Orleans, horns were out, guitars were in. "That's what happened to me," New Orleans promoter and disc jockey manager Jim Russell said. "I'd had eighteen disc jockeys and sixty bands. Three to six months after the invasion, we were completely disintegrated. Nothing. Because all of our bands had saxophones. How the hell do you find a guitar player overnight, when there's only two or three in the whole city?"

"The British invasion," Earl King confirmed, "that was different times right then." New Orleans singers Frankie Ford and Irma Thomas ("Ruler of My Heart," "It's Raining") were reeling, too. "Believe me," Ford said, "they were motor-pooling out of this town. When I got back from the Army in '65, there wasn't a horn player working in the French Quarter." Ford adapted via a cabaret act on Bourbon Street, but Irma Thomas bristled when people accused her of copying the Rolling Stones. "Anything somebody from Britain did was a hit, whether they could sing or not," she said. "But I was fine with that until one night I did my song, 'Time Is on My Side,' and somebody said, 'Oh, you're doing the Rolling Stones' tune.' I said, 'That's it. I won't be doing this song anymore!'" Johnny Vincent's teen idol, Jimmy Clanton, suffered, too. "Everything changed overnight, so I went into hiding," he said.

Lloyd Price, the singing star from nearby Kenner who, unlike most musicians from the New Orleans area and black artists in general, had moved successfully to the business side of music by founding and buying record and publishing companies in the mid- to late 1950s, cited the British for decimating American rhythm-and-blues on an international level. "We couldn't get back on the radio," Price said. Even Ernie K-Doe's No. 1 national hit, "Mother-in-Law," meant nothing. An especially flamboyant character from a city filled with characters, K-Doe had seen his career cool when Huey and driver Ike Favorite picked him up for a gig in Baton Rouge. "Watch K-Doe when he gets in here," Ike told Huey. "He go' say he got a hit coming out. Watch him." "I got a hit coming out!" K-Doe announced as he opened the car door. "Wait till Larry McKinley [an important New Orleans disc jockey and cofounder of Minit Records] hear it!"

"That's all his mind was," Huey said later. "When the people hear this new record, he go' be Ernie K-Doe again. So he went down there to the alimony court judges, he's telling them he's Ernie K-Doe and he's making a million dollars a night. So that's what the judge orders him to pay his ex-wife, Shirley. And then he's staying in jail because he wasn't making *nothing*. They were back there in jail joking about K-Doe, making him sing about Shirley, because that's why he was in there." The *Times-Picayune* reported in May 1965 that Ernest Kador Jr., "a young Negro entertainer known for his song, 'Mother-In-Law,' sang the alimony blues Monday" in Civil District Court. The judge sentenced K-Doe to ten days in jail for "ignoring the legal process."

Torch song queen Connie Francis, too, was among the formerly big-selling non–New Orleans stars stung by the invaders. "American artists, we cried a lot," she said. "Even Elvis stopped selling records."

Back in New Orleans, the downturn touched rank-and-file musicians. At forty, Alvin "Red" Tyler, the baritone saxophonist who'd played classic sessions for Fats Domino, Little Richard, Shirley and Lee, Huey, and many more, took a full-time gig in 1965 as a liquor company sales rep. "I realized that musicians only live as good as their last gig," he said. "There's no hospitalization, no retirement." On the up side, Tyler's day job income and benefits allowed him to pursue his true love, jazz. "I didn't have to go on Bourbon Street and play tourist music."

The mid-1960s were particularly troublesome for Johnny Vincent and Ace Records. The distribution, sales, and promotion deal Vincent made with Chicago's Vee-Jay Records in 1962, which he'd had enormous hopes for, turned sour. The mismanaged Vee-Jay went bankrupt in 1965, Vincent went broke, and the once mighty Ace went out of business. "I hit hard times," he said. "My wife divorced me. I had four kids to support. I started all kinds of businesses. None of them did any good. I sold the publishing rights to four big songs for $20,000. I blowed it all."

As for Huey's career, it dipped to the point that he didn't need a manager. "There was nothing to manage," he said.

As his fellow New Orleans musicians hit hard times, Dr. John, still known as Mac Rebennack, did hard time. Busted for heroin possession, he went to Orleans Parish Prison and then to a federal institution in Fort Worth, Texas. Sprung in 1965 and ordered to stay out of Orleans Parish, he migrated to the show business capital of Los Angeles. He and other talented New Orleans expats found recording studio work there.

Even before the British invasion, the New Orleans music community experienced a locally inflicted wound. Dr. John blamed crusading New Orleans district attorney Jim Garrison for the quick decline of the city's nightlife and music. "A twenty-four-hours-a-day happening city was being closed," he mourned. "The lights had gone dim in the joints, the music slammed in the gutter." By late 1962, Garrison had cited twenty-four French Quarter establishments, including bars and strip joints, for vice violations. The offenses included B-drinking, a scam in which dancers and waitresses promised sex to men who bought overpriced liquor. The district attorney's office padlocked a dozen of the cited nightspots in early 1963. Meanwhile, Garrison saw no irony in the fact that he patronized the joints himself. "It's not that I am against stripping," he told the *Washington Post*. "It just happens that B-drinking and prostitution are against the law."

Despite the difficulties faced by many New Orleans musicians in the mid-1960s, Clowns singer Curley Moore found some profitable new work. Willie Nettles (a drummer with Huey and Guitar Slim in the early 1950s) exported Curley to the Midwest to impersonate Motown star Marvin Gaye, just as Earl King had impersonated Guitar Slim a decade before. The ruse earned Curley a few thousand dollars. Such lucrative impersonation was common in the years before photos of hit recording artists were ubiquitous. Curley nearly blew his cover, though, as he sat at a nightclub bar with a young lady after the show. "Look, baby, I'm Curley Moore!" he boasted. Nettles quickly shushed him. "Shut up, boy! People think you're Marvin Gaye! And you're hollering you're Curley Moore?!"

Now a solo act, Curley did have a local hit to brag about, 1966's "Soul Train." Earl King wrote the song and Wardell Quezergue produced and arranged it. Deacon John Moore, a guitarist who did sessions for many New Orleans hits, including Aaron Neville's "Tell It Like It Is" and Lee Dorsey's "Working in the Coal Mine," worked with Curley during his "Soul Train" fame. He remembers the singer looking up to King as a new mentor. "Curley used to hang with Earl at all the places we used to hang," Moore said. "Curley worshiped Earl King. So he started looking like Earl, sounding like Earl, and having all of Earl's little mannerisms. He's like a carbon copy of Earl King!"

During the difficult period that followed the British invasion, Huey's wife, Doretha, concluded that he didn't want her to help support their family. "Huey is a proud man," she said. "He thought people would talk about him if I worked. I told Huey I was more concerned about keeping what we had than what people were saying about us. But every time I got a job, Huey would come and mess things up for me or make noise at night to keep me up so I would be unable to go to work. It was not Huey's fault that life gave us a bad hand, but I could not play the game anymore with the cards that were being dealt to my family. Life was getting too far out of balance for me. There were too many people pulling strings and none were in our favor. I knew Huey loved his family. Huey wanted us to have the best of everything and he worked hard to provide for us. But I decided to give my husband his freedom to achieve his dreams. I took my children and we started a new life. To leave the children with him would have interfered with his music career. I wanted him to be all that he wanted to be."

Following a final series of Ace singles in 1962 and 1963—including "Quiet as It's Kept," a little-known gem featuring one of New Orleans's most elegant vocalists, former Spiders singer Chuck Carbo—Huey and Carlton H. Pecot formed Pitter-Pat Records and Pitter Music. Pecot had a long record of achievement behind him. In 1950, this civil rights pioneer became one of the first two

African American patrolmen to join the New Orleans Police Department in forty years. By the 1960s Pecot was a prominent member of the city's black business community, the president of the Carver General Insurance Agency, Carver Realty Company, and Carver Development Securities, Inc. In 1963, he staged an abbreviated run for the U.S. House of Representatives.

Huey, hoping to escape the stigma attached to Ace Records and Johnny Vincent, gave himself and his groups new names. He recorded as the Pitter Pats, the Hueys, and Shin-Dig Smith and the Soul Shakers. His Pitter-Pat Records debut, "It Do Me Good," became a regional hit. In 1966, Huey and Pecot leased "It Do Me Good," a haunting love song, to Joe Banashak's Instant Records. A record sales and distribution veteran who'd cofounded Minit Records in 1958 with Larry McKinley, Banashak experienced much success with his Instant and Minit labels thanks in part to in-house producer, songwriter, and pianist Allen Toussaint. The labels' national hits included former Clowns drummer Jessie Hill's "Ooh Poo Pah Doo," Ernie K-Doe's "Mother-in-Law," Benny Spellman's "Fortune Teller," Chris Kenner's "I Like It Like That," and one of the most regionally revered recordings of the era, a Toussaint-penned ballad sung by Art Neville, "All These Things." Banashak also issued sides by Aaron Neville, Irma Thomas, Eddie Bo, Lee Dorsey, and Huey associates Curley Moore and Raymond Lewis.

Gloria Franklin sings the female vocal for "It Do Me Good," a rare love song from Huey and a highlight of his mid-1960s recordings. Alex Scott performs the striking "doo-doo, doo-doo" falsetto, which prompted Curley Moore to nickname Scott "the doo-doo boy." Huey hoped "It Do Me Good" would reach beyond New Orleans. There was reason to be optimistic. In 1966, three New Orleans recordings—Robert Parker's "Barefootin'," Lee Dorsey's "Working in the Coal Mine," and Aaron Neville's "Tell It Like It Is"—moved high into the national charts. With a potential national hit for Huey and his Pitter Pats looming, Ike Favorite lobbied to be the group's road manager, a job he also did for Chris Kenner and Fats Domino. But momentum for "It Do Me Good" stalled. "Ike got some placards printed and we hit a few places, try to do something with 'It Do Me Good,'" Huey said. "The thing started getting some airplay. We fixing to start again. We promoted a dance over in Donaldsonville, but it poured down raining. 'It Do Me Good' didn't make it nationally and Ike had me owing people in Baltimore. We didn't schedule no more."

Despite his disappointment over "It Do Me Good," Huey continued working with Banashak and Instant. Banashak, lacking the money to hire session musicians, asked Huey to write new lyrics for an instrumental track originally used for the Chris Kenner recording "Stretch My Hand to You." Working with the existing music, Huey produced one of his most popular Instant singles. The label released "Coo Coo over You" in 1968 as a single by the Hueys. In the recording, a passionate Edward "Little Buck" Ross shouts out his love above a steely groove while girl singers chirp, "I love ice cream, I'm wild about cookies, too."

"Coo Coo over You," popularized by disc jockey Shelly Pope, became a New Orleans hit just as a jail sentence took Ross, the song's lead singer, out of circulation. Huey visited the incarcerated vocalist and asked Carlton Pecot to see if he could get him released. But Ross remained imprisoned, thwarting the chance to fully exploit "Coo Coo over You." Meanwhile, the song earned five mentions in *Billboard,* beginning with a prediction in the April 20, 1968, issue that it would reach the magazine's R&B chart. *Billboard's* June 15 issue listed "Coo Coo" as a regional breakout. The following week William Roy Brown, program director for KJET in Beaumont, reported that the No. 3 record in New Orleans was becoming "a stone monster in Texas."

But when Atlantic Records offered to distribute "Coo Coo" in the United States, Banashak wouldn't let it go. "I'm go' hold out," he told Huey. "I'm a' try it myself, to build Instant back up." "We thought we had a breakthrough with 'Coo Coo over You,'" Huey said later. "But that's when Joe got sick and went in the hospital. Well, after the song had played and played, the big companies weren't interested in it no more. Joe admitted he made a mistake." A licensing deal Banashak made with the United Kingdom's London Records, however, got the song a British release in April 1969.

The mighty Pearl Edwards, a girlfriend of Chris Kenner, sang for many of Huey's mid- to late 1960s recordings. He met her at a bar while she was singing along as the jukebox played Esther Phillips's 1962 hit, "Release Me." "Pearl was sounding like she'll run Little Esther out of town," Huey remembered. "Gloria [Franklin] had a good voice, but it couldn't reach the depths of Pearl. Pearl would run Aretha Franklin off the stage." Indeed, Pearl and Huey played a ballpark with a band that had just toured with Franklin, the Atlantic Records soul star. "Pearl, boy, had the people screaming all over the ballpark," he said.

Huey, once again casting his singers in songs designed for them, featured Pearl's gospel-fired conviction in such horn-powered soul scorchers as 1967's "Bury Me Dead (Deep in My Grave)" and 1968's "Smile for Me." His mid-1960s recordings also include Roosevelt Wright, the bass-singing member of the

1950s-era Clowns who'd moved back to New Orleans from Baton Rouge. Roosevelt returned to music even though his family told him the stroke he'd suffered had been his punishment for singing the blues.

Huey's Instant years also yielded one of his few Mardi Gras–specific songs, "Twowaypocaway." The 1969 single features the traditional Carnival season call for beads and trinkets: "Hey, mister! Throw me something!" Huey particularly enjoyed having drummer Joseph "Smokey" Johnson on the "Twowaypocaway" session. Johnson's studio credits include Professor Longhair's Carnival classic "Big Chief" and Earl King's pioneering funk number "Trick Bag." "Twowaypocaway" didn't catch on, not even locally, but it's one of Huey's personal favorites among his recordings. "Today, like for the dancers, that's one of the best things I ever did," he said. "It's just got that beat and everything in it. If they'd played that around Carnival time it would have hit."

Pearl Edwards, Gloria Franklin, Edward "Little Buck" Ross, Alex Scott, and the other singers Huey made recordings with in the 1960s represented a continuation of the vocal ensembles he'd led featuring Dave Dixon, Bobby Marchan, Gerri Hall, John Williams, Curley Moore, Roosevelt Wright, and others in the 1950s and early 1960s. "So, like all them songs what I have, only one individual created them and that's Huey Smith," he said.

In an example of Huey's studio methods, Jesse Thomas, one of Huey's singers concurrent with Pearl Edwards, joined his boss at a Jackson studio to add vocals to previously recorded instrumental tracks. "Huey just retracks, because the old tracks were made at Cos's studio with Lee Allen and all the fine musicians," Jesse explained. "And a lot of times Huey might put some fresh piano or something on there with the voice." The latter productions include "I'm Boss, Yeah," released by Ace in 1964 as a Jesse Thomas solo single. Johnny Vincent, always looking for an angle, suggested that "I'm Boss, Yeah" be credited to Lil' Jesse Brown. "I was to be James Brown's little brother," Jesse said with a laugh. "Yeah, that's Johnny Vincent!"

With so many singers passing through Huey's groups, music writers of the not-so-distant future, admiring though they were, got confused. Many books, articles, and liner notes perpetuate the errors. The names of Billy Brooks and Roosevelt Wright, for instance, were frequently blended into the nonexistent Billy Roosevelt. Other New Orleans singers were falsely reported to be members of the Clowns, one of whom Curley Moore saw performing in the French Quarter. "Yeah," Curley told Huey, "he be down there on Bourbon Street singing and he stop and say, 'Just a minute, wait. Excuse me, y'all—let me get this booger out my nose!' Yeah," Curley continued, "them white people flip over that." Huey shook his head over the incident. "They threw him big tips when he did stuff like that," he marveled. "But he didn't even come up to the standard of a Clown."

Regarding singers, Huey's brother, Melvin, suggested something his older brother had not considered in all the years he'd been leading groups. "I understand why you don't let nobody in the group stand out front too long," Mel said. "If you let somebody get too much power, they be wanting to take over." Huey saw his brother's point. "I changed girls a couple of times," he recalled. "Sometimes it's Gloria Franklin, sometimes it's Pearl Edwards. They don't own the Pitter Pats, Soul Shakers, or Clowns name. That's what you are when you're up there with me. When you leave, you're back to you, sing with who you want. Yeah, be whatever you want to be, but you're not a Clown and neither a Pitty Pat and [lowering his voice] you're certainly not a Huey!"

Singers for hire though they were, Huey strived to compensate them well. "I like to pay the people because I want a good session," he said. "Like one time Johnny gave me a certain amount of change and he thought that he was going to see a squabble, because I hadn't given the money to them."

"I gave Huey $25 dollars apiece for y'all!" Vincent bragged to Pearl Edwards at the session's end. Pearl simply stared at Vincent, as if he were crazy. She started walking out. "Hey, Pearl!" Vincent yelled. "I gave Huey $25 apiece for y'all!" "What you talking about?" she asked. "Hewitt gave us $50!"

"I gave them my own money," Huey recalled. "Because they needed it. And I buy drinks for them and we be partying. I want the people to be happy, and they got a little change in their pocket, too. That still wasn't nothing neither."

Wary of his earlier business dealings with Vincent, Huey credited himself and his then common-law wife, Brenda Brandon, and even his son, Huey Jr., as the cowriters of some Instant Records 45s. "I could be Peter Pan, but I'm Brenda Brandon," he explained. "My little brother, too, Melvin, I credited him for songs. So, when I go to getting sued, they can't take all my eggs. I got some sitting over here."

In the midst of Huey's years at Instant Records, on February 23, 1967, Johnny Vincent registered the Huey P. Smith compositions "Rocking Pneumonia and the Boogie Woogie Flu," "Sea Cruise," "High Blood Pressure," "Roberta," and "Don't You Know Yockomo" with the U.S. Copyright Office, in the name of E. M. Mc-Daniel, his father-in-law. Vincent listed himself as the composer of "Sea Cruise" and "Rocking Pneumonia" and Huey as lyricist. He subsequently registered "Don't You Just Know It" on March 15, 1967, also in his father-in-law's name.

The value of Huey's compositions beyond his and other Ace recordings of them was made clear as early as 1963, the year Chubby Checker ("The Twist") sent a remake of Huey's "We Like Birdland" to No. 12 on the pop charts. Countless more artists, many of them major stars, would record "Sea Cruise," "Rocking Pneumonia," "High Blood Pressure," and lesser-known Huey songs. Jerry Lee Lewis, a rock 'n' roll pioneer from northeast Louisiana, cut "Rocking Pneumonia" in May 1965 for Mercury Records' Nashville subsidiary, Smash. Lewis, who'd recorded the explosive late 1950s rock 'n' roll hits "Whole Lot of Shakin' Going On," "Great Balls of Fire," "Breathless," and "High School Confidential" for Sun Records in Memphis, hadn't yet produced a hit for Smash. Even though he performed "Rocking Pneumonia" for ABC-TV's *Shindig* on June 30, 1965, it, too, didn't chart. Oft-recorded though "Rocking Pneumonia" already was, its highest chart position and sales were yet to come. Meanwhile, Huey Smith and the Clowns' influence could be heard in the Lovin' Spoonful's comic 1966 hit, "Did You Ever Have to Make Up Your Mind?" From New York City, the John Sebastian–led Spoonful sent seven consecutive hits to *Billboard*'s Top 10. "Did You Ever Have to Make Up Your Mind?" features a bass vocal part à la Roosevelt Wright. "We wanted to do a record that sounded like Huey 'Piano' Smith and the Redheads," Sebastian explained.

At Instant Records, Huey wrote and produced recordings for others as well as himself. Joe Banashak told him that production work would provide him with rent money until something developed with his own recordings. His productions include Curley Moore's Huey-composed throwdown "Sophisticated Sissy," a New Orleans hit in 1968. That same year he wrote and produced "Son of a Son of a Slave," a late civil rights–era song performed by Larry Darnell. "I'm wearing a bush, it's looking nice, my favorite food red beans and rice," Darnell proclaims.

Ohio native Darnell, a powerful and elegant vocalist, had been a regular Dew Drop Café performer in the late 1940s, his hits including 1949's recitation-fueled "I'll Get Along Somehow." Darnell's much later "Son of a Son of a Slave" is another of Huey's favorites among his own productions. "It was very good," Huey said. "Larry, he had the vocals." Unfortunately, the session's recording engineer failed to balance Darnell's great voice with the instruments. Besides the record's audio shortcomings, the "Son of a Son of a Slave" lyrics made it a hard sell for Banashak. Christian conservatives in Texas found a phrase in the song, "stomp down soul," offensive. "No, we can't fool with something saying 'Stomp down soul!'" they insisted. "Look," Banashak explained, "like y'all say, 'Pure D beef?' That's what we're talking about here. Not the verb 'stomp' it down, but like one hundred-percent genuine soul!"

Darnell stayed with Huey in New Orleans, running his producer's phone bill up. Huey noticed that Darnell drank day and night but his voice stayed strong. Also in the summer of 1968, the singer played a month-long engagement at the Dew Drop. Columnist Joe Emery noted the engagement in the *Louisiana Weekly*: "Frank Painia is holding LARRY DARNELL over for the fourth week. Larry is a sensational singer. He still has his magnetism." Great singer though Darnell was, he was a bad speller. Lifting a line from Bo Diddley's "I'm a Man," the angry Darnell was overheard arguing outside of the Dew Drop. "Let me tell you right now! I want you to know! I'm a M-A-I-N. Man!"

Remembering the short musical films he'd seen Louis Jordan in, Huey approached Joe Banashak about doing the same for his recordings, especially 1969's "Epitaph of Uncle Tom," a blistering sociopolitical minidrama featuring gospel-style female singers and bass vocalist Roosevelt Wright. Huey recited the verses himself. The lyrics describe an illiterate black man who tipped his hat, flashed his teeth, and scratched his head. "We are gathered here today," Huey announced. "Uncle Tom is dead!" Two decades before the music video–based MTV premiered, Banashak instantly rejected Huey's idea to make a promotional film for "Epitaph of Uncle Tom." "Huey!" the incredulous Instant owner said. "Let me tell you this: They made this movie somewhere in Hollywood and do you know what a guy did? He pressed a button and they were out $20 million!"

Besides not having money to produce music videos, Banashak wrote a bad check for sessions at S. J. Montalbano's Montel Studios in Baton Rouge. Montalbano reported the bounced $300 check and the police arrested the humiliated Banashak at his New Orleans office on Camp Street. Attorney Charles Levy Jr. came to his rescue, Huey recalled. "Joe never had nothing to do with Levy, but Levy was the only person to see the judge to have Joe out on bail. That's who they go to when they need help, Mr. Levy."

Levy was said to be the only white lawyer in New Orleans who'd work with black musicians. Besides Huey, his clients included Fats Domino, Ernie K-Doe, Jessie Hill, Irma Thomas, and Chris Kenner. Convicted of simple kidnapping and simple rape, the troubled, alcoholic Kenner entered the Louisiana State Penitentiary (aka Angola) on January 10, 1969. Huey was in Levy's office when the attorney grabbed his hat in a rush to reach Angola. Levy told Ernie K-Doe, who was there looking for a royalties advance, that he didn't have time to deal with him. "But I—," K-Doe protested. "Look," Levy cut in, "Chris is in and you're out. I got to go. I'll see you when I get back. I've got to plant money down to keep Chris alive!"

Levy feared that Kenner's fellow inmates would harm him because he'd been convicted of raping a minor. "Men gets holy in jail," Huey explained. "They all want to become heroes in there, so they go' kill Chris for doing what he did. But that's not justified, I don't care what you do. Levy can't let Chris get killed, so he's up there looking after him. Nobody touched Chris. Levy was a good lawyer."

14

Jehovah's Witness

Here came a point in his life as a musician when Huey thought he was beyond redemption. He changed his mind after talking with a Jehovah's Witness in his neighborhood about the Bible. She told him that Jehovah is a forgiving God. It was good news, indeed, and all the news he needed to know. "You strip off the old personality, make your mind over again," he explained. "You don't participate in the same activities. You dedicate yourself to God, your life belongs to Jesus." Huey phoned his mother, a longtime Jehovah's Witness, to tell her of the Bible discussion he'd had and his new direction. "I'm putting drinking and so forth behind me," he said. "I want to be one of Jehovah's Witnesses."

Huey felt deep regret about the way he'd lived to that point. "One time, I must of was out about three or four days," he said of an incident that troubled him. "I was standing in front of the Dew Drop and then Annette, my girlfriend, came over there. So, Doretha, my wife, she came and choked Annette because she thought she had been with me. I had never even seen anything like that before. I felt very bad about that. So, that, basically, was my badness. That's not me now. A lot of things, I wish I could undo them, but I know I can't."

Guitarist Deacon John Moore, for one, found Huey's transformation astounding. "He liked to hang out, just like the rest of the guys, man," Moore remembered. "He wasn't no angel. That's what's so strange because, back in the game, he was having a good time. Because all his music was just having a party, good times roll."

Jehovah's Witnesses believe that those who fit Jehovah's purpose will flourish in perpetual paradise on Earth once the present system ends with the battle of Har-Magedon. The wicked shall be destroyed and a chosen 144,000 will ascend to heaven and rule with Christ. If Jehovah's Witnesses grow old or die before

Har-Magedon, the Bible holds a hope for a resurrection. In God's new world, paradise on Earth, Jehovah's Witnesses will be restored to perfect life.

"An intelligent creator put you here for a reason," Huey emphasized. "And that reason is to do His will. The problem is everybody on this Earth is not doing that. Some people on Earth might say, 'I don't want to do His will!' No problem— you just won't be here," Huey said and laughed. "The devil got all those religions out there, but now is the time for people to know what God really has in store, what it's really all about, instead of the moneymaking activities, Jimmy Swaggart and them."

Witnesses study the Bible continuously, from Genesis to Revelation, round and round, year after year. They call their place of worship a kingdom hall rather than a church. God does not dwell in manmade temples, the Witnesses believe. The true church is a spiritual temple of living stone, a global brotherhood that cannot be destroyed. Nor are there titles among the Witnesses. "Jesus said do not you be called rabbi or father," Huey said, "for one is your father, one is teacher, which is Jesus Christ. You all are brothers. No titles, no bishops. And we do what Jesus did, as he instructed. We go house to house, door to door. And all human government is in opposition to Jesus' government. He said my kingdom is no part of this world. And if everybody was a Jehovah's Witness there could be no war. You might be wondering why I'm telling you this—that's my job. I cannot not tell you these things."

One of Huey's fellow Witnesses thought Brother Smith might like to meet a young woman who'd recently joined the congregation. "I'm not interested," Huey told him. The brother persisted. "Her name is Sister Riley," he said. "Naw," Huey insisted. "She nice, yeah," the man continued, "and you got to meet her." "I don't want to meet her," Huey countered. But when Sister Riley's name was announced at the kingdom hall along with the names of other new members, Huey noticed her. He moved behind her seat in the kingdom hall and asked her name.

Margrette Riley told Huey she'd been studying with Sister Dickerson. Huey happened to have shot some home movies with Sister Dickerson in them. Sister Boyd, another lady in the congregation, also had an eight-millimeter movie camera, but she was having trouble with it. "I brought the film to have it developed,"

Sister Boyd told Huey, "but I must have had the camera backwards." "No, Sister Boyd," Huey said, "how are you going to have a camera backwards?" "I'm telling you I had the camera backwards!" "That's impossible. You can't have a camera backwards!" "I'm telling you I did," Sister Boyd insisted. "Come on down, I'll show you," she added. So Huey went to Sister Boyd's house to watch her home movies. When she turned her projector on, a giant eye filled the screen. "You're right!" the astounded Huey said. "You sure did have it backwards!"

Back at the kingdom hall, Huey spoke with Margrette's daughter, seven-year-old Kathy. He noticed Kathy had some candy. "Bring me some candy when you come back next week," he told the child. The following week Huey asked Kathy if she'd brought candy for him. "Well," the child admitted, "I had it, yeah, but I ate it."

When Huey's mother told him a woman in the congregation had started a rumor that he was getting married, he confirmed the forthcoming union. He also went to see Joe Banashak to tell him he needed money for wedding rings. But his mother expressed her concern. "You know, that's a big step, getting married," she said. "Let me tell you something, mother," the confident Huey replied. "See, like a female, any female in the world, I don't have too much trouble with us getting along. But, now, you're talking about a female looking at the Bible—I ain't go' have no trouble. Because I know how to yield. That's what Christianity means. That's what Jesus is. You bend, you yield, like clay."

Huey and Margrette married in 1971. He came to rely upon her tremendously. "She is me," he explained. Curley Moore dropped by the newlyweds' house shortly after their marriage. It was Margrette's and Curley's first meeting. He watched as she straightened her new husband's tie. "That used to be my job," Curley said with uncharacteristic seriousness.

"When we fixing to go on stage," Huey remembered with affection, "Curley dressed me, patted my hair. When we get up there, he wants me to look good. That was Curley."

Being a Jehovah's Witness didn't stop Huey from making music. His fellow Witnesses even accepted free copies of his records. "I heard you was giving away your records," a sister in the congregation said. "Give me some of them!" Nor did the presiding overseer object to him performing. "Yeah, Brother Smith, we have brothers who play music. Now, of course, you wouldn't be drinking, like you at the Dew Drop Saturday night and then knocking on the kingdom hall door Sunday morning. You wouldn't do it like that now." The overseer also knew Huey had recently made a new record. "Let me hear it," he said. Huey played

"The Whatcha Call 'Em," an Instant Records 45 released in 1970. The song was rather risqué.

> You might be good, might be bad, might be happy, might be sad.
> I want to play with that—Boomt, T-boomt, T-boomt—whatcha call 'em!

"Ahhhh!" the overseer exclaimed. "Did you say you have some other kind of work you might like to do?!" But "The Whatcha Call 'Em" is the exception among Huey's songs. "I never did anything like that before," he said. "But you can have records. It all depends on what it is. I wasn't doing nothing like Redd Foxx! But there's nothing wrong with playing music. We got a lot of brothers playing music. George Benson and, at that time, the Jackson 5. And the burning of records? That's radical, like it's some kind of evil. Jehovah's Witnesses don't do foolish, hypocritical stuff like that. Music is to be enjoyed, but now you don't sit there and sing something immoral."

Even as Huey's career wound down in the late 1960s, the Flamin' Groovies, a San Francisco rock group that preferred 1950s and mid-1960s rock 'n' roll over the psychedelic jams performed by their peers the Grateful Dead, Jefferson Airplane, and Santana, recorded a faithful rendition of "Rocking Pneumonia and the Boogie Woogie Flu," including hand claps. Released by Epic Records in 1969 as the Flamin' Groovies' debut single, it became a hit in the San Francisco area. Flamin' Groovies lead singer Roy Loney had bought a copy of the original "Rocking Pneumonia" during his rock 'n' roll-loving childhood. Finding the title to be amazingly strange, he purchased the disc before he'd even heard it. "I got it home and, I gotta admit, at first I went, 'What the heck is this?'" Looney said. "But then, by the third listening, I was so locked in. I was like, 'This is the coolest thing I've ever heard!' It is a real high point for me. Huey 'Piano' Smith has this groove that you just can't mistake. It just grabs you and you can't get away from it."

Skip Easterling, a white singer born in New Orleans and raised in nearby rural Slidell, signed a recording contract with Joe Banashak at fourteen. Full of dreams, full of himself, Easterling nevertheless was awed by the record company boss who'd released national hits by Ernie K-Doe and Chris Kenner as well as many regional hits. "Yep," Banashak told Easterling after listening to his audition tape, "you got a lotta talent. You're a nice-looking young man. You'll make them skirts fall right on off. We're gonna make a lot of money."

Banashak ran four labels in the 1960s: Minit, Instant, Alon, and, named in honor of the Banashak family, Seven B. From the early 1960s through the early 1970s, Easterling recorded for Alon and later Instant. Three of New Orleans's most significant songwriter-pianists—Allen Toussaint, Eddie Bo, and Huey Smith—produced his recordings.

At Banashak's behest, the then eighteen-year-old Easterling recorded vocals for "Don't Let Him," a music track produced by the absent Toussaint, then serving in the U.S. Army. "Don't Let Him" became a local hit in 1963, but then the British invasion of 1964 eroded Easterling's momentum. Banashak, seeing that the Brits had driven local artists from New Orleans's pop radio stations, set a new course for Easterling that defied his skin color. "I'm go' put you in the black bag," he told the young singer. "That way we can make money in the regional market."

Following a rocky recording session led by the recently discharged Toussaint, Banashak paired Easterling with Eddie Bo. Bo composed a soul throwdown, "Keep the Fire Burning (In Your Heart)," and the sorrowful "The Grass Looks Greener (On the Other Side)" for the 45's flipside. They cut the tracks at Cosimo Matassa's studio. The space was packed with a huge horn section, arranger Bo at the piano, Matassa as engineer, and Banashak riding shotgun in the control booth. Bo, sensing that Easterling was nervous, took him aside. "Look, Skip, just sing your song, 'The Grass Looks Greener,' the way that you feel it. Don't listen to Joe. Don't listen to nobody. You sing the way the way you feel it in your heart. That's called soul. What you white people call feelings, we black people call soul."

Extroverted expression came naturally to the Pentecostal-raised Easterling, and Banashak's decision to take him in an R&B direction proved fruitful. Black audiences in the Deep South embraced "The Grass Looks Greener," making it a regional hit for Alon Records in 1967. But Bo and Easterling's follow-ups failed to match the team's initial success. Huey Smith framed the singer's next hit.

A few years later Banashak phoned Easterling with two specific, previously famous songs in mind for him. "Look," he said, "it's time for you to do another session. I got two songs for you. One of them is 'Hoochie Coochie Man.'" Hearing the song he was to record, Easterling felt his heart sink. He preferred the upbeat musical styles from his home state, such as New Orleans funk and southwest Louisiana's zydeco and Cajun music. Jimmy Reed's easy-rolling country blues was okay, too, but Easterling never liked the rigid, foot-stomping blues from Chicago and Mississippi.

Easterling grew even more distraught when Banashak summoned him to Instant's Camp Street office and played Muddy Waters' classic Chess Records rendition of "I'm Your Hoochie Coochie Man." "Mr. Joe, please, man, don't make me do that!" "Look," Banashak assured him, "don't worry about it. Huey Smith is reworking the thing. It's gonna be a completely different arrangement by the time you get it." But there was still more bad news. His new single's flipside would be a remake of Jessie Hill's 1960 Carnival season hit, "Ooh Poo Pah Doo." "Are you kidding me?" the floored Easterling asked Banashak. "Only Jessie can do it like that!" But being under contract, Easterling could do no more than state his objection. "I really thought it was gonna be a waste of my time," he said later.

Before Easterling recorded his vocals for "I'm Your Hoochie Coochie Man" and "Ooh Poo Pah Doo," Banashak gave him a tape of the rhythm tracks Huey had recorded with drummer Little Joe Lambert, guitarist Mike DeMary, and the recordings' coproducer, bassist Tex Liuzza. "Huey had 'Hoochie Coochie Man' all mapped out," Liuzza recalled. "He told me, 'Play the lick like from 'Groove Me' [by King Floyd]. And 'Hoochie Coochie Man,' it's an old, old song and it's always been a twelve-bar blues. But we didn't do it as a blues. We did it with those 'Groove Me' changes, one-[chord] to four to one to four. Huey just kept it in these four-bar phrases and we didn't ever go to the five-[chord] change."

In addition to rhythm tracks for "Hoochie Coochie Man" and "Ooh Poo Pah Doo," Liuzza, Lambert, DeMary, and Huey recorded an entire album's worth of music, probably in a single day, including music tracks for remakes of "Sea Cruise" and "Rocking Pneumonia." "Me and Huey got along well," Liuzza said. "Nice cat. Very focused. He told us what he wanted, we did it, and he left. I mean, it's like he thought about what he was gonna do before he came into the place. Either that or he just had a phenomenal sense of keeping it going."

Easterling, still unenthusiastic after having listened to the tapes Banashak provided, phoned Instant's owner to say he was ready to cut his vocals for "Hoochie Coochie Man" and "Ooh Poo Pah Doo." Banashak booked an early-afternoon recording session. "We went in there and I was sober," Easterling recalled. "Usually, I would have done a little drinking. I drank too much. But it was something strange that day. It was like everything went right. My voice did everything I wanted it to do." He recorded only two takes of "I'm Your Hoochie Coochie Man." Banashak released the first take.

With the vocals down, Huey phoned Liuzza, who then made wind arrangements, including a "Hoochie Coochie Man" score featuring multi-instrumentalist Liuzza's trumpet and raspy flute and a second flute played by Otis Bazoon. But Easterling remained unmoved even after he heard the finished "Hoochie Coochie Man." "The only things I liked about it were the little horn riff, the beat, and the flutes," he said.

Instant's "I'm Your Hoochie Coochie Man" remake followed two similarly funky recent records by New Orleans artists, Jean Knight's "Mr. Big Stuff" and King Floyd's "Groove Me," both arranged by Wardell Quezergue. Both records were hits. In their wake, "Hoochie Coochie Man"—featuring Easterling's otherworldly tenor, Huey's electric piano, an irresistibly funky rhythm section, plus the novel flutes and trumpet—became an Instant hit, rising to the top of black radio charts throughout the Gulf Coast. Easterling suddenly found himself performing alongside such black entertainers as Barbara Lynn at nightclubs, pavilions, gyms, and political events. Black audiences were surprised that the singer of "Hoochie Coochie Man" was white, but they embraced him anyway. In fact, Huey is the recording's only black musician. "It really threw them for a flip," Easterling said of his skin color. "But I never had one problem playing in any black club anywhere. They treated me like a star, made me feel like I was the second coming of Moses. I got used to making at least $1,500 a night, for doing one forty-minute show. For somebody who was used to playing four to six hours at Papa Joe's and the Green Room for $18 a night, I mean, gee, I couldn't believe it."

Thirty-five years from his days as a southern soul star, Easterling deflected credit for "Hoochie Coochie Man." "It wasn't me that made that song No. 1 on the black charts in the South," he said. "Mainly it was the syncopated beat. King Floyd had 'Groove Me' before that, so what Huey Smith did—and he was very calculating in this and smart—he used that same kind of groove on 'Hoochie Coochie Man.' Put a little salt in the stew, a little Creole, a little redneck—and presto." Regardless of Easterling's humility, "Hoochie Coochie Man" coproducer Liuzza recognized soul when he heard it. "Skip's a naturally singing white boy," he said. "I mean, just as soulful as anybody singing at the time."

Despite the southern success of "I'm Your Hoochie Coochie Man" and the regional popularity of Huey's Instant records "It Do Me Good" and "Coo Coo over You," music was not paying his bills. "An artist is as hot as his last record," he explained. "Well, if you ain't in the charts, where you at? Wherever you at in New Orleans. Okay, so the man in New Orleans pays you whatever little change, maybe for two months or so forth. Well, after that, then what you go' do?" He needed a new source of income. For a time he worked as a funeral home driver. His coworkers' behind-the-scenes nonchalance astonished him. Jokesters beyond public view, they turned instantly earnest in the presence of mourners. Huey learned to do the same, but he still never approved of one coworker who, during the course of preparing bodies, stored lit cigarettes between the deceased's lips.

After doing yard and garden work at an apartment complex managed by one of the Witnesses, Huey started his own gardening business. Attorney Charles Levy acquired a truck and equipment. Huey operated Smith's Dependable Gardening Service with his wife, Margrette, a lover of flowers. Following their day's labor, they'd drive around in the evening to admire their work. The couple's customers included Cosimo Matassa. In the meantime, Huey's new spiritual direction and exit from music inspired rumors and criticism. "Ike Favorite and Chris Kenner," he remembered, "told me some people in New York were saying I was on the corner with sackcloth and a big, raggedy Bible and a bottle of wine. People told that type of lie."

A woman once told Huey's mother that she'd heard that Jehovah's Witnesses are celibate. "Where you think all these children come from?" the incredulous Mrs. Smith asked. Joe Jones, the New Orleans recording artist who later got into the music business, challenged Huey's membership in the nonworldly, politically indifferent, and pacifist Witnesses. "Y'all want to use our streets," Jones complained. "We pay our taxes, too, like everybody," Huey countered. "Just because we don't vote, well, Jehovah's Witnesses do vote, but for the government of Jesus Christ. Like Red China didn't used to be viewed as a recognizable government, but now the United Nations accepts them. Just because you didn't believe it, it still was there. Well, Jesus Christ is *the* rightful ruler over the Earth."

Huey and Margrette were studying the Bible with his father when their neighbor, Mr. Seaberry, ridiculed them. "They ain't go' be no change!" he claimed. "Things will continue just as it was since the world began to turn!" Hearing that, Huey turned to Margrette and said, "Hey, you heard what he said? He's fulfilling what it says here in the Bible, that there'll be ridicule. 'Things will continue just as they were since our forefathers fell asleep.' Wow." Huey's elderly, ailing father told his son and daughter-in-law to ignore Mr. Seaberry.

"Don't pay no attention to him," Arthur Smith said. "I'm go' tell you—since y'all been talking to me the last few weeks, I learned more about the Bible than I did all my life!"

Robert "Catman" Caffrey, former bandleader with Shirley and Lee, phoned Huey after hearing the Witnesses ridiculed on a radio talk show. "Huey!" Caffrey said. "Man, ooh. They talking about y'all like a dog!" "That isn't strange to me," Huey replied. "We expect to be persecuted. Jesus said, 'If they persecute me, they will persecute you.' If you're not persecuted, you're not in. Yeah, that's a mark. Know what our prize is? He gave us the strength to endure it."

Some friends and associates reacted positively to Huey's becoming a Witness, including former Clown Jesse Thomas. "I'm a very spiritual person, but I'm nondenominational," Jesse said. "But I can say being a Witness helped save Huey. Yeah, because Huey was pretty wild at one time. But, like I say, he was always cool, because he wouldn't hurt nobody but hisself." Earl King had similar thoughts. "Huey and his wife both Jehovah's Witnesses, and that's when he changed his whole thing," Earl said. "And I said maybe it was for the best. At the rate Huey was going, he wasn't go' be here long." And master pianist and former Clowns band member James Booker surprised Huey by revealing his true thoughts about the Witnesses. "Huey, like when you be talking to me, about the Bible," Booker confided, "I know what you telling me is the truth. I know that! I want to tell you this now, because, see, like when Earl [King] and other people around, I'm go' give you stupid answers about what you're talking about, but don't think I don't know no better!"

Singer Pearl Edwards studied the Bible with Huey at her home. "Huey," she confessed, "I used to study before, yeah." "Yeah?" Huey asked. "Remember, Huey, when you and Rayfield and them was coming to my house to pick me up?" Pearl asked. "Well, I would hide the Witness books." "Why you did that?" "I thought that's what you supposed to do."

Acting upon his Jehovah's Witness duty, Huey spoke to Instant Records owner Joe Banashak about the Bible. "Huey," Banashak said, "when you're talking to me, you worry me." "Oh, Joe, I didn't mean to disturb you with the kingdomness," Huey apologized. "We're not supposed to do that." "No, no," Banashak said. "I don't mean when you're here. I'm talking about after you leave! And then when I'm at home, too."

"God's word is alive," Huey later said of the Bible's impact on receptive listeners. "See, like a certain incident happens to me, when I open the Bible, maybe the incident wasn't in there yesterday, but it's in there today, because it's for me, because this is the Word."

Being a Witness also led Huey to quit smoking. Years before doing so, when Sidney Rayfield announced that he was kicking the habit, Huey, then smoking three packs of Pal Malls a day, claimed no such ambition. "I'm smart," he told Rayfield. "See, that's one of my pleasures in life." But he'd later choose to quit smoking because nicotine addiction isn't accepted among the Witnesses. "If you stop for seven days," someone counseled him, "you will have no problem with smoking, but the urge will still be there." "How long will that urge be there?" Huey asked. "Forever," the man answered. In his first attempt to stop smoking, Huey went six days without a cigarette. "Before that sixth day, I still had a pack of cigarettes," he recalled. "And because I had wanted one, I balled them up and threw them under the house. Then, about three o'clock in the morning, I'm crawling under there to get them. It was sloppy, with snails all down there. I prayed and I cried. And I found the pack and I lit them."

A few months later he tried again. "I went seven days and I had it," he said. Like other ex-smokers, though, he turned to food. He gained so much weight that people didn't recognize him. "A lot of people weren't speaking to me," he said. "Well, I didn't even know how I looked. I thought they just weren't speaking. I had got to 215 pounds, where originally I was 118 pounds." When Eddie Bo, Huey's peer from the Dew Drop Café and Club Tiajuana days, encountered the heavier Huey, he couldn't believe it. "That's Huey?! That's Huey?!" he repeated.

In contrast to Huey's relatively quiet new life, former Clowns driver Rudy Ray Moore created a high-profile new identity as X-rated comic Dolemite. Moore's homemade comedy album, 1970's *Eat Out More Often*, became an underground hit. More albums and then movies followed. Huey wasn't impressed. "When Rudy Ray Moore got famous, people were accepting underground cussing and stuff like that," he recalled. "But like Richard Pryor and them, off the top of their hat, they'll make you laugh. I never saw that in Rudy Moore. He just had the nerve and the vulgarity."

15

Rocking Pneumonia, Part II

Johnny Ramistella, a singer-guitarist from Baton Rouge, moved to Los Angeles in the 1960s and hit the big time. Performing with the stage name Johnny Rivers, Ramistella fueled his frequent visits to the Top 10 with remakes, including Chuck Berry's "Memphis," the Four Tops' "Baby I Need Your Lovin'," and Smokey Robinson and the Miracles' "The Tracks of My Tears." In 1971, Rivers cut "Sea Cruise," the Huey Smith song that had been a pop and rhythm-and-blues hit for Frankie Ford in 1959. Ramistella's "Sea Cruise" got only as high as No. 84 in *Billboard*'s pop singles chart, but he sailed back into the Top 10 in November 1972 with a remake of Huey's 1957 rhythm-and-blues hit, "Rocking Pneumonia and the Boogie Woogie Flu." Ramistella had performed the song years before in Baton Rouge with his high school band, the Spades. Also in 1972, British rocker Dave Edmunds, another fan of New Orleans rhythm-and-blues, expressed his appreciation for his American music heroes in his high-charting remake of Smiley Lewis's 1955 hit, "I Hear You Knocking." During the record's instrumental break, the jubilant Edmunds shouts the names of Lewis, Chuck Berry, and the pianist on the original "Knocking" recording, Huey Smith.

A soulful new Huey Smith and the Clowns recording of "Rocking Pneumonia"—featuring original vocalist "Scarface" John Williams—appeared in 1972 on Atlantic Records subsidiary label Cotillion. It had been recorded in 1970 along with remakes of "High Blood Pressure," "Don't You Just Know It," and "We Like Mambo." John had become a chief of the Apache Hunters Mardi Gras Indian tribe, and, fittingly, the new version of "We Like Mambo" contained Indians references.

"Joe Banashak got some money from them to do a session on me because Jerry Wexler [the Atlantic Records partner and producer behind recordings by Big Joe Turner, Ray Charles, the Drifters, Otis Redding, Aretha Franklin,

Led Zeppelin, Professor Longhair, and many more] had heard a slow version of 'Rocking Pneumonia.' I remember doing it almost like a different song, but with the same words." But like so many of Huey's projects, the promising sessions he recorded for Atlantic didn't reach their commercial potential. His new "Rocking Pneumonia" was pressed into promo singles, but the record never got off the ground. "Somebody told somebody to sit on it," Huey remembered. "You know, people present themselves as experts on records, like they know what'll happen. They mighta just stopped it right there, shelved it."

It was in 1972, too, that Johnny Vincent sold the publishing rights for Huey's most successful songs—"Rocking Pneumonia and the Boogie Woogie Flu," "Sea Cruise," and "Don't You Just Know It" as well as the latter song's original 45 rpm flipside, "High Blood Pressure"—to Cotillion Music, Inc., the publishing division of the Atlantic Recording Corporation. Warner Bros.-Seven Arts, later known as Warner Communications, Inc., and later still as Time Warner, Inc., had purchased Atlantic and Cotillion in 1967, but the company's cofounder, Ahmet Ertegun, continued to run his still-flourishing label and publishing business.

An assignment of copyright for Huey's four songs states that Vincent's father-in-law, E. M. McDaniel, sold the compositions to Ace Publishing Co., Inc., eight days prior to Vincent's own sale of the same songs to Cotillion Music, Inc. The songs had been registered at the U.S. Copyright Office to McDaniel since 1967. But McDaniel having died, his participation in the 1972 sale of the songs to Ace was impossible. Regardless, the copyright registrations are frauds, Huey maintains, because the 1957 publishing contract that Vincent purported to be legitimate has a fraudulent Huey Smith signature. Huey surmised that Vincent lifted the signature from mass-produced thank-you letters sent by Ace Records to disc jockeys. In addition to the fact that Ace Publishing Company was not formed until March 1959, the 1957 "general agreement" has an especially obvious flaw: Huey did not live at the Pontchartrain Park address listed on the contract until 1958. His lawyer, Charles Levy, later demanded that Vincent turn over all of the copies of Huey's signature in his possession. "Never been one statement of money paid on that 1957 general agreement," Huey recalled. "But every judge, every lawyer, they hold to that and say it is legitimate and that Johnny had a right to sell my songs."

In a September 12, 1972, letter to Cotillion Music, Inc., however, Levy acknowledges Vincent's sale of the four songs to Cotillion. Levy's letter also states that Cotillion would not be held responsible for songwriter royalties Huey did not receive from Vincent. "Huey Smith reserves all his rights against Ace and shall look solely to Ace Publishing Co., Inc., for payment of royalties, if any, to Huey Smith from Ace prior to the date Cotillion Music, Inc., was assigned copyrights from Ace Publishing, Inc."

Vincent's sale of the songs came in a busy year for Huey's compositions. In addition to Johnny Rivers's hit rendition of "Rocking Pneumonia" and rock 'n' roll revivalist group Sha Na Na's "Sea Cruise" remake, Dr. John's New Orleans–inspired ATCO Records album *Gumbo* contains a Huey Smith medley featuring "High Blood Pressure," "Don't You Just Know It," and "Well I'll Be John Brown," plus an introductory piano quote from "It Do Me Good." Recorded at Sound City Studios in Van Nuys, California, and coproduced by Atlantic Records principal Jerry Wexler and New Orleans maestro Harold Battiste, *Gumbo* also features Huey's "Little Liza Jane" and "Blow Wind Blow," James "Sugar Boy" Crawford's "Jock-A-Mo," Professor Longhair's "Tipitina," and Earl King's "Those Lonely, Lonely Nights." A West Coast krewe of New Orleans expats including Lee Allen, David and Melvin Lastie, Ronnie Barron, Shirley Goodman, Tami Lynn, and Alvin "Shine" Robinson guaranteed the project's Crescent City vibe.

"My enthusiasm for the album was unbounded," Wexler said. "Mac and I saw eye to eye, groove to groove. Authenticity was the key—real songs with real players playing with real feeling." Wexler, during a phone conversation later with Earl King, mentioned seeing Johnny Vincent while he'd been working on the Dr. John album. Earl asked how Vincent was doing. "He's doing bad," Wexler said. "Man, he sold us a couple of songs. Huey Smith stuff." "How much money y'all paid Johnny?" "Oh, we gave him about twenty thousand bucks."

Remembering the call later, Earl said Vincent shot himself in the foot. "Johnny didn't have to sell that. Johnny Rivers had released 'Rocking Pneumonia' overseas but it just hadn't hit America yet. 'Rocking Pneumonia' was hot as a firecracker but Johnny didn't know it because he wasn't buying the *Billboard* then to notice that it was in there. And I asked Jerry, 'Man, I sure wish Johnny had sold you some of my Ace stuff. At least then I'd get paid.' Warner Bros. and them kind of folks, they go by the letter, the book. Ain't none of that trying to rip nobody off for no pennies."

The year 1972 also brought tragic news about "Scarface" John Williams. Shortly after Mardi Gras, the thirty-three-year-old chief of the Apache Hunters Mardi Gras Indians tribe was stabbed in the heart as he tried to stop a fight between two men at a Dryades Street bar. The incident happened a few blocks from Sidney Rayfield's barbershop. Rayfield ran to the scene and lifted his slain fellow Clown from the gutter. John, the *Times-Picayune* reported on March 5, 1972, "wounded in the chest and the neck, was pronounced dead at the scene. . . A seven-inch butcher knife was used."

"John was meek," Huey said. "I never heard of John in a squabble, ever. That wasn't his makeup. It wasn't. But Rayfield saw him in the gutter right behind that barroom on that corner with his throat cut." John's widow, Mary, remembers seeing his body lying by a street drainage portal. "The blood was running down in the drain," she said. "That blood stayed in that spot for years. Even the rain didn't wash it away."

The city's fabulously colorful, feather- and headdress-attired Mardi Gras Indians honored John with a special funeral procession. Chanting, dancing, and banging tambourines, the Apache Hunters, Wild Magnolias, Black Eagles, Golden Eagles, White Eagles, Yellow Jackets, and Yellow Pocahontas tribes accompanied his body from Fourth and Danneel streets to Melpomene Street and South Claiborne Avenue. The procession stopped at the bar where the chief was slain. "We gonna do our thing outside where he got killed," Golden Stars Indian Warren Williams told a *Times-Picayune* reporter. "That's soul. You don't know nothin' about that."

George Landry, aka Big Chief Jolly of the Wild Tchoupitoulas tribe, wrote a song in memory of John. "Brother John" appears on the 1976 album *The Wild Tchoupitoulas,* featuring the great New Orleans funk band the Meters, as well as Landry's nephews, Art, Aaron, Charles, and Cyril Neville. "There have been many songs about John," Cyril said. "I hope mine expresses that weird mixture of violence and beauty that was part of our R&B street life." The *Wild Tchoupitoulas* album, a landmark fusion of New Orleans funk and Mardi Gras Indians music, precipitated the formation of the Neville Brothers band.

Johnny Vincent continued making recording offers to Huey. "He offered you $300?" the skeptical Joe Banashak asked. "Let me tell you something, Huey. If Johnny offered you $300, somebody must have offered him $30,000." The wary Huey warned Vincent not to make more forged contracts. "So, what Johnny does, he just pays me a visit," Huey recalled. "Then he goes by the K&B drugstore where Earl King and them hang out. 'Ha-ha-ha-ha. Yeah, y'all, I bought Huey half a pint of whiskey and he signed with me again!' So Johnny had another one of them forged papers. It's just propaganda, but everybody believes that I signed these things. And I know Johnny passed a remark, 'You don't know what you signed. I got ya!'"

While Vincent plugged away at the music business, a heart attack sidelined Banashak, signaling the end of Instant, one of New Orleans's great independent labels. "I'm not leaving Joe, Joe left hisself," Huey said. Banashak, despite his aversion to the Catholic religion in which he was raised, grew interested in Christian spirituality following his illness. "The heart attack put some fear in him," Huey said.

Meanwhile, Huey's musical activities declined to the point that he sold his electric piano to Skip Easterling. "I had played that piano so long and it was not in too good a shape," he said. "It just cost $500 and Joe Banashak gave me, I think, pretty close to $400 for it. Skip wanted one. He could have bought a new one, but Joe just said he wondered whether I needed the money. So I said, 'He can have it. Give it to Skip.'"

James Booker, former pianist for the Clowns' band, visited Huey and Margrette often. Booker would drop by the Smiths' house early on a Wednesday morning, for instance, on his way to teach piano to Orleans Parish district attorney Harry Connick Sr.'s son, Harry Jr. "The boy was about five or six years old," Huey remembered. "I never saw him, but Booker told me about him. 'Ooh, he doing good.'" Growing into a handsome crooner and skilled pianist and arranger, Harry Connick Jr. became a recording star and actor. Former Clown Gerri Hall always wondered how he got so good. "Booker, huh?" she marveled when the laughing Huey told her that Booker had been Connick's piano professor. "I don't believe it! Booker gave all our soul away. Booker laid it on him."

Unfortunately, Booker fell in with bad companions. "He was enthused about some of the older gentlemen around where he lived," Huey said. "They mostly were using drugs. He liked to be in that crowd. I know he wanted to be accepted among them." A drug bust sent Booker to the Louisiana State Penitentiary at Angola. "Everybody else, they catch the train," he boasted. "But Harry Connick Sr. *flew* me to Angola!" Many more Louisiana musicians served time at Angola. The list includes Shreveport folk singer Leadbelly, Baton Rouge blues man Robert Pete Williams, and New Orleans's Chris Kenner. Another New Orleans musician, Charles Neville of the Neville Brothers, got sentenced to five years' hard labor at Angola for the possession of two marijuana cigarettes. "The terrible irony of prisons in the South," said Nick Spitzer, folklorist and host of the *American Routes* public radio music show, "has been that African culture has been preserved in prisons because most of the people imprisoned were African-Americans."

Huey signed an employment contract with New Orleans attorney Charles Levy on January 31, 1973. It granted Levy authority to represent him "in all claims I may have against record companies, publishing companies, and individuals and performing rights societies, as the result of songs written by me in the past and records made by me in the past. . . . For and in consideration of the legal services that he has already rendered and to be rendered by said attorney, CHARLES LEVY, JR., who also does agree to advance any and all monies necessary to investigate, audit and to file legal action and to pursue same in my behalf, I do hereby transfer to the said attorney, CHARLES LEVY, JR., in perpetuity, Thirty-Five (35%) PerCent interest in and to all songs I have written and all records I have produced. This includes both mechanical and performance rights." Huey gave Levy authorization to collect his artist's royalties from record companies and songwriter's royalties from music publishers as well as performance rights organization BMI. Huey believed that music companies were more likely to pay a white attorney fairly than a black artist and songwriter. "Other words, and everybody knew, if I get $10, Levy's going to get $50. He's not going to let them play him penny-cheap. So that's why everybody was letting Mr. Levy get it for them. And he was good at that. If Mr. Levy was your lawyer, you were going to make something."

Billy Diamond, who'd worked with Levy while he was road manager for Huey Smith and the Clowns, Fats Domino, Shirley and Lee, and others, gave Levy a mixed review. "He was a giant with the New Orleans musicians," Diamond said. "Yeah, because everything went to him, he controlled everything. He was a good operator—but if he only would have played square." Huey, on the other hand, considered Levy a friend as well as a lawyer. The Jewish attorney and the musician-turned-Jehovah's Witness even discussed the Bible together. But other musicians, especially James Booker, despised Levy. "You got all that confidence in Levy!" Booker barked at Huey. "But I got lawyers *watching* lawyers. I got a battery of lawyers! You need somebody watching Levy!"

"A lot of them hated Mr. Levy," Huey recalled. "They hear about my relationship with him, they resented it, Ike Favorite and them. 'You think Levy's so much.' They said it just out of thin air. I don't know what they know, except that I'd be in Levy's office. A lot of people didn't like me because of me and Mr. Levy. But that man didn't steal *nothing* from me. Now, I believe that he was involved in doing things like that. But we sat down and talked together, often. Mr. Levy, certain things he'll sit and tell me he won't tell Chris Kenner or K-Doe. All the time. He told me how he was going to donate his body to science."

Huey thought of Instant Records owner Joe Banashak as a friend, too. And unlike Johnny Vincent and Joe Caronna, Banashak never claimed to be a cowriter of Huey's songs. The two men talked often, chitchatting, as Huey called it. "Joe told me why his wife left: He couldn't have sex anymore. He had that heart attack. He said an angel standing at his hospital bed told him if he had sex again, he would die. Joe said, 'I told my wife I ain't doing nothing!'"

Levy wanted to sue Banashak for royalties the attorney suspected were owned to Huey for his Instant singles. "I'm going after Johnny Vincent," the lawyer said. "Want me to get Joe Banashak, too?" "Uh-uh, no," Huey replied. "I'll get him right now, yeah," Levy insisted, "tell him to account for the records he's sold." "No, Joe okay," Huey insisted. "Don't sue him or nothing like that." "Come on. Let me get Joe." "Leave him alone." "Let me get Joe—*please.*" "No."

"Joe didn't have any money," Huey said of Banashak, another example of an important New Orleans music figure who made bad business decisions. "Joe was scuffling. Johnny Vincent used to be joking about Joe got broke playing the racehorses. But I know Johnny was a gambler, too. He used to have them card games up there [in Jackson, Mississippi], talking about high stakes."

Like Vincent and Banashak, Cosimo Matassa hit bottom, too, losing his recording studio after financial struggles and tax troubles. The studio owner and engineer who'd recorded decades of hits from New Orleans blamed himself. "I wasn't as good a business man as I should have been," he said in characteristic, matter-of-fact style. "I set myself up for a fall." Banashak told Huey that he'd lent Matassa, a future Rock and Roll Hall of Fame inductee, money to get a haircut.

Johnny Vincent, meanwhile, reissued the Ace catalog on compilation LPs during the 1970s. He had a problem, though—his only photos of Huey were a few portraits that saxophonist Alvin "Red" Tyler, an amateur photographer with a small camera, snapped in 1959 on the Pontchartrain Park golf course, just across the street from Huey's house. The best-known photo made its debut on the cover of Huey's first Ace album, 1959's *Having a Good Time*. The same image appeared on the cover of Huey's second Ace LP, 1961's *For Dancing*, albeit with the original's trees stripped out. Huey had no input in either album or any subsequent Ace albums. Ironically, few vintage photos of Huey exist, even though he loved getting his picture taken. "Catman," he remembered, "used to say, 'Them Japanese'll love you. You be right there.' Because every time Catman takes a picture, I jump in it." Tragically, the boxes of images photographer and saxophonist Robert "Catman" Caffrey took of Huey and his New Orleans music peers apparently are lost. As for Alvin "Red" Tyler's hundreds of images, they were destroyed by the flooding that followed Hurricane Katrina.

Vincent rectified his lack of photos during a visit to Huey in New Orleans. "We were letting him see a bunch of slides, and he slipped one of them in his pocket," the laughing Huey said. Vincent used the stolen image for the cover of the 1974 album *Rock and Roll Revival!* He also exploited the hit-maker status Dr. John finally achieved with 1973's "Right Place Wrong Time" by re-releasing Huey's 1962 Christmas album under the revised credit "Dr. John Band with Huey 'Piano' Smith." In fact, Dr. John had been merely a session player for the album.

Levy and Vincent signed a consent agreement with the U.S. District Court, Eastern District of Louisiana, in January 1974. The agreement stated that Levy's client, Huey P. Smith, and John Vincent Imbragulio had reconciled their differences. The judgment further stated that all songwriter mechanical royalties due from Cotillion Music, Inc., for "Sea Cruise," "Rocking Pneumonia and the Boogie Woogie Flu," "High Blood Pressure," and "Don't You Just Know It" are "as of the date of this judgment due and owing to John V. Imbragulio, and he may receive them without any obligation to Huey P. Smith. It is further ordered, adjudged and decreed that Huey P. Smith pay the sum of $1,000 to John V. Imbragulio immediately upon receipt of royalty statements from Broadcast Music, Inc., for the period January 1, 1973, to March 31, 1973. It is further ordered, adjudged and decreed that there be judgment herein in favor of Ace Records Company, Inc., and against Huey P. Smith, dismissing plaintiff's suit at his costs."

The judgment in favor of Vincent angered Huey, prompting the only falling out he and Levy ever had. "In favor of Johnny Vincent against Huey Smith?" the incredulous musician read from the judgment in Levy's office. "I wrote that," the lawyer responded. "I drew that up. I'm go' make money with these people [Cotillion Music Publishing]. I'm go' let them go ahead and make money. You go' start getting some money. Take my word. I know what I'm doing." Despite Levy's promises, Huey slammed the office door on his way out. He also wrote to BMI, instructing the performance rights society to send his songwriter royalties directly to him rather than Levy. But, as time passed, Huey's anger toward Levy faded. "I can understand him now," he reflected. "He told me that Johnny said he was broke, that there wasn't nothing left of Johnny. Levy figured if they go sooner through the big publishers he can start making money. But it wasn't his intention to steal. I know that."

Punk-rock poet Patti Smith briefly quoted lines from Huey's "We Like Birdland" in "Birdland," a track on her 1975 debut album, *Horses*. She spends most of "Birdland" spouting stream-of-consciousness poetry while her band jams. The song ends with a hushed, elongated twist on the "We Like Birdland" lyrics. The *Horses* album also features a remake of Chris Kenner's "Land of 1000 Dances." Just a few months after the release of the much-praised album, Kenner, Huey's long-troubled New Orleans music peer, died of an apparent heart attack. Neighbors found the forty-six-year-old singer-songwriter's body in his Jackson Avenue apartment on January 28, 1976. Kenner's family kept his demise and funeral secret, publishing no obituary in the local newspapers. Friends of the singer said he'd been frequently depressed and drinking heavily. "It's a sad thing about Chris," Huey said. "He was very, very mild tempered and nice. But, you know, some things you get involved with and it just be like the wrong place at the wrong time with the wrong people. Things like that happened to Chris. I miss him."

Kenner's 1961 hit, "I Like It Like That," sold seven hundred thousand copies for Joe Banashak's Instant Records, reaching No. 2 on both the rhythm-and-blues and pop charts. It won *Billboard* awards for best rock 'n' roll record of the year and best writer of the year. "I Like It Like That" returned to the charts in 1965 in a remake by British invasion group the Dave Clark Five. Soul star Wilson Pickett and Mexican-American rock band Cannibal and the Headhunters also released hit renditions of "Land of 1000 Dances" in the mid-1960s. Decades after Kenner's barely noticed death, his songs were still making money, one example being "I Like It Like That" in a national television commercial.

When James Booker toured, he would phone Huey and others from wherever he might be in the world. Wondering if Booker was in trouble, Huey always took the collect calls. "But he's just calling for to chitchat," Huey said. "We got the bill." Once during a visit with Booker in Charity Hospital's mental ward, Huey and Margrette thought they'd kill two birds with one stone by sharing Jehovah's good news with the other patients. "I'm God," a man next to Booker claimed. "You're God?" Huey asked. "He God," another patient said, "and I'm Jesus!" The offended Huey looked at Margrette and said, "Come on." Speaking later of the mental patients, he said: "They were walking around freely. They could have been jokesters. They ain't had no straitjackets but, if they really meant what they said, they needed some."

New Orleans entertainers Booker, Huey, Earl King, Ernie K-Doe, Irma Thomas, and Aaron Neville traveled to Baton Rouge in 1978 to do a local television show called *Louisiana Magazine*. The program was shot at the Kingfish, a popular nightspot named after Louisiana's assassinated governor, Huey P. Long. An image of Long, his arms outstretched in populist embrace, served as the stage backdrop. Huey performed with two of his most distinctive Clowns, the high-pitched Bobby Marchan and bass vocalist Roosevelt Wright. But prior to the show he worried about the fifth of whiskey he'd seen atop the piano during Booker's set. "If you expect me go get anywhere near that piano," he warned backstage, "you go' have to move that fifth of whiskey off of there!"

"They want to make the Jehovah's Witness be a drunk!" Huey complained later. "That's what they were really trying to do, paint a bad picture. Something that was fifty years ago, yet they're like, 'This is now.'" Removing Booker from the stage, however, proved more difficult than removing the whiskey bottle. He exceeded his allotted twenty minutes and, finally, John Fred Gourrier, the six-foot-five-inch Baton Rouge singer who led John Fred and the Playboys to fame with "Judy in Disguise (With Glasses)," carried the pianist backstage.

In early 1978 Huey was asked to come to a studio and lip sync some of his songs for video. Curley Moore showed him the way to the studio but also warned his old boss that these people from Memphis were trying to put something over on him. "We go' give you $2,000," the video producer told Huey. "Whatever you're going to give me," Huey replied, "whatever kind of document it is, you have to let some legal people know what that is." "Ah, I can tell you what it is!" the producer replied. "I can read," Huey said, "but I'm going to bring this to my lawyer and let him tell me what it is." He took the still-unsigned contract to attorney Charles Levy. "Huey," the lawyer said, "if you'd signed this junk you'd have signed your life away. What they had in mind, if you sign that, that'll mean they'll own your songs. I'll take care of all of this. I'll fix it."

Levy drafted a contract dated May 2, 1978, that stated the composer had transferred his right, title, and interest in "Sea Cruise," "High Blood Pressure," "Don't You Just Know It," and "Rocking Pneumonia and the Boogie Woogie Flu" to Jane Alshuler, Levy's wife, for the sum of $2,000. The agreement assigned mechanical rights due from Cotillion Music, Inc., the songs' publisher, to Alshuler, but specifically added that Huey retained his BMI performance rights.

Huey later believed that the contract was executed to protect him from the Johnny Vincents of the world, and the songs' royalties were held in an account for him. "Mr. Levy didn't ask me to sign it," Huey recalled. "He had one of the signatures Johnny Vincent was using. So it has 'signed to Jane Alshuler,' but she didn't know nothing about it. See, it was a document to deal with somebody who comes and says, 'Well, see, we gave Huey some drinks and he signed over his songs.' Johnny Vincent had a habit of doing that. So this was an avenue for protection when somebody comes up with that. That's all Levy was doing, functioning as attorney for Huey Smith."

At a tax preparer's office after Levy's death in 1980, the woman handling Huey's file noted that the attorney had filed papers and paid money to qualify his musician client for Social Security. "I see what he was doing," she said. "It's very seldom somebody pays somebody's Social Security and sees that they're taken care of. Not no lawyer!"

"No Social Security tax had ever been paid till Levy paid it in," Huey said in 2001. "But Levy did that. That's the only reason I get Social Security now."

16
Disaster at Sea-Saint

The 1970s saw a revival of interest within New Orleans in the city's classic 1950s and 1960s rhythm-and-blues music. The New Orleans Jazz and Heritage Festival began in 1970 at Congo Square and the Municipal Auditorium. Although poorly attended in its first two years, the festival gradually became a major event. Producer George Wein, who'd previously founded the Newport jazz and folk festivals, convinced the publisher of the city's major newspaper to recognize the festival's increasing importance. "I explained that New Orleans had international heroes walking the street every day," Wein wrote in his autobiography. "Men and women who were glorified in Europe and Japan—and the *Times-Picayune* only acknowledged them in obituaries. Mr. Phelps heard what I had to say, and the response was immediate." The debut of WWOZ, a community radio station dedicated to New Orleans music, on December 4, 1980, also contributed to the city's belated embrace of its greatest cultural export.

In the climate of renewal, Huey began playing the occasional gig at an Uptown club founded in 1977 by young fans of the soon-to-be-famous-again Professor Longhair. Longhair's fans named the club at 501 Napoleon Avenue after his song "Tipitina." Huey's reason for performing again was more practical than artistic. He needed the money.

Like Professor Longhair, James Booker had devoted followers. Variously dubbed the Black Liberace, the Emperor of Ivory, and the Piano Prince, Booker began believing the flattering things said about him. Huey did not appreciate such hero worship. "Yeah, Booker got cocky, too, after they start telling him he's a pope," he said. "They go to telling them they kings of this or kings of that, and that go' to their heads. K-Doe been like that. He made *hisself* like that. They come up with that Muhammad Ali stuff, 'I'm the greatest.' Yeah, exalting themselves as something to be worshiped."

Ernie K-Doe's egotism became legendary in New Orleans and beyond. During his acceptance speech at the 1998 Rhythm & Blues Foundation's Pioneer Awards in New York, he announced: "There have only been five great singers of rhythm and blues—Ernie K-Doe, James Brown, and Ernie D-Doe!" That year, too, in another example of K-Doe's decades of comically surreal self-aggrandizement, the singer declared himself Emperor of the World and even dressed the part, wearing crowns and robes. As for Booker's ego, it was showing at one of the New Orleans venues where he and Huey shared the bill in the late 1970s. Booker performed every song that Huey had rehearsed before continuing with his own repertoire. "Oh, boy," Huey reacted. "He changed. This is a brand-new Booker." Booker had moved into a house with white musicians, one of whom was his piano student. "He come in there cussing everybody out, and they didn't want to open their mouth. He was throwing his weight around."

Unlike Huey, many singers and musicians in New Orleans and throughout Louisiana named themselves the king, queen, or prince of this or that musical style. Journalists, too, often bestowed faux crowns. Beyond the insular Louisiana music scene, however, Jamaican music star Peter Tosh's distaste for hero worship echoed Huey's view precisely. Following the 1981 death of reggae's biggest star, Bob Marley, Tosh rejected journalists' descriptions of him as the new king of reggae. "I don't want no one tell me that," he said. "I don't want no title from men, 'cause I don't work for men. I work for the Almighty."

Charles Levy approached Huey in 1977 about recording again, this time for Sansu Enterprises, the New Orleans production company founded in 1965 by pianist, songwriter, producer, and arranger Allen Toussaint and his business partner, Marshall Sehorn. Toussaint and Sehorn had their own recording studio, Sea-Saint, as well as the record labels Sansu, Deesu, and Tou-Sea. Between the two of them, Toussaint and North Carolina native Sehorn had years of success behind them, including Sehorn's late 1950s and early 1960s promotion and talent scout work for Bobby Robinson's Fire and Fury labels (Wilbert Harrison's "Kansas City," Lee Dorsey's "Ya-Ya" and "Do-Re-Me") and Toussaint's hit-yielding stay at Joe Banashak's Minit and Instant labels (Jessie Hill's "Ooh Poo Pah Doo," Ernie K-Doe's "Mother-in-Law," Benny Spellman's "Fortune Teller," Chris Kenner's "I Like It Like That," Irma Thomas's "Ruler of My Heart," Art Neville's "All These Things"). The team's subsequent Sansu and Sea-Saint projects included hits by Lee Dorsey, the Meters, and Dr. John's "Right Place Wrong Time," as well as hits by non-New Orleanians Betty Harris, the Pointer Sisters ("Yes We Can Can"), and Labelle ("Lady Marmalade"). Even Paul McCartney and his post-Beatles band, Wings, came to New Orleans to record their 1975 album, *Venus and Mars*, at Sea-Saint.

"Huey," Levy said, "you know how Johnny Vincent does back-pocket business? Now, Marshall and them have a little operation, but they're not penny-ante like that. We can do something, money-wise, with this. I'll make an appointment for you to go down there and maybe do a little recording." "Okay, I'll give it a try," Huey replied, "but if I'm doing this, I'm not going to be cutting nobody's yard." "Okay," Levy agreed.

Huey asked Sehorn for a $10,000 advance, adding that he would grant Sehorn and Toussaint half of the publishing rights for his newly composed songs. Sehorn said he needed to consult with Toussaint. "Actually," Huey further told Sehorn, "I just told you that part about the publishing for to butter the whole thing up, so you can feel like you want to do this. But I'm thinking you'll come back and say, 'Well, look. Allen says we don't even want half the publishing. That's yours, and we will give you this $10,000 anyhow, because it's you, out of respect.' So," Huey concluded, "you go back to Toussaint and tell him that's what I say."

Huey started recording the album without a contract. Working with a young white band, Skor, he recorded about a dozen songs at Sea-Saint, located on Clematis Street in Gentilly, a neighborhood near the Fair Grounds Race Course, site of the annual New Orleans Jazz and Heritage Festival. Huey sang spirited lead vocals for the album, veteran Clown Roosevelt Wright sang bass, and Huey's wife, Margrette, contributed the highest vocals heard on a Huey Smith recording since Bobby Marchan's falsetto. The songs included remakes of "Rocking Pneumonia and the Boogie Woogie Flu," "Don't You Just Know It," "Little Chickie Wah Wah," and "High Blood Pressure." The session's new compositions were "Witcha Way to Go"; "I'm So Blue Without You"; a wry morality tale recited by Huey, "Hip Little Monkey"; and an after-hours jam featuring a howling wolf, "Fore Day in the Morning." Huey also showed his affection for Hank Williams with a remake of "Jambalaya" (featuring Dr. John playing slide guitar) and revived a Coasters song he performed for the Clowns' 1957 stage debut, "Young Blood."

Backing band Skor had a recording contract with Sehorn. They also toured with the Toussaint-produced Lee Dorsey. "Four white teenagers," Huey recalled.

"Nineteen, maybe the oldest twenty, one sixteen, one fifteen. They mama and them brought the instruments. That's their ages now, and here I am, playing with them, but the record still sounds like Huey. That's what amazed me. You can take just one person in a group of five and he dominates."

In the studio, Skor guitarist Louis Kahl recalled, "Huey'd show us the song, we'd go through it once and then he'd go, 'All right, roll the tape.' And we'd go, 'Whoa, whoa! Wait, Huey.' We wasn't used to that, but Huey wanted that rawness and, when you think back to his early records, that's how they were. Like some people at a party, sitting around the piano and just having a good time."

Curley Moore subsequently visited Sea-Saint and taunted Sehorn about teaming Huey with inexperienced white boys. "What y'all trying to do? Make Hu-ree white? Why you didn't get George Porter and the Meters to play behind him?" Curley had a point. The Meters—featuring bassist George Porter Jr., keyboardist Art Neville, guitarist Leo Nocentelli, and drummer Joseph "Zigaboo" Modeliste—weren't just the city's premier funk band of the late 1960s and 1970s; they were prolific Sea-Saint session players who backed visiting stars Paul McCartney, Robert Palmer, and Patti LaBelle as well as locals Earl King, Lee Dorsey, Dr. John, and the 1976 Neville family and Mardi Gras Indians project, *The Wild Tchoupitoulas*. A project pairing Huey Smith with the Meters would have had historic potential. Unfortunately, the Meters, embittered by their business dealings with Sehorn and Toussaint, had disbanded.

Building on his forthcoming album, Huey embarked on reunion gigs with his classic Clowns. Gerri Hall thought Huey should buy a new stage costume for her. When she and Margrette went shopping at Sears, Gerri selected an expensive outfit, but the budget-conscious Margrette talked her into something less pricey. "Gerri wanted a dress with wings under the arms, like Diana Ross," Huey said and laughed.

Once songs for the new album were recorded, Skor backed Huey and Clowns Bobby Marchan, Roosevelt Wright, Gerri Hall, Curley Moore, and new group member Margrette Smith in November 1978 at a packed Tipitina's. That night, Curley told his boss man that Cosimo Matassa had been marveling about Huey's ability to turn ordinary people into entertainers. "You know something?" Curley said. "You can make anybody a singer." "Huey would school cats," Dr. John confirmed. "He was about the show. It was about presenting something and making it fun." "Really," Huey said two decades later, "if somebody pass by,

I say, 'Come here. I wonder—can you dance? Well, you can talk. You come let me show you this.'"

Although Louis Kahl and the other members of Skor thought the Tip's show went well, reviewer Vincent Fumar criticized it in New Orleans's afternoon newspaper, the *States-Item*. "Huey 'Piano' Smith at Tipitina's had all the earmarks of a hastily called practice session," Fumar wrote. The reviewer, apparently unaware that Huey had played electric pianos since the 1950s, knocked him for playing an electric keyboard at Tip's. "Unless he changes the instrument he was playing, people just might forget his middle name."

Fumar's bad review hurt Huey deeply, Kahl recalled. "He called when that came out and he read the whole thing to me over the phone, with disgust in his voice. I thought he was to the point of tears. It really devastated him." "Like I had some gentleman," Huey recalled, "talking about this 'comeback of Huey Smith,' way back there then. I said, 'See, if it was a comeback of Huey Smith, there'll be a tour set up. We play thirty days or so. Now, the first few jobs, that is rehearsal.' And they told me to come to Tipitina's. 'See, these kids there, they want to see how y'all played in years past.' Okay, then, I'm go' do this now. But coming back? Well, where have I been? Then the newspaper got cheeks enough to write, 'It sounds like a rehearsal,'" Huey said before laughing through the pain.

More unfortunate developments followed. Huey got an unpleasant surprise when he returned to the Sea-Saint Recording Studios. His new recordings had been mixed without his input. "You didn't even know what to do on it!" he protested. "How are you going to already mix my session and you don't know? I've got to tell you how it goes." But the studio's door did not open for him again. "No contract," he lamented. "They took the recordings. They just take your things when you're not finished yet. That's how disrespectful they are." The surprised Huey and Margrette later found an album of songs from their Sea-Saint sessions on sale at the 1984 World's Fair in New Orleans. England's Charly Records released the sessions with the title *Rockin' and Jivin'*.

Skor, unaware of behind-the-music events, had been thrilled about recording with Huey, so much so that being paid was not a priority. "Huey was one of our heroes," Kahl said. "We were just happy to make music. But when it came time to pay, Marshall Sehorn said, 'Well, I got these speakers.' We already had some of the studio mics, and he said, 'Take them, too.' The guy that he was dealing with in our band said, 'Yeah, we'll just take that.'"

n the late 1970s, Huey met Jonathan Foose, a filmmaker from Mississippi who loved New Orleans music. Foose and New Orleans writer Jason Berry produced a documentary about two musical New Orleans families, the Nevilles and the Lasties. Historian Tad Jones served as the pair's research partner. The trio, realizing there was much more to tell, later collaborated on the book *Up from the Cradle of Jazz: New Orleans Music since World War II.* "Huey was a childhood hero of mine," Foose recalled. "When I got down to New Orleans and started doing music research, I was knocked out that he wasn't doing anything. I encouraged him, but he was tentative. And I had met Bobby Marchan and Curley Moore, James Booker and Roosevelt Wright and Gerri Hall. So I kept trying to get everybody together. We were able to get together for a couple of brief, shining moments."

Huey, Bobby, Gerri, Roosevelt, and Curley and a band featuring saxophonist David Lastie, his drummer brother, Walter, bassist George French, and guitarist Walter "Wolfman" Washington rehearsed for the 1979 New Orleans Jazz and Heritage Festival at Foose's three-room French Quarter apartment at 1229 Royal Street. The group not only practiced in the tiny space, they played for a party there, too. "Getting them up there was like herding snakes," Foose said. "Not the Lasties, but some of the Clowns. Curley Moore was so crazy. I guess he was all drunked up, but we were able to get some rehearsals in and, you know, it's like falling off a log for those guys, once they were doing it."

Lively though the short, wiry Curley was, Foose remembers him being overshadowed by Bobby Marchan. "Bobby was total old-school show business," he remarked. "When we put the bunch back together, a lot of the stuff that we did was through Bobby's work and encouragement. And Roosevelt was a beautiful, quiet, passive, big bear of a guy with that incredible voice. Gerri, she's a trip. I guess Huey enjoyed it. It's hard to gauge him. He had a desire to have attention and another desire to not have it, depending on where the wind's blowing. I love Huey, man. We went through a lot of stuff together."

Huey "Piano" Smith and the Clowns made their belated New Orleans Jazz and Heritage Festival debut on Saturday, May 5, 1979. The group shared a 12:30 P.M. set on Stage 4 with the Lastie Brothers and Al "Carnival Time" Johnson. British writer Clive Richardson, attending his first Jazz Fest, was astonished when he saw the reunited Clowns listed in the festival's program. "Their performance was superb, like a dream come true, with strong support from the Lastie Brothers' band," Richardson reported in England's *Juke Blues.*

F rom the 1970s onward, growing appreciation for rhythm-and-blues and rock 'n' roll pioneers made Huey "Piano" Smith and New Orleans music in general the subjects of books and articles. In 1978's *Stranded: Rock and Roll for a Desert Island*, twenty major music writers and critics, including Lester Bangs, Dave Marsh, Nick Tosches, and Robert Christgau, expounded upon which recordings they'd take to a desert island. Jay Cocks, whose screenplays for the Martin Scorsese–directed *The Age of Innocence* and *Gangs of New York* would later receive Academy Award nominations, picked *Rock and Roll Revival!*, the Huey compilation album Johnny Vincent released in 1974. Cocks's thirteen-page essay reveals a thorough knowledge of the music of New Orleans and Huey Smith. "The joy of Huey Smith's records is retroactive and regenerative, self-perpetuating past any arbitrary limits," he wrote. "That spirit travels well, too, because, like Huey's keyboard skill, it seems so spontaneous and effortless, so true."

Much of what was written about Huey was much less true, and when mistakes were printed, other writers echoed them again and again. A well-meaning early chronicler of New Orleans music, for instance, tangled up the names of two Clowns. "I named Billy [Brooks] and then Roosevelt [Wright] and Bobby [Marchan]," Huey recalled. "So some kind of way he wrote somebody is named Billy Roosevelt. Now I can pick up a million papers about this person in the group, Billy Roosevelt. Nobody's named Billy Roosevelt! And one article wrote I was born in 1924. Must have been talking about Joe Jones, because it also said I went to Xavier University. . . . If you're going to do it, get it accurate as possible. And everybody they interview is the greatest! I view all of that like you're saying this red is a prettier color than this blue. But you can't make a claim one way or another. This one does what he does and this other one does what he does. Like Tuts Washington said he knew he was the greatest. I don't believe he said that. That's him, the writer, saying that."*

H uey went by Tipitina's one night in late January 1980. "I don't know why," he reflected. "I didn't even know who was there, but I walked in. Nobody was up there on the piano but Professor Longhair. The very next day they say Fess died!" Longhair left this world's stage at three in the morning. "He didn't moan,

---

*Born in 1907 and mentored by pianist Joseph Louis "Red" Cayou, Isidore "Tuts" Washington was a brilliantly versatile but rarely recorded New Orleans pianist emulated by younger pianists Professor Longhair and James Booker.

he didn't groan," his wife, Alice, said. "He just slept away." The Orleans Parish coroner's report cited chronic bronchitis, pulmonary emphysema, and advanced cirrhosis of the liver as the causes of death. The sixty-one-year-old singer-pianist died when his fortunes were brighter than ever. He'd been making a living playing music and shooting a documentary film with Allen Toussaint and Tuts Washington. Chicago's Alligator Records released his new album, *Crawfish Fiesta*, the day he died. "Fess was unique," Huey said softly. "I liked Fess, all the time."

During Longhair's wake at the Majestic Funeral Home on Dryades Street, Toussaint played an instrumental rendition of "Big Chief." Brothers Earl and Wilson "Willie Tee" Turbinton performed a heartfelt saxophone and keyboard duet. Righteous testimony erupted near the open casket while the professor's children and grandchildren wept. Atlantic Records principal Jerry Wexler delivered one of the many eulogies Longhair would receive that weekend. Wexler hailed Longhair's keyboard innovations and traced a line from him to five surviving New Orleans pianists—the apostles who, as he put it, brought the piano gospel according to Fess to the world. "They are well known to every one of you here," he said. "I have had the privilege of knowing all of them and even working with some of them in the recording studio. My life has been enriched by knowing Professor Longhair and Allen Toussaint and James Booker and Mac Rebennack, Huey Smith and Fats Domino."

I n early 1980, attorney Charles Levy told Huey that he was taking his wife to a special doctor in Texas. "I really was thinking he was going there for himself," Huey recalled. "Because he told me, 'If something happens to me, that boy knows what to do.' He was talking about his son, Clifford. 'If something happens to me, your things here, that boy knows what to do.'" Levy died April 7, 1980. The sworn descriptive list of assets and liabilities in his succession papers, dated November 26, 1980, included royalties from Cotillion Music, Inc., valued at $30,000.

W hile Huey's membership in the Witnesses gave him a new direction, his old friend Curley Moore continued playing dangerous games. Curley's Uncle Austin told Huey that the gun-toting Curley got himself in a standoff with an armed stranger. Fortunately, the two talked and neither fired. Austin warned Curley not to play with guns, but Curley reveled in the gangster life-style. At Tipitina's, for instance, he tried to impress a girl by opening his over-coat and revealing the big gun in his waistband. "One time he unholstered it," Huey said.

onathan Foose interviewed Huey's friend and former piano player James Booker in December 1980:

"You like Huey Smith?" the languid Booker asked Foose.

"I don't understand him, but I like him," Foose replied.

"I don't understand Huey Smith," Booker said. "I don't understand anybody."

"What do you think about Huey's Smith's playing?"

"He's one of the people that really got me to play in the fashion that let every-body know you got more than one influence. Huey Smith. Huey Smith could play!"

On November 8, 1983, Booker sat down in the waiting room of Charity Hos-pital. He frequently visited the hospital for various ailments. The staff made lit-tle note of him. After waiting a few hours, New Orleans's "Piano Prince" passed quietly away. The official cause of death was intestinal bleeding and heart and lung failure. "All we found out is that he went into Charity and was sitting in a wheelchair," Orleans coroner Dr. Frank Minyard said. "They don't know who brought him there." Booker's demise made the front page of the *Times-Picayune*. He was forty-three. Booker had lived for a year with Jerry Brock, a record pro-ducer, documentary filmmaker, cofounder of local radio station WWOZ, and one-time co-owner of the city's great record store the Louisiana Music Factory. "James Booker was complex on many levels," Brock recalled of the mytholo-gized New Orleans musician he knew as a friend. "He made astonishing music, so natural and effortless, yet he struggled to find harmony in life. Thirty years after his death, people are still trying to catch up to Booker's genius."

17

Red Stick

Huey, important figure that he is in New Orleans music, unsurprisingly found himself the main attraction at Tipitina's one night. Much of the attention came from women. They'd sit in his lap two at a time. Another played with his neck. He was already feeling vulnerable, following the recent death of a family member due to high blood pressure, a condition he himself had recently been diagnosed with. After Huey allowed himself to be the center of female attention that night, he concluded that he'd crossed the line and broken his integrity. He'd disappointed himself. "But it wasn't what Almost Slim, that writer, said," he clarified. (Almost Slim is the pseudonym for music journalist Jeff Hannusch.) "Sure wasn't about drinking. It was about sexyology. I repeated back far into my old life."

If a Jehovah's Witness conducts himself in a way unbecoming of a Christian, he is subject to disfellowship from the congregation. Although the Witnesses were not aware of Huey's behavior at Tipitina's, he told them about it. They did indeed disassemble him, but soon, Huey having shown himself repentant, the congregation welcomed him back.

Wanting to make a new start, Huey and Margrette moved to Baton Rouge in late 1980. Margrette had relatives there. A deeply conservative place compared to Huey's celebratory, music-loving hometown, Baton Rouge is Louisiana's lawyer-, politician-, and petrochemical plant–heavy capital city. The town's mood swings most of all on the fortunes of the Louisiana State University football team. Barry Armstrong, one of Guitar Slim's and Albertine Armstrong's sons, helped the Smiths move to a house on Royal Street in the city's second-oldest neighborhood, Beauregard Town.

Soon after his arrival, Huey approached Tabby Thomas about performing at Thomas's new blues club. Thomas, along with such colorfully named acts as Slim Harpo, Lazy Lester, Lonesome Sundown, Whispering Smith, Lightnin'

Slim, and Schoolboy Cleve, was among the Baton Rouge–area swamp-blues acts J. D. Miller recorded in the 1950s and 1960s in Crowley, Louisiana, for Nashville's Excello Records. Thomas told Huey that his new club wasn't for stars from New Orleans; it was for Baton Rouge talent. The fledgling club owner also gave Huey his card. It read "Tabby 'Piano' Thomas." Nor were the Smiths' new neighbors particularly welcoming. When the expensive gardening equipment Huey had stowed in his backyard was stolen, the police told him, "We can't prove it, but your neighbors took that." "Now," Huey wondered, "why they took it, I don't know, because they never seen a weedeater before."

Margrette's aunt, who lived nearby, chided Huey and Margrette for landscaping their yard. "Them too many flowers," she complained. Nor was she pleased when Huey cut her grass free of charge after he'd heard her lamenting the $2 some boys charged her for the service. "Ah, Hu-ree," she said. "My yard look-ed so bad, till you did mine, huh?" One of Margrette's cousins charged the couple $3 for jump-starting their car on nearby Highland Road. When the same cousin needed jump-starting on the street in front of the Smiths' house, Margrette refused to take the $5 he handed her. "Call your husband," the man insisted. She replied, "He'll tell you the same thing." Coming from New Orleans, Huey sensed the differences between the people in his hometown and residents of Baton Rouge. "We're different," he said. "We're not like Baton Rouge people."

Still new in town, Huey and Margrette went to see a movie at the city's soon-to-be-demolished downtown movie palace, the Paramount Theater. The local newspaper's music critic told Huey about *American Hot Wax*, a biopic about pioneering rock 'n' roll disc jockey Alan Freed. One scene in the film features Frankie Ford lip-syncing "Sea Cruise" in a recording studio as a group of white actors pretend to be session musicians. After seeing the film, Huey told promoter-turned-vintage record dealer Jim Russell, "Yeah, you saw that guy in the movie behind the piano? That was supposed to be me!"

In its November 1980 issue, New Orleans music magazine *Wavelength* reported Johnny Vincent's plan to re-release classic New Orleans rock 'n' roll. Vincent, the story added, also was opening a nightclub in Jackson, Mississippi, called the Bon Ton, and hoping to do so with Huey "Piano" Smith.

"Come up here to Jackson, Huey," Vincent said in phone call. "I got something for you." When Huey got to Jackson, Vincent showed him a bombed-out former nightclub in a black neighborhood within walking distance of the old Vincent Building. The place appeared to have recently been a parking garage. Huey spent three weeks cleaning it up. Vincent sent him to apply for a liquor license, and Huey sent for former Clown Jesse Thomas. Vincent also asked Bill Sinigal—the bandleader, bassist, and saxophonist who wrote and recorded the Mardi Gras classic "Second Line"—to lead the club's band. But this latest collaboration between Vincent and Huey slipped off the rails almost instantly when Vincent introduced Huey to the young woman he'd hired to handle money for the venue.

"Yeah, this the girl go' be on the cash register," he said. "On my cash register?" Huey asked. "Yeah," Vincent said, adding, "how I'm go' be able to keep up with my money? You'll be in here drunk and we don't know where the money at." The offended Huey immediately canceled the club's liquor license and called Jesse Thomas to tell him not to come to Jackson after all. Placards had been printed, however, advertising the appearance of Huey and Sinigal. Band leader Sinigal did play opening night, and in a subsequent phone conversation with Huey, he defended Vincent. "Johnny may have not paid for records, but he opened up a lot of doors for gigs," he said. Huey didn't want to hear it.

Sinigal and Frankie Ford held similar views of Vincent. "I'm sure they stole," Ford said. "I'm certain of that—but they didn't steal as much as they gave me a chance. I still did business with Johnny Vincent, OK, up until his death."

W riter and filmmaker Jonathan Foose interviewed Bobby Marchan in January 1981 during an engagement Bobby and his band, Higher Ground, played at Prouts Club Alhambra in New Orleans:

FOOSE: What was it about Huey's songwriting that made him infectious? What made it good?

BOBBY: Well, he was stupid and he wrote stupid. And it just caught—

FOOSE: I disagree! I don't think Huey's stupid.

BOBBY: I don't mean stupid that way. I mean he wrote—

FOOSE: Simple?

BOBBY: Yeah, he wrote simple stuff, that's what I mean. And it was simple stuff that be happening every day and it just caught on. After all, you have to be very silly to say you want rockin' pneumonia and have a boogie woogie flu. Nobody wants no rockin' pneumonia and no boogie woogie flu. But it caught on like wildfire. Everybody caught it. And then Huey come with another sick record, which I led, called "I Get High Blood Pressure." And I had high pressure ever since. I got it right now!

FOOSE: What makes New Orleans such a musical city?

BOBBY: New Orleans just a born musical city. I don't know what makes it. It's just like asking what makes red beans and rice.

England's Charly Records released *Rockin' and Jivin'*, an album culled from Huey's Sea-Saint Studios sessions, in 1981. When Huey and Margrette finally heard the album three years later, in addition to being disgusted with the bad business they associated with the record, they found its production appalling. Margrette wished Toussaint and Sehorn had let them re-record the project from scratch. The ten-track lineup also is missing what Huey considers his best recording of "High Blood Pressure." He especially likes Margrette's contribution to the remake. "I think it's the best record I ever made in my life, was that 'High Blood Pressure,' but it hasn't showed up nowhere," he said.

All of the LP's tracks, the Charly sleeve states, were licensed to Charly Records by Sehorn and Toussaint's Sansu Enterprises. Ironically, the sleeve notes, attributed to Phil A. Gumbo, wish Huey well. "Because of its recent vintage this album may, at first sight, appear to be for Huey Smith completists only," Gumbo writes. "But, believe me, it is an essential addition to any discerning R&B collection. If only it could change Huey's dismal fortunes." Defending himself in 1981, Sehorn sounded much like Johnny Vincent. "I read article after article about how the Meters got beat out of money, and how I built a house on the lake and Allen bought a Rolls Royce," Sehorn complained. "Shit! The Meters owed me $190,000. . . . And those records that come out on Charly overseas, these guys [recording artists] think they sell millions. Hell, they only sell between five and ten thousand at the most."

Huey rarely performed after moving to Baton Rouge. An appearance with Robert Milburn, brother of early rhythm-and-blues star Amos Milburn, and Irma Thomas at Louisiana State University's Union Theater was advertised in 1981, but Huey didn't perform. For two weeks, the local newspaper reported, "students of legendary New Orleans piano man Huey 'Piano' Smith waited like expectant bridegrooms for the man with the magic left-hand rhythm to walk down the aisle and help take charge of the March 29 Louisiana Purchase concert. But shortly after he was supposed to join Robert Milburn's Blue Notes' opening set, word came that Smith wouldn't show after all." Huey explained his absence, saying: "In Bible times they had what they called the bride price. If the groom didn't come up good, he didn't get the bride. When Robert Milburn told me what they wanted to pay, I told him, 'Well, I need more than that to get my clothes out the cleaners.' I'm not a teenager who wants to be on somebody's stage for fun." A follow-up newspaper story revealed that the Louisiana Purchase concerts never had a contract with Huey. "We never spoke to him," the program adviser said. "The matter of money was strictly between Milburn and Smith."

That same year, however, Huey and the Clowns performed for the Uptown Gator Ball, an annual Mardi Gras concert series in New Orleans, and later at Tipitina's and the Jazz and Heritage Festival. The group rehearsed at saxophonist David Lastie's house. Former Meters bassist George Porter Jr. joined the musicians who backed Huey and the Clowns for the gigs. "Rehearsal," Porter recalled, "probably started, like, three hours late, because we were dealing with the Clowns, you know. We sat around and talked and talked for hours and hours. Not *we* talking, but *they* talked. I did a lot of listening, because they were talking twenty years over my head. But I knew all of those guys from the stories that I heard from Earl King and hanging with Chris Kenner when I was a kid, too. They talked about the antics of the Clowns."

A successful show at Tipitina's was a warm-up for a Jazz Fest appearance featuring Huey and classic Clowns Bobby Marchan, Roosevelt Wright, and Gerri Hall. Curley Moore joined, too. The group's audience at Tipitina's included Jon Cleary, a newly arrived young Englishman smitten with New Orleans rhythm-and-blues. "I think Huey Smith was pretty true to form in that the piano was almost tucked in the back," Cleary said of Huey on stage at Tip's. "The Clowns were lined up in the front. Huey was just back there near the drummer. You hardly even saw him. But it was a great gig. Zigaboo [Modeliste] and George [Porter Jr.] were playing with them. It was basically Huey Smith with the nucleus of the Meters." Cleary soon switched his primary instrument from guitar to piano. Staying in New Orleans, he worked as a side man for Huey's peers Earl King, Ernie K-Doe, Jessie Hill, Tommy Ridgley, Johnny Adams, Eddie Bo, Snooks Eaglin, Dr. John, and Walter "Wolfman" Washington. Cleary later established a solo career and backed New Orleans piano fan Bonnie Raitt for ten years. Of course, Cleary couldn't know that the Huey Smith and the Clowns show he saw at Tipitina's would be among the final gigs Huey would ever play.

Huey and the Clowns performed at Jazz Fest on May 9, 1981, on Stage 1, backed by Lastie's band, A Taste of New Orleans. "It went great," Jonathan Foose said, giving particular props to George Porter Jr. "I was sort of music director," Porter said. "I organized who did what and when and where and how and just kept everybody talking together musically. The gig was absolutely a gas. We played all of the songs. I was absolutely happy just to be a part of that traditional thing."

Huey didn't mention it to anyone at the time, but a disastrous sound check preceded his Jazz Fest set. "See this ear?" he explained while pointing to his left ear, the only ear in which he'd had hearing. "It's not the Jazz Festival's fault, but that's where I lost my hearing," he said. "I had the earphones on and I asked the gentleman, the engineer, 'Can you turn up the piano a little bit? . . . Can you turn it up a little bit more?' He must have got irritated, because after that I barely touched the piano and, *boom*, it liked to break my head open. It was the most painful thing I ever experienced. I didn't complain. I went on and played the thing. I didn't think it would be serious at the moment, but I know that's when my hearing went to dwindling fast."

Although Porter enjoyed his Huey and the Clowns experience, he has an unpleasant earlier memory of Curley Moore. Of course, drugs were part of many musicians' lives in the 1960s, 1970s, and 1980s. Porter would get clean and sober in 1988, but prior to that he was no exception to the rule. "Curley Moore spiked the first joint that I ever smoked in my life," he recalled. "It was some cheap weed with some angel dust in it. That stuff messed me up so bad. I remember coming out of the stupor that I was in. Cosmo Matassa was on the studio floor holding me in his arms, I guess to keep me from freaking out. Cosmo said I was out for like six hours. It was my first experience with angel dust. My first and last. I wanted to kill Curley."

Shortly after Huey and the Clowns' 1981 Jazz Fest appearance, the *Baton Rouge Morning Advocate* quoted Foose as saying Huey might perform more often and record again, too. "Huey's always considered himself a songwriter-pianist and he'll only perform regularly if the situation is comfortable for him," Foose told the reporter. As for recording, "everybody's very much for the idea, but we'll see what develops." Despite Foose's cautious optimism, Huey's career took another hiatus. By July it seemed unlikely he'd return to the stage or the studio, especially after the cancellation that month of a show scheduled for Tipitina's. "Every bridge that I get to," he told the *Times-Picayune/States-Item,* "I want to see what the water is like underneath and how the structure of the bridge is. As far as recording, I haven't heard anything that interests me." Fortunately, his songwriting provided him with income. A few months after Jazz Fest, a BMI royalty check enabled him to pay cash for a house in Beauregard Town. The funds arrived after soul star Patti LaBelle recorded "Rocking Pneumonia and the Boogie Woogie Flu."

Huey's name didn't appear in the *Morning Advocate*'s weekly entertainment section again until June 1982. A photo showed him beaming in cap and gown on the occasion of receiving his GED at Baton Rouge High School. Obtaining the diploma, he told the newspaper, "knocked a fly off my nose about not having that piece of paper." He was writing new songs, the story added, but had no plans to return to music because his Jehovah's Witnesses ministry was more rewarding than anything he had done before.

Meanwhile, the Smiths were raising their granddaughter, Tyra. Her toddler talk inspired Huey's illustration of his metamorphosis from a crawling musician to a saved Jehovah's Witness. "Ty couldn't say the word 'butterfly' right," he said. "She was talking about the caterpillar out of the cocoon. 'Oh, now he a beautiful bubba-fly!' So that's what happens. There's a lesson in the Bible dealing with transformation of your personality. And you got to continue cultivating it."

R obert "Catman" Caffrey, in addition to being a saxophonist and bandleader with Shirley and Lee during the 1950s, was an amateur photographer who snapped countless images of his New Orleans music peers. He later worked as a photographer for the *Louisiana Weekly.* Asked one year to bring his photos to a concert at the long-closed Dew Drop Inn, Caffrey arrived with huge prints of New Orleans music stars. But seeing the sad state of the once-great nightclub, he didn't have the heart to hang them. "Man," Caffrey told Huey, "I saw how ragged and tore down the Dew Drop was. I put all my pictures—I had life-size pictures of you and Fess, Earl, all of y'all—I loaded my stuff in my car and went on back home."

18

You Are Entitled To and Can Collect Your Royalties

C huck Rubin worked in the music business during the 1960s and 1970s as a booking agent, manager, talent packager, and artist consultant. His management clients included pop singing group the Happenings ("See You in September," "I Got Rhythm") and singer-songwriter and former Fury Records artist Wilbert Harrison ("Kansas City," "Let's Work To-gether"). In court papers and on the witness stand decades later, Rubin cited his work as agent for the Beatles, the Four Seasons, Sam Cooke, Fats Domino, James Brown, and Roy Orbison. In 1970, Rubin and Wilbert Harrison were part-ners in a Mercury Records–linked production company, Action City. Harrison's quest for unpaid royalties, Rubin later said, inspired the founding of the Artists Rights Enforcement Corporation in 1981.

Rubin pitched his Artists Rights services via a mailed solicitation to Huey Smith in March 1982. The letter from New York City read like a Publisher's Clearinghouse promise of cash. "Please allow this letter to introduce our com-pany to you," Rubin wrote. "Artists Rights Enforcement Corp. is a research and investigative service within the record industry. Our purpose is the representa-tion of the Artist and writer in the recovery of royalties. Mr. Smith, in related searches for other clients we have located several areas of activity in which you are entitled to, and can collect your royalties. It would be in your interest to contact us by letter or phone at your earliest."

Rubin had good timing. During the 1980s and 1990s, hits from the 1950s and 1960s were dusted off for television commercials, oldies radio, and such high-profile and highly profitable movie soundtracks as *Dirty Dancing, The Big Chill,* and *Stand by Me.* The 1980s also saw vinyl LPs and 45s replaced by the compact disc, a new format that allowed record companies to resell their cata-logs. With millions in old gold to be collected, Rubin contacted potential clients by mail and phone. His list of clients eventually read like a mid-twentieth-century rhythm-and-blues and rock 'n' roll hall of fame: Ruth Brown ("Mama, He Treats Your Daughter Mean"); the Coasters ("Charlie Brown," "Yakety Yak"); Hank Ballard ("The Twist"); Richard Berry ("Louie Louie"); the Dixie Cups ("Chapel of Love," "Iko Iko"); Sam and Dave ("Soul Man"); the estate of Huey's late friend Chris Kenner; and hundreds more. Recording artists and songwriters of the 1950s and 1960s, particularly black artists, widely believed that they had not been compensated fairly. Rubin could mail hundreds of solicitations to potential clients, confident that the income-promising pitch letters would grab their attention.

Huey's fellow Louisiana recording artist John Fred Gourrier ("Judy in Disguise," "Shirley") was among the recording artists and songwriters Rubin contacted.* Gourrier didn't find the offer persuasive. "They saying fifty percent of something is better than one-hundred percent of nothing. . . . Yeah, see, that's no good, man. That's too much. I wouldn't hire them, because all you doing is getting shystered by another shyster."

Huey, having never heard of Rubin or Artists Rights Enforcement, was suspicious at first. Rubin quickly followed the letter with a phone call. Charles Levy Jr. having died nearly two years before, Huey signed a contract with the New York company without consulting an attorney, days after he'd received the company's introductory letter. The contract states that Rubin would receive 50 percent of all sums that may come into Artists Rights Enforcement's hands or may be realized as a "proximate" result of the company's activities. (*Black's Law Dictionary* defines *proximate* as "immediately before or after" and "very near or close in time," and "proximate consequence" as a result that follows an unbroken sequence from an event.) If necessary, the agreement adds, Artists Rights will hire accounting firms and recommend attorneys to its clients. Both the accounting services and attorneys shall be paid from Artists Rights' 50 percent share of the proceeds.

Huey hoped that Artists Rights Enforcement would collect recording artist royalties from Johnny Vincent. Rubin, however, said he was most concerned

---

*Huey Smith met John Fred Gourrier in 1959 when he produced a session for the teen singer from Baton Rouge at Matassa's New Orleans studio. They recorded a remake of "You Made Me Cry," Huey's recording debut. "John Fred said I recorded something with him, but I don't recollect it," Huey said. "A lot of people come through the studio. You don't remember them all. You just help get it together, play, and they be gone and then somebody else. Like the young people, you do what you can to help them."

about Huey's more recent activity with Marshall Sehorn, the ill-fated Sea-Saint Studios sessions released by England's Charly Records in 1981. Rubin asked his new client to put the details of his dealings with Sehorn in a letter as well as the names of the songs he'd recorded. Sehorn and Rubin had at least one recording artist other than Huey in common. While working as a talent scout and promotion man for Bobby Robinson's Fire and Fury record labels, Sehorn brought Wilbert Harrison and his future hit, "Kansas City," to Robinson.

Huey grew wary of Rubin almost immediately, especially after speaking to the Nashville office of Broadcast Music, Inc. (BMI). This nonprofit performing rights society collects income from radio and television broadcasts, in-concert performances, jukebox play, and more for songwriters and publishers. "BMI said, 'A man says he's to collect your BMI money,'" Huey recalled. "I said, 'Oh, no! I'm looking for him to collect from Johnny Vincent!' So the man at BMI told me, 'Send him a telegram and tell him he's not authorized to get your BMI. And then send a copy to me and I'll put a halt to that.'"

Huey dispatched a Western Union mailgram to Rubin:

I WAS UNDER THE IMPRESSION OUR AGREEMENT IS FOR YOU TO COLLECT MONIES I AM NOT RECEIVING AT THE PRESENT, MECHANICAL, RECORDING, ETC. I AM ALREADY RECEIVING MY B.M.I. DIRECTLY AND DO NOT WISH TO CHANGE THIS. LET THIS MAILGRAM SERVE TO AMEND OUR AGREEMENT TO EXCLUDE B.M.I. MONIES.

HUEY P. SMITH

The language in the contracts that Artists Rights Enforcement clients signed was such that Rubin could have claimed 50 percent of Huey's performance royalties if BMI had redirected his checks to Artists Rights. The contract states that Rubin shall receive 50 percent of all sums that come into his hands. For instance, Carl Gardner, cofounder of one of Atlantic Records' most successful 1950s vocal groups, the Coasters, signed with Artists Rights for the purpose of retrieving money from bootlegged recordings and unauthorized use of his group's image. The Coasters' former manager, Lester Sill, was no longer collecting royalties for them because he'd left the group's employment. Gardner writes in his autobiography that Rubin contacted Atlantic Records, which told him it didn't have a current address to send the Coasters' checks to. Rubin gave Atlantic his address. Henceforward, the record company sent the Coasters' royalty checks to Rubin. He deducted his 50 percent fee plus $100 out-of-pocket expense for accounting and forwarded the divided balance to the individual group members.

After Huey ensured that Artists Rights Enforcement did not collect his BMI royalties, he heard nothing from Rubin. He thought Artists Rights Enforcement had lost interest in him until Rubin called again about five weeks later. Rubin had turned his attention to Huey's late lawyer, Charles Levy, focusing on a contract Levy drew up in 1978 for a transfer of "Rocking Pneumonia and the Boogie Woogie Flu," "Don't You Just Know It," "High Blood Pressure," and "Sea Cruise" from Huey to Jane Alshuler, aka Mrs. Charles Levy Jr. In dramatically phrased letters dated May 7, 1982, one to Levy's widow and the other to his son, Clifford, Rubin threatened civil and criminal litigation against the Levy family. The letter to Mrs. Levy states that Rubin had been advised by Huey that the composer was receiving neither mechanical royalties from publishing company Cotillion Music, Inc., nor performance royalties from Broadcast Music, Inc. In fact, the composer was receiving BMI royalties and had seen the need to explicitly tell Rubin not to collect those royalties.

The letter to Mrs. Levy reads in part:

> . . . We at present do not have proof of your personal role in this activity, but your appearance as a benevolent stranger in the May 2, 1978 sale, to our thinking, paints you a vital part of the alleged conspiracy to strip HUEY SMITH of his herinmentioned Copyrights.
>
> Further, with respect to performance royalties which were pay to HUEY SMITH and his rightful monies also, BROADCAST MUSIC, INC. records indicate that between June 26, 1978 (just 2 months after the sale) and April 27, 1979 $9,000.00 in advances were requested by as yet person unknown in the name of HUEY SMITH. None of this was made known to HUEY SMITH by you or Levy & Levy. . . .
>
> Accordingly, without separating your personal role in this very serious activity we respectfully request the following:—
>
> 1. Your immediate voiding of the May 2, 1978 sale.
> 2. Return of the $23,799.80 you received as a result of the May 2, 1978 sale.
> 3. Ten percent interest or $2,380.00 in addition to the monies mentioned in #2.
>
> We expect to receive your response within the next ten days. If we do not hear from you by mail (please forward response to our New York City address) within that time, we will proceed to take whatever action available on behalf of our client under the laws of this land.

"When I met Huey he was tending to Mr. Levy's garden," Rubin said later. "He told me he had no money, he lost all his money and sold his rights away to some person that Mr. Levy recommended. He was getting zero. Zero." Furthermore, Rubin added, his hunch about what Charles Levy had done proved correct. But as Huey recalls it, his late lawyer's estate was in succession, the Cotillion songwriter royalties were in a fund set aside for him, and the surviving Levys were his friends. Most importantly, the 1978 document regarding a transfer of his songs to Mrs. Levy, aka Jane Alshuler, was an instrument to protect his copyrights. "If somebody got your signature on a forged contract, this'll beat it," he said. "It was for when somebody says, 'Ha-ha-ha. You signed your songs away!' 'No, you ain't neither. Let me send you this. It's for Jane Alshuler.' So that's how Mr. Levy was protecting his client. But when Mr. Levy died, Mrs. Levy didn't know nothing about it. And I didn't talk with Mrs. Levy during that particular time because of what Mr. Rubin is telling me they saying about me while he's telling them I'm saying they crooks and thieves."

Within four months of Rubin's letter to Mrs. Levy and Clifford Levy, the family rescinded the apparent transfer of the songs to Mrs. Levy. The September 1982 out-of-court settlement mentions nothing of Rubin's claim that the family conspired to strip the composer of his copyrights. Instead, the settlement characterizes the 1978 transfer as a mistaken assignment. The Levys further agreed to pay Huey $24,000 in royalties. Rubin collected the latter sum, from which he took 50 percent before sending the balance to Huey in Baton Rouge. Although Clifford Levy characterized the settlement as a simple accounting matter, Rubin now had basis to claim a 50 percent share of Huey's songwriter royalties.

With the Levy matter settled, Huey's Artists Rights–recommended lawyer, Richard Linn, began pursuing royalties for the Sea-Saint Studios recordings. The Washington, D.C.–based attorney, seeing that separate recording and publishing contracts provided by Marshall Sehorn had identical "Huey P. Smith" signatures, questioned the contracts' validity. The attorney concluded that one or both of the signatures were fraudulent. It was déjà vu for Huey, a repeat of the 1957 general agreement with Johnny Vincent's Ace Music Publishing. In fact, the signature that appears on the Sehorn contracts is unmistakably identical to the signature on a decades-old thank-you note sent by Ace Records and Huey P. Smith to New Orleans radio station WBOK. Sehorn responded to Linn by saying Huey's rights had not been violated and that production costs for studio time and musicians exceeded $20,000, expenses that had not nearly been recouped. Sehorn's claims of high costs and "months and months" spent on the project conflict with session musician Louis Kahl's account of minimal studio time and the band's being paid with used speakers and microphones.

While Huey continued hoping Rubin would collect royalties from Johnny Vincent, Cotillion Music routinely sent songwriter publishing royalties for "Rocking Pneumonia," "Sea Cruise," "High Blood Pressure," and "Don't You Just Know It" to Rubin, who deducted 50 percent and sent the balance to Huey. "I could have stopped him at first," Huey reflected. "I knew better, but I was letting him make money so they can get what I was looking for from Johnny Vincent. But that's all ignored, so, evidently, they were really after my four songs from the beginning."

Meanwhile, Rubin continued soliciting clients. Two members of Motown singing group Martha and the Vandellas, Rosalind Holmes and Annette Sterling, signed with Artists Rights Enforcement in January 1984. Their contracts are identical to Huey's except for an additional paragraph that grants Rubin the authority to collect the Vandellas' royalties.

"Chuck's a smart guy," said Fred Wilhelms, a Nashville attorney who was the national director of health and retirement funds for the American Federation of Television and Radio Artists when he met Rubin. "Early on he had a marvelous reputation as a white knight. He helped many people, he got some great press—but the details of his arrangements with the artists, that never came up."

19

You're Fired

I n the late spring of 1984, two years and two months after Huey signed a contract with Chuck Rubin's Artists Rights Enforcement Corporation, Rubin paid half of a $6,000 IRS levy against Huey's Cotillion Music songwriter royalties. Huey subsequently told Rubin that he would terminate his Artists Rights Enforcement contract unless the company paid the levy in full. After paying the levy in total, the composer added, Rubin could then take $3,000 from the composer's next quarterly royalty check from Cotillion. "So if he pays my levy for me, I can sleep like him," Huey recalled. "But then he's on the phone with me, he says—and this the first time I heard it—'Half of that is mine's anyhow!' I say, 'Well, you collect half of it from now on then!' He wasn't collecting for me."

On May 25, 1984, Huey put his demand that Rubin pay the entire IRS levy in a Western Union mailgram:

TO WHOM IT MAY CONCERN:

STOP ALL LEGAL ACTIONS. IF BALANCE DUE THE IRS BY HUEY P. SMITH IS NOT PAID IN FULL BY MR. CHUCK RUBIN IMMEDIATELY LET THIS MAILGRAM SERVE NOTICE OF TERMINATION OF AGREEMENT BETWEEN HUEY P. SMITH AND ARTISTS RIGHTS ENFORCEMENT CORP. OTHER NECESSARY LEGAL STEPS WILL FOLLOW.

HUEY P. SMITH

CC. ATTORNEY RICHARD LYNN [sic]

Richard Linn subsequently informed Huey that he had instructed Rubin to pay the IRS levy in its entirety. The attorney added that Rubin apparently did not fully understand the IRS garnishment's legal effect. Linn also explained that money used to pay the IRS would have to be repaid to Rubin from Huey's next royalty payment. But Rubin refused to pay the levy balance, Huey's promise to fire Artists Rights Enforcement stood, and Cotillion Music honored his directive to stop payment of his songwriter's royalties to Rubin. Three months later, Rubin wrote Jerry Bursey in Cotillion's royalty department, demanding that the publisher send 50 percent of Huey's royalties as well as royalty reports to Artists Rights Enforcement. Cotillion attorney Raymond Brody sent a terse reply. "Mr. Smith has formally notified our client that he has terminated his relationship with you, and is no longer represented by Artists Rights Enforcement Corp., or its attorneys, including Richard Linn, Esq. He has instructed our client to render all accountings and payments directly to him, and to no one else."

F ollowing a month of European touring in 1984, Frankie Ford called Huey from London to apologize for recording his song "Don't You Know Yockomo." "What you sorry for?" Huey asked. "I get paid. You know, BMI. What you sorry for?!" Released by England's Ace Records, Ford's *New Orleans Dynamo* LP includes Huey compositions "Don't You Know Yockomo" and "Rockin' Behind the Iron Curtain," plus Chris Kenner's "Sick and Tired," Ernie K-Doe's "A Certain Girl," and Benny Spellman's "Lipstick Traces (On a Cigarette)."

O n October 23, 1985, Joe Banashak, owner of two of New Orleans's most successful independent record labels of the 1960s, Minit and Instant, had a fatal heart attack at the Atlanta airport. Shortly before his death, Banashak told one-time Instant Records artist Skip Easterling that he needed to apologize to him. Like The Hueys' "Coo Coo over You" before it, Easterling's regional hit, "I'm Your Hoochie Coochie Man," potentially could have been a much bigger record than it was. "Skip, I really feel bad," Banashak said. "'Hoochie Coochie Man' could have been your meal ticket, but I screwed it up for you." "How'd you do that?" Easterling asked. "Well, you weren't there that day that Jerry Wexler from Atlantic Records said he wanted to put you on ATCO [Records]. He wanted to distribute 'Hoochie Coochie Man.' But I wouldn't let you go. I wanted to keep the record for myself. But I wasn't big enough to handle it and the distribution killed me." Interviewed in 2002, the Mississippi-dwelling Easterling expressed no bitterness about Banashak's mishandling of the song. "If it would have went to Atlantic, into Jerry Wexler's hands, I might not be living on a frog pond today," he said. "I might be dead or I might be living in a fine mansion. Whatever be the case, I'm happy that I'm with my wife and my family. I'm glad I gave up the road."

By the 1970s and 1980s, another of Huey's former musical associates, Curley Moore, was more about trouble than music. Bad boy Curley was sent to the Louisiana State Penitentiary. Huey heard he'd set a woman's house afire. Curley was also caught shoplifting dental glue for his broken dentures in a K&B drugstore. The concealed weapon the police found on him brought more trouble. Huey tried to be a good influence by giving Curley a Bible.

Curley had recorded three singles for Allen Toussaint and Marshall Sehorn's Sansu Records in 1966 and 1967. During a 1985 phone call to Huey in Baton Rouge, Curley claimed that an enraged Sehorn had threatened him. "Yeah, Marshall picked me up and throwed me against the wall. He say, 'I'm a' *knock* you off.' They do that, yeah. See, I had called Marshall 'plastic.'" Sometime later, an anxious Curley knocked on the door of Huey's eldest sister, Oddress, in New Orleans. "I got to find Doc," he said repeatedly. But Curley never saw Huey again. The *Times-Picayune/States-Item* reported his murder on December 17, 1985, at the bottom of page A-22: "Moore's body was found in Algiers when police answered an ambulance request about 8:50 p.m. Police found the body face down at Powder and Alix streets, near the river. It appeared Moore had been shot in the chest and arm and his body dumped from an automobile. . . ." The report made no mention of forty-two-year-old Curley being a singer and recording artist. Curley's newspaper obit ran ten days after his murder, two days after Christmas. It invited Sea-Saint Studios, the Fats Domino Organization, and all other New Orleans recording groups to his wake and funeral service. *Billboard* noted the singer's death in its January 18, 1986, edition. The story credited Curley as the lead vocalist for "Pop-Eye" and mentioned his local solo hits "Soul Train" and "Sophisticated Sissy."

"Now, who picked up the funeral tab was Sea-Saint and them," Huey recalled. "They buried him like the gangsters do in the movies. Al Capone and them. They send flowers and stuff. So I start staying inside." Concerned for his own safety, Huey wondered why no one contacted him about Curley's murder. He called Crime Stoppers in New Orleans. "They said, 'You can't say Marshall did this!' I said, 'No, but nobody asked me nothing else. Maybe you know something already. I ain't got nothing to do with it. That's your job to find out who did it!' But many people didn't like Curley anyhow."

Singer-guitarist Deacon John Moore is one among many who suspect Curley's murder was drug-related. "Curley was like a slick dude, always trying to con people," Moore said. "I guess that's how he just messed over the wrong person. Some drug deal went sour and, *boom,* they blew Curley away. Somebody shot him and just threw him in the gutter on the West Bank."

In the years after Curley's death, Bobby Marchan told Gerri Hall how much he missed the mischief-making singer. "Oh, Miss Gerri," Bobby lamented. "I sure need Curley. I wish Curley was here." "Yeah, Bobby, not just you," Gerri replied. "I been up there in Baton Rouge where Huey's at. He wish Curley was still here."

"When we had the first group," Gerri said of the classic Huey Smith and the Clowns years, "it was like me, Bobby, Eugene [Harris], and Roosevelt [Wright]. We had good Clowns. But when the Clowns start falling away, Huey got Curley. He say, 'With Curley, I know I can hold the group together and do the things that we do. Curley will sing everything that needs to be sung.' That was fine and that worked, but then Curley went South and East and North and West, starting getting married and everything!"

A s the 1980s progressed, national publications presented glowing accounts of Chuck Rubin's work with aging rock 'n' roll and rhythm-and-blues stars. The *New York Times* characterized him as a white knight who jousted with corporations and returned honor and royalties to rock 'n' roll pioneers. *Maclean's* proclaimed that, at last, "artists have someone to champion their cause. He is Chuck Rubin." The *Los Angeles Times* cited Artists Rights' work with "Louie Louie" composer Richard Berry as "another hit for Chuck Rubin." All of the stories took the feel-good angle of long-delayed justice being finally served. Later, the differences between early rhythm-and-blues star Ruth Brown's attorney, Howell Begle, and Rubin were covered amid an otherwise favorable depiction of Rubin in the singer's 1996 biography, *Miss Rhythm.* "Howell was uncomfortable with the fifty percent Chuck demanded," Brown wrote.

Music journalist Dave Marsh gave an epic account of "Louie Louie" in his 1993 book of the same name. Berry sold his "Louie Louie" publishing and songwriting rights to Max Feirtag's publishing company, Limax Music, in 1959 for $750. "I've never ever accused them of stealing the song from me," Berry told Marsh. "I went to them. I said, 'I need some money to get married.'" In 1983, singer Darlene Love, Berry's friend and former schoolmate, told him that Rubin wanted to speak with him about regaining rights to "Louie Louie." Berry, knowing nothing illegal had transpired, was not optimistic. But when a profitable licensing deal for "Louie Louie" loomed in 1985, Limax Music, not wanting to lose money because the song was held hostage in litigation, reassigned 75 percent ownership of it to Berry's publishing company, American Berry Music. Artists Rights then took 50 percent of Berry's 75 percent share henceforward.

When the *New York Times* and *National Law Journal* cited Huey "Piano" Smith as another of Rubin's success stories, neither publication mentioned the composer's heated 1984 breakup with Artists Rights. *Maclean's* also reported, falsely, that Huey was earning royalties for his compositions for the first time thanks to Rubin. But subsequent coverage of Artists Rights wasn't always laudatory. "Like any bounty hunter, he is viewed as savior by some, scum by others," Stephen Fried wrote in his January 1990 *GQ* column. "I'm not sure either description is entirely unfair."

"I found I can do this great," the upbeat Rubin told Fried. "I can see things, I can understand things. . . . I don't think that these record-company people believe that they're doing anything that's really wrong. I think that they have found a way of justifying what they do as a smart way of doing business. I don't think I'm doing anything wrong, but if you speak to some of these record companies, they'll say that I'm a real bad guy because I'm an opportunist, or I take advantage of my own clients because they don't really need me. There *is* a need, and I seem to have filled it."

I n October 1987, historian Donald J. Mabry interviewed Johnny Vincent at the North Park Mall in Jackson, Mississippi. Mabry described Vincent as "generous to a fault, unsophisticated and living an unusual life." Vincent would not reveal his address to Mabry. "Each time I went to Jackson to talk with him I had to call various people," the historian recalled. "He did not live with his wife, but she had no hesitation in telling me where he was. Most of the time I called Malaco Records and left word that I was looking for him. He had helped Tommy Couch and Wolf Stephenson create Malaco. I guess they felt an obligation to him. We met in a variety of places. I never understood why and was afraid to ask."

Meanwhile, Joe Jones, one of Huey's New Orleans music peers, came to see him in Baton Rouge. Jones, after cutting the novelty hit "You Talk Too Much" in

1960, moved into music production and management in New York. His clients included New Orleans acts the Dixie Cups ("Iko Iko," "Chapel of Love") and Alvin "Shine" Robinson ("Something You Got"). He moved to Los Angeles in 1973 and formed a music publishing company. Back in Louisiana, Jones told Huey that Hollywood wanted to use his music. "Your boat come in," Jones said. "People got this movie, *The Big Easy,* coming out. All you have to do is sign here and then they go' be sending you some money about the movie. Give you $2,000."

Huey signed the agreement Jones provided. His father-in-law, Willie Clay, signed as witness. "Then Mr. Clay went to complaining, grumbling about he don't know what he signed," Huey remembered. "So I asked Joe Jones to send it back to let my father-in-law see it, and then I could bring it to a lawyer. Joe, he had difficulty doing that." When Jones finally did send a copy of the agreement, Huey showed it to Baton Rouge attorney W. Steven Mannear. "You didn't assign it to the movie people," Mannear explained. "The paper you signed, Mr. Jones made it to himself, and he assigned it to the movie company." Mannear contacted Jones but was taken aback by the hostile reaction. The lawyer told Huey that Jones was "a very, very angry man."

Two 1987 films, the New Orleans–set *The Big Easy* and Ritchie Valens's biopic *La Bamba,* feature "Don't You Just Know It." *The Big Easy* also contains "Fore Day in the Morning," one of the songs Huey recorded at Sea-Saint Studios in 1978. The film's on-screen credits cite Huey "Piano" Smith as composer and performer, Huey's Cooley Publishing, Inc., and "Courtesy of Joe Jones." Another 1987 film, *Less Than Zero,* features a remake of "Rocking Pneumonia" by Aerosmith. The popular rock band recorded the song at the suggestion of producer Rick Rubin during sessions for *Permanent Vacation,* the best-selling album of Aerosmith's career. Also in 1987, Coca-Cola licensed "Sea Cruise" for its "Taste the Good Life" television commercial and in-store promotion. "Sea Cruise" had previously appeared in the 1986 Robin Williams movie *Club Paradise.* And in 1985, the mostly female British ska group Amazulu reached the United Kingdom's Top 20 with a distinctly 1980s rendition of "Don't You Just Know It."

Diane M. Grassi was general manager of Cotillion Music, Inc., the publishing division of Atlantic Records that had been established at the time of Atlantic's incorporation. Cotillion Music hired Grassi in the mid-1980s to help the underutilized Cotillion song catalog generate new revenue. "Cotillion wanted to generate as much revenue as it could for those songs being used in a lot of movies and commercials," Grassi said. "That's where I came in." Huey's "Sea Cruise" proved an especially valuable copyright, she added. "It was a hot commodity when the cruise lines were doing startups with their lines. Everyone wanted 'Sea Cruise.'"

With Grassi at Cotillion's helm, licensing fees for songs Huey had written and recorded more than twenty-five years earlier were producing impressive revenue. But Rubin, fired by the composer in 1984, was missing the boat.

"When I did those films, they were like $15,000 a film," she said. "I was told that Huey was entitled to half of that. We're talking about thousands and thousands of dollars. And I remember getting screamed at by Chuck Rubin a number of times. I think he wanted a say in how much money was being negotiated. I asked him what relationship he had to Huey. He said that he owned the copyrights. It was toward the end of my time there [at Cotillion Music]. I don't know how all that ended. But the royalty department at Atlantic Records added up the checks, put them in an envelope, and mailed them somewhere. They didn't know whether or not they were mailing things to the appropriate place. I would be asked to go back to contracts that were thirty-four years old to try to decipher them and try to get people's addresses out of them. A lot of these people had died or their heirs had died. When someone didn't get paid, once in a blue moon they'd float to the surface and call Atlantic Records. They weren't getting paid because the addresses Cotillion had hadn't been updated in thirty years by various estates, heirs, and in some cases the songwriters themselves."

Grassi didn't know if Cotillion royalty checks for Huey's songwriting were reaching him directly. "The royalty department only had a P.O. box for him," she said. "That's when Huey must have called me, because he wasn't getting his checks but people would call him up and say, 'Gee, Huey, do you know your song was in this movie? Did you know it was in this radio commercial?'"

Cotillion Music's general manager developed a personal fondness for Huey. "He's a very nice gentleman and he wrote great songs and he brought people a lot of joy," Grassi said. "When 'Sea Cruise' was originally written, I don't think that Huey knew, because nobody knew, that it would still be around today. He was ahead of his time in a lot of ways. He combined some of the best types of music and put them all together and made it phonetically easy to sing and to listen to. That's the beauty of a good song. You don't have to be Frank Sinatra to sing it."

20

Artists Rights vs. Artist

On March 23, 1988, Chuck Rubin sued Huey "Piano" Smith and Cotillion Music, Inc., in New York. Rubin claimed the composer owed Artists Rights Enforcement 50 percent of the songwriter royalties earned by "Sea Cruise," "Rocking Pneumonia and the Boogie Woogie Flu," "High Blood Pressure," and "Don't You Just Know It" since 1984. He put the latter amount at more than $400,000. The suit also claimed that Rubin was entitled to 50 percent of the royalties in perpetuity.

"I never heard nothing from Chuck Rubin whatsoever, till somebody dreamed up they can do whatever they do," Huey said. He hired Baton Rouge attorney W. Steven Mannear to represent him. Mannear's office was in Beauregard Town, blocks from the Smiths' house.

"I heard his music over the years growing up," the soft-spoken Mannear said years after the suit. "That music was very old by the time I got involved, but one or two of his songs had been used in promotional campaigns. That generated some income for Huey, which raised the red flag for the folks in New York who had a file bank of contracts that they had signed with artists from all over. Every time the contracts looked like they were gonna make some money, they pulled them out. It was nothing but a moneymaking opportunity for the operators of that—who knew the business much better than their clients did—to basically get a windfall."

On the contrary, Rubin and his associates say they fight and win great victories for their clients. "Well," Mannear said, "there is an argument that if you are successful in helping somebody recover their royalties, you should be compensated. But it seems to me, just like attorney-client contracts, 50 percent is rarely ever approved by the court as being fair and reasonable, except under very, very strange circumstances."

Richard Linn, Huey's former attorney, now representing Rubin and Artists Rights Enforcement, conducted a deposition of the composer for Artists Rights on the morning of November 1, 1988. "Richard Linn," Huey marveled later, "had been *my* lawyer, but he questioned me for Artists Rights!" Chuck Rubin arrived late to Mannear's law book–lined conference room. When he finally arrived, Huey rose to shake his hand across the table. It was their first in-person encounter.

During the deposition, Huey told Linn that he'd given his late attorney, Charles Levy, permission to collect his royalties. Levy, as far as he could remember, was the only entertainment lawyer in New Orleans.

Throughout the deposition, Linn repeatedly asked, to the point of insisting it must be so, if Huey had initiated contact with Rubin to ask for help in collecting royalties. "Isn't it true that you first contacted Chuck Rubin before you received anything in the mail?" the attorney asked. "Positively not, definitely not," Huey answered. "It was a surprise. I'd never heard of Chuck Rubin." "Didn't you receive recommendation from another artist or songwriter to contact Artists Rights or Chuck Rubin at some time in '82?" "I never received any recommendation from any artists concerning anything before or after '82." "Did you have any discussions about royalties with [fellow Ace recording artist] Jimmy Clanton?" "I haven't had a discussion with Jimmy Clanton in my life."

"Did you pick up the phone and call Mr. Rubin?" Linn continued.

"I probably got a call from him," Huey said. "First of all, I was suspicious of who is this person. Usually, it's people come from across the world to interview me and so forth."

Nor did Huey have trouble collecting royalties from BMI. "I have always said they were the only people connected with the music business that really was legitimate," he said.

"Isn't it true that you were attempting to collect back money that was paid by BMI to Charles Levy?" Linn asked. "No." "And that you tried to enlist the aid of Artists Rights to recover that money?" "No. Only thing, you know, with regard to a possibility of that aspect, it could be a mere suggestion or some fantasy from Chuck Rubin. BMI always been legitimate." "Well, how about Cotillion, did you seek the aid of Artists Rights in recovering back royalties?" "I never seeked the aid of Artists Rights, period."

Linn continued to insist otherwise.

"And after you had contacted Mr. Rubin and Artists Rights, you got your money back; isn't that true?" he asked. "I'm going to say," Huey explained again, "I'm going to say it all, for, I think, about the fifth or fourth time—I never contacted Mr. Rubin, period."

Turning to the rescission, reconveyance, and reassignment agreement the Levy family agreed to in a 1982 out-of-court settlement, Linn asked if the settlement was the result of Rubin and Artists Rights Enforcement's efforts to recover royalties owned to Huey by his late lawyer.

"I don't think it was the efforts," Huey said. "I think it was to look as if [there were] efforts to recover them. . . . I feel like he was telling me what he wanted me to think was going on."

Hoping to undermine Huey and Mannear's first line of defense, lack of legal jurisdiction in Louisiana, Linn asked if Huey refrained from doing business in the state of New York. "Did you ever take any steps to contact anybody at Cotillion to tell them not to sell any records in the state of New York?" Linn asked. "I didn't even know Cotillion sell records," Huey said. "Why am I going to tell them don't sell no records in the state of New York?"

"I have no further questions at this time," Linn announced. "I would request of Mr. Smith and his counsel that the document identified during the course of the deposition as the introductory letter from Artists Rights back in 1982 be produced by hand or by facsimile on or before November 4, 1988."

"How about now?" Huey's attorney asked.

"Now would even be better, if you have it," Linn replied.

"We'll furnish a copy to you before we close the deposition," Mannear said of Rubin's letter of solicitation to Huey.

Johnny Vincent sent a letter to the music clearance administrator at Warner Bros. in December 1988 stating that, despite decades of claiming otherwise, he was not the cowriter of "Rocking Pneumonia and the Boogie Woogie Flu." Vincent copied the letter to Huey's attorney and informed Mannear that Ace Publishing Company was attempting to locate its original contract with Huey P. Smith, but should that contract be in Huey's files, would Mannear please forward a copy of it to Vincent.

"He's supposed to be sending me the copy of the contract!" Mannear told Huey.

Even though Vincent didn't form Ace Music Publishing until March 1959, the general agreement-contract between Ace Music Publishing and Huey Smith that Vincent eventually produced is dated October 3, 1957. Curiously, too, the contract lists a New Orleans address for Huey—6011 Congress Drive in Pontchartrain Park—that the composer did not reside at until the summer of 1958. Huey is certain the contract is fraudulent. "I knew Johnny legally wasn't the publisher of my songs," he said. "I had never assigned them to him. The 1957 contract was made recently. That's why it was so much confusement."

Rubin lost his first lawsuit against Huey due to lack of personal jurisdiction. "Insofar as plaintiff contends that defendant Smith has been 'doing business in New York' in connection with the contract sued upon," the Supreme Court, New York County, ruled on March 17, 1989, "defendant Smith has provided proof that he terminated the agreement in May, 1984, and it is undisputed that he executed the contract in Louisiana after being solicited by plaintiff."

21

A New Suit

M oving to the U.S. District Court in Baton Rouge, Chuck Rubin and Artists Rights Enforcement sued Huey P. Smith for breach of contract a
second time on September 22, 1989. The suit again claimed the songwriter owed the company more than $400,000. The new suit, however,
dropped Cotillion Music as a defendant.

Though W. Steven Mannear had helped Huey win the suit that Artists Rights
filed in New York, the composer had come to fear that Mannear was sympa-
thetic to Rubin. He sent the attorney a letter saying he appreciated his services,
and then he and Margrette searched through the telephone book for new representation. A yellow-pages ad citing an "Equal Opportunity Lawyer" caught their
eye. "So I talked to her," Huey recalled. "She said, 'Look, you been talking now.
You owe me $300.' I gave her a check for $300. She looked at the Artists Rights
contract and said, 'Where the rest?' I said, 'That's it.' 'No, it got to be more than
this!' I said, 'No, that's all.' 'No, it got to be more than this!' 'No, that's all.' She
was supposed to think about if she'll represent me, but she was going somewhere, like for Christmas. She came back and said, 'No, I won't be able to help.'
But she kept my $300." Searching the phonebook again, the Smiths found David
Ferguson Sr. The many piles of paper in the lawyer's office troubled Huey, so
much so that he wondered how Ferguson could find even a phone number amid
the clutter. Nonetheless, he hired this attorney who was adamantly proud of the
phonebook ad that stated his areas of practice included entertainment law.

C iting lack of clarity in Artists Rights Enforcement's contract, Judge John V.
Parker—a sixty-one-year-old native of Baton Rouge best known for presiding over the East Baton Rouge Parish Schools desegregation suit, the sec-
ond-longest running desegregation suit in U.S. history—denied Chuck Rubin's

motion for summary judgment on July 13, 1990. "The definition of 'realize' in Webster's dictionary, includes 'to make real or apparently real . . . to convert into actual money. . . .' The definition of 'proximate' includes 'soon forthcoming; imminent.' In view of these commonly understood definitions, it is not clear that the provision of the contract, 'which may be realized as a proximate result of your activities,' was intended by the parties to include the right to collect future royalties as a result of the settlement negotiation of Smith's attorney."

Rubin's new suit came at time when Johnny Vincent, the reason Huey signed with Artists Rights Enforcement in the first place, was again doing well in the music business. By 1990, Ace Records was releasing new soul material and reissues of the label's classic catalog. "Suddenly, everything I did was right," Vincent said of his comeback. "I lived out my dream, man—making records. Now Ace does $2 million, $3 million a year. But I'm older. I just wanna play with the label. I'm gonna sell and try to stay on in some capacity. I guess it's time. I'm a diabetic. I've had triple bypass surgery. I've got cataracts tremendously, to where I can't see good. I wobble when I walk, but I still love the record business. It's all I have left."

I n the market for an electric piano in 1990, Huey stopped at the BeBop Music Shop on Government Street in Baton Rouge to look at pianos. Store owner Mike Armshaw, one of Dr. John's cousins, told this new customer the prices. "He walked around the store," Armshaw remembered, "and came up to the counter and pointed at one and said, 'I'm gonna get that one.' But he hadn't played it or anything." Armshaw didn't know who he was talking to. "He finally asked me to turn the keyboard on so he could hear it," Armshaw said. "He played a walking bass figure with his left hand. The second he did I realized he was from New Orleans. He never played the midrange or the treble side of the piano at all, but you could tell he was a player because he had an unbelievable left hand. And then I saw his check. It said 'Huey P. Smith.'"

A rtists Rights hired a new lawyer in September 1991. Baton Rouge attorney Ralph E. Hood's specialties included creditor bankruptcy and mortgage lien foreclosure. Huey, saying the deadline for enrollment had expired, unsuccessfully objected to the new counsel. Huey's own counsel was highly changeable. His list of lawyers eventually included W. Steven Mannear, David Ferguson

Sr., Robert Oliver, Philip J. Dugas, Daniel Keys III, and New Orleans attorney Ellis J. Pailet. Huey also filed papers stating that he'd never given a pair of New Orleans attorneys, James G. Burke Jr. and Robert D. Hoffman Jr., authority to be his counsel. They withdrew. Ralph Hood complained about the many lawyers, telling Judge Parker that each attorney he'd discussed the case with and required pretrial stipulations from had been allowed to withdraw. "Ralph Hood had the nerve to say," Huey recalled, "'Your honor, he keeps changing lawyers!' Yet Artists Rights got *chains* of lawyers. And once I see my lawyer ain't saying what I'm saying, he's saying what Mr. Rubin's attorney wants him to say, it's time for him to go, because he's working for Mr. Rubin now!"

Huey has a test for lawyers. "A lady got a billion dollars," he tells his prospective counsel. "At her death, she wants that billion dollars to go to her cat. Now, she dies. Where you go' see this money goes? Her kids or the cat?" If the lawyer says the children get the cash and the cat's in the cold, Huey says, "Well, I can't use you. I don't want you to tell me what's best for me. I want you to do what I want you to do. By the way—I'm not a cat lover."

One of his attorneys, the composer said, asked why he didn't simply pay Artists Rights Enforcement. Again, Huey suspected that this particular lawyer and Rubin's lawyer were overly friendly with one another. "My counsel was talking with Ralph Hood, just calm," he recalled. "That's how they be doing. And these movies I see where people are dedicated to exposing corruption—like journalists and officials who don't want no hanky-panky—you can't go by that. That's like dreams. Years back, that might have been, but it don't work like that no more."

Huey sent a telegram voicing his ethics concerns to Judge Parker in August 1991. "Knowing that you are a man of integrity, I entreat you to personally monitor case # 89-723 section A. Please, please, I am in fear of collusion."

The telegram sparked a blistering reply from the court's chief deputy clerk. "NO CORRESPONDENCE OR CONTACT SHALL BE MADE DIRECTLY TO THE JUDGE'S CHAMBERS. Any correspondence mailed directly to the Judge's chamber shall be returned to you." Huey subsequently believed Judge Parker developed a personal dislike of him. "Just by his actions, he must have taken a hatred for me." One of Huey's new attorneys, Suzette Becker, noted Judge Parker's animus as well.

C ontrary to Chuck Rubin and Artists Rights' glowingly positive image in the national press, U.S. District Judge Morey L. Sear found Rubin's 1991 testimony in New Orleans for a long-running dispute over the 1956 Shirley and

Lee hit, "Let the Good Times Roll," to be evasive. The case arose from Shirley Goodman's claim that she deserved publishing royalties for cowriting "Good Times" with her late singing partner, Leonard Lee. Richard Bennett, a lawyer who worked with Rubin in the early years of Artists Rights Enforcement, represented Goodman. Rubin and Bennett had clashed previously during a royalty dispute involving three women who each claimed to be the widow of 1950s singing star Frankie Lymon ("Why Do Fools Fall in Love?"). Rubin and Bennett also were adverse parties in a California suit involving Goodman and Capitol Records. Artists Rights began as an altruistic endeavor, Bennett said in 1989, but "as soon as there's big bucks, the greed factor sets in and the artist gets screwed again. Artists Rights now masquerades as an investigative organization."

In the Shirley and Lee case in New Orleans, Judge Sear, a respected jurist with a no-nonsense reputation, found that, "based upon his demeanor on the witness stand, his inability to support his testimony with credible business records . . . and his bias and animus toward Goodman and Bennett, I am convinced that Rubin did not testify truthfully."

A renewed motion for summary judgment against Huey emphasized Chuck Rubin's 1960s experience—including being an agent for the Beatles, the Four Seasons, Sam Cooke, Fats Domino, James Brown, and Roy Orbison—as well as his investigation of the late Charles Levy and the Levy family. Richard Linn, Huey's former attorney, filed a declaration, too, writing, "the entire arrangement was simply an effort to dupe Smith out of his future songwriter royalties in their entirety. . . . [Levy] left a complicated mess of incomplete documentation and a very uncertain state of affairs with respect to his estate and those administering his estate who might be responsible for setting the record straight."

Neither Rubin's nor Linn's accounts impressed Huey. "You can't go in a lawyer's desk and see this there and then say he was stealing," he said. "The man is dead and that's how they doing him. But in the court Chuck Rubin says, 'By means of our investigation.' He up there saying beautiful words."

Huey still speaks fondly of Levy. In an early 1990s testimonial to the attorney, he wrote: "The time has come to vindicate the name of Charles Levy Jr., a southern Jewish lawyer, the only one in the South that was willing to help poor black musicians and songwriters."

The late New Orleans music historian Tad Jones, unlike many in the New Orleans music community, refused to cast Levy as a villain. "Most everything he knew was privileged," Jones said. "But I'm sure he did a lot of good things for people. I mean, he's the type of guy, if a musician died, he took care of the funeral. And he got a lot of clients simply because he was the only attorney in town in the 1950s who would even take on a black client. And Levy was like the only entertainment lawyer in town, so he became the man in the '50s and '60s. Even into the '70s, there still was virtually nobody who dealt with the music business. I'm sure he learned by the seat of his pants as he went."

As the Artists Rights suit against Huey wound its way to trial, Huey's influence in the music world he'd left behind continued. Robbie Robertson, former member of The Band, recorded his second solo album, 1991's New Orleans–inspired *Storyville*, in the city with the help of such local talent as Art, Aaron, Cyril, and Ivan Neville, Mardi Gras Indian chiefs Bo Dollis and Monk Boudreaux, arranger Wardell Quezergue, the Rebirth Brass Band, the Zion Harmonizers, and former Meters Art Neville, George Porter Jr., Leo Nocentelli, and Joseph "Zigaboo" Modeliste. "Making a record that incorporated the mystery and spice of New Orleans has been a dream of mine ever since I heard Smiley Lewis and Huey 'Piano' Smith as a kid in the '50s," Robertson said.

Following two failed attempts at summary judgment against Huey, Rubin's suit received a trial date of January 31, 1992. At a pretrial conference on December 16, 1991, Judge Parker told Suzette Becker, Huey's newly enrolled attorney from New Orleans, that her client would not be allowed to call witnesses. The defendant had failed to comply with the court's pretrial order, the judge said.* Becker sent Judge Parker a motion asking him to reconsider the decision "on the grounds that defendant complied with the pretrial order as soon as it was practically and chronologically possible to do so." Huey wanted to call himself, Jane Alshuler (Mrs. Charles Levy Jr.), Clifford Levy, Chuck Rubin, and Richard Linn as witnesses. Becker also asked that the trial be postponed because only minimal, incomplete discovery had been made on her client's behalf. Judge Parker denied both requests. "This action has been pending for more than

---

Black's Law Dictionary defines "pretrial order" as a court order that establishes the claims and defenses to be tried, the stipulations of the parties, and the procedural rules that have been agreed to by the parties or mandated by the court.

two years, and the record shows that defendant has had a series of lawyers," he scrawled over Becker's draft order.

Artists Rights Enforcement's attorney, Ralph Hood, dominated the subsequent nonjury trial in the federal courthouse at the edge of Baton Rouge's small downtown. His presentation was less a discussion of the merits of Rubin's case than a public relations presentation aimed at an audience of one, Judge Parker.

Ellis J. Pailet, one of Huey's two New Orleans attorneys, brought Becker in as co-counsel. Pailet argued the case, while Becker prepared the defense. It was her first music business case.

Hood, forgoing an opening statement, called plaintiff Rubin to the stand. Rubin gave a lengthy history of his music business experience and the origin of Artists Rights Enforcement Corporation. Judge Parker grew impatient with Hood's many questions about Artists Rights' modus operandi and told Hood to move on to the issues before the court. Hood finally asked Rubin about his work for Huey "Piano" Smith.

Rubin's explanations of why he contacted Huey varied through the years. In a 1990 affidavit, he said he learned that Huey had complained of being cheated out of his songwriter rights. In a 1991 declaration, Rubin said he heard rumors in the music industry that Huey was not receiving royalties and might need his help. In his emphatic March 1982 letter of introduction to the composer, Rubin wrote, "Mr. Smith, in related searches for other clients we have located several areas of activity in which you are entitled to, and can collect your royalties."

On the witness stand in Judge Parker's courtroom, Rubin offered a new variation on the theme. Because Johnny Vincent had not paid Jimmy Clanton, a former Ace Records artist and songwriter who'd signed with Artists Rights Enforcement, Rubin assumed that other Ace artists, including Huey Smith, "suffered the same fate." Subsequent conversation with Huey, Rubin added, had confirmed that Huey had not been treated fairly and had been cheated out of his royalties. Huey was delighted that someone would attempt to correct his problems with Ace Records, Rubin said.

In addition to being cheated by Vincent, Rubin continued, Huey did not receive a fair accounting of his songwriter royalties from his late attorney, Charles Levy Jr. The lawyer also deprived Huey of songwriter's publishing royalties and performance royalty income from Broadcast Music, Inc., and eventually recommended that Huey sell his songwriting rights to, as Rubin described, a benevolent lady. "Mr. Levy continued to tell him that there was no money and that his songs were not earning very much money."

Hood and Rubin moved on to the contract for the sale of Huey's songs "Rocking Pneumonia," "High Blood Pressure," "Don't You Just Know It," and "Sea Cruise" to Jane Alshuler. "For him [Levy] to convince Huey that this benevolent lady is offering $2,000 for his song rights," Rubin said, "this is terrible, this is a real bad deal." After Clifford Levy stopped cooperating with Artists Rights' effort to recover the songs for Huey, Rubin continued, the company was forced to threaten legal action against the Levy family. Four months after Rubin's legal threats to the Levys, the family reached an out-of-court settlement that nullified the 1978 transfer of the songs from Huey to Mrs. Levy.

Rubin and Hood told their lengthy backstory about the Levys to justify the 50 percent share of the money Artists Rights received from the Levy family as well as the company's subsequent continuous receipt of 50 percent of the songs' royalties. Having made that argument, Hood returned to more discussion about the day-to-day operations of Artists Rights. Forty-eight pages into the 126-page trial transcript, Hood and Rubin reached the dispute between Rubin and Huey that precipitated the composer's 1984 firing of Artists Rights, the action that, four years later, led Rubin to file his first breach-of-contract suit against the composer.

Artists Rights received an IRS levy on Huey's royalty income from Cotillion Music. After Rubin informed Huey that Artists Rights must pay the levy, Rubin testified, the composer demanded a $4,000 to $5,000 advance. Rubin refused, saying he'd given Huey many advances and would no longer do so. "I received a telegram from him about a day or so after I had to pay the levy . . . that basically said that if I don't receive the money and you don't pay the IRS in full . . . that he was going to fire me. And he did."

During Rubin's cross-examination by Huey's attorney, numerous questions from Pailet about the royalty account listed in Levy's succession papers left Rubin baffled. Following an explanation that succession papers are the same as estate papers, Rubin finally said he had not known the royalty account existed and had never seen Levy's estate papers.

Important though obtaining royalties from Ace Records was to Huey, Rubin told Pailet that Huey's songwriter's royalties from Cotillion Music were more worthy of pursuit. Rubin also told Pailet that Huey brought his recording misadventures with Marshall Sehorn and Sansu Enterprises directly to his Artists Rights–recommended attorney, Richard Linn. In fact, Rubin, in his March 1982 communication with Huey, said that he was most concerned about his new client's recent activity with Sehorn.

Just as Hood exhaustively covered Artists Rights' history and activities on behalf of its clients when Rubin was on the stand, Hood likewise extensively covered the personal history and credentials of his second witness, Linn. Hood included peripheral details about Linn's love for rock 'n' roll music. "Some of the songs he [Huey] wrote," Linn said, "are some of the greatest rock 'n' roll songs ever written." Linn ultimately echoed Rubin's account of Charles Levy's reassignment of songs from Huey Smith to Mrs. Levy. During Pailet's comparatively brief cross-examination, Linn, unlike Rubin, said he did not recall a "benevolent lady" who, as Rubin testified, offered to buy the songs for $2,000.

Linn, presenting himself as a hardworking, conscientious attorney, said Huey's firing of him and Artists Rights Enforcement left him stunned. "I have some recollection of dictating some kind of mailgram to send to Mr. Smith, basically saying, 'Listen, I don't know what's happening, but I'm here in Europe, I'll be back soon.' . . . As I said, I really looked up to Mr. Smith. He was a childhood idol."

Asked by Pailet if he helped Huey with the IRS levy that caused the rift between the composer and Rubin, Linn contradicted the written communication he'd sent to Huey in late May 1982. In that mailgram the attorney had told his then-client that he'd spoken to Rubin and instructed him to pay the IRS levy in its entirety. But in Judge Parker's courtroom Linn said: "I wasn't fully familiar with the details of this IRS situation . . . I did discuss with Mr. Rubin, this IRS situation and I surmised—"

"You actually weren't involved with it, is that correct?" Pailet asked.

"I was not involved with it at all," Linn said.

Pailet's further questioning of Linn revealed that Levy filed and paid income taxes on behalf of his client for the Cotillion royalties account. "But not giving the sum to Mr. Smith—is that correct?" Pailet asked. "That's correct," Linn replied. "It was a very strange set of circumstances."

Hood focused his closing argument on simple breach of contract. "Mr. Smith agreed to pay Artists Rights fifty percent of all sums which may come into his [Rubin's] hands or which may be realized as a proximate result of Artists Rights' activities on behalf of Mr. Smith," he said.

Pailet's closing argument claimed unauthorized practice of law by Rubin, and while he did not dispute Artists Rights' mandate to collect royalties for Huey, he argued that the contract says nothing about collecting royalties in perpetuity.

"They already have collected their funds for the money that they have already collected," Pailet said. "Let them keep it. But they certainly don't have a right to future monies which, in essence, would be the same as ownership."

Hood responded: "The court cannot ignore the fact that Mr. Rubin was instrumental, and as a proximate result of his activities on behalf of Mr. Smith, Mr. Smith recovered the Cotillion songwriter royalties."

Judge Parker ruled that Artists Rights Enforcement Corporation was entitled to receive 50 percent of all previously paid songwriter's royalties, as well as royalties that might become due and payable from all present and future owners and holders of the copyrights for "Rocking Pneumonia and the Boogie Woogie Flu," "Sea Cruise," "Don't You Just Know It," and "High Blood Pressure." He further agreed with Rubin and Linn that the late Charles Levy Jr. defrauded his client, Huey Smith.

"Mr. Smith," the judge said, "you have probably been ill-served by the legal profession. The evidence before the court certainly demonstrates that your original lawyer, Mr. Levy, did. And you probably were not served very well by a series of lawyers that came in and represented you from time to time, excluding your present counsel. It's the ruling of the court that you owe future royalties to the plaintiff in this case."

Pailet's courtroom performance disappointed Huey. "He got up there like Columbo, dropping the papers all over the floor," Huey recalled. "And Ralph Hood jumped up, like he had rehearsed this: 'But your honor, it was ruled on appeal that that was permitted!' Ellis Pailet said, 'Oh.' Like he got a law lesson from Mr. Hood!"

"The whole thing," co-counsel Becker said a decade after the trial, "came down to a breach of contract, as opposed to a copyright case. I adored Huey. I adored Margrette. I wanted to win for them so badly. If the judge had looked at it other than strict breach of contract, we had a lot of possible arguments. I tried to make the case against Artists Rights that they were practicing law without a license. The judge didn't buy it. He focused narrowly on one issue and that was the end of it."

As Becker remembers it, Charles Levy was the principal source of Huey's troubles. "The story that I recall is that Huey needed $500, and Levy supposedly said I know someone that can give you $500 for the copyrights of these four songs. I remember that being from—I guess it would have been Chuck [Rubin], huh? If that's what happened, that's quite upsetting, but it may have been that, at the time, that would have been considered permissible. It's hard to judge people's actions that far in the past. But don't forget that Huey agreed with Chuck and needed Chuck at that point and entered into that contract. . . . I guess the initial injustice is what's the most upsetting to me, if, in fact, that is true."

In the same year Huey lost the suit Rubin brought against him, Dr. John (aka Mac Rebennack) gave him a shout of support in the liner notes of his new album, *Goin' Back to New Orleans*. Released June 23, 1992, by Warner Bros. Records, the eighteen-track disc did indeed take Dr. John back to New Orleans. Recorded in the city at Ultrasonic Studios, the project's bunch of local talents included all four Neville brothers, vocalists Shirley Goodman and Chuck Carbo, singer, guitarist, and banjo player Danny Barker, trumpeters Al Hirt and Clyde Kerr Jr., tenor saxophonist Herbert Hardesty, baritone saxophonists Alvin "Red" Tyler and Roger Lewis, and arrangers Wardell Quezergue and Edward Frank. "The most important thing to remember is this," Rebennack wrote of his hometown's music. "New Orleans music was not invented, it just kind of grew up naturally, joyously. No deep psychological traumatic jive. Just plain, down to earth, happy times music."

The latter words apply to New Orleans music in general, and Huey's music in particular. As for the brilliantly rendered *Goin' Back to New Orleans*, it features such local standards as "Basin Street Blues," "My Indian Red," "Milneburg Joys," "I'll Be Glad When You're Dead, You Rascal You," a Rebennack-penned tribute to Professor Longhair titled "Fess Up," and a medley featuring Huey's "Scald Dog" (flipside of 1962's "Pop-Eye"), and Fats Domino's "I Can't Go on, Rosalie." "I'd like to give a big plug," Dr. John wrote in the album's liner notes, "to the author of 'Scald Dog,' Huey Smith, who's working so hard while someone's trying to stiff him out of his writer's money on songs like 'Sea Cruise.'" *Goin' Back to New Orleans*, a No. 1 jazz album in *Billboard*, also won a Grammy award for best traditional blues album.

The Smiths appealed Judge Parker's ruling to the U.S. Court of Appeals for the Fifth Circuit in New Orleans. The appeals court, agreeing with Judge Parker, upheld his ruling in November 1992. Charles Levy clearly had not paid Smith properly, the court concluded, and he also convinced the composer to sell his songs for a fraction of their value. The contract with Rubin, the court continued, was clear and Rubin's Artists Rights Enforcement Corporation continued to have vested rights to half of the royalty payments received for the subject songs. Nonetheless, the appeals court stopped short of declaring Rubin owner of a 50 percent share of the songs' royalties. "AREC does not have a real right or right in rem in the royalties themselves, but has a personal right or right in personam against Smith for half of the proceeds of those royalties."

Back in U.S. District Court in Baton Rouge on November 9, 1993, Judge Parker fixed the monetary judgment amount against Huey P. Smith: For song-writer royalties collected between August 14, 1984, and May 11, 1993, Huey was ordered to pay Artists Rights Enforcement $233,191.74. It was a much smaller sum than Rubin's original claim of more than $400,000.

D espite Artists Rights' courtroom success, Warner/Chappell Music attorney Milton A. Rudin accused winning attorney Ralph Hood of misleading him. "You have been less than forthright in your communications to me," Rudin wrote in a 1993 letter. "The prior judgment you sent me is not binding upon Warner/Chappell Music, as it was not a party to that lawsuit and, as the Appellate Court upheld, the judgment was not an 'in rem' judgment, but a personal judgment against Mr. Smith." Rudin's clients through the years, in addition to Warner/Chappell, included Marilyn Monroe, Groucho Marx, Lucille Ball, and Frank Sinatra. He also helped Jett Williams, the long-lost daughter of Hank Williams Sr., obtain a share of her country music legend father's estate. "He knew more than the biggest law firm put together," she said.

The Smiths did not file a second appeal. "Ralph Hood called to tell me," Huey remembered, "'Yesterday was your last day to file an appeal with the Supreme Court.' Well, he know it wasn't filed. So they just depend on technicality. But doing this to me ain't no different than going in that drugstore and saying, 'Give me that money out that register.' They feel like they shrewd. I don't see how they can sleep at night, doing people like that. I don't see how Judge Parker can sleep with hisself. But I ain't got no lawyers, ain't nothing I can do."

I n 1986, three artists with deep connections to New Orleans—Fats Domino, Ray Charles, and Little Richard—were among the first wave of Rock and Roll Hall of Fame inductees. In June 1993, the Hall of Fame broke ground for its museum in Cleveland, Ohio. The mission of the hall and its museum includes the education of visitors, fans, and scholars about the history and impact of rock 'n' roll music. To that end, the museum collects, preserves, archives, and displays rock 'n' roll artifacts and memorabilia.

The same year that the Rock and Roll Hall of Fame broke ground for the museum, it hired New Orleans writer and drummer Ben Sandmel to seek donations of New Orleans music artifacts from area record companies. Sandmel traveled to Jackson, Mississippi, to see Johnny Vincent. "I spent a couple of hours talking with him," Sandmel said. "I figured he probably had all kinds of old publicity photos, contracts, promotional items, etc. He gave me a hard time at first but then ended up being very friendly. He took me to eat at Shoney's and told me a lot of stories. Didn't donate any artifacts, though."

"Huey," Vincent later told his Ace composer during a phone conversation, "they go' put me in the Hall of Fame." "Yeah? Bring a big donation wit' you," Huey replied. New Orleans studio owner and engineer Cosimo Matassa, who'd be inducted into the Rock and Roll Hall of Fame in 2012, contributed nothing to it either. "When they came down here a few years ago looking for artifacts and mementos, we didn't give them anything," he said in 2000. "Me, I just didn't save photographs or historic items that I probably should have."

Prior to his 1992 trial in U.S. District Court, Huey tried to retain his songs by transferring them to his wife, Margrette, for $2,000. The all-in-the-family sale mirrored the transfer Charles Levy drafted in 1978. After the 1992 trial, Huey obtained new copyright registrations from the U.S. Copyright Office for "Rocking Pneumonia," "Don't You Just Know It," "High Blood Pressure," and "Sea Cruise." He assigned the songs to his own Cooley Publishing, Inc. Before it issued the new registrations, the Copyright Office explained that it does not determine which registrations among conflicting registrations are valid. Nonetheless, the office explained that it issues second copyright registrations only if there is reason to believe the earlier registrations are fraudulent.

On February 22, 1995, Margrette faxed Don Biederman, executive vice president and general counsel for Warner/Chappell Music, a letter telling him of the new copyright registrations. "I am directing this letter to you, inasmuch as, I feel that you are a reasonable man and will place this information into the proper hands," the letter reads. "This is to notify you that the copyrights obtained by Johnny Vincent, assigned to Cotillion, and now in the hands of

Warner/Chappell Music, are frauds. . . . The new copyright registrations has been issued to the writer. If you would like to legally continue to publish these songs, we will be happy to negotiate this arrangement with you." Biederman responded the same day. "There is a statute of limitations on fraud," he wrote, "and the law provides certain protections in some instances to those who acquire rights from those who might have acquired these fraudulently."

Rudin wrote Margrette in April 1995, saying the new copyrights she listed in her earlier letter were invalid and that Warner/Chappell would take action should she attempt to collect royalties for the compositions or license them. Rudin added that, due to the conflicting claims by the Smiths and Artists Rights Enforcement, royalties for the songs that had accrued and had not been paid, and royalties that would accrue, would be paid to the appropriate U.S. District Court that has jurisdiction over Margrette Smith or Artists Rights Enforcement. Through this interpleader action initiated by Warner/Chappell Music, the U.S. District Court in New York City ultimately paid Artists Rights Enforcement $81,647 on June 17, 1997.

"Their registrations are lies, but they don't care," Huey complained. "Johnny Vincent told me he sold something that didn't belong to him. E. McDaniel was dead when Johnny signed E. McDaniel's name assigning them to himself. He doesn't try to disguise the different signatures. It's obvious E. McDaniel sold them to Johnny Vincent and the witness is Johnny! All that's Johnny! And it's the next week after that Johnny Vincent sells them to Cotillion. Johnny Vincent's is no good, so that makes Huey Smith the sole owner."

Chuck Rubin, successful in Louisiana courts though he was, didn't win everywhere. In March 1994, the Superior Court of the State of California for the County of Los Angeles ordered Capitol Records to pay Huey's former employer, Shirley Goodman of the New Orleans duo Shirley and Lee, "the balance of her share of funds remaining in the 'Shirley and Lee' account and all future royalties that accrue to her share of that account. . . . Cross-defendant Artists Rights Enforcement Corporation is to take nothing." Relieved, Goodman said, "Yes, Lord. Thank God. I am retired. I'm finished. I don't want to be bothered with none of this. I go to church now, just me and Jesus."

Also in 1994, Artists Rights Enforcement, finding itself unable to collect from Cotillion and Warner/Chappell, asked the Supreme Court of New York to authorize garnishment of Huey's BMI-administered performance royalties in the amount of $233,000 plus interest. In the meantime, Huey hoped to get legal mileage from a claim Rubin made in a 1993 declaration. "Each of the Songs was originally registered in the name of E. M. McDaniel (also known professionally as Bo Diddley). . . . I DECLARE UNDER PENALTY OF PERJURY THAT THE FORGOING IS TRUE AND CORRECT."

Although the E. M. McDaniel named on the songs' copyright registrations was not Bo Diddley, the influential singer, guitarist, and songwriter who recorded early rock 'n' roll classics for Chicago's Chess Records was one of Rubin's clients. Born in Mississippi as Ellas Otha Bates, Diddley was adopted and raised by his mother's cousin, Gussie McDaniel, whose surname he assumed. An agitated Huey mentioned Rubin's claim about Diddley to Johnny Vincent during one of their phone conversations. "E. M. McDaniel is *not* known professionally as Bo Diddley," he said scornfully. "That's my ex-wife's daddy." "If I had a lawyer," the excited Huey responded, "he could tell the judge that and make him throw it out! That's perjury! You show that to your lawyer!" "I'm going to," Vincent said. "I'm gonna send you some money, Huey, for to buy you some groceries."

During the mid- to late 1990s, Vincent periodically sent Huey checks ranging from $50 to $500. A $150 check dated July 16, 1998, for example, was drawn on the account of Vincent's new label, Avanti Records. "But I'm still saying I didn't never ever get a royalty statement," Huey said later. One check that Vincent sent, in the amount of $50, bounced. Suspicious of Vincent's motives though he was, Huey's legal and financial troubles compelled him to accept the checks. "Well," he speculated, "Johnny might say, 'Look at there! See, I been paying Huey!' Yeah, well, I needed the change. But whatever his purpose was, I know that wasn't no whole lot of money."

Willie Clayton, a Mississippi-born, later-generation rhythm-and-blues and soul singer who recorded two albums in the 1990s for the resurrected Ace Records, said Vincent sent checks to many ex-Ace artists. "From Frankie Ford to Earl King, Huey, Charles Brown, they all would still call Johnny," Clayton recalled. "I know this because I was there running the company when Johnny had a triple bypass. Some of them would ask for funds and Johnny Vincent would send it to them. And I don't mean it was pennies either. It was for real money. But, you know, I can't speak for them, but I can honestly say Johnny Vincent was a jewel in my life."

Vincent, promoting his newly recorded music and repackaged classic material, placed a two-page ad in New Orleans music magazine *Offbeat*'s 1995 New Orleans Jazz and Heritage Festival issue. He devoted the first page to Frankie Ford's CD, *Hot and Lonely*. The ad's second page characteristically boasted "the greatest collection of original New Orleans hits" and "the latest soul, rhythm & blues hits." The reissues included collections by Huey, Ford, Jimmy Clanton, Earl King, Alvin "Red" Tyler, and volumes one through five of the *Ace Story*.

Former Clowns singer Bobby Marchan was among 1995's Jazz Fest performers. Bobby also was running his rap- and hip-hop–based Manicure Productions from suburban New Orleans. "The Jazz Fest wants me to be on their panel down there on Sunday, talking about hip-hoppers and rappers and all that," he complained. "You know how people be in there free to listen to you talk? Sort of like *The Ricki Lake Show*. They offered me $100, but I won't do it for that little chicken-change." The frankly speaking Bobby made it clear why he'd gotten into the rap music business. "I'm not interested in rap. I'm interested in what they do, bring the money in. Off the job, I stay home and watch TV. There's too much violence in the street for me to be running around out there."

Bobby, to his old singing mate Gerri Hall's surprise, rejected the homosexual lifestyle he'd previously been so open about. "After all those years, he did not want to come off as or say anything gay," she marveled. "Bobby say, 'By the way— I'm saved. I been going to church. I been saying my prayers, regular. Prayers to Jesus, prayers to St. Joseph, rosary beads. I'm saved, Miss Gerri.' And from then on you didn't say nothing concerning being gay. You didn't call him Miss Bobby."

22

Bankruptcy and Farewells

O
n July 28, 1997, Huey filed for bankruptcy. He believed that bankruptcy's automatic stay provision would halt Artists Rights Enforcement Corporation's lien on his BMI royalties. If his BMI income were restored, he'd have money to hire a new lawyer and pay for his family's basic needs. Artists Rights' returning attorney, Ralph Hood, responded by requesting the dismissal of the new Chapter 13 bankruptcy case and/or its conversion to Chapter 7. The Chapter 7 bankruptcy code gives control of a debtor's assets to a trustee, who then liquidates the assets for the benefit of creditors. On the contrary, the Chapter 13 bankruptcy protection the Smiths chose to file under includes opportunities for debtors to save their homes from foreclosure, reschedule secured debts, and extend those debts through the life of the Chapter 13 plan.

Huey read about bankruptcy in the book *This Business of Music*. When a record company or artist goes bankrupt, the book states, established public policy dictates that honest debtors be helped and granted a new financial life. He soon converted his original Chapter 13 bankruptcy filing to Chapter 11, the bankruptcy code chapter that provides for the reorganization of a corporation or partnership. He'd founded his music publishing company, Cooley Publishing, Inc., in the 1960s. Chapter 11 allows a debtor corporation to propose a reorganization plan that keeps the business functioning while creditors are paid over time. But the benign description of bankruptcy Huey read about in *This Business of Music* does not reflect the Smiths' bankruptcy. Having pawned many of their possessions, for instance, the Smiths lost them after their bankruptcy lawyer told them to stop paying interest on the items. "She said, 'This'll be through the court now. You're not supposed to pay it.' I gave her the stack of pawn tickets—my wife's ring, grandmother's expensive ring, my piano. We had been paying interest on them for a couple of years. So we stopped. Then the man from the pawnshop come to the court with a lawyer. The judge told him all this stuff go' to the pawnshop. My lawyer, Ms. Magee, said, 'Huey, I'm sorry. I didn't know that.' And we got no compensation, even with the steady BMI money coming. The bankruptcy trustee could ask the judge to let my family have a couple of hundred bucks a month to eat." Nor did Huey get the BMI check he anticipated receiving through bankruptcy's automatic stay provision.

The bankruptcy clerk of court assigned the Smiths' case to Judge Louis M. Phillips. A 1992 survey conducted by the *Baton Rouge Advocate* of members of the Baton Rouge Bar Association and other legal organizations ranked the forty-four-year-old Phillips, then in his fourth year as a bankruptcy judge, last among the five federal judicial officials serving East Baton Rouge Parish. Although survey participants described Judge Phillips as the brightest judge on the federal bench, they also characterized him as arrogant, inefficient, discourteous, and sarcastic. Judge Phillips told the newspaper that he would "take each one of these different responses to heart and think about them."

Huey wrote Judge Phillips about his attorney, Pamela Magee, complaining that she'd spoken falsely at a creditors' meeting. "She told the lady I contacted Artists Rights," he recalled. "I told the judge that wasn't true. That was a known fact, documented. I didn't contact Artists Rights. Mr. Rubin's letter says, 'Allow me to introduce myself.' And I know Ms. Magee knew better than that. But she looked at Ralph Hood and said, 'Mr. Smith contacted Artists Rights to assist him in getting his rights back.'"

Another reason Huey's bankruptcy filing disappointed him was that having his income out of his reach meant he couldn't afford a new hearing aid for the one ear in which he had some hearing left. The Smiths wrote Judge Phillips in November 1997, requesting funds from their bankruptcy estate:

Dear Sir:

We are asking you to please grant us 5 minutes of your time to speak with you.

The problem is we just cannot believe, while the court is now holding around $30,000 payable to us that the court is depriving us of emergency necessities for our family of four. . . .

Since, we only teach the Bible, I understand that we do not render any other service to the estate. But the income that is being generated is service rendered earlier by the author of the compositions, which Congress granted to encourage others to pursue this type of contribution to society. . . .

The Smiths missed a bankruptcy court hearing in November 1997. Pamela Magee, representing the absent debtors, and Artists Rights' attorney Ralph Hood were present. Hood expressed his opposition to allowing the Smiths compensation:

> HOOD: They can go and get jobs. If they do that, we wouldn't have any objection. We do have an objection, though, to money that is otherwise property of the estate that could be used to pay creditors, principally my client, from being used to pay their living expenses.

Hood quickly presented what he likely hoped would be the hearing's bombshell, a faxed draft court order that had been superimposed upon Magee's letterhead.

> HOOD: This was sent, it's my understanding . . . in response to the debtors learning that Warner/Chappell had decided to pay Artists Rights half [of Huey Smith's songwriter's royalties] and pay the other half that was due to Mr. Smith into the registry of the court. Mr. Wisner [of Warner/Chappell] says he was advised that there had been an order entered by this court that said, "No, no . . . All the money was supposed to go to the registry of the court." . . . The order . . . cuts out all the portions that I had proposed about recognizing Artists Rights' rights to half of the money . . . doesn't even have a signature . . . flip it back over and you can see that the center has been basically cut out and it says, "Dear Mr. Wisner: The following documents speaks for themselves."
>
> MAGEE: That wouldn't be my—
>
> JUDGE PHILLIPS: We would hope that would not be your use of the verb "speak."
>
> HOOD: . . . at this point, I would like to get an order recognizing our right to get the half [of the songs' publishing royalties].

Prior to Hood's introduction of the draft into the November hearing, the draft order had circulated between Hood and Magee while they debated its wording. Hood wanted Warner/Chappell Music to send half of Huey's songwriter royalties income directly to Artists Rights, as if the company were the songs' half-owner. Magee disagreed. She drew a line in the draft through wording that called for direct payment to Artists Rights, thereby changing the order to read that all money be sent to the court. Meanwhile, Huey spoke with Gary

Roth, an attorney with BMI in New York. Their conversation led him to believe he could collect his BMI performance royalties if he established the fact that he was a Chapter 11 debtor. The Chapter 11 designation was clearly stated on the Hood-Magee draft.

"Gary Roth told me if I show him anything that says Chapter 11, he'll send me my money tomorrow," the composer recalled. "I called Ms. Magee and told her what he said. She was in a hurry. So then I faxed it [the draft order] to Gary Roth. If you read it, it says the money should be sent to the court. Well, what's the problem?" Judge Phillips, however, maintained in court that Huey used the draft order in an attempt to convince Warner/Chappell to send money to him. Ultimately, Huey's intended recipient of the fax, BMI, told him they never received it.

> JUDGE PHILLIPS: . . . you [Magee] can't hardly represent these people. They're going around behind your back faxing stuff, using your letterhead, jimmying it all up to try to lie about the state of affairs here in this court . . . using an official lawyer fax sheet and changing up a form of a draft judgment that was never signed to convince people to send him money. . . . I'm not going to conduct my own investigation because I think I know what happened. But I've got to send this over to the U.S. Attorney's office . . . The motion [for compensation to the Smiths] is denied without prejudice. Next.

Things went badly again for the Smiths during a December 16, 1997, bankruptcy hearing. The couple's lawyers asked to withdraw as counsel. Hood again sought to convert Huey's Chapter 11 bankruptcy to Chapter 7, the code that installs a trustee to liquidate a debtor's assets and property for the purpose of paying creditors' claims.

During the hearing, Judge Phillips rebuked Huey after he raised his hand to ask a question. Deaf in one ear since childhood and mostly deaf in the other due to years of performing, Huey wanted to ask the judge if his wife could whisper what was being said in the courtroom into his ear. As it was, he heard almost nothing that was said.

Magee asked for a continuance of the hearing, in part so Huey and Margrette could obtain new counsel. A music publishing company executive and the Rhythm & Blues Foundation, an organization that provided various forms of assistance to artists in addition to presenting an annual awards show, indicated that they would help the Smiths find a new lawyer. Judge Phillips questioned the existence of both the music executive and the Rhythm & Blues Foundation.

JUDGE PHILLIPS: But you understand my concern about whether there is a real "they"?

MAGEE: Yes, sir.

JUDGE PHILLIPS: As a result of the Smiths' apparent attempt to defraud everybody here, I mean, I've got a problem getting a letter from the Smiths that says it's from somebody else, because they faxed this stuff off and played like they were you and lied to everybody. . . . Why can't we just convert the case now and get them out of it? . . . I mean, you know, if the United States Attorney ever gets their act together on Edwin Edwards [regarding corruption charges against the former Louisiana governor], they're just liable to say, "Well, let's just go see Huey and Margrette Smith and start investigating them." . . . So, you just want to convert the case to a 7 and let it take its—wind its way through, Mr. Hood?

HOOD: Yes, sir, your honor.

JUDGE PHILLIPS: They [the Smiths] are not going to be faxing anything to anybody, saying that they ought to, you know, that the court is issuing orders and documents "speaks for themselves." . . . They [the Smiths] are not getting any money now from me or from this. They won't be getting any money from the Chapter 7 estate.

All right, Mr. and Mrs. Smith, come up here, please. . . . Number one: These lawyers can't represent you. Number two: I can't believe anything you say. Number three: You've absolutely violated your duty to this court and to your bankruptcy estate. Number four: You have shown me that you are incapable of trying to come up with a sensible, self-benefiting way out of the last number of years worth of financial difficulties and contractual disputes with Artists Rights. Five: You have convinced me of your intention to do anything to frustrate the rights of Artists Rights . . . I, in no way, shape or form, could conceive of letting you remain debtor-in-possession without a lawyer. . . .

What happened before Judge Parker issued his judgment, it's not relevant anymore. It has not been relevant for years. What's relevant now is that you are, as of today, going to be two Chapter 7 debtors with no claim to any of the income generated from anything that's been done in the past, period. But I wish you hadn't done what you did, but you did it, and, if you, being grown, made the decision, then you, being grown, can live with the consequences. We're through here.

When Huey went to the local FBI office to speak to someone about the faxed draft order that Judge Phillips and Ralph Hood discussed so extensively, he was told to contact the FBI's office in New Orleans. "But I couldn't get to no New Orleans," he recalled. "I really went there in Baton Rouge to see if I done something, if the FBI want to talk to me about this. I showed him the transcript where they mention the U.S. Attorney and Edwin Edwards. So they didn't say no more about the fax, but I was convicted anyhow, no hearing or nothing, for whatever Ralph Hood told them I had did."

A federal fraud investigation, as suggested by Judge Phillips, would be enough to intimidate most debtors. Judges and officials in East Baton Rouge Parish often questioned the legitimacy of documents, just as Judge Phillips did in the Smiths' bankruptcy case, only to not follow through with their threats of referrals to the U.S. attorney.

In more ways than one, Huey felt left in the dark. "I asked them while the power company was cutting my lights off could they allocate anything to a person in bankruptcy," he said. "They said, 'That's your problem,' and hung up." The family's lack of funds forced Huey and Margrette's granddaughter, Tanisha, whom they had raised, to drop out of Southern University and Baton Rouge Community College. The Smiths could no longer afford tuition. Tanisha soon moved out. "She said, 'Daddy, I'm just not used to being poor.' And she wasn't. Tanisha had to go to work."

Johnny Vincent's lawyer, Robert Arentson, suggested Huey seek legal aid from Baton Rouge's Capital Area Legal Services Corporation. But he'd tried that already. "They told me they can't help me. But him [Arentson] and Johnny, they was supposed to be on their way here, before Johnny got sick the last time. Johnny kept saying, 'I'm go' get your things back, chief. Me and Bob coming up there. You see, I wanna sell out. It ain't for my wife. I'm just trying to get this for you.'"

Vincent suffered from diabetes, which caused him to lose feeling in his feet, making it difficult to walk and impossible to drive. He next lost his peripheral vision. Even so, he continued recording acts for his latest label, Avanti. "He would be back in the studio," his lawyer recalled, "just rocking along with the tracks they were laying down."

Seeking help elsewhere, Huey asked his friend Dr. John to tell 60 Minutes newsman Ed Bradley, a lover of New Orleans and its music, about his troubles. Huey wrote to Bradley as well, sending copies of his many legal papers. Bradley didn't reply. "Dr. John said Ed Bradley's bosses told him, 'If you get something from Huey Smith about the music industry, just sit on it.'"

If the Smiths had collected Huey's performance royalties from BMI and publishing royalties from Cotillion Music in 1997, the couple and their two dependents could have lived comfortably. His compositions earned nearly $70,000 that year.

Contradicting the U.S. Court of Appeals for the Fifth Circuit's 1993 ruling that Artists Rights Enforcement Corporation had no ownership rights in Huey's Cotillion Music royalties, Judge Phillips signed an order, "Partial Judgment Entered As Final Judgment," on April 27, 1998. The order approved a joint motion by Artists Rights attorney Ralph Hood and the Smiths' recently appointed bankruptcy trustee, Dwayne Murray, to declare that 50 percent of the songwriter publishing royalties for "Rocking Pneumonia," "Sea Cruise," "High Blood Pressure," and "Don't You Just Know It" was not the property of the Smiths' bankruptcy estate. The judge ordered direct payment of those royalties to Artists Rights. In September, the judge discharged Huey's bankruptcy. The action did nothing to ease the Smiths' financial difficulties and, in fact, allowed the Louisiana Department of Revenue to garnish the small salary Margrette Smith earned at a telemarketing company. "If we get a hold of a penny, they go' take it?" Huey asked.

Also in 1998, Johnny Vincent and Frankie Ford collaborated on a new project that wasn't exactly new. Echoing 1959's "Sea Cruise" and "Roberta," Ford's Avanti Records album A New Orleans Tradition features the singer's newly recorded vocals superimposed on original Ace music tracks from the 1950s and early 1960s. The songs include the Huey Smith recordings "Rocking Pneumonia," "Don't You Just Know It," "High Blood Pressure," "Sea Cruise," and "Havin a Good Time," Earl King's "Those Lonely, Lonely Nights," Roland Stone's "Just a Moment," and Chuck Carbo's "Promises." Vincent characteristically pumped up the publicity. "The Hottest Little Record Company in America is Avanti Records . . . and Frankie Ford has made us #1 in Louisiana with his new CD!"

B obby Marchan, a regular performer at the New Orleans Jazz and Heritage Festival, appeared at the event again on April 30, 1998. It was his sixty-eighth birthday. Following a 3 P.M. show by Bobby and his group, Higher Ground, local writer-musician Ben Sandmel conducted a public interview with the singer at the festival's Music Heritage Stage. "I had a splendid show today," Bobby told the crowd in the horse track's air-conditioned grandstand. "Yes, indeed. I had so many people in front of me—pitiful!"

Sandmel introduced Bobby as the singer of some of New Orleans's greatest rhythm-and-blues hits, both with Huey Smith and the Clowns and as a solo act. The interview covered his early days in New Orleans as a female impersonator and Bobby's current work as an outrageous emcee and rap and hip-hop booker and promoter. Operating from an office in Metairie and employing two secretaries, Bobby worked with such acts as the Hot Boys and DJ Jubilee. "They selling records so fast make you wanna buy one!" Bobby bragged. "I don't ask for but 10 percent because, you know, I'm not trying to make all the money. Just pay the bills and things, keep me going. That's good enough for me."

Bobby's history with Huey Smith and the Clowns was a recurring topic during the fifty-minute session that included questions from the audience.

"People get a kick out of old stories," Sandmel said.

"I get a kick out of them, too, because I be young again," Bobby said. "Feel free to join in," he told his audience. "Don't be bashful."

An audience member asked if the Clowns' recordings were rehearsed or simply thrown together. "Yes, they were rehearsed!" Bobby said. "You can't just jump up and play anything. Huey would do it. That's the reason they call him Huey 'Piano' Smith. And Bobby Marchan did the singing. Huey would write the words and then he would find me and say, 'Bobby, hum this tune.' And I would hum the tune. Pretty soon he say, 'We go' record this.' I said, 'Well, I'm for it.' And nine out of ten times he was right." Huey, Bobby added, "he was sensational."

Bobby revealed that he'd been diagnosed with cancer in 1985. "I've been quite lucky," he said. "But you can't get away from everything, so next I was at the dialysis machine. I didn't mind, because you got to live some kind of way. I go three times a week. I went this morning. They said, 'How you go' do Jazz Fest and you got to go to the dialysis machine?' I said, 'I betcha I be there to do it.'"

In strong voice despite his morning dialysis and afternoon show, Bobby led the crowd in the call-and-response chorus of "Don't You Just Know It." "See how nice it is?" he asked Sandmel afterward, obviously delighted to be on yet another stage. "I'm having so much fun today, on my birthday. So if y'all got any questions, you better ask them while I'm here."

U p in Baton Rouge, the Smiths' new lawyer, Cleo Fields, a thirty-five-year-old star among Louisiana's African American politicians, expressed disbelief that Judge Phillips had compared the Smiths' case to former governor Edwin Edwards's federal corruption investigation. "This is a judge talking like this?" the attorney asked. Hiring Fields in August 1998, Huey had high hopes for the former state senator, two-term U.S. congressman, and 1995 gubernatorial candidate. "I'm calling everybody, telling them Cleo Fields representing me," he said. "I thought he done heard about injustice."

But his enthusiasm for Fields soon faded. Unable to afford new tires, Huey couldn't attend a memorial service in New Orleans for his son, Huey Smith Jr. "We can't catch up with Cleo Fields to ask him to ask the court [for funds]," he remembered. "We couldn't trust our tires to drive to New Orleans. And when my brother, Mel, died, it wasn't no sense in me asking the trustee, Dwayne Murray, for anything. The same situation."

Huey suspected Fields wanted to sell his compositions. "They said, 'See, what we trying to do is help you,'" he recalled. "So I told them, 'Don't nobody talk about selling nothing of mine.' Well, from then on they were through with me, because they know they weren't go' be able to sell my songs."

W hen the Smiths' resources dwindled to the point they could not afford an attorney, the couple spent eight-hour days poring over countless books in the nearby Louisiana State University law library. "Anytime Ralph Hood filed something, I run there and get copies of the same thing and reply similar to that," Huey explained. "I didn't have no more money for lawyers. I can't come and match them dollar for dollar. But that's how they do. They drain you. So they had me crippled like that."

Huey realized Artists Rights Enforcement was a fertile source of employment for lawyers, his own former lawyers included. Suzette Becker, one of his attorneys in the 1992 U.S. District Court trial he'd lost to Artists Rights, later worked as co-counsel for Artists Rights clients the Dixie Cups in their success-ful suit against their former manager, Joe Jones, over the ownership of "Iko Iko."* "I got a GED," Huey mused. "I ain't no lawyer. Lawyers, they go and see if a mail truck hit you or if the doctor left something in during your operation. All I want to see about is my copyrights. I learned that you can't take them from nobody. They're mine unless I sign that particular copyright from me to him."

Justin Zitler, adjunct professor of music and entertainment law at Loyola Law School in New Orleans and attorney for SongByrd, Inc., the company es-tablished by heirs of Professor Longhair, said Huey's efforts to defend himself against Artists Rights' professional litigators had merit. Zitler reviewed the songwriter's legal file in 1998. "I can't tell you how personally devastating it was for me to look through his box of papers," he said. "He thought of everything that any lawyer could have done during the '90s, any form of relief. But every avenue he tried, they killed him in court on procedure."

"New Orleans has more poor rhythm-and-blues legends per capita than any place in the world," Zitler told the *Times-Picayune* that year for a story about the pursuit of royalties for the heirs of Professor Longhair. "It's part of our charm, but it's also really sad."

Exhausted after a decade of courtroom conflict, Huey finally gave up. "I said, 'Look, I'm not fighting this anymore.' What happens is that it be like kangaroo courts. A lot of people been sentenced to death by kangaroo courts!" But unlike some other Artists Rights Enforcement clients, Huey never objected to Rubin's 50 percent collection fee. "I don't think that's too much," he said.

H uey's bandmate from the Dew Drop days, Earl King, came to Baton Rouge in October 1998 to play for Baton Rouge Blues Week, an annual event pro-duced by local music entrepreneur Johnny Palazzotto. Earl had spent years

---

*James "Sugar Boy" Crawford wrote and recorded "Jock-A-Mo" in 1953. He based the song on two Mardi Gras Indian chants. Released in time for the 1954 Mardi Gras season, it became Sugar Boy and His Cane Cutters' biggest hit. New Orleans group the Dixie Cups later claimed to have writ-ten the song. Crawford sued Barbara Ann Hawkins, her sister, Rosa Lee, and Marilyn Jones in 1965 after their "Jock-A-Mo" remake, "Iko Iko," became a national hit. A 1967 settlement between Craw-ford and the Dixie Cups resulted in both the Hawkins sisters and Jones being named the song's writers. The settlement, however, gave Crawford 25 percent of the song's performance royalties. "I don't even know if I really am getting my just dues," he later said. "I just figure 25 percent of something is better than 100 percent of nothing."

away from performing and recording, but *Glazed,* his Grammy-nominated 1988 album for New Orleans label Black Top Records, and a 1990 follow-up, *Sexual Telepathy,* helped make him a busy international attraction. "I've got too much work," he complained in 1992. "Since May of '89, I haven't stopped."

Earl hoped to see Huey while he was in Baton Rouge, but Palazzotto cautioned him about phoning from the promoter's office phone. Huey had grown suspicious of Palazzotto in the early 1990s, believing he was connected to Chuck Rubin. "Johnny say, 'Earl, if you dial him from my number, he ain't go' answer,'" Earl said a few years later. The two New Orleans music peers whose careers had intertwined so closely had not seen each other in some twenty years. "Yeah, I miss Doc," Earl said. "That's why, when I was in Baton Rouge, I said, 'Oh, man, I'll get a chance to holler at Huey!' But Huey is maybe similar to Allen Toussaint, in a way, because he's kind of offset in his ways with people. Now, when he was playing music with you, everything was an everyday thing. But once he stopped, he got kind of distant."

The consequences Judge Louis Phillips spoke of in bankruptcy court included Huey's inability to afford blood pressure medicine. "The prescriptions, they were very high," he remembered. "He [the bankruptcy trustee] taking all the BMI. The little Social Security, that's all we was left."

The Smiths wrote to the judge again on December 14, 1998, requesting funds from their bankruptcy estate:

Dear Judge Phillips:

We have repeatedly asked Mr. Dwayne Murray, the trustee, for funds in emergency situation only. Each time, that we ask, he would say to us "I am sorry, but you know what the Judge said he was going to do to you." Why, we still do not know what crime that we have committed for these harsh actions. We are, again appealing to you, especially, since we received the enclosed copy of the "discharge" (September 4, 1998) signed by the Bankruptcy Judge. We simply cannot believe that you intended for Atty. Dwayne Murray, in favor of a creditor, whose debts we contest, not allow us money for medical needs. So, we beg of you to instruct Mr. Murray, as he is still collecting money due to be paid to us, least of all, if nothing else, emergency money for medicine (enclosed copy of prescription). Mr. Dwayne Murray may not be aware of it, but in this country this is cruel and inhumane. We, truthfully, do not believe that you instructed Mr. Murray to proceed in such a harsh way against a fellow human, who filed bankruptcy after we read about the automatic stay where we were so disappointed to find out how the legal system really works.

Thank you,
Huey P and Margrette Smith

I n 1999, surviving Clown Bobby Marchan got booked for a rock 'n' roll oldies show in Pittsburgh, the city said to be America's oldies music capital. The show's producer wanted a Clowns reunion. Bobby told them he'd find as many Clowns as possible. "So, Miss Gerri, whyn't you come go?" he asked his old singing partner. "I can't find nobody else. I'm go' take you up there, let these people see you, since you still here and you still capable."

Just before the show, Bobby lavished compliments on the one Clown he'd found for the trip. "Oh, Miss Gerri!" he gushed as she opened her door. "Look at you! You transformed! You go from just plain and peaceful Gerri into a stage presence. You're a star!" The extravagant praise cracked Gerri up. Later, the seriously ill Bobby insisted that the video cameras stay on Gerri. "Bobby could barely make it," Gerri said. "We were only in Pittsburgh three days and he went to dialysis twice." Gerri and Bobby performed, but the promoter refused to pay them, ostensibly because Bobby hadn't brought enough Clowns. It was a disappointing outcome, especially considering the strain the trip placed on Bobby. At least he and Gerri shared the stage one more time. "I got to know Bobby more in the last three years he lived than I ever knew him before," she reflected. "I got to know him when he was getting ready to get out of here. . . . But Bobby would not give up. At the home he say, 'Where's my shoes? Didn't that boy leave my things in that closet, Miss Gerri?' 'No, Bobby.' 'I have to be ready for to catch the plane at two o'clock. I'm going to Florida!'"

Bobby Marchan—recording star, irrepressible performer, personality, and cornerstone of New Orleans rap and hip-hop—died at sixty-nine on December 5, 1999, at Stonebridge Convalescent Center.

"When Bobby was in a nursing home," Huey recalled, "Almost Slim [Hannusch] was telling us he sick-sick. So, if we going to see him, we got to hurry up. Next thing you know, they say he had died, yeah. . . . We could have toured Japan, anywhere. You got Gerri Hall, Roosevelt, and the Clowns. It'd been just like new. It wouldn't been nothing for Bobby to do, if he wasn't so sick."

Bobby was not buried until January 8, 2000, more than a month after his death. The *Times-Picayune* made brief mention of the services. "Friends have finally raised the money needed for a funeral, and Marchan will be laid to rest this weekend." Grand Marshal Henry Alexander, Bobby's business partner in Manicure Productions, and the Soul Rebels Brass Band led a crowd of several hundred people during Bobby's jazz funeral parade. "The procession ended at Kemp's bar on LaSalle Street," Geraldine Wyckoff reported in *Gambit Weekly,* "just a block away from the Dew Drop Inn, where Marchan entertained so many people. The parade should have stopped to pay tribute at the legendary club, but perhaps the young Soul Rebels didn't grasp its significance in the life of Bobby Marchan."

Gerri, visiting Huey in Baton Rouge in 2001, told him that Bobby's spirit broke after he found that his bank wouldn't cash a big check he'd received from Cash Money Records, the hugely successful, Universal Music–linked New Orleans rap label that he helped launch. "That's what did it, they wouldn't cash his money," she said. "That hurt Bobby's health," Huey agreed softly. "Yeah," Gerri said, "his health was *gone.*"

I n November 1999, Judge Louis Phillips signed an order entitled "Engagement of Attorney for a Special Purpose." The order approved San Francisco attorney Steven Ames Brown's representation of the Smiths' bankruptcy trustee, Dwayne Murray, for the pursuit of unpaid songwriter royalties. The order stated that Brown would work closely with Artists Rights Enforcement in connection with his special purpose and was not entitled to compensation from the estate. The order did not state who was responsible for Brown's compensation.

In January 2000, Murray again warned the Smiths of a possible federal investigation. He demanded that their state and federal tax refunds be sent to him to be prorated for the benefit of their creditors: "If you spend a refund that belongs to the estate, I will it be necessary that I ask the FBI to investigate this matter and make a referral to the U.S. Attorney for possible criminal prosecution."

W hile Huey lamented perceived injustices done to him, Richard Linn, the lawyer who represented him when he was an Artists Rights Enforcement client but later conducted a deposition of his former client for Artists

Rights and later still testified against him in Judge John V. Parker's Baton Rouge courtroom, was sworn in as a judge for the U.S. Court of Appeals for the Federal Circuit on January 1, 2000. President Bill Clinton made the lifetime appointment. As Chief Judge H. Robert Mayer administered the oath to Linn, fireworks celebrating the turn of the millennium could be seen bursting around the Washington Monument from the court chambers.

O n February 4, 2000, two months after Bobby Marchan's death, Johnny Vincent Imbragulio died of heart failure in Flowood, Mississippi. The brief Associated Press obit that appeared in Baton Rouge's daily newspaper listed only two songs from the hundreds released by Vincent's record labels: "Rocking Pneumonia and the Boogie Woogie Flu" and "Sea Cruise." Vincent's promised meeting with Huey and attorney Robert Arentson never took place. But the two men who'd shared so much music history, the attorney said, talked by phone until Vincent's death. "It seemed like they were fighting with each other a lot, but I think that was part of their relationship. Johnny valued Huey as a friend and as a musician. He felt that Huey was an integral part of the history of rock 'n' roll out of New Orleans."

"The last thing Bob Arentson told me," Huey said, "he say, 'I tell Johnny what to do and he just does what he wants to do anyhow.'" Despite his financial disappointment in Vincent, Huey still considered him a friend. Earl King, for one, didn't cry over Vincent: "He ain't treat nobody good, man. I was sorry for him, but, you know, he messed over a lot of people and didn't have no reasons to do it. Because he was making the money and, see, when the tax people got hold to Johnny, he couldn't write off nothing because he hadn't paid nobody." Frankie Ford, however, dedicated his Web site to "Mr. Johnny." And in a letter to *Offbeat*, Ford both thanked Vincent for giving him a shot and defended music business executives in general. Vincent, Cosimo Matassa, Dave Bartholomew, Lew Chudd, Art Rupe, Joe Caronna, Joe Ruffino, and others, Ford wrote, "dealt the cards and it was up to us as to how we played the hand."

Two years prior to Vincent's death, VCI, a multimedia publishing group in the United Kingdom, paid him $2 million for his entire Ace Records holdings of about one thousand record masters plus music publishing rights.

23

Pioneer Days

I n April 2000, Tuff City Music Group, a New York City company that specializes in soul, funk, and rhythm-and-blues reissues, asked Huey "Piano" Smith to make a solo record. The company's Night Train Records catalog was heavy with New Orleans music rarities, including a collection of Huey's Imperial and Pitter-Pat recordings titled *Snag-a-Tooth Jeanie*. Tuff City owner Aaron Fuchs, a producer of early 1980s rap recordings coveted by major labels for old-school rap compilations, had a winning formula for selling vintage African American music in foreign markets. "Reissue the most obscure music you can find and there's a good chance it will become a hit in Japan," he said in 1996.

But Huey wasn't enthusiastic about doing a solo record. He'd made a career, after all, of recording songs and arrangements featuring vocal ensembles, not to mention the great studio musicians of New Orleans. He'd also heard a solo record by James Booker and thought it inferior. Nonetheless, Huey was impressed that Fuchs had an encyclopedic knowledge of Joe Banashak's Instant Records catalog. "He almost was singing some of the words to stuff nobody had heard," Huey said. "Like 'Ballad of a Black Man.'"

Fuchs raised his original four-figure offer for a solo piano record and offered an advance if Huey would permit Tuff City to administer his catalog. And if the composer would agree to transfer a third of his copyrights to Tuff City, the company would raise the advance to five figures. During a subsequent phone conversation, Huey brought up the CD that Tuff City previously released, *Snag-a-Tooth Jeanie*. He asked Fuchs what right he had to issue the material. Fuchs replied that he'd licensed it. "Who licensed them?" Huey asked. The discussion turned adversarial. From Huey's perspective, the *Snag-a-Tooth Jeanie* collection was one more example of him being cheated. "If Johnny Vincent didn't have any rights, see, none of them have rights. They just have my stuff for free!"

Even while his legal troubles multiplied through the 1990s, record labels throughout the world continued reissuing Huey's recordings. Many imports from England and Japan showed up in New Orleans, at Tower Records as well as the locally owned Louisiana Music Factory. Both stores were located in the tourist-filled French Quarter. The CDs' image of a smiling Huey—often the same Pontchartrain Park–set photo Johnny Vincent used as the cover for Ace's first two Huey Smith and the Clowns albums—and cheery liner notes gave no hint of the composer's dire straits. As usual, too, he received no royalties from the CDs' sales. "They could put 'Licensed through Peter Pan,'" he said. "Well, if somebody say, 'Pull up your papers. Where you got this from?' Well, you ain't got papers. Dr. John told me them record companies don't care what it sounds like. Somebody told him, 'We just make money with it. We don't like none of it!'"

I n June 2000, Huey got a notice from the IRS that said he owed $24,628.16 for tax year 1997, the year he filed for bankruptcy. It read, "We contacted you twice but have no record of receiving your response. Your 1997 tax return does not report the same income or deductions reported to us by your payers or trustee."

Huey replied by letter:

I have repeatedly responded to all communications with the IRS. On my initial call to the IRS about this matter, an unnamed gentleman, in essence, found hard to believe that the unnamed source who reported sending me money did not send it to me. In essence, he said that I was a liar. The last lady that I spoke with gave me 30 days to send documents to prove that I did not receive the money reported to me.

Enclosed please find documents that would show those who had previously sent me money had discontinued it: Levy and garnishments to BMI; payments made to the US District Court, by Warner/Chappell Music (see check where the court awarded payments to someone else). Also, included is a notation of Bankruptcy Filed on July 28, 1997 by the Smith's where the IRS is listed as a creditor. Besides, all royalties from BMI, I am enclosing a document which shows that the bankruptcy trustee just recently picked up $200,000 belonging to the Smith's estates. What confuses me is that, if this was truly a debt due the IRS, why was this information not sent to the Bankruptcy Trustee, Dwayne Murray.

I hope these documents satisfies you. Incidentally, we filed bankruptcy, hoping, to get the automatic stay provide by law, only to be ignored, preventing us from being able to acquire legal counsel. . . . I feel that it is shameful for a government agency to function in this manner, especially since copyright laws that protect musical compositions by the author Huey P. Smith are simply being ignored.

Better news arrived at the Smiths' home via a June 29, 2000, letter from Washington, D.C. In recognition of his lifelong contribution to rhythm-and-blues music, the Rhythm & Blues Foundation was giving him its Pioneer Award. The honor, to be presented September 6 in New York City, would be accompanied by a $15,000 monetary award. He could keep the money, the letter explained, or donate it to the foundation's financial assistance program benefiting rhythm-and-blues artists. The foundation's stated mission is "to pay tribute through honorariums and awards to those legendary rhythm-and-blues artists from the 40s, 50s, and 60s who have made a significant contribution to the development of the music." But the foundation has its critics, music journalist and former foundation board member Dave Marsh among them. "[The] institution's main mission appears to be covering up the felonies record companies committed against R&B and soul artists." Nonetheless, it was easy for the financially ruined Huey to accept the honorarium. "Now, I know Toussaint able to give his back," he said with a laugh. "John Lee Hooker gave his back. Some people not able to!"

When asked whom he would like to present him with his Pioneer Award at the ceremony in New York City, Huey named Dr. John. He asked Mike Armshaw at the BeBop Music Shop if he could contact his famous first cousin. "They were looking for Mac, but they didn't get in touch with him in time," Huey said later. "But he would have been happy to do that. I've always communicated with Dr. John." "Yeah, I was trying my ass off to make it," Dr. John said. "That really bothered me because, if there's anybody I would like to give something to in my life, it's Huey. He's always been the most givingest cat I know."

Huey also suggested that his old boss, Shirley Goodman of the singing duo Shirley and Lee, present the award. "But the lady at the foundation said, 'Oh, well, she's not big enough,'" he recalled. "Yet they go suggest Frankie Ford. Ain't that something? Frankie Ford."

On August 18, 2000, nineteen days before the Rhythm & Blues Foundation gala in New York, the Smiths were back in bankruptcy court in Baton Rouge. The hearing concerned bankruptcy trustee Dwayne Murray's sale, for the benefit of creditor Artists Rights Enforcement Corporation, of "Don't You Just Know It," "High Blood Pressure," "Sea Cruise," and "Rocking Pneumonia and the Boogie Woogie Flu" to Cotillion Music, Inc., care of Warner/Chappell Music, Inc. The price was $1 million, less an unrecouped $390,000 balance in Huey's royalty account. The sale made the music publishing company the 100 percent owner of the United States and Canadian songwriter and performance royalties for the songs. Huey would receive 100 percent of the songs' foreign royalties. The sale further gave Artists Rights Enforcement a direct payment of $179,000.

Appearances were made by Murray and Artists Rights Enforcement's attorney, Ralph Hood. Pamela Magee, Huey's most recent attorney, was listed as appearing for Artists Rights. The Smiths had no counsel. Judge Louis Phillips, demonstrating a change of tone toward the Smiths, expressed his desire that they receive funds from the bankruptcy estate and that their case be thoroughly resolved in the best way possible.

In addition to the sale of Huey's songs, the proceeds that the sale would generate, and the amount of money the trustee was holding, the hearing contained much discussion of taxes. Hood stated that Artists Rights Enforcement, unbeknownst to Judge Phillips, had paid no taxes on royalty income sent by Cotillion Music—in accordance with the judge's 1998 order declaring that 50 percent ownership of the songs was not the property of the Smiths' estate—directly to Artists Rights. Murray told the judge that, under the law, it had been clear to him that Huey Smith owed taxes on only 50 percent of the income generated by songs, but the matter had slipped from his attention.

> MURRAY: Just for the record, judge, Mr. Smith is present. I've had an opportunity to talk with him about what is going on. It's my understanding, also, that the other fifty-percent owner of the rights in this matter have also been discussing what we are trying to accomplish today. Pursuant to my conversation with Mr. Smith, I have put a signature page for him to sign. . . .
>
> JUDGE PHILLIPS: What say you about this motion, Mr. Hood?
>
> HOOD: . . . this motion will allow the estate to receive a substantial amount of money, about $430,000, which should provide enough funds for the trustee to pay all the unsecured claims. That will allow Mr. Smith's bankruptcy case to be closed and Mr. Smith to then be revested with whatever rights he has in those songs. . . . it should give us enough money to

pay the taxes on everything, pay all the creditors, unsecured creditors, and basically let Mr. Smith back out into the real world and hopeful with a right to pursue some substantial money from foreign royalties.

JUDGE PHILLIPS: Tax consequences? . . . have we ever gone back and looked at Mr. Smith's prior year tax returns? . . . Because he's paying gazillions of dollars in taxes. . . . I was under the impression—I don't know whether I'm remembering correctly—that Artists Rights was paying taxes and Mr. Smith was paying taxes, Artists Rights on its part, Mr. Smith on all of it. . . .

MURRAY: Judge, I put it in the hands of counsel who no longer represents Mr. Smith . . . under the law, it was clear to me that he [Huey Smith] only owned fifty percent and maybe only should be paying taxes on fifty percent. But that lawyer is no longer representing Mr. Smith. So, I don't know what happened with respect to that. . . .

JUDGE PHILLIPS: The question I have, I still have, because I think the estate has an interest in getting Mr. Smith's prior-year tax returns straight, because I think you're right and I think I ruled that you were right, that Artists Rights owned a half-interest in this thing. . . . I was understanding that Artists Rights was doing tax returns, accounting for it or something.

HOOD: For the money they received, no, they did not pay taxes on it. . . .

JUDGE PHILLIPS: I think the estate has an interest in it, and I don't know why, because Mr. Smith tried to get around—I'm interested in whatever he can get out of this, making sure he gets. But it's mostly that the trustee needs to do the trustee's job about tax liability and who pays what. It's been a kind of long road, longer for some of us than others, but once it gets over with, let's have it really over with the best way it can be. . . . Mr. Murray is going to do everything he can do to get all the taxes straight. And I think you heard what I was saying, Mrs. Smith, if Mr. Smith didn't. . . . Mr. Smith is a party to this, because of the prospect of a residual interest and also because the residual interest, even if it doesn't generate monetary relief now, hopefully will give him the foreign royalties over and above everything, right?

MURRAY: That's correct, judge.

JUDGE PHILLIPS: And, for his interest in the foreign royalties—but I'm not interested in that, right?

MURRAY: Right, judge . . .

JUDGE PHILLIPS: Well, I don't have an interest in it. My orders are my orders. Whatever my orders have said, they say. Whoever my orders bind—and I tried to bind as many people as I can grab—my orders bind. And I'm understanding that this assumes the existence of all prior orders and is consistent with it.

HOOD: That's correct.

I n *Backbeat,* the 1999 book about his life, the great New Orleans and Los Angeles drummer Earl Palmer recalled the dangers of being black in Jim Crow–era New Orleans. "You didn't want to go to jail in New Orleans," he said. "You might never come out. You don't know how those days were. They could kill you if they wanted and say you committed suicide. Who was going to argue? Who was going to investigate?"

Huey lived through that time, too, and incidents of the kind Palmer speaks of were known to him, too. When his bankruptcy trustee called him out of the courtroom on the day of the hearing that granted the million-dollar sale of his songs to Cotillion Music, Huey felt intimidated. A recent, high-profile example of a jailhouse death came to his mind. On August 7, 1995, the *Baton Rouge Advocate* reported the demise of one of the city's notorious characters. Just before her death, convicted madam Sylvia Landry hinted that she'd rather die than spend six years in prison. "Daddy, this is the last time you'll talk to me," she said during a phone call to her parents. Shortly thereafter, officials announced that the woman known as the Baton Rouge Madam had hung herself in a Brazos County jail cell in Bryan, Texas.

"Mr. Murray," Huey remembered of his meeting with his bankruptcy trustee, "he told me, 'I'm trying to help you. Now, you got to sign these things.' The newspaper said the madam hung herself in her cell. I didn't want to find myself hanging in my cell, so I signed the papers, stack by stack. But I told Mr. Murray, 'I'll sign them, but if I read them I can't sign them, because I know what's in here is not the truth.' I didn't have no 'For Sale' sign on my songs. But I can't say one word. They'd lock me up then for contempt of court, for the night. Well, you dead then. They'll say, 'Well, he tried to escape,' or, 'He was despondent,' something. Yeah, they do that. I'm telling you, people don't know what's going on."

Artists Rights Enforcement's years of litigation against him ultimately led to the liquidation of the composer, pianist, and recording artist's most valuable assets—his four most popular and profitable songs. The parade of lawyers he hired after winning the original 1988 Artists Rights suit failed him. "Nobody, they didn't never hear nothing I had to say," he explained. "A lot of people, they have their minds set already. They don't see what you're really talking about and cut you off. I think they trained at that. And they looking for something in the law to handle the court."

Throughout his legal trials and financial hardships, Huey found hope and consolation in the Bible and his Bible study with his Jehovah's Witnesses friends. "There is a God who cares about you," he said. "It almost go' to one of Frankie Lymon's songs. 'Why do birds sing?' Jehovah made it like that. When you taste honey, why does it taste good? Jehovah made it like that. And why are flowers not just all white? Some red, some blue. It's something beautiful for you. So there's not just a God, there's a God who cares. Things happen, though, but He will take care of all the rest of it very soon. Rest assured, he go' do us right."

Huey's reservation for his flight to the Rhythm & Blues Foundation Pioneer Awards ceremony in New York City, booked by the foundation, listed him as Huey P. Newton. The error startled him. Former Black Panther leader Huey P. Newton had been murdered in 1989. "That's a militant that the police were going to kill," Huey said. "It really scared me, but I went there ahead of time and they changed it. I got it straight and I finally got to New York." A car sent by the foundation picked up Huey, Margrette, and their granddaughter, Tyra, at LaGuardia International Airport. Huey got a half-hour rehearsal with the band for the two songs he was to perform, "Rocking Pneumonia" and "Sea Cruise." Having lost his piano to the pawnshop, he'd had only twenty minutes of practice before the flight to New York. "I went to a lady's house because I didn't know exactly how to do the introduction to 'Rocking Pneumonia.'"

A well-attended afternoon press conference at the Crystal Ballroom in the New Yorker Hotel preceded the awards gala. The questions mostly were what Huey expected. Some members of the press suggested that being a Jehovah's Witness led him to reject music. "A lot of people try to make it like I feel that music is a type of evil," he countered. "I cut them short with that." Someone else asked if a line from "Rocking Pneumonia"—"I wanna jump but I'm afraid I'll fall"—was a plea to drug companies to develop a 1950s version of Viagra. "No! Y'all just now coming up here with that!" Huey said. "A lot of times the public will take what you say and come up with a twisting thought on it. But a while back I had a song called 'Rockin' Behind the Iron Curtain.' Sure enough, that's what occurred."

One of the attendees was the well-spoken thirteen-year-old reporter Jake from Soul-Patrol.net, a website dedicated to "great black music from the past to the future":

JAKE: New Orleans has a jazz festival coming up and I think they want to see Huey "Piano" Smith come back.

HUEY: The Jazz Fest, you couldn't live off of a thing like that. Like one gentleman had asked me, "Would you do such and such a thing?" I said, "Sure—if it's right." But everybody tries to make like playing music is something unholy. Many occasions it do be, but it all depends on where it's at and what they doing. Like Huey Smith, I'm not dancing with the dead like Michael Jackson! I try to stay clean and everything have to be in harmony with Bible principles.

JAKE: What are we gonna see from Huey in the near future?

HUEY: The same thing you saw in the past, except, while I'm here, I was hoping to talk to some people from the media. It's so much corruption with lawyers and judges and without any kind of thing to make it exposed to what's really going on. They don't need new laws. They need to enforce the ones already on the books!

The many interviews wore even Huey down. "Must have been about twenty-five interviews," he remembered. "I said, 'Miss, I'm tired.' I really was."

While in New York, Huey met Glenn Gaines, a young man from New Orleans. Gaines managed the Wild Magnolias Mardi Gras Indians and gospel and rhythm-and-blues singer Marva Wright. He was a second-generation New Orleans music businessman, his father having been a principal of NOLA Records, the label that released Robert Parker's 1966 hit, "Barefootin'."

"He said where he come from," Huey said later. "That man ain't stopped talking yet!"

Besides Huey, honorees at the Rhythm & Blues Foundation's eleventh annual Pioneer Awards were Johnnie Johnson (pianist with Chuck Berry); songwriter and producer Clyde Otis; Sylvia Robinson, part of the duo Mickey and Sylvia ("Love Is Strange") and cofounder of the pioneering Sugar Hill rap music label; singer Betty Wright; and vocal groups the Impressions and the Chi-Lites.

Stevie Wonder received a lifetime achievement award, the foundation posthumously awarded its legacy tribute to Marvin Gaye, and Atlantic Records executive Ahmet Ertegun received the Founder's Award.

Former Clown and longtime New Yorker Jesse Thomas joined Huey, Margrette, and Tyra at a table with gospel singer BeBe Winans. Also seated at the table were singer-songwriter Brenda Russell ("Piano in the Dark," "So Good, So Right"), former Supreme Mary Wilson, and Sylvia Robinson. "It really was a great time," Jesse said. "A matter of fact, everybody was saying this one was one of the best that they had since they started it."

Motown star Smokey Robinson acted as master of ceremonies. The all-star presenters included Bonnie Raitt, Natalie Cole, Aretha Franklin, Ashford and Simpson, Isaac Hayes, Gerald Levert, Brian McKnight, John Sebastian, Brenda Russell, Sister Sledge, BeBe Winans, and Mary Wilson. When the time arrived to give out the awards, Robinson announced, "Our first recipient is a man whose middle name is literally 'Piano'—Huey 'Piano' Smith." Applause greeted Huey's name as his 1950s black-and-white headshot loomed on screens above the stage. "Yeah!" Robinson agreed. "Huey wrote so many wonderful songs. He wrote 'Rocking Pneumonia and the Boogie Woogie Flu.' We all got a case of that. Here he is, Mr. Huey 'Piano' Smith."

Without his Clowns, Pitter Pats, Hueys, or Soul Shakers, Huey sang and played "Rocking Pneumonia" with a big band featuring *Late Night with David Letterman* bandleader Paul Shaffer. Sitting at a grand piano, he characteristically didn't sing close enough to the microphone. The band's dreadlocked conductor ran over to move it closer. "All right, kick it!" Huey interjected during his "Rocking Pneumonia" piano solo. "Now, step on it!" Near the song's end, he added a few questions that seemingly addressed the hazards of the music business. "How do you get on the other side of somewhere over the rainbow? I can't tell. Why don't you go and ask Patti LaBelle?" Next came "Sea Cruise," the rock 'n' roll classic Huey thought should have been among his, not Frankie Ford's, chart hits. After "Sea Cruise" he walked across the stage to the podium, waving and blowing kisses, passing a grinning, applauding Shaffer. The night's audience included Suzette Becker, his former attorney from New Orleans. "I was cheering the loudest from way up high," she said. "I was so delighted when I saw that Huey was being awarded. I always wished him the best."

Fellow New Orleanian Lloyd Price presented Huey's award. "Huey Smith and his group, the Clowns," Price said as he stood next to the honoree, his arm around Huey's shoulders, "were the finest example of romping, stomping—in

New Orleans that made the sound what it was. His organization featured some of the greatest and the finest music of New Orleans—and I'm gonna forget this teleprompter because I happen to know Huey real good. He played in one of my first bands in New Orleans. Huey Smith, one of the great, all-time pianists of New Orleans, the Rhythm & Blues Foundation is proud to present this Pioneer Award to you for all the contributions you've made to our great music. Thank you for preserving the soul!"

"Actually," Huey said softly during his acceptance speech, "you might not believe it, but this is a debut for me. It was Huey Smith and the Clowns, men like Curley Moore, Bobby Marchan, Roosevelt Wright, and John Williams. They're not with us, but they certainly would enjoy this. Seeing that the foundation is the one who makes miracles, I honor you all. Thank you, Rhythm & Blues Foundation." Huey kept his speech brief, just as the foundation had asked. Others took their time. "Aretha Franklin talked for, *ooh,* like a hour!" he recalled. "Of course, she donated $700,000 to it. But I got tired of listening at them, really."

Jesse Thomas told his former boss that Paul Shaffer was a big Huey Smith fan. "Ooh, boy, he crazy about you! All Paul Shaffer know is Huey Smith!" Jesse said. "Yeah?" Huey asked, thinking Jesse was pulling his leg. Most of the lawyers he'd dealt with over the decades said they were big fans. So did Chuck Rubin.

Before Huey and his family left New York, Jesse gave him a copy of his latest CD, *Easy in the Apple.* The disc includes Earl King's "Those Lonely, Lonely Nights," Chris Kenner's "Sick and Tired," James "Sugar Boy" Crawford's "Jock-A-Mo," Guitar Slim's "The Things That I Used to Do," and "Rocking Pneumonia." Listening to the CD later, Huey was amazed that Jesse didn't know the correct lyrics for "Rocking Pneumonia." "He sang, 'Young man rhythm's got a hole in my tooth!'"

Delighted by his Rhythm & Blues Foundation honor though Huey was, the organization's revision of the biographical notes he sent to New York dismayed him. The revised bio included the oft-repeated myth of a 1950s New Orleans studio house band that supposedly played for every hit the city produced. "I wasn't in no house band," Huey said later. "Dave Bartholomew wasn't no house bandleader for Imperial Records. Yeah, he was a bandleader, all right, but not for the record company and then you hear him on everybody's records."

I n the days after the Pioneer Awards ceremony, Chuck Rubin put a positive face on his dealings with Huey: Artists Rights Enforcement had successfully extracted Huey from bankruptcy and put the composer on the path to financial good times. When the Smiths got back to Baton Rouge, Rubin's calls were waiting on their answering machine. "I didn't answer," Huey said, "because I don't want to get in no argument about that last letter he sent, about how I asked him to help me get out of bankruptcy. I didn't. I told him I wasn't go' fight him anymore about that. Whatever you go' take, you're too powerful for me because I'm without any lawyer to represent me."

Huey also got a visit from Glenn Gaines, the musicians' manager from New Orleans he'd met in New York. And he gave the local newspaper an interview. "There I was and I enjoyed every minute of it," he said of his trip to New York. "Those people were so friendly. It was baffling to me. I hadn't been there in years. I said, 'I can't even believe this.' They were all over me."

Though Huey disagrees with Frankie Ford's often-published versions of events surrounding "Sea Cruise," he told the *Advocate* he had no grudge against Ford. He even hoped to stage a concert featuring Ford and himself. "Like Stevie Wonder recorded whatever it was for the Rhythm & Blues Foundation. So I can benefit the foundation, just like Stevie Wonder, with the production of the First Annual Sea Cruise. Me and Frankie Ford in New Orleans. Robert Parker and Irma Thomas, whoever else, K-Doe, and conclude with Huey Smith and Frankie. It could be on one of the big riverboats, casinos. It could be anywhere." Huey suggested that the First Annual Sea Cruise could be promoted through billboards depicting Huey and Ford nose-to-nose in the manner of feuding WWF wrestlers. But the confrontational advertisement would be just for show. "See, rather than Huey Smith opposing Frankie, it'll be Huey Smith with Frankie Ford. When we actually do a duet, it will be tremendous."

During the newspaper interview, Huey unleashed a blitz of names, events, and, most of all, legal battles, jumping through decades with no thought of chronology. The resulting article revealed that Huey "Piano" Smith did not have a piano. "After they cut off my funds completely, I had to sell my piano," he said. "They were talking about cutting my lights off. . . . It's so much corruption in the world. It's not just the drug dealers. Like, the ambulance-chasing lawyers, now that's accepted. It's a corrupt society."

Watching a video of the Rhythm & Blues Foundation Awards some months later, the sixty-six-year-old Huey was pleased with neither his performance nor his appearance beneath the bright stage lights. "I didn't do such a good job on the thing," he judged. "And I don't know what they did to my hands. Made them look like Miss Jane Pittman, in that movie. Looking at that, I see my daddy!"

But as Huey told the audience that night, his performance there was his debut. On stage, Huey had always worked with groups of singers performing songs that he, in most cases, had composed and arranged for them. Working solo had never been his style. In fact, he asked the Rhythm & Blues Foundation if Jesse Thomas could join him. Jesse was willing to sing on stage or even backstage. The foundation organizers, apparently not understanding Huey's art, refused.

H uey wrote his bankruptcy trustee shortly after returning from New York:

Dear Mr. Murray:

IRS agent on September 13, 2000 instructed me to forward this bill to you that demands your immediate attention.

I have a question for you—Why, as long as you have been receiving Huey Smith royalty statements with Huey Smith's social security number, that you never bother to report this to the IRS? . . . I am sure that you are aware of what is happening with former Governor Edwin Edwards and you know the federal government is not something for you to play with. So, I strongly suggest that you clean up your act.

An American Citizen and Taxpayer denied of the automatic stay upon filing bankruptcy.

Huey P Smith
Cc: IRS
Rhythm & Blues Foundation Legal Dept.

Huey believed the question of his owing the IRS approximately $25,000 for income received in 1997 had been resolved until another letter from the IRS arrived in December 2000. "To prevent collection agency, please pay the current balance now," the letter warned. The IRS claimed the Smiths owed $26,192 for tax year 1997, including a $481 penalty and $1,082 interest. Huey wrote a letter to Gary Roth at BMI entitled "Erroneous IRS Report." Roth earlier had promised to contact Murray, and then, if Murray advised that he'd reported income under Huey's tax number, BMI would send the Smiths a corrected 1099. "My Dear Mr. Roth," Huey replied. "You misinterpreted my letter. I am not concerned of who, where, or why you send anyone any money. But, I am pleading with you to please do not report to the IRS, using my name or social security number, that you sent me any money, unless you actually send it to me." A later letter from the IRS took Huey off the hook. "They made a change," he explained. "They sending us $8, rather than we owing them $24,000." Nevertheless, IRS claims that the Smiths owed the agency five-figure sums continued to plague them in the years after their bankruptcy case closed.

Glenn Gaines continued his courtship of Huey. "Gaines keep talking about how many times the Neville Brothers play in New Orleans and the amount of money they get, when they just play a few times," Huey said of his suddenly frequent visitor. "He's telling me this lady from the foundation said Johnnie Johnson took advantage of getting that award and now he's playing. But Gaines got to come up with some figures. Be specific. Tell me what you can do and put a price there."

In January 2001, Huey heard that Chuck Rubin had said the Smiths' bankruptcy case would be concluded in three weeks. "Well," he reacted, "they go to squabbling over dividing somebody's money the last ten years. Yeah, why don't y'all just go shoot each other and be done with it?" Barbara Hawkins of the New Orleans singing group the Dixie Cups offered muted praise for Chuck Rubin and Artists Rights Enforcement. "She don't want to get in no trouble," Huey surmised. "That's sad. Other words, she's in bondage." Steven Ames Brown, the San Francisco attorney hired by the Smiths' bankruptcy trustee on Rubin's recommendation to pursue foreign royalties, defended Rubin in a torrent of praise. "People don't like Chuck Rubin because he's done very well for people," Brown said. "And some of his own clients—apparently Huey—seem to forget that the reason that they're getting their money is because Chuck fought for them for years."

When Phil Brady, a former Baton Rouge bar owner and blues fan who'd moved south from Brooklyn, heard about Huey's legal problems, he wondered if an attorney friend of his in New York City could help. Brady was upbeat about Huey's prospects. "These guys in New York, they know what to do," he told Huey. "Yeah," Huey said, "so I'll round up the papers for you. That's no problem for me. I done did it a hundred times before." His many years of tangling with Rubin, Huey told Brady, seemed unreal: "This is like a horror movie." He sent a package of documents to Brady's lawyer friend in New York. Reading a bankruptcy hearing transcript, however, the lawyer was taken aback by Judge Phillips's threats to have the U.S. attorney investigate the Smiths. Brady's friend wanted nothing to do with the case.

Huey wrote his congressman, Richard Baker, in January 2001. "I am writing to you to ask for your help. . . . Copyright law to protect composers creating intellectual works to encourage others has been abused. The courts is treating my property as a material object, even ignoring quantum meriut, which, in that respect, is a terrible injustice that is taking place. I feel, that it would be well worth it if someone would look into this matter that make the United States Copyright Laws Worthless. For this reason, I am asking for your help, please help me."

Some months later Huey got a call from Dr. John, his ever-traveling friend. "Dr. John was apologizing about not being able to make the Rhythm & Blues Foundation awards. He was so disappointed he didn't make that. He talked about Joe Caronna an hour, and Johnny Vincent, and him, Mac hisself, the problem he had, just like some of the things in his book." Huey had found parts of Dr. John's 1994 autobiography astounding, especially the California years spent with such wild New Orleans characters as Dave Dixon and Jessie Hill. "Wow! I ain't even know that was Dr. John's lifestyle. Me, I know he cursed a lot, but I thought he was kind of conservative like."

"Listen," Dr. John explained. "Most of the stuff in the book was conversation between Red Tyler and myself, Google Eyes, whoever was around that day. This poor guy writing the book gotta understand New Orleans-ese, musician-ese, and all the rest of it at the same time, and nothing connects. It ain't easy."

Frankie Ford, a regular at the New Orleans Jazz and Heritage Festival, appeared at the 2001 festival dressed like a pirate in billowing golden sleeves, an oversized earring, and vest and hat covered by faux gold coins. "That's why Glenn Gaines say he prancing around like a peacock," Huey said and laughed. Naturally, "Sea Cruise" was the highlight of Ford's set. The song drew people off the Fair Grounds Race Course infield, out of their chairs, up to dance. Huey wondered why Ford hadn't invited him to join him at Jazz Fest. "I know he had to read the newspaper article [containing Huey's idea for a joint concert with Ford]. He could contact me and let's get together. The sea is deep enough for both of us to cruise together in unity."

Other classic New Orleans performers appearing at the 2001 Jazz Fest included Fats Domino, Ernie K-Doe, Eddie Bo, Allen Toussaint, Irma Thomas, the Neville Brothers, Pete Fountain, and Earl King. Earl rarely performed in New Orleans, but he made an exception for Jazz Fest, even though his agent protested that he could make more money elsewhere. Before he played Guitar Slim's "The Things That I Used to Do" at the blues stage, Earl suggested Slim's mischievous spirit had detuned his guitar strings while he wasn't looking. "I'm optimistic," he told the crowd. "I like to think Slim's up there."

24

Piano Night

n 2001, Eddie Bo, Huey's keyboard peer from the Dew Drop Café and Club Tiajuana days, invited him, Earl King, and Dr. John to be special guests at the annual New Orleans piano-playing marathon called Piano Night. Set for the Monday between the two weekends of the New Orleans Jazz and Heritage Festival and billed as "A Tribute to Eddie Bo," the show was a benefit for radio station WWOZ. Scheduled performers included Bo, Dr. John, Hadda Brooks, Marcia Ball, Bonnie Raitt pianist Jon Cleary, Reggie Hall, and James "Sugar Boy" Crawford's grandson, Davell Crawford.

Huey told Bo he'd be there. But as piano night approached, he wondered why Bo hadn't asked him to perform. Suddenly, he feared his not performing would make Piano Night attendees angry. Bo, upon hearing Huey wished to play, was enthusiastic. "It'd be nice if he would play."

"That's the only way I'll be there," Huey said. "I'm a' be there and I'm go' play." Huey liked Piano Night's concept of continuous piano playing by multiple pianists. He also planned to introduce his new, never-heard composition, "Tipitina's Baby Sister," and perform songs by Big Joe Turner, Charles Brown, and Roy Brown. "I want to conclude with the 'Sea Cruise,' by myself," he said. "Turn the lights out and the band be gone and just me up there with 'Sea Cruise.' So, me, I'm looking forward to playing."

Huey hoped to join two of his old bandmates, guitarist Earl King and saxophonist Robert Parker, at Piano Night. "Most of the solos on the records, like 'Havin a Good Time,' that's Robert. So, if he's there, we be sounding just like the record. Earl King, that's Earl on 'Little Liza Jane.' Like the introduction on 'Don't You Know Yockomo,' that's Earl. Yeah, so the whole thing will be just like the original—if they're there. But that's why I would have called for a little rehearsal. The musicians need to know what they're doing. Not be up there, *sss, sss, sss,* and the audience looking. That's not professional."

Though Huey hadn't played piano regularly for years, it came back to him easily. "It's just something you don't forget, like walking," he said. "But if you play every day, you'll get repetitive. Then you have to put it down. If you leave it alone and then come back to it, it'll be brand new."

Huey sent Glenn Gaines an email message asking him to inquire about exactly what was expected of him at Piano Night. Gaines replied via email from Australia, where he was touring with Marva Wright. She was killing her Aussie audiences, and a promoter there was interested in booking Huey "Piano" Smith and the "New" Clowns. Gaines reassured Huey that everything would be in order for Piano Night.

Piano Night, taking place at the church-like Generations Hall, was a big event. But Huey Smith, the quintessential New Orleans songwriter and pianist many were hoping to see and hear for the first time in twenty years, did not appear. His former band member saxophonist James Rivers was among the disappointed attendees. "Huey was gonna be there!" Rivers said. "That's one of the reasons I accepted the gig." Earl King didn't attend either. "I was out sick," he explained. "After that, I said, 'I wonder if Huey made it down there.'" Others never expected Huey to appear, Deacon John Moore among them. "Everybody said, 'Man, don't believe it. Huey ain't showing up. Him, neither Earl.' And both of them didn't show up, just like they said! It was just a ruse to get people coming out thinking that they might show up. But I knew they weren't contracted to perform."

"Robert Parker wasn't there," Huey said later. "Earl wasn't there. So who was go' play for me? Well, what I'm go' do when I got up there? I'm there to look stupid. So Gaines say he go' make these young white piano players know exactly what's going on with this, too." Rumor had it that the Piano Night organizers refused to give Huey a hotel room for the night. "They couldn't afford Huey Smith, one of the originators of the New Orleans piano sound, a hotel room?" Moore asked. "They shoulda sent a limousine for him. Come on, they wouldn't do that to Elvis!" Moore laughed long and loud.

Piano Night producer Stephanie Lawrence said incorrect information had been given to Huey. Eddie Bo found Huey's change of heart baffling. Bo's manager was simply angry.

O n April 24, 2001, six days before Piano Night, the Tractors, the Oklahoma country band that got a Top 10 hit in 1994 with "Baby Likes to Rock It," released a new album, *Fast Girl*. Tractors singer-guitarist Steve Ripley based one of the album's songs on "Rocking Pneumonia and the Boogie Woogie Flu." A Huey Smith fan, Ripley had attempted to send a fan letter to the songwriter-pianist on many occasions. "Actually," Ripley confessed, "I know a few really big stars, but I was just too in awe to send the letter to Huey Smith. To me, it might as well be Elvis Presley. I finally just drove around listening to his things so many times that I took that 'Rocking Pneumonia' form and wrote some new words and pretended he was here [in the studio]. It was a long ordeal to get the Warner/Chappell clearance on that, but then I said, 'Hey, I am so thrilled to have my name alongside his.'"

A hillbilly joke inspired the lyrics for the Smith-Ripley song, "Nine Eleven." "The hillbilly was supposed to call 9-1-1," Ripley explained. "But he thinks of it as nine-eleven and there's no eleven on the phone." Even though "Nine Eleven" was an album track rather than a single, it became a hit in that regional stronghold of beach music, the Carolinas. "It came out gangbusters in that region as a dance thing," Ripley said. Huey heard Ripley's reworking of "Rocking Pneumonia" and voiced his approval. "That's what you're supposed to do," he said.

25

The Money's Still Funny

T he proposed distribution of the Smiths' bankruptcy estate funds included $501,000 to creditor Artists Right Enforcement Corporation; $51,000 to bankruptcy trustee Dwayne M. Murray for his reported 32.2 hours of work for the estate; $163,000 to the IRS; $16,000 to the Louisiana Department of Revenue and Taxation; and $7,100 to Pamela Magee, the attorney who'd left the Smiths' employment three years prior. The trustee objected to ten creditor claims, including Emergency Medical Services, Baton Rouge General Hospital, and Margrette Smith's mother. Following Murray's lead, Judge Phillips struck the claims. "Mr. Murray took my mother-in-law and all of them off," Huey said. "So we got to scuffle and pay them ourselves, however we could."

In May 2001, Chuck Rubin found himself at the other end of a lawsuit. Rosemary Prater, an Artists Rights client and widow of the late Dave Prater, half of the soul-singing duo Sam and Dave, sued Rubin and her late husband's record company, Atlantic, in New Jersey. "AREC, and its principal, Charles 'Chuck' Rubin," the complaint stated, "engage in the predatory practice of approaching unsophisticated musicians who are in financial difficulty, obtaining their confidence, and then inducing them to enter into oppressive, burdensome and unconscionable contracts, whereby AREC will participate in the royalties due to the artists in perpetuity. Atlantic is aware of AREC's unsavory practices . . . in furtherance of its predatory practices, as part of its scheme to control the artists it purports to represent, AREC employs the Courts and the judicial process by bringing lawsuits which have no merit, knowing that the defendants do not have the financial ability or the business skills necessary to properly defend themselves."

The complaint asked for a judgment against Artists Rights Enforcement and Atlantic Records for all royalties attributable to Dave Prater. The latter funds included "the double payment to attorney [Steven Ames] Brown for the monies that were wrongfully taken by Brown." The suit also asked that Prater's contract with Artists Rights be terminated and have no further force and effect. Rubin told the *Record* newspaper of Bergen County, New Jersey, that he was dismayed by the suit. "I don't understand why she is doing this. If it were not for Artists Rights, she'd be receiving nothing. . . . I just feel that she is bitter she can't take it all." The much-publicized suit was settled out of court.

Dwayne Murray came to the Smiths' Baton Rouge home early one hot, spring evening in 2001 to deliver Huey's distribution from his bankruptcy estate. Following years of financial deprivation and Judge Phillips's December 1997 pronouncement that the Smiths would receive nothing from the Chapter 7 estate, it was a comparatively positive development. Nevertheless, the composer's share of the estate's distributions, substantial though it was, was less than one-tenth of his songs' $1 million sale price. Sitting in the Smiths' den, Murray handed the sixty-seven-year-old musician the check and shook his hand. As Huey walked with Murray to his car, the trustee advised him to call Chuck Rubin, saying Artists Rights Enforcement could swing another $85,000 or $90,000 his way. "Yeah, like Mr. Murray is his agent," Huey said afterward. "I'm just sorry he didn't say that in front of somebody. A lot of things like that, but you can't prove it." Rubin phoned Huey soon thereafter. The composer didn't answer. "I ain't got nothing to say to him. He writes letters and he sends email. I ain't talking to him."

Glenn Gaines made one of his increasingly frequent visits to Huey in May 2001. Huey enjoyed the visits. Gaines told his host that people in New Orleans believe that Huey Smith lives in a one-room shack in Baton Rouge and wants nothing to do with the music business. "Well," Huey replied, "usually, like with me, when they call me they're not saying who they are. 'I'm somebody at the Queen Mary,' whatever." Meanwhile, word had gotten around New Orleans about Gaines's association with Huey, something he wasn't keeping secret. The conversation also turned to Piano Night. In Gaines's view, honoree Eddie Bo had not made it the big payday for himself it should have been, especially after calling in favors from such big-name friends as Dr. John, Hadda Brooks, and Bonnie Raitt.

nvited by his ex-wife, Doretha, Huey made a rare trip to New Orleans to attend a family reunion. The occasion was a combination reunion and birthday party for their grandson, Noble. Being a Jehovah's Witness, Huey doesn't celebrate birthdays. But Doretha told her ex-husband her intention was that he'd only attend the reunion that would follow the party. Although his grandchildren sang Huey's local hit from 1968, "Coo Coo over You," at the event, Huey was the star attraction. "He played his piano for the family, which added his special touch," Doretha said. "Huey's children, grandchildren, great-grandchildren danced and clowned like never before. It was like the old days again. Everyone had a good time."

On September 11, 2001, nineteen al-Qaeda–trained militants launched attacks that killed more than three thousand people on the U.S. mainland. The fiery way things were going, Huey said, Armageddon was near. "Ain't no going to heaven or hell, like the hell-fire preachers say, but there will be a ruling class with Jesus. That's the Kingdom, 144,000 chosen ones from the Earth. But people don't want the truth. They want to do what they want to do."

A few days after 9/11, Gerri Hall visited the Smiths. She was surprised that Huey had set microphones and his electric piano up in his den. "Yes, indeed!" she exclaimed. "Huey go' play! Yeah, you right. How you feeling today, mister?" "I don't know exactly," the recently ill Huey said. "But I thought I might get a few keys straight with you. 'Little Chickie Wah Wah' and things. For Monday, huh?" "For Monday? What's happening Monday?" Gerri asked. "That's the induction of the Blues Hall of Fame," Huey said.

Given recent world-shaking events, Huey wondered if the Louisiana Blues Hall of Fame, which picked him as one of its 2001 honorees, would hold its ceremony as planned. "Many things canceled," he told Gerri. "I know the Rhythm & Blues Foundation at the Apollo cancelled. That was Toussaint and them, Al Green. But I want to get to the man who's sponsoring this Blues Hall of Fame and ask him is he going to have any kind of rehearsal. And another thing, in specific. I'm go' say I need money for you, Gerri. That's what I told Gaines. Now I wish I knew where Roosevelt was."

Huey and Gerri—the original voices on "Sea Cruise" and many more recordings—ran through "Sea Cruise," "Don't You Know Yockomo," "Don't You Just Know It," and "It Do Me Good."

"All right," Gerri said. "So we gotta have another rehearsal. We can't just do this."

"I want to see your voice," Huey said.

Gerri snapped back: "You ain't no good! You always tell me, 'You know what to sing!'"

"You do!" Huey said.

Taking a break, Huey and Gerri talked about the Dew Drop days, the people they knew, the times they had. Blues-shouter Big Joe Turner, Gerri remembered, got round like a balloon in his middle. They called him "Rockin'" Joe Turner, Huey said, because he rocked in his chair while he ate.

Gerri exclaimed: "He roll like a big wheel in a Georgia cotton field! And all of his middle just dance. I say, 'Oh, no!' We used to have a time in the Dew Drop! Huey, them days will never be the same, man. We'll never see all that beauty again."

"They're not here no more," Huey agreed.

"The music ain't here, people ain't here," Gerri said. "They don't have no more people no more. Everything is robots. Everybody want to be into stuff that they no part of. Everybody's not part of the music."

A year after the Rhythm & Blues Foundation Pioneer Awards, the Louisiana Blues Hall of Fame gave Huey another honor at the Varsity Theatre in Baton Rouge. His fellow honorees included Clarence "Gatemouth" Brown, Fats Domino, Baton Rouge blues men Chuck Mitchell and Oscar "Harpo" Davis, and Chicago and Baton Rouge radio personality E. Rodney Jones. Cosimo Matassa also presented a lifetime achievement award to Quint Davis, director and producer of the New Orleans Jazz and Heritage Festival. Davis traveled from New Orleans for the ceremony, but Domino stayed home. To the surprise of many, Huey did attend, despite his walking pneumonia. He was the last inductee called to the stage by Louisiana Blues Hall of Fame director Gary Daigle.

Echoing his Pioneer Awards acceptance speech, Huey said this latest honor mainly belonged to the Clowns. "I had the group the Pitter Pats and also the Hueys, but, now, very important is the members of the Clowns. Mr. Bobby Marchan, he's not with us. And another important gentleman, Curley 'Soul Train' Moore, is not with us. And John Williams. Gerri Hall—I thought Gerri was go' be with us, but, evidently, she couldn't make it." Huey cracked the crowd up with memories of his early musical partner, Guitar Slim. "Slim said, 'Hewitt! One day I'm go' get a Pontiac station wagon like Gatemouth Brown!' But when he did 'The Things That I Used to Do' he got an Oldsmobile. He ran into a bull-doozer and left out the hospital premature. I think that's why he's not with us. So, I do want to thank everyone and I don't want to forget anyone, like Sidney Rayfield, Roosevelt Wright. I love those fellows and I really miss them." Huey also expressed his disappointment in Fats Domino's absence. "About fifty-two years ago, I ventured over to Canal Street to the Saenger Center," he said. "I looked up, it was a big upright piano, and a gentleman was getting it! And then he went to yodeling, 'They call me the Fat Man!' But Fats is not well and he's not with us tonight. I'm sorry about that. I figured one day I would get on the same stage with Mr. Fats Domino."

When Quint Davis accepted his award that evening, he said, "Huey, you can come down to our festival in New Orleans. We'll get you where Fats Domino is."

"They say Fats was sick," Huey reflected later. "I heard that every time Fats have a date, he don't go. He don't care where it's at. They say Fats wouldn't help me neither, I'm like competition for him. But I had often said, way later on, Fats, with his name, like Barnum and Bailey, that circus, a show with Fats and others could have toured the nation, the world, forever. But Fats just wanted to be Fats, that's all. He wasn't interested. He wanted to be the only one, nobody else but him."

Although 9/11 didn't stop the Louisiana Blues Hall of Fame, it absolutely stopped any chance that the Tractors' "Rocking Pneumonia"–based song, "Nine Eleven," would become a national hit. The band and its record company had picked "Nine Eleven" to be among the singles from *Fast Girl*, released April 24, 2001. "We didn't release 'Nine Eleven' first," lead Tractor Steve Ripley explained, "because we thought it was the better song. We wanted it to come out two or three singles deep into the album." But then the September 11 terrorist attacks happened, and Ripley's happy dance number got shelved. "By the time we got two or three singles deep, that thing had happened," he said. "Of course, the whole music business died. Yeah, it stopped everything, the real 9/11."

Glenn Gaines printed cards citing himself as management for "Huey 'Piano' Smith: Rock & Roll Legend." He also assembled a record company–style bio of Huey, dated November 2001. The bio reported that Huey would be celebrating his fiftieth anniversary in the music business in 2002, release a new record, and tour the United States, Europe, and Australia.

Anticipating an Australian tour by Huey, Gaines arranged a rehearsal at Sound Services Recording Studio in New Orleans. He enlisted smoky-toned New Orleans vocalist John Boutte and a band including Wild Magnolias guitarist June Yamagishi and Deacon John Moore's bass- and classical guitar–playing brother, Charles. Boutte, a singer from the city's Seventh Ward who is often compared to Sam Cooke, would later find fame through his performance of the theme song for the HBO drama set in post-Katrina New Orleans, *Treme*. Waiting at the studio well past the scheduled starting time, Boutte grew impatient. "I was sitting around two hours, man," he said. "I was about to get up and leave and then I stopped and said, 'Oh, wait a minute. I'm about to meet a legend. If he shows up, it's worth it.' I figured they were late not because Huey was sitting around at home but because Glenn got there late to pick him up."

Gaines and Huey finally arrived, bringing an entourage of Smith family members with them. "And they all stepped out of a PT Cruiser," Boutte said. "It looked like a clown car because they must have been about twenty people came out that car! And they all sat around on the studio couches and they were very cool. I started working with them and doing Huey's stuff. 'Don't You Know Yockomo.' The words make no sense at all, man, but it's just so funny. 'Om my lady, two-way-poc-a-way.' And then we went to 'Coo Coo over You.' We did 'High Blood Pressure.' We did all of his tunes, man. I really was having fun. His tunes are not hard, but they don't have to be hard to be good, man. I mean, they simple and just timeless. You can't get those tunes out of your head."

The sixty-seven-year-old Huey was nothing like Boutte expected. "People say he's such a recluse, he's this, that, and the other. That gave me the impression that he was difficult. But I found him to be very normal and entertaining. At first I was, like, 'Maybe he's a little bit old.' But he didn't look that old!"

Pearl Edwards, the powerfully expressive singer heard on many of Huey's 1960s recordings, died in New Orleans in November 2001. She was sixty-seven. Her obituary listed her as "a professional singer with Huey 'Piano' Smith and the Clowns and the Tick Tocks music groups."

"Curley Moore," Huey said after learning of Pearl's death, "he laid up there when nobody was burying him. Tell me Toussaint and Marshall Sehorn picked up the tab. Of course, I plan mine to be cheap. If I go before Armageddon and I have to be resurrected, I plan cremation. And like they do memorials? Uh-uh. A lot of people get cremated with no announcement, memorial, nothing. Just see you later. Say like Bobby Charles, 'After while, crocodile.'"

T he Smiths' bankruptcy case closed November 27, 2001. Judge Phillips's days as a bankruptcy judge were about to close as well. In January 2002, the U.S. Court of Appeals for the Fifth Circuit declined to reappoint him. The court does not publish its reasons for a judge's dismissal, but a reporter at the *Baton Rouge Advocate* who covered the federal courts said Phillips's "judicial tempera-ment" led to his discharge. Within the Baton Rouge legal community, it was suggested that Phillips's contradictions of the Fifth Circuit's opinions contrib-uted to the end of his federal appointment. Phillips contradicted the appeals court in 1998, for instance, when he signed an order declaring that 50 percent of the songwriter publishing royalties for "Rocking Pneumonia," "Sea Cruise," "High Blood Pressure," and "Don't You Just Know It" was not the property of the Smiths' bankruptcy estate.

W hen the New Orleans Jazz and Heritage Festival released its schedule on February 17, 2002, Huey "Piano" Smith was the second performer listed on a press release containing hundreds of acts, just after the top-listed jazz trumpeter and composer Wynton Marsalis. Huey's name preceded those of rock star Lenny Kravitz, Jimmy Buffett, and homegrown stars the Neville Broth-ers, Dr. John, and Allen Toussaint. *Times-Picayune* music writer Keith Spera made special note of Huey's pending festival return in a story about the lineup. Gerri Hall mentioned the interest in Huey during a visit to Baton Rouge. "They want Huey to come out and put that bottom in our music so bad they can taste it like red beans and rice!" An *Advocate* reporter who'd gotten an advance list of the Jazz Fest performers sent an email message to Huey about his announced appearance. The surprised Huey replied: "I would not have known about the appearance at the Jazz Festival if you had not informed me." Huey sent another message to the reporter six days later. "It's all really baffling to me, inasmuch as, no one bothered to mention this engagement to me, still, up to this day."

As the Jazz Fest approached, Huey got an offer one evening to perform in

New Orleans. "Glenn Gaines was outside across the street," he remembered. "Sit out there about a' hour. Then he knocked on the door and hand her [Margrette] that. He say this got to be accepted before midnight tonight. The offer was for $8,000. And it was never a Jazz Festival mentioned to this day by Glenn Gaines. It was the House of Blues."

On April 5, 2002, the *Times-Picayune* reported that the much-anticipated return of Huey "Piano" Smith to the Jazz and Heritage Festival had been canceled. "The announcement that he would perform at the 2002 New Orleans Jazz and Heritage Festival on May 4 was hailed as the return of one of New Orleans's lost legends," Keith Spera wrote. "However, Jazzfest said this week that Smith decided not to perform. Smith's manager, Glenn Gaines, was traveling overseas at press time and was unavailable for comment."

On May 4, the *Times-Picayune* ran a lengthy story about Huey's absence from the Jazz Fest that day. "I was really looking forward to it," Huey told Spera. "I wanted to see Dave Bartholomew and all of them. It's disappointing to me. . . . Glenn hurt me to my heart." Gaines told the newspaper that he suspected Huey made excuses for not joining the Wild Magnolias during a March tour of Australia. Huey objected to the comment. "Why have I got to make an excuse for something I don't want to do?" he asked. "I ain't chasing no career. I ain't sleeping on no floor. I ain't trying to hustle no red beans and rice."

Earl King, Robert Parker, and others believed that, though Huey wasn't performing in public, his creativity must be intact. "I think he got a lot of stuff in his head right now he created that he ain't come forward with," Earl said. "He don't write stuff down, like I do. I don't know how he keep all that stuff crammed up in his head. Because I think I would go berserk. But that's Huey. If somebody came in to him and say, 'I want you to do an album,' he would have the material in his head to do that album. I'm just sorry that Huey stopped."

Dr. John felt differently than his friend Earl. After the heartache Huey experienced in the music business, Dr. John wouldn't blame him if he never stepped on a stage or in a studio again. "Look, how many times can you accept that you've been screwed and you 'bout to get screwed some more, and feel any kind of way good about anything? Really, Huey don't owe music nothin'. He just owes Huey somethin'."

Singer John Boutte was disappointed that Huey's Jazz Fest performance didn't happen, but not surprised. "We had like two, three rehearsals, man," he said. "And no one never calls me back to say why it wasn't gonna happen. Nothing. I'm just sitting there in a lurch. I don't know if it was Glenn, if it was Huey, if it was the Jazz Fest, or who knows? In New Orleans you never can figure that stuff out, man. It's like reading tea leaves on who gets on, who doesn't get on, who gets paid, who doesn't get paid. I ain't lying to you." Even so, Boutte's brush with Huey put a potent new song in his repertoire. "Every time I play 'Coo Coo over You,' with my country guys, my jazz guys, or whoever it is, people lose it, man. Everybody's right on it." Bassist Charles Moore, part of the band that rehearsed for the gig that never was, said Huey's heart wasn't in it. "It was a good idea," Moore said. "Glenn got on him, to make Huey think about his fans, but he was more worried about what God would think. You can't tell him how wonderful he is or speak of his part in the music of New Orleans. He don't care nothing to that. You can't praise him because he gives all praise to God."

Like Huey, Rock and Roll Hall of Fame inductee Dave Bartholomew did not play the 2002 Jazz Festival. "I wasn't there because we were never asked," he said. "Quint Davis and I, we're not on the same page." Told that the *Times-Picayune* reported that Huey was offered $3,500 to play Jazz Fest that year, Bartholomew couldn't believe it. "You mean $35,000?" he asked. No, $3,500. "Aw, shit!" Bartholomew said before erupting in a long spell of deep laughter. "That's a joke! That's a joke, man. But one thing I know about the Jazz Fest: I've been to all of them, almost all over the world, and this is the greatest one, this one here. You can't take that away from it."

When Bartholomew, Huey Smith, Deacon John Moore, Dr. John, and their peers from New Orleans's classic era of rhythm-and-blues reminisce, they tap experiences others can't begin to understand. "Listen," Dr. John said. "If I'm sitting and talking with a bunch a guys, all of us from New Orleans, we be laughing about shit that ain't even funny to somebody else. We don't want to remember it as a *drag*."

As early as the 1980s, promoter and deejay manager turned vintage records dealer Jim Russell was angry about what he saw as the lack of New Orleans and Louisiana talent at the Jazz and Heritage Festival. He told Huey he wanted to start an alternative festival. "Even today," the then eighty-two-year-old Russell said in 2002, "I'm still hoping that I can get something together and we'll have our own jazz fest. But I could not get all of them together at any one time. Huey was enthused, but he couldn't help me. You see, the New Orleans recording artists are helpless. From the beginning of time to the end of time, they're all helpless!"

n July 2002, W. Steven Mannear, the lawyer Huey hired when Artists Rights Enforcement sued him in New York in 1988, remembered his former client, but not much about the case. "It's not often that you are fortunate enough to have clients who have some celebrity, as opposed to some infamy," Mannear said. "I don't recall what gigantic percentage Huey was supposed to pay him [Chuck Rubin] and I don't recall if that company actually did anything." The years of continued legal woes that followed his representation of Huey, the attorney added, "dramatically display the pitfalls of the system and how people were taken advantage of, which was fairly uniform for black artists."

In Los Angeles in June 2003, Dr. John spoke about Huey's misfortune again. "I mean, it's tyrannical that even after all this time, it's like the money is still funny. Johnny Vincent's done passed away and somebody is still making the money, but it ain't nobody that actually made the music. I remember I was so glad to see Huey get out from under Johnny and do the thing for Lew Chudd. When does he do it? Right when Lew Chudd's selling Imperial Records. It was just like he couldn't catch the right breaks, even though he caught breaks."

John Fred Gourrier, Huey's fellow songwriter and Baton Rouge resident, also sympathized. "Man, look, just 'Rocking Pneumonia' and 'Sea Cruise,' those two right there, are millions of dollars. You got to remember, man, Huey wrote these songs, but Johnny Vincent put his name on there as cowriter, which was a lie. I'm not sure Huey ever signed any publishing agreements. Johnny just took the publishing. I collected a lot of my money, but poor Huey, I don't think he collected much of his."

Deacon John Moore felt for Huey, too. "I guess as a businessperson, much can be said about Johnny Vincent," he said. "He produced a lot of hit records from New Orleans. But I wasn't privy to the deals they made to do all these records. I was just a guitar player. I wouldn't know what to say about things like that, except to express the sentiments of a lot of the artists who fooled with those kind of producers in those days. 'Hey, we got messed over, man.'"

Complaints from Huey, Earl King, James "Sugar Boy" Crawford, the Meters, and other New Orleans recording artists and songwriters about not receiving just compensation for their songs and recordings were echoed by countless others from coast to coast. Bo Diddley, who recorded for Chicago's Chess Records, was one more example. "I don't hate the Chess people for giving me the opportunity to be who I am today," the seventy-four-year-old who popularized the much-imitated Bo Diddley beat said in 2003. "But I've never seen a royalty check from them. I trusted them to do the right thing and it didn't happen. You're looking at a dude who should be a millionaire. Chess Records helped a lot of people and then destroyed them."

Like Huey, the classic rhythm-and-blues vocal group the Coasters found themselves at the losing end of a lawsuit brought by Chuck Rubin. "It appears like he's helping you, and on the other hand he's destroying you," Coasters co-founder Carl Gardner said. "He collects 50 percent of anybody's money. I just can't stand the man, but he caught me in a trick bag like." When Coasters member Billy Guy died in November 2002 in Las Vegas, his body lay unclaimed in a mortuary for weeks. The *Las Vegas Sun* reported that the singer's friends were not surprised that Guy died without funds to pay for his burial. After Jerry Leiber and Mike Stoller, composers of many Coasters' hits, volunteered to contribute to the cost of the singer's burial, Rubin announced that he'd match them. "We have an obligation, a moral responsibility, to get involved," Rubin said. "Billy entertained millions of people with a beautiful expression of Leiber and Stoller's music, giving it a voice that will live forever."

Earl King, singer, guitarist, and composer, died April 17, 2003, of complications from diabetes. His newest CD—a great group of songs cut for Marshall Sehorn and Allen Toussaint in 1972 that had never before been issued in the United States—was released the day before his memorial service at New Orleans's grand Gallier Hall on St. Charles Avenue. Earl's surviving rhythm-and-blues peers joined his family to honor one of their own, making the service a musical gathering that could happen only in New Orleans. Dave Bartholomew was there, as were Gerri Hall, Earl Palmer, Dr. John, Irma Thomas, "Guitar" Joe Daniels, Raymond Lewis, Smokey Johnson, Wilson "Willie Tee" Turbinton, Wardell Quezergue, Jim Russell, George Porter Jr., Lloyd Washington of the Ink Spots, Antoinette K-Doe, pianist Henry Butler, Deacon John Moore, Quint Davis, and Cosimo Matassa.

"It's not easy when you have to turn somebody loose," Matassa said as he viewed Earl's body in one of Gallier Hall's ornate, high-ceilinged rooms.

Attendees were given ribbons to wear, the same shade of purple as the deceased blues man's suit and the huge bouquet of roses at the foot of his coffin. The memorial's music included Aaron Neville's emotion-choked renditions of "Amazing Grace" and "Ave Maria." Dave Bartholomew led the crowd in "Down by the Riverside" and then blew his muted trumpet for "Just a Closer Walk with Thee." "Earl King," Bartholomew said, "is the only one who could get a crowd out this early in the morning." Dr. John, rather than sing or play, said a few words from a stage above the open casket. His account of Earl educating local musicians about the music business inspired laughter from a room full of singers, players, songwriters, and recording artists who largely believed they had not been paid fairly for what they'd created. "We all just wanted to play music," Dr. John reflected before adding that it was Earl who, realizing music wasn't only about music, founded his own publishing company in 1962. "If you don't own the publishing for your songs, guess what? You ain't gonna see the money. It's a very simple equation."

Producer and jazz musician Harold Battiste, whose credits include Sonny and Cher hits and Dr. John's landmark early albums, dubbed Earl a philosopher. "Whenever I was in the presence of Earl, I felt like I would learn something you couldn't learn in school or from a book," he said. King's closest friend, "Guitar" Joe Daniels, coaxed to the stage by the master of ceremonies, Tony Owens, could summon just a few words. "He was a great, great, great man." Willie Tee, who recorded Earl's song "Teasin' You," sounded a cautionary note. "One of the things we have to do is find a better way to give the flowers to our legends before they pass."* Raymond Lewis, another friend and fellow recording artist, said, "Everything I have heard about Earl today is the Gospel truth."

Following the service, hundreds of people outside on St. Charles Avenue watched as Earl's coffin was carried down Gallier Hall's steps to a horse-drawn, glass-paneled hearse. On a hot spring day in New Orleans, Dr. John led the traditional second-line parade to Louis Armstrong Park. Wiping a tear from her eye, Gerri Hall said, "When people like Guitar Slim, Earl King, and Professor Longhair pass, there's no music in New Orleans no more. Nobody can make the noise they make."

Despite Dr. John's many attempts to contact Huey about Earl's memorial service, he didn't reach him. Huey's oldest sister, Oddress, in fact, had died four days earlier.

---

*Influential singer-keyboardist Wilson "Willie Tee" Turbinton died four years later at sixty-three. His sixty-five-year-old saxophonist brother, Earl, died five weeks before him. Both musicians were exiled from New Orleans after Hurricane Katrina and the flood of August 2005.

n April 2003, two years after Rosemary Prater's suit against Artists Rights Enforcement, two more of Chuck Rubin's clients, Rosalind Holmes and Annette Beard Sterling of the Motown group the Vandellas, sued him. Claiming Rubin and attorney Ira Greenberg were not entitled to a perpetual share of their recording artists royalties, the plaintiffs sought to terminate their Artists Rights contracts. The pair's other claims against Rubin included substandard accounting, lack of efforts to find new sources of royalties, and an unfair return on the cost of being his clients. Vandellas attorney Gregory J. Reed conducted a deposition of Rubin in Detroit. The transcript contains much discussion of the wording of the disputed contract:

> REED: . . . it doesn't say "thereafter" or "forever." So then where is the conclusion of the collection?
>
> RUBIN: It's in the explanation that we gave to the young ladies.
>
> REED: . . . It is not written in your agreement?
>
> RUBIN: It is, in that language.
>
> REED: If I am not mistaken, you said it was in your explanation to the ladies?
>
> RUBIN: As well.
>
> REED: Why wasn't it written in English?
>
> RUBIN: It is written in English.

Reed questioned Rubin about his suits against the Coasters, the Tams, the Richard Berry estate, Donald Storball (composer and, as a member of the Capitols, performer of "Cool Jerk"), Rosemary Prater, and Huey Smith. Rubin, speaking of Artists Rights Enforcement's work for Huey, described the company's 1982 out-of-court settlement with the Levy family, executed over a period of four months, as a bitterly fought case in which his company prevailed on behalf of its deprived client. "Our job is to help artists," he insisted. But Rubin's deposition answers contained multiple inaccuracies. He told Reed that Huey attempted to terminate his contract with Artists Rights Enforcement six to twelve months after the September 1982 collection from the Levy settlement. Actually, Huey unambiguously fired Rubin and Richard Linn twenty months after the collection. Also inaccurate was Rubin's claim that Judge John V. Parker found that Huey could not fire Artists Rights Enforcement. The judge said the contract with Rubin could be terminated but that payment for services rendered by Rubin prior to termination must be made in perpetuity. Nor was Cotillion Music,

Inc., as Rubin told Reed during the deposition, a party in the suit tried in Parker's court. Of the Smiths' bankruptcy, Rubin said, "we interceded on his behalf again, we worked it out so that he could become whole and escape bankruptcy. . . . He collected a huge amount of money in the beginning, and then, at the end, he collected well over a hundred thousand dollars, escaping bankruptcy as a result of our coming to his aid." U.S. District Court Judge Robert H. Cleland in Detroit ruled in favor of Rubin. The judge refused to stop Rubin from collecting 50 percent of the Vandellas' royalties, rejected the singers' claims that Artists Rights Enforcement's percentage was unconscionably high, and found there was no evidence of fraud or deceit.

In January 2011, Artists Rights Enforcement's website reported that the company had five hundred clients. But that same month another of Rubin's clients, the Guy Mitchell and Betty J. Mitchell Family Trust, expressed its displeasure with the company through a lawsuit. Guy Mitchell, a white pop star of the 1950s, recorded hits for Columbia Records, including "Singin' the Blues," "My Heart Cries for You," and "Heartaches by the Number." Filed in Spokane, Washington, the complaint includes conversion of property, breach of fiduciary duty, common law fraud, and negligent misrepresentation. The action seeks accounting, injunctive relief, declaratory judgment, and damages. At the time of this writing, the trial had been delayed.

Huey "Piano" Smith believes that federal courts in Louisiana erred in deciding two suits against him in favor of Artists Rights Enforcement. He further believes, as he has for decades, that Johnny Vincent never had legitimate ownership of his songs. "My wife, she be, 'Shhh.' I say, 'No. It's like the light. If the light is on something people are doing wrong, the public will try to do us right. But that judicial system is horrible. I read something about what a judge was paid—a pork chop dinner! That's all, not no lot of money. But in a case like mine, the judges and lawyers don't care nothing about me—but I know congressmen who wrote federal copyright laws do care. This is the United States, that other countries look to, to follow. If the United States is to take the lead in regulating music activity, it's got to do a little better. They can't let this go like this. They making a fool out of the United States."

Spoken in 2001, the composer's words about systemic corruption among elected and appointed officials in Louisiana rang true many times thereafter.

The state's more spectacular recent corruption prosecutions include the U.S. Senate's 2010 impeachment of New Orleans federal judge Thomas Porteous. The Senate convicted Porteous of accepting cash from lawyers and gifts and favors from bail bond executives, and of lying during his personal bankruptcy case. In Porteous's defense, Georgetown University professor Jonathan Turley argued that the sixty-three-year-old jurist's acceptance of money, gifts, and favors is business as usual in Louisiana.

Coda

To me he was the man that got more out of simplicity than anybody in New Orleans," drummer Earl Palmer said nearly fifty years after he recorded Huey Smith's "Little Liza Jane" and "Everybody's Whalin'" at Cosimo Matassa's studio. "And everything Huey did was just wrapped in New Orleans. We used to always say he sounds like those downtown piano players down in Tremé, where I came up. I hope he can come out of his shell enough to perform some more. Because he can get heard by some more people, man, and they can find out who really instigated a lot of that music."

Like Palmer, John Boutte, the soulful New Orleans singer who rehearsed with Huey in 2002, noted the economy in Huey's music. "Such simple stuff with so few chords," he said. "Not all this complicated bullshit, man. Just something that hits a groove that's so heavy that you can't help but want to rock to it."

"Huey is like Professor Longhair and Fats Domino," Gerri Hall said. "They the only ones who have the rhythm in their fingers."

Huey's name, said Austin, Texas–based singer-pianist and New Orleans music lover Marcia Ball, has never left the lips of those who know the history of the city's music. "If you play 'Rocking Pneumonia,' people dance," she said. "They just can't help it. I do 'Don't You Just Know It' for the same reason. I guess that's the magic of Huey."

A gift for writing songs that combine humor with instinctive, infectious groove, Tractors leader Steve Ripley said, plus natural-born New Orleans piano playing, have earned Huey a place in the Rock and Roll Hall of Fame. "It's not something you can practice and grow up to be," Ripley said. "It's in you already. It's in Huey. He should be in the Hall of Fame. Lesser people get in there, but he is a logical candidate because he's a prime mover of rock 'n' roll. He's an originator of something and that's so rare. He's where the roots of this tree run."

"The guys up here in New York," Jesse Thomas said, "they just love Huey's piano playing. They all say they can't get that sound, can't get their fingers to play like that. He really has a special touch. If you do a big study of music, Beethoven and stuff like that, it's sometimes limiting to you. But when you play from a feeling, or a touch, you just hit something and, *boom*, find out that it's right. I call it 'playing definitely.'"

"His touch is just impeccable, as far as the genre was played down here," Allen Toussaint said. "A very smooth, funky feeling."

"Yeah," Jesse added, "drummers and piano players from New Orleans. The New Orleans drummers say, 'Look, it's just something we feel.'"

A drummer from James Brown's band who'd periodically visit New Orleans drummer Bob French told him, "I want you to show me how to do that New Orleans thing." French demonstrated the style many times, but Brown's drummer never mastered it. "But I can take a kid from New Orleans," French explained, "who's eight years old and show him the same lick and he'll play it in five minutes. Because he's been hearing it all his life! We bring the New Orleans street beat to the bandstand. It's our thing!"

Saxophonist Alvin "Red" Tyler said much the same at the 1995 New Orleans Jazz and Heritage Festival. "Whether we playing rhythm-and-blues, gospel, straight ahead jazz, we all hear second line."

Robbie Robertson, one of fifty artists asked in 2010 by *Rolling Stone* to pick their personal Top 10s, listed fifteen recordings by New Orleans acts. "Rocking Pneumonia and the Boogie Woogie Flu" is No. 2 on his list, just behind the Wild Tchoupitoulas' "Hey Pocky A-Way." Beneath the latter two songs are Fats Domino's "Blue Monday," Professor Longhair's "Tipitina," and other classics by Dr. John, Lloyd Price, Aaron Neville, the Neville Brothers, the Meters, Lee Dorsey, Clarence "Frogman" Henry, Shirley and Lee, Jessie Hill, Clarence "Gatemouth" Brown, and the Dixie Cups. "It's such feel-good music," Robertson said of the city's music. "You don't care about finding deep meaning. It's a celebration of life."

As the Smiths' bankruptcy left them progressively poorer in the 1990s, Davis Rogan, the singer, pianist, and leader of the eight-piece New Orleans funk band All That, recruited musician friends to join him in tribute nights at the Mermaid Lounge. Before doing Rolling Stones and Ramones nights, he devoted his first tribute show to classic comic rhythm-and-blues vocal group the Coasters. Rogan decided to honor a New Orleans act during his second tribute night, one contemporary with the Coasters. Huey "Piano" Smith and the Clowns was an easy choice. Performed June 21 and July 11, 1997, the show featured songs by both Huey and the Coasters.

Rogan, a long-time deejay at WWOZ, later inspired a principal character in HBO's *Treme*. In the series, Davis McAlary is an aspiring songwriter, music scenester, and fervent defender of New Orleans music and culture. The real Rogan, like other WWOZ deejays through the decades, has a knowledge of local recordings that stretches into the deepest corners of the individual artists' vinyl discographies. Digging past Huey's relatively accessible Ace Records catalog, Rogan owned a collection of his Instant label 45s as well, acquired from Jim Russell's vintage record store on Magazine Street.

"I chose Huey Smith over [Allen] Toussaint for a tribute because his songs have the same childlike but amazingly funny value that the Coasters have," Rogan explained. "There's a youthful playfulness about 'Coo Coo over You' and 'Free, Single and Disengaged' and 'You Ain't No Hippie.'" Rogan also admired the way Huey wrote songs for a cast of singers, just as Jerry Leiber and Mike Stoller had for the Coasters.

The musician friends Rogan enlisted to play the Huey tribute at the Mermaid Lounge included guitarist Alex Chilton. The reclusive rock 'n' roll legend of Box Tops and Big Star fame had moved to New Orleans in 1982. Rogan, Chilton, and music journalist Robert Palmer all lived within blocks of each other. Chilton agreed to participate in the tributes as long as he didn't have to be front man. "A little five-man collaboration was about as much work as Alex felt like doing," Rogan said. "I remember both he and [Astral Project bassist James] Singleton remarking on how it was great to take Huey's tunes apart, see how they tick and how well-crafted they were. Huey was a soundtrack for them when they grew up."

The tribute's set list featured songs Rogan and such fellow WWOZ deejays as Jivin' Gene and Billy Delle played during their weekly programs. "It's a shame," Rogan said, "that above and beyond the [Johnny Rivers] cover of 'Rocking Pneumonia,' everybody in the United States and the world doesn't know all of these songs." Rogan recorded the tribute night performances on DAT tape. But like thousands of recordings, scores, instruments, photos, and other irreplaceable

New Orleans music and memorabilia, the tape was lost in the floodwaters that followed Hurricane Katrina's landfall on August 29, 2005.

A few weeks before the storm, Gregory Tyler, son of saxophonist and amateur photographer Alvin "Red" Tyler, decided he had better buy a scanner and digitize the many volumes of photos his father took of his New Orleans musician peers. Before the Alaska-dwelling Tyler could return home to follow through, his father's house, photos included, became one of the 275,000 Gulf Coast homes destroyed by Katrina and its flooding aftermath.

Sundays at the West Congregation Kingdom Hall in Baton Rouge—fifty-some years after the hits, the nights at the Dew Drop Café, Club Tiajuana, and the Apollo, and the recording sessions at Cosimo Matassa's studios—Huey "Piano" Smith softly sings the lyrics of the gentle, nonsyncopated hymns in his Jehovah's Witnesses hymnal. The man whose middle name is Piano finds peace and comfort in the promise of a new life far greater than anything mortal existence can give.

Don't you just know it.

NOTES

INTRODUCTION: NEW ORLEANS

1   **"Blues is kind of a revenge"**: Lomax, *The Land Where the Blues Began*, 461.

2   **"The smallest you've ever seen"**: Palmer, Rock and Roll Hall of Fame interview.

3   **"When I was a kid"**: Delle, "Wavelength Interview: Robert Plant," 7.

1. ROBERTSON STREET BOOGIE

5   **"Every man a king"**: Long, "Carry Out the Command of the Lord."

5   **Dearly loved his father**: Roberts, WBRH-FM interview with Huey "Piano" Smith.

9   **"We stress equality of opportunity"**: "Negro Says He Will Seek Post of Governor," 8A.

9   **Huey heard Dixieland bands**: Roberts, WBRH-FM interview with Huey "Piano" Smith.

9   **Blackface minstrel shows**: Tosches, *Where Dead Voices Gather*, 271.

10 **Biggest star of the 1940s**: Whitburn, *Top R&B/Hip-Hop Singles, 1942–2001*, 309.

12 **He preferred simply playing**: Roberts, WBRH-FM interview with Huey "Piano" Smith.

12 **To finance music lessons**: Berry, Foose, and Jones, *Up from the Cradle of Jazz*, 46.

12 **Huey's interest in the piano**: Roberts, WBRH-FM interview with Huey "Piano" Smith.

12 **"We played little games at school"**: Wirt, "Smith's Legacy Rooted in '50s Rock 'n' Roll," Fun, 10.

14 **Many Darnell hits**: Penny, *The Chronological Larry Darnell, 1949–1951*.

14 **"Fess" kicked the piano in rhythm**: Roberts, WBRH-FM interview with Huey "Piano" Smith, 1988.

14 **"I was just listening with admiration"**: Coleman, unpublished interview with Huey "Piano" Smith.

14 **"Just deep down funk"**: Jones, "Living Blues Interview: Professor Longhair," 24.

15 **"You're great!!"**: Winslow (aka Dr. Daddy-O), "Boogie-Beat Jive," 13.

2. NEW ARRIVALS

17   "I want you to meet him": Roberts, WBRH-FM interview with Huey "Piano" Smith.

17   Hoping to become a recording artist: Berry, Foose and Jones, "Huey 'Piano' Smith and Guitar Slim," 22.

17   "Nobody knew about this boy": Scott, "New Orleans' Cousin Joe," 22.

19   Slim's shadow: Roberts, WBRH-FM interview with Huey "Piano" Smith.

19   An exact copy of Clarence "Gatemouth" Brown: "Guitar Slim Bows at Painia's: Held Over for 2nd Big Uptown Week," 14.

19   Outhouse: Coleman, unpublished interview with Huey "Piano" Smith.

19   "Aesthetic guidepost": Zappa and Occhiogrosso, The Real Frank Zappa Book, 179.

19   "I wanted to be Guitar Slim": Guy and Ritz, When I Left Home, 42.

20   "Feeling very proud of him": Butler, letter to Huey P. Smith, September 16, 2001.

20   "Maybe next time": Coleman, unpublished interview with Huey "Piano" Smith.

21   The officers stopped musicians: Ibid.

22   Extended engagement at Grady's: Coleman, Blue Monday, 74.

22   "Business started coming": Berry, Foose, and Jones, Up from the Cradle of Jazz, 84.

23   Bullet's best sellers came in the late 1940s: James, The Bullet Records Story, 1–4.

23   Slim's real name, Eddie Jones: Hawkins, A Shot in the Dark, 108–109.

23   Huey couldn't wait to tell Johnny Vincent: "Specialty Buys Out Champion, Opens Brand," 17, 48.

24   "He's very friendly to us": Broven, Record Makers and Breakers, 478.

24   "You boys ought to be singing the blues": Hannusch, "Masters of Louisiana Music: Earl Silas Johnson IV," 21.

26   "We began to call patterns": Coleman, unpublished interview with Huey "Piano" Smith.

26   Vincent hired Ray Charles: Mabry, "An Interview with Johnny Vincent of Ace Records."

26   "He got in some trouble": "Making a Hit," 33.

26   A few dollars to sit in with the band: Jordan, "Ray Charles: An Offbeat Interview," 64–65.

26   "One of the very first cities that was good to me": Fumar, "Rapping with Ray," 116.

26   "Kept the reins on Slim": "Ray Charles, 1930–2004," 47.

26   "A pint and a half of gin: Hannusch, "Talkin' 'bout New Orleans," Offbeat, October 1998, 25.

27   "Black clubs in this town had big bands": Wirt, "Cosimo Matassa," Fun, 10.

28   "Congregating in a Negro saloon": "Zachary Scott Booked in Raid: Nine Held for Drinking in Negro Establishment," 19.

28   "You can put this in your memoirs": "Judge Acquits Zachary Scott in N.O. Court," 1, 6.

28   "A new show is on tap this week": "New Show Opens Friday, Band on Stand Nitely at Dew Drop," 4-B.

28   "We jammed, enjoyed each other": Wirt, "Jazz Lives in Eddie Bo," Fun, 12.

29   "Whatever club, it was morning till night": Wirt, "Smith's Legacy Rooted in '50s Rock 'n' Roll," Fun, 21.

29   "I've been on shows with them": Wirt, "K-Doe and 'Mother-in-Law' Ready to Go Another Round," Fun, 8.

29   "New Orleans is, to me, the capital of music": Spera, "A Little Bit of . . . Little Richard," 27.

29   "That's where I met Earl King": White, *The Life and Times of Little Richard,* 35.

30   "When I was a kid I listen at Professor Longhair": Coleman, unpublished interview with Huey "Piano" Smith.

30   "Go ahead, Slim. Make it": Ibid.

30   "Heading to New York City's famed Apollo Theater": "On Tour," B6.

30   Outdrew Sammy Davis Jr.: Berry, Foose, and Jones, *Up from the Cradle of Jazz,* 91.

30   "The dazzling splendors of the Negro genius": Schiffman, *Uptown,* 21.

3. THEY GOT ANOTHER GUITAR SLIM

31   "We need somebody to play guitar": Roberts, WBRH-FM interview with Huey "Piano" Smith.

31   "Saying things that people want to hear": Hannusch, "Masters of Louisiana Music: Earl Silas Johnson IV," 21.

32   "Show them how the piano work!": Hannusch, "Huey 'Piano' Smith," 20.

32   "As close to his records as possible": Coleman and Hannusch, *Shame, Shame, Shame,* 24.

32   "A white girl cut him out completely": Hilburn, "Bartholomew," 52.

32   "We just couldn't break him nationally": Coleman and Hannusch, *Shame, Shame, Shame,* 27.

34   "I figured Ace would be first": Hannusch, *I Hear You Knockin',* 130.

34   "I had me some royalties coming": Mabry, "An Interview with Johnny Vincent of Ace Records."

34   "That's not important": Jones, "Earl King," 19.

35   "I liked to die when I heard it": "Making a Hit," 34.

35   "I want to be me": Berry, Foose, and Jones, *Up from the Cradle of Jazz,* 86; WWOZ Earl King interview by Jeff Hannusch (pseud. Almost Slim).

36   "Real hard and groovy": WWOZ, interview with Frank Fields.

36   "All of them the best in New Orleans": White, *The Life and Times of Little Richard,* 47.

36   "You've *got* to sing it": Ibid., 50.

36   Richard's wild piano was essential: Ibid., 50, 51.

36   "It never struck me as a song you'd *record*": Ibid., 55.

36   "They had to stop and get the tuner": Coleman, *Little Richard: The Specialty Sessions,* box set notes, 24.

37   "Nobody has to tell you it's him": Wirt, "Cosimo Matassa," Fun, 10.

4. ACE RECORDING ARTIST

39   "Most of the recording artists didn't even write songs": "Interview with Huey 'Piano' Smith," *Louisiana Magazine,* WRBT-TV, Baton Rouge, 1978; *Artists Rights Enforcement Corp. against Cotillion Music, Inc., and Huey P. Smith,* Supreme Court of the State of New York, County of New York, November 1, 1988, deposition of Huey P. Smith.

41   **"I was the only white man in there"**: "Making a Hit," 33.

42   **"They took the road by storm"**: Coleman and Kruppa, *The Sweethearts of the Blues,* 16.

43   **Leaping from a coffin**: Morris, "Legendary Screamin' Jay Hawkins Dies at 70," 8.

43   **"2 Are Slain"**: "2 Are Slain Amidst Mardi Gras Gaiety," *Louisiana Weekly,* March 9, 1957, 1; "Mardi Gras 'Reveler' Is Fatally Shot," *Louisiana Weekly,* February 14, 1959, 1; "2 Die in Mardi Gras Crash," *Louisiana Weekly,* February 25, 1961, 1.

44   **"Breaking every attendance record on the seaboard circuit"**: "Shirley, Lee and Co. Here Jan. 6th," 10.

45   **Separate white and black seating arrangements**: Act No. 579, Acts of the State of Louisiana Regular Session (1956), 1054–1055.

47   **He danced for tips on Bourbon Street**: Payne, *The Great Drummers of R&B, Funk and Soul,* 11.

5. ROCKING PNEUMONIA

49   **"I wanna holla but the joint's too small"**: Wirt, "Smith's Legacy Rooted in '50s Rock 'n' Roll," Fun, 10.

50   **"Baptist mule"**: Jones, "Charles 'Hungry' Williams," 22–24.

51   **"It won't no big thing"**: Tyler, New Orleans Jazz and Heritage Festival Heritage Stage interview.

52   **Backed Bobby for "Helping Hand" and "Pity Poor Me"**: Hannusch, "Talkin' 'bout New Orleans: Bobby Marchan—The Ace Years," 65.

52   **He was ready to quit show business**: "Bobby Marchan Almost Gave Up; Now a 'Name,'" 8.

52   **"I ain't making no money here"**: Sandmel, interview with Bobby Marchan.

53   **"R&B Territorial Best Sellers" Top 5 for New Orleans**: "This Week's R&B Best Buys," 56; "R&B Territorial Best Sellers," 57.

54   **"It tore the house down"**: Foose, unpublished interview with Bobby Marchan.

55   **From behind the auditorium curtains**: "Jim Crow Spectre Nearly Floors Rock & Roll Show," 1, 8.

55   **"We were always clowning"**: Foose, unpublished interview with Bobby Marchan.

56   **"It's the sound"**: Hannusch, "Johnny Vincent Imbragulio, 1927–2000," 94.

56   **"That's where Johnny ends"**: WWOZ Earl King interview by Jeff Hannusch (pseud. Almost Slim).

6. ROCKIN' AND DRIVIN'

58   **"One laugh after another, all the time"**: Butler, letter to Huey P. Smith, September 16, 2001.

59   **"I don't want your sister!"**: Moore, *Hully Gully Fever,* CD notes, 9.

61   **"Had a stomp-down-party good time"**: Berry, Foose, and Jones, *Up from the Cradle of Jazz,* 88.

61   **"I handled all the business, period"**: Grady, "Singer Gave Voice to R&B Original: Marchan Takes Care of Business," B-1.

7. DON'T YOU JUST KNOW IT

65   **"Every time we would go somewhere"**: Sandmel, interview with Bobby Marchan.
66   **120,000 copies had been shipped**: Whitburn, *Joel Whitburn Presents Billboard Singles Reviews 1958*, 20.
66   **"It *scared* Johnny Vincent!"**: Sandmel, interview with Bobby Marchan.
66   **800,000 copies**: McNutt, *Guitar Towns*, 42.
66   **"I don't need to sell masters"**: "Ace Rejects 25G Bid for 'Know It' Master," 3.
67   **She refused to use the home's electric washing machine**: "New York Beat," 64.
67   **An eighteen-hole golf course**: City of New Orleans, "Pontchartrain Park Neighborhood Profile," 3.01–3.02.
68   **"Everybody just joined in"**: Roberts, WBRH-FM interview with Huey "Piano" Smith.
69   **"I'd like to be able to market *my other stuff*"**: "Up to His Ears in Tunes," *Times-Picayune*, Dixie Roto, 16, 19.
69   **"Those records were real big all through the Delta"**: Jordan, "Levon Helm," 89.
70   **A neighborhood band called Little Caesar and the Consuls**: Hoskyns, *Across the Great Divide*, 15.

8. CLOWNS ON STAGE

71   **"The most entertaining frantic-type acts on the bill"**: Bundy, "Avalon a Standout in Feld's New R&R Pkge," 7.
72   **"I'd make it go over big!"**: Foose, unpublished interview with Bobby Marchan.
74   **"Each individual was at liberty"**: Berry, Foose, and Jones, *Up from the Cradle of Jazz*, 90.
74   **"It'll make people laugh"**: Foose, unpublished interview with Bobby Marchan.
75   **"I know he'll never be a sissy!"**: Wirt, "Smith's Legacy Rooted in '50s Rock 'n' Roll," Fun, 10.
75   **"We went out so much without Huey Smith"**: Foose, unpublished interview with Bobby Marchan.
76   **"Little James Booker played piano"**: Ibid.
76   **"You got curls in your hair"**: Sandmel, interview with Bobby Marchan.
77   **"'Sock-O' job with plenty of punch"**: "Rock-Jamaica-Rock," *Daily Gleaner*, July 15, 1959, 7.
77   **Cliff recorded Jamaican hits**: Katz, *Solid Foundation*, 38.
78   **"Smiley Lewis, Professor Longhair, all the jazz people"**: Oumana, *We Are All One: The Best of Jimmy Cliff*, CD notes.
78   **"The Jamaican attempt to play the grooves of New Orleans R&B"**: Bordowitz, *Every Little Thing Gonna Be Alright*, 264.

78   The postponement of "Rock Jamaica Rock": "Rock-Jamaica-Rock," *Daily Gleaner,* July 30, 1959, 7.

9. SEA CRUISE

80   "Strong prospect for R&B coin": "The Billboard Spotlight Winners of the Week," *Billboard,* November 10, 1958, 36.

80   "John Brown was a slave liberator": Hannusch, *That'll Get It (Even More of the Best),* CD notes, 6.

80   "He paints something for the audience to appreciate": Roberts, WBRH-FM interview with Huey Smith.

80   "Yockomo" led the week's fifteen new arrivals: "Hot 100 Adds 15," 4.

81   Among 1958's million-sellers: "Bumper Crop of 45s Sold in '58," 4, 10.

81   "The horn of the boat made me feel": Smith, biography prepared for the Rhythm and Blues Foundation.

81   "'Loberta' was a street song": Roberts, WBRH-FM interview with Huey "Piano" Smith.

82   "You hear something you think is congas or bongos": Jones, "Living Blues Interview: Earl King," 19.

82   "I was always able to tell a hit": Smith, biography prepared for the Rhythm and Blues Foundation.

83   "'Sea Cruise' is a rocking blues": "The Billboard Spotlight Winners of the Week," *Billboard,* December 22, 1958, 38.

84   "'Sea Cruise' was cut to be the follow-up": Berry, Foose, and Jones, *Up from the Cradle of Jazz,* 114.

85   "We decided we were gonna get some of that market": "Making a Hit," 35.

85   "We were trying to git the white crowd": Mabry, "An Interview with Johnny Vincent of Ace Records."

85   "White records were selling a lot more than black records": Ford, New Orleans Jazz and Heritage Festival Heritage Stage interview.

85   "He would go into Cosmo's studio": Sandmel, interview with Bobby Marchan.

85   "I didn't think he had a chance": Grevatt, "On the Beat," 30.

85   "My hair did not turn red": Wirt, "'50s Teen Idol Frankie Ford Cruises in BR," Fun, 9.

86   "It was very nice to be in their company": Roberts, WBRH-FM interview with Huey "Piano" Smith.

86   Multiple weekends at the Dew Drop Café: "Charles Brown, Amos Milburn Open La. Tour," 15.

86   "I thought he was a good singer": Hannusch, *That'll Get It (Even More of the Best),* CD notes, 1, 2.

86   "I'll buy the whole box": WWOZ, interview with Chuck Carbo and Earl King, May 1, 1982.

87   Eddie "Guitar Slim" Jones died: Berry, Foose, and Jones, *Up from the Cradle of Jazz,* 91–92.

87   "He didn't take care of himself": Hannusch, "Lawrence Cotton," 29.

87   "He got two sons": Grady, "Bluesman's Done Got over Bad Luck, Trouble; The Things He Used to Do He's Not Doing Anymore," Metro, 1.

87   "Lord, have mercy": Foose, "Lord have mercy that was a good man!," 22.

88   "There's nothing I can do": Hannusch, "Talkin' 'bout New Orleans: Bobby Marchan— The Ace Years," 65.

88   "'You'll be sorry.' And he was": Sandmel, interview with Bobby Marchan.

89   "It was so different": Robinson, The Fire/Fury Records Story, box set notes, 8.

89   "We knew it was a smash": Sandmel, interview with Bobby Marchan.

89   "That was really one of the first raps": Robinson, The Fire/Fury Records Story, box set notes, 8.

89   "That was the funniest thing that happened to me": Foose, unpublished interview with Bobby Marchan.

10. THE MONEY'S FUNNY

90   1 percent royalty rate per record sold: "Making a Hit," 36.

90   the total cost for recording a session in the mid to late 1950s: Mabry, "An Interview with Johnny Vincent of Ace Records."

91   mechanical licenses . . . synchronization licenses: Krasilovsky and Shemel, This Business of Music, 192.

92   "Every artist thinks their record sells a million": Mabry, "An Interview with Johnny Vincent of Ace Records."

93   "I was scrupulous in paying the royalties": Frame and Howlett, In His Own Words.

93   "He's a hell of a promoter": Vera, The Specialty Story, 30.

93   Vincent formally established Ace Recording Company: Mabry, "The Rise and Fall of Ace Records," 438–39.

94   "This broke my back and it broke my heart": Berry, Foose, and Jones, Up from the Cradle of Jazz, 111–12.

94   "There were a lot of midnight sessions": Saperstein, The Best of Spinett, CD notes, 2.

95   They butchered the bodies: Akerman, "Who Killed Lumumba?"

95   "Everybody was talking about the Sputniks": Hannusch, "Talkin' 'bout New Orleans: Bobby Marchan—The Ace Years," 27.

96   Among the labels that practiced payola: Mabry, "The Rise and Fall of Ace Records," 446.

96   "Y'all got the wrong guy": Mabry, "An Interview with Johnny Vincent of Ace Records."

96   The sell-off cost him millions: Webber, "Dick Clark, 1929–2012," A-24.

98   "We thought that this would never end": Broven, Rhythm and Blues in New Orleans, 122.

98   "Fats had to have priority": Wirt, "Cosimo Matassa," Fun, 10.

98   "I could go in the studio": Dahl, "Fats Domino," 17, 71.

98   He might also miss sessions: Coleman, Blue Monday, 192, 193.

98   "He was a pain in the ass to record": Broven, Rhythm and Blues in New Orleans, 16.

98   **A white Steinway concert grand piano**: Hychew, "Dig Me!," 7.

99   **"It's the day for anybody"**: Ibid.

99   **Nabbed for buying marijuana**: Wright, "Mardi Gras Sad Day for Prof. Long Hair," 1, 15.

99   **"I wasn't making a living off of the music"**: Jones, "Living Blues Interview: Professor Longhair," 28.

100 **"It was Jones's version"**: Hannusch, *The Soul of New Orleans*, 159.

100 **The troupe included**: Dahl, *Motown*, 270–71.

11. POP-EYE

102 **New Orleans record stores also were getting requests**: "N.O. Twist Gives Way to Popeye Muscles," 1.

102 **"Pop-Eye" among the top three sellers**: "Record Ramblings," 18.

102 **"Imperial didn't record me no more"**: Roberts, WBRH-FM interview with Huey "Piano" Smith.

103 **"He thought the label should be one-track"**: Coleman, *Blue Monday*, 193.

12. CHRISTMAS BLUES

107 **Not the usual Christmas fare**: "Strong Sales Potential," 16.

109 **"Made Sugar Boy get out of the car"**: Hannusch, "Backtalk," 100.

109 **A second operation several weeks later**: Berry, "Davell Crawford Comes of Age," 44.

109 **"They hit me in my head"**: Berry, Foose, and Jones, *Up from the Cradle of Jazz*, 78.

109 **"I had a brain injury"**: Stroup, "'Jock-A-Mo' Composer Will Sing at Jazz Fest," D-4.

109 **"I looked for other things to do with my life"**: Hannusch, "Backtalk," 100.

112 **"John Fitzgerald Kennedy, our symbol of hope"**: "A Martyr to Freedom," 1, 12.

13. PITTER PATTING

113 **In Great Britain**: Spitz, *The Beatles: The Biography*, 448.

113 **The parade of shaggy British invaders**: Gould, *Can't Buy Me Love*, 250, 251.

113 **"That was different times right then"**: *New Orleans Soul '60s: Watch Records*, CD notes, 4.

114 **A cabaret act on Bourbon Street**: Wirt, "Ford Has Lifetime Ticket aboard 'Cruise,'" Fun, 10.

114 **"I won't be doing this song anymore!"**: Wirt, "Time Really Is on Irma Thomas' Side," Fun, 8.

114 **"I went into hiding"**: Wirt, "Teen Idol Jimmy Clanton Still Rocking, Rolling," Fun, 9.

114 **"We couldn't get back on the radio"**: Price, New Orleans Jazz and Heritage Festival Heritage Stage interview.

114 **"Sang the alimony blues Monday"**: "Alimony Blues Sung for Judge," 11.

114 **"American artists, we cried a lot"**: Wirt, "Connie Francis Is Everybody's Baby but the Hit-Maker Is Nobody's Fool," *Fun*, 8.

115 **"There's no hospitalization, no retirement"**: "New Orleans Jazzman 'Red' Tyler Dies," 6A.

115 **"I blowed it all"**: McNutt, *Guitar Towns*, 43.

115 **"The lights had gone dim in the joints"**: Dr. John and Rummel, *Under a Hoodoo Moon*, 2.

115 **"It's not that I am against stripping"**: Clayton, "Crusader or Opportunist?" A1, A6.

116 **"Huey is a proud man"**: Butler, letter to Huey P. Smith, September 16, 2001.

118 **Thwarting the chance to fully exploit**: Coleman, unpublished interview with Huey "Piano" Smith.

118 **The song earned five mentions in *Billboard***: "Spotlight Singles," 73.

118 **Regional breakout**: "Regional Breakouts," 34.

118 **"A stone monster in Texas"**: "Radio-TV Programming," 79.

121 **It, too, didn't chart**: Tosches, *Hellfire*, 194.

121 **"We wanted to do a record that sounded"**: Sebastian, *The Lovin' Spoonful Anthology*, CD notes.

122 **Running his producer's phone bill up**: Coleman, unpublished interview with Huey "Piano" Smith.

122 **"Larry is a sensational singer"**: Emery, "Dig Me! . . . ," section 1, page 10.

14. JEHOVAH'S WITNESS

125 **"We go house to house, door to door"**: Wirt, "Smith's Legacy Rooted in '50s Rock 'n' Roll," *Fun*, 10.

128 **"You got a lotta talent"**: Wirt, "Easterling an Unsung Regional Music Standout from '60s," *Fun*, 18.

128 **Eroded Easterling's momentum**: Coleman, *Taking Inventory*, album notes.

128 **"That's called soul"**: Wirt, "Easterling an Unsung Regional Music Standout from '60s," *Fun*, 18.

130 **"Put a little salt in the stew"**: Ibid.

15. ROCKING PNEUMONIA, PART II

135 **Levy acknowledges Vincent's sale of the four songs**: Levy, letter to Johnny Vincent, September 12, 1972.

136 **"Mac and I saw eye to eye"**: Wexler and Ritz, *Rhythm and the Blues*, 257.

137 **"Wounded in the chest and the neck"**: "Woman Is Shot to Death Mistakenly by Husband," sec. 1, p. 2.

137 **"We gonna do our thing outside where he got killed"**: Lee, "Chief's Funeral Held Saturday," sec. 1, p. 22.

137 "There have been many songs about John": Neville et al., *The Brothers Neville*, 280.

139 "The terrible irony of prisons in the South": Wirt, "Symposium Gives Angola Inmates Musical Encouragement," Fun, 10.

139 Huey signed an employment contract: Levy, contract for legal representation of Huey P. Smith.

140 "I set myself up for a fall": Berry, Foose, and Jones, *Up from the Cradle of Jazz*, 139.

141 "It is further ordered, adjudged and decreed": *Huey P. Smith v. John V. Imbragulio*. U.S. District Court, Eastern District of Louisiana. January 1, 1974.

142 Frequently depressed and drinking heavily: Pattison, "Chris Kenner," 8.

142 "It's a sad thing about Chris": Roberts, WBRH-FM interview with Huey "Piano" Smith.

16. DISASTER AT SEA-SAINT

145 "International heroes walking the street every day": Wein and Chinen, *Myself among Others*, 369.

146 "Only been five great singers of rhythm and blues": Sandmel, *Ernie K-Doe*, 179.

146 Emperor of the World: Ibid., 6.

146 "I work for the Almighty": Steffens, "In the Tracks of the Stepping Razor," 51.

149 "People just might forget his middle name": Fumar, "Music—Huey 'Piano' Smith," *States-Item*, November 11, 1978, Lagniappe, 6, 28.

150 "Their performance was superb": Richardson, "The 'Comeback' of Huey Smith, 1979–1980," 15.

151 "The joy of Huey Smith's records is retroactive": Marcus, *Stranded*, 157.

152 "He just slept away": Berry, Foose, and Jones, *Up from the Cradle of Jazz*, 24.

152 Jerry Wexler delivered one of the many eulogies: Ibid., 26.

152 "My life has been enriched": Palfi, *Piano Players Rarely Ever Play Together* (DVD).

153 "Huey Smith could play!": Foose, unpublished interview with James Booker.

153 "They don't know who brought him there": Fumar, "'Piano Prince of N.O.' James Booker Dies at 43," sec. 1, p. 1.

153 He was forty-three: Berry, Foose, and Jones, *Up from the Cradle of Jazz*, 174.

153 "James Booker was complex on many levels": Brock, unpublished manuscript.

17. RED STICK

156 "I'm sure they stole": Wirt, "'50s Teen Idol Frankie Ford Cruises in BR," Fun, 9.

156 "I don't think Huey's stupid": Foose, unpublished interview with Bobby Marchan.

157 "If only it could change Huey's dismal fortunes": Gumbo, *Rockin' and Jivin'*, album notes.

157 "How I built a house on the lake": Hannusch (pseud. Almost Slim), "Marshall Sehorn," 50.

158 "Waited like expectant bridegrooms": Eddy, "Baton Rouge Billboard," *Morning Advocate*, April 3, 1981, Fun, 4.

158 **"We never spoke to him"**: Eddy, "Baton Rouge Billboard," *Morning Advocate,* May 1, 1981, Fun, 4.

159 **He was no exception to the rule**: Swindle, "Half-Frettin' with George Porter," 48.

160 **"We'll see what develops"**: Eddy, "Baton Rouge Billboard," *Morning Advocate,* May 15, 1981, Fun, 4.

160 **"I haven't heard anything that interests me"**: Matthews, "Vreeland-King Top Big Music Weekend," 8.

160 **Had no plans to return to music**: Eddy, "Baton Rouge Billboard," *Morning Advocate,* June 11, 1982, Fun, 4.

18. YOU ARE ENTITLED TO AND CAN COLLECT YOUR ROYALTIES

161 **"Please allow this letter to introduce our company"**: Rubin, letter of introduction to Huey P. Smith, March 12, 1982.

162 **"They saying fifty percent of something is better than one-hundred percent of nothing"**: Wirt, "Sour Notes," Magazine, 16.

162 *Black's Law Dictionary* **defines** *proximate*: Garner, ed., *Black's Law Dictionary,* 1346.

162 **50 percent share of the proceeds**: Contract between Huey P. Smith and Artists Rights Enforcement Corporation.

163 **Huey dispatched a Western Union mailgram**: Smith, Western Union mailgram to Chuck Rubin, April 1, 1982.

163 **He deducted his 50 percent fee**: Gardner, *Yakety Yak I Fought Back,* 113, 114.

164 **"We at present do not have proof of your personal role"**: Rubin, letter from Artists Rights Enforcement Corporation to Mrs. Jane Alshuler, May 7, 1982.

165 **"He was getting zero"**: Wirt, "Sour Notes," Magazine, 16.

165 **$24,000 in royalties**: Rescission, reconveyance, and reassignment agreement between Huey P. Smith, Marjorie A. Levy, aka Jane Alshuler, the estate of Charles A. Levy Jr., Charles A. Levy III, Richard A. Levy and Clifford J. Levy, September 9, 1982.

165 **Sehorn's claims of high costs**: Matthews, "Vreeland-King Top Big Music Weekend," 8.

166 **Their contracts are identical to Huey's**: Contract between Artists Rights Enforcement Corp. and Martha and the Vandellas, January 12, 1984.

166 **"Chuck's a smart guy"**: Wirt, "Sour Notes," Magazine, 16.

19. YOU'RE FIRED

167 **Huey put his demand**: Smith, Western Union mailgram to Artists Rights Enforcement Corporation, copied to Richard Linn, May 25, 1984.

168 **"He has terminated his relationship with you"**: Brody, letter to Chuck Rubin, August 17, 1984.

168 **A month of European touring in 1984**: Broven, *Cruisin' with Frankie Ford,* CD notes, 7.

169   **"Moore's body was found in Algiers"**: "N.O. Shooting Victims Identified," A-22.

169   **Curley's newspaper obit**: June "Curley" Moore, obituary, A-23.

169   *Billboard* **noted the singer's death**: "Lifelines," 61.

170   **A white knight who jousted with corporations**: Pareles, "Tracing Lost Royalties," C-13.

170   **"Artists have someone to champion their cause"**: Jennings, "The Fight over Golden Oldies," 36.

170   **"Another hit for Chuck Rubin"**: Snowden, "Fighting for Artists' Publishing Rights," Calendar, 82.

170   **"Howell was uncomfortable with the fifty percent"**: Brown and Yule, *Miss Rhythm*, 254.

170   **"I've never ever accused them of stealing the song from me"**: Marsh, *Louie Louie*, 193–196.

171   **The composer's heated 1984 breakup with Artists Rights**: Soocher, "Attorneys Make Tracks for Rockers' Royalties," 1.

171   **"I found I can do this great"**: Fried, "You're Cheatin' Art," 60, 63.

171   **"I never understood why and was afraid to ask"**: Mabry, "An Interview with Johnny Vincent of Ace Records."

20. ARTISTS RIGHTS VS. ARTIST

176   **"We'll furnish a copy to you"**: *Artists Rights Enforcement Corp. against Cotillion Music, Inc., and Huey P. Smith*, Supreme Court of the State of New York, County of New York, November 1, 1988, deposition of Huey P. Smith.

176   **Would Mannear please forward a copy of it to Vincent**: Vincent, letter to W. Steven Mannear, December 16, 1988.

177   **"Defendant Smith has provided proof"**: *Artists Rights Enforcement Corp. v. Cotillion Music, Inc., and Huey P. Smith*, Supreme Court of the State of New York, County of New York, March 17, 1989, order.

21. A NEW SUIT

178   **The suit again claimed the songwriter owed the company**: *Artists Rights Enforcement Corp. v. Huey P. Smith*, U.S. District Court, Middle District of Louisiana, September 22, 1989, complaint.

179   **"It is not clear that the provision of the contract"**: *Artists Rights Enforcement Corp. v. Huey P. Smith*, U.S. District Court, Middle District of Louisiana, July 13, 1990, ruling on motion for summary judgment.

179   **"I still love the record business"**: McNutt, *Guitar Towns*, 43.

180   **"Knowing that you are a man of integrity"**: Smith, telegram to U.S. District Clerk of Court, Middle District of Louisiana, August 19, 1991.

180   **The telegram sparked a blistering reply**: Chief Deputy Clerk, U.S. District Court, Middle District Court of Louisiana, letter to Huey P. Smith, August 20, 1991.

181 **"The greed factor sets in"**: Fried, "The Three Mrs. Lymons," 108.

181 **"Based upon his demeanor on the witness stand"**: *Shirley Goodman v. Audrey Lee, et al.,* U.S. District Court, Eastern District of Louisiana, August 13, 1991, 64, 65.

181 **A renewed motion for summary judgment against Huey**: *Artists Rights Enforcement Corp. vs. Huey P. Smith,* U.S. District Court, Middle District of Louisiana, November 14, 1991, declaration of Chuck Rubin in support of plaintiff's renewed motion for summary judgment.

181 **"The entire arrangement was simply an effort to dupe Smith"**: *Artists Rights Enforcement Corp. v. Huey P. Smith,* U.S. District Court, Middle District of Louisiana. November 13, 1991, declaration of Richard Linn.

181 **"The time has come to vindicate the name of Charles Levy Jr."**: Huey Smith and Margrette Smith, "High-Tech Copyright Piracy in the Rocking Pneumonia Rip-Off," undated.

182 **"Ever since I heard Smiley Lewis and Huey 'Piano' Smith as a kid in the '50s"**: Hoskyns, *Across the Great Divide,* 396.

182 **"As it was practically and chronologically possible to do so"**: *Artists Rights Enforcement Corp. v. Huey P. Smith,* U.S. District Court, Middle District of Louisiana, January 7, 1992, *ex parte* motion to reconsider decision.

182 **Only minimal, incomplete discovery**: *Artists Rights Enforcement Corp. v. Huey P. Smith,* U.S. District Court, Middle District of Louisiana, January 7, 1992, *ex parte* motion to continue trial.

182 **"This action has been pending"**: *Artists Rights Enforcement Corp. v. Huey P. Smith,* U.S. District Court, Middle District of Louisiana, January 9, 1992, order.

182 **Black's Law Dictionary defines**: Garner, ed., *Black's Law Dictionary,* 1307.

183 **In a 1990 affidavit**: *Artists Rights Enforcement Corp. v. Huey P. Smith,* U.S. District Court, Middle District of Louisiana. April 11, 1990, affidavit of Chuck Rubin in support of plaintiff's motion for summary judgment.

183 **In a 1991 declaration**: *Artists Rights Enforcement Corp. vs. Huey P. Smith,* U.S. District Court, Middle District of Louisiana, November 14, 1991, declaration of Chuck Rubin in support of plaintiff's renewed motion for summary judgment.

186 **"You have probably been ill-served"**: *Artists Rights Enforcement Corp. versus Huey P. Smith,* U.S. District Court, Middle District of Louisiana, February 5, 1992, trial transcript.

187 **"To the author of 'Scald Dog,' Huey Smith"**: Dr. John, *Goin' Back to New Orleans,* CD notes, 11.

188 **"AREC does not have a real right or right in rem"**: *Artists Rights Enforcement Corporation versus Huey P. Smith,* U.S. Court of Appeals for the Fifth Circuit, November 9, 1992, ruling.

188 **Huey was ordered to pay Artists Rights Enforcement**: *Artists Rights Enforcement Corporation v. Huey P. Smith,* U.S. District Court, Middle District of Louisiana, ruling, November 9, 1993, fix amounts due under final judgment.

188 **"You have been less than forthright in your communications"**: Rudin, letter to Ralph E. Hood, July 19, 1993.

188 **"He knew more than the biggest law firm put together"**: Wirt, "Jett Williams' Life Story Straight out of a Country Song," Fun, 8.

189 **"Me, I just didn't save photographs or historic items"**: Hannusch, "Cosimo Matassa," 58.

189 "This is to notify you that the copyrights obtained by Johnny Vincent": James, letter to Don Biederman, February 22, 1995.

190 "There is a statute of limitations on fraud": Biederman, letter to Margrette R. James, February 22, 1995.

190 Through this interpleader action: Rudin, letter to Margrette R. James, April 10, 1995.

190 "Artists Rights Enforcement Corporation is to take nothing": *Shirley Goodman v. Capitol Records, Inc., et al.*, Superior Court of the State of California. March 28, 1994, judgment.

191 "Each of the Songs was originally registered": *Artists Rights Enforcement Corporation v. Huey P. Smith*, U.S. District Court, Middle District of Louisiana, October 11, 1993, declaration of Chuck Rubin.

192 "I'm not interested in rap": Grady, "Singer Gave Voice to R&B Original: Marchan Takes Care of Business," B-1.

22. BANKRUPTCY AND FAREWELLS

193 The Chapter 7 bankruptcy code gives control: Uscourts.gov/FederalCourts/Bankruptcy, "Chapter 7: Liquidation under the Bankruptcy Code."

193 The Chapter 13 bankruptcy protection the Smiths chose to file under: Ibid., "Chapter 13: Individual Debt Adjustment."

193 Chapter 11 allows a debtor corporation: Ibid., "Chapter 11: Reorganization under the Bankruptcy Code."

194 "Take each one of these different responses to heart": Talley, "Attorneys Rate Federal Magistrate Best: Survey Finds Differing Opinions of Officials on Federal Bench," 1A.

194 "We are asking you to please grant us 5 minutes": Smith and Smith, letter to Judge Louis M. Phillips, November 11, 1997.

196 "You [Magee] can't hardly represent these people": Huey P. Smith and Margrette R. Smith bankruptcy, U.S. Bankruptcy Court, Middle District of Louisiana, November 21, 1997, hearing transcript.

197 "But you understand my concern": Huey P. Smith and Margrette R. Smith bankruptcy, U.S. Bankruptcy Court, Middle District of Louisiana, December 16, 1997, hearing transcript.

201 "I'm having so much fun today": Sandmel, interview with Bobby Marchan.

202 "I just figure 25 percent of something is better than 100 percent of nothing": Hannusch, Sandmel, and Ferguson, "Anatomy of a Carnival Song," L-17.

202 "Every avenue he tried": Wirt, "Sour Notes," Magazine, 16.

202 "It's part of our charm": Spera, "Heirs Fight to Reclaim Rights; La Musicians Often Exploited," A-1.

203 "I've got too much work": Clark and Spera, "The Blues Brothers," 17.

203 "Dear Judge Phillips": Smith and Smith, letter to Judge Louis M. Phillips, November 14, 1997.

205 "Marchan will be laid to rest this weekend": Spera, "Rest in Peace," Lagniappe, 11.

205 "The procession ended at Kemp's bar": Wyckoff, "Marchan Memories," 37.

205 **The order stated that Brown**: Huey P. Smith and Margrette R. Smith bankruptcy, U.S. Bankruptcy Court, Middle District of Louisiana, November 20, 1999, order approving engagement of attorney for a special purpose.

205 **"If you spend a refund"**: Murray, letter to Huey and Margrette Smith, January 27, 2000.

206 **Was sworn in as a judge for the U.S. Court of Appeals**: "And the Last Shall Be First."

206 **"It was up to us as to how we played the hand"**: Ford, "Ace up His Sleeve."

206 **Paid him $2 million for his entire Ace Records holdings**: "Newsline . . . ," 46.

23. PIONEER DAYS

207 **"Reissue the most obscure music"**: Hannusch, "Talkin' 'bout New Orleans," *Offbeat*, August 1996, 26.

208 **Huey got a notice from the IRS**: Internal Revenue Service, letter to Huey P. Smith Sr. and Margrette Smith, June 19, 2000.

208 **"I have repeatedly responded to all communications"**: Smith and Smith, letter to Internal Revenue Service, July 10, 2000.

209 **"[The] institution's main mission appears to be"**: Marsh, "No Future for Who?"

210 **"Just for the record, judge"**: Huey P. Smith and Margrette R. Smith bankruptcy, U.S. Bankruptcy Court, Middle District of Louisiana. August 18, 2000, hearing transcript.

212 **"You didn't want to go to jail in New Orleans"**: Scherman, *Backbeat*, 95.

212 **The *Baton Rouge Advocate* reported the demise**: Baughman, "Landry Hinted of Suicide to Family," 1A.

214 **"New Orleans has a jazz festival coming up"**: Soul-Patrol.net, interview with Huey P. Smith, September 6, 2000.

216 **Chuck Rubin put a positive face**: *Rosalind Holmes and Annette Beard Sterling v. Artists Rights Enforcement Corp., Charles Rubin, Summit Rovins & Feldesman, and Ira Greenberg*, U.S. District Court, Eastern District of Michigan, October 20, 2003, deposition of Charles David Rubin, 58, 59.

217 **"Those people were so friendly"**: Wirt, "Smith's Legacy Rooted in '50s Rock 'n' Roll," Fun, 10.

217 **"I had to sell my piano"**: Ibid.

218 **Huey wrote his bankruptcy trustee**: Smith, letter to Dwayne M. Murray, bankruptcy trustee, September 14, 2000.

218 **"To prevent collection agency"**: Internal Revenue Service, notice to Huey P. and Margrette Smith, December 11, 2000.

218 **"You misinterpreted my letter"**: Smith, email to Gary Roth at BMI, January 29, 2001.

219 **Barbara Hawkins of the New Orleans singing group**: Wirt, "Sour Notes," Magazine, 16.

219 **"People don't like Chuck Rubin"**: Ibid.

220 **"I am writing to you to ask for your help"**: Smith, letter to U.S. Rep. Richard Baker, January 2001.

221 **"I like to think Slim's up there"**: Wirt, "Louisiana Talent Rocked Final Day of Popular Music Event," Fun, 10.

25. THE MONEY'S STILL FUNNY

225 **"The double payment to attorney [Steven Ames] Brown"**: *Rosemary Prater against Artists Rights Enforcement Corp. and Atlantic Recording Corp.*, Superior Court of New Jersey, May 21, 2001, complaint.

226 **"I don't understand why she is doing this"**: Hughes, "Blues Star's Widow Suing for Royalties: Dispute with Label, Collection Agency," L1.

227 **"It was like the old days again"**: Butler, letter to Huey P. Smith, September 16, 2001.

230 **Her obituary listed her as**: Pearl Louise Smith Edwards, obituary, B-4.

231 **"I would not have known"**: Smith, email message to *Advocate*. February 15, 2002.

231 **"It's all really baffling to me"**: Smith, email message to *Advocate*, February 21, 2002.

232 **"The announcement that he would perform"**: Spera, "Spare Notes: Jazzfest Changes," Lagniappe, 29.

232 **He suspected Huey made excuses**: Spera, "The Comeback That Wasn't," E-1, E-3.

234 **"I don't hate the Chess people"**: Weinraub, "Pioneer of a Beat Is Still Riffing for His Due."

235 **"Billy entertained millions of people"**: Koch, "Fund-Raiser to Help Pay Costs of Singer's Burial."

237 **Two more of Chuck Rubin's clients**: *Rosalind Holmes and Annette Beard Sterling v. Artists Rights Enforcement Corp., Charles Rubin, Summit Rovins & Feldesman, and Ira Greenberg*, U.S. District Court, Eastern District of Michigan, January 8, 2004, declarations of Rosalind Holms and Annette Sterling.

238 **"We interceded on his behalf again"**: *Rosalind Holmes and Annette Beard Sterling v. Artists Rights Enforcement Corp., Charles Rubin, Summit Rovins & Feldesman, and Ira Greenberg*, U.S. District Court, Eastern District of Michigan, October 20, 2003, deposition of Charles David Rubin.

238 **Ruled in favor of Rubin**: *Rosalind Ashford Holmes et al., v. Artists Rights Enforcement Corp. et. al.*, U.S. District Court for the Eastern District of Michigan, Southern Division, March 3, 2004, judgment.

238 **The complaint includes conversion of property**: *The Guy Mitchell & Betty J. Mitchell Family Trust v. Artists Rights Enforcement Corporation.*, U.S. District Court, Eastern District of Washington, Spokane, January 19, 2011, complaint.

239 **Business as usual in Louisiana**: "Thomas Porteous Is the Eighth Federal Judge to Be Convicted and Removed from Office by the Senate."

CODA

240 **"I guess that's the magic of Huey"**: Wirt, "Sour Notes," Magazine, 16.

241 **"His touch is just impeccable"**: Spera, "The Comeback That Wasn't," E-3.

241 **"He's been hearing it all his life!"**: Matthews, "Bob French," 25.

241 **"We all hear second line"**: Tyler, New Orleans Jazz and Heritage Festival Heritage Stage interview.

241 **"It's such feel-good music"**: Robertson, "Fifty Artists Pick Their Personal Top 10s."

BIBLIOGRAPHY

INTERVIEWS BY THE AUTHOR

Arentson, Robert. Telephone interview, April 2002.
Bartholomew, Dave. Telephone interview, April 2001.
Bo, Eddie. In-person interview, April 2001, and telephone interview, May 2001.
Boutte, John. Telephone interview, October 2002.
Clayton, Willie. In-person interview, March 2010.
Cleary, Jon. In-person interview, April 2012.
Delle, Billy. Telephone interview, March 2001.
Diamond, Billy. Telephone interview, July 2008.
Easterling, Skip. Telephone interviews, May and July 2003.
Foose, Jonathan. Telephone interviews, March and April 2002.
Gardner, Carl. Telephone interview, April 2001.
Goodman, Shirley. Brief telephone interview, April 2001.
Gourrier, John Fred. Telephone interview, April 2003.
Grassi, Diane M. Telephone interview, October 2001.
Hall, Gerri. In-person interview, September 2001.
Harrison, Herreast. Telephone interview, November 2010.
Henry, Clarence "Frogman." Telephone interview, July 2003.
Holiday, Herb. Telephone interview, February 2001.
Jones, Tad. Telephone interview, June 2001.
Kahl, Louis. Telephone interview, June 2001.
King, Earl. Telephone interview, June 2001.
Lawrence, Stephanie. Telephone interview, May 2001.
Liuzza, Tex. Telephone interview, August 2009.
Loney, Roy. Telephone interview, September 2010.
Mannear, W. Steven. Telephone interview, March 2001.
Montalbano, S. J. In-person interview, September 2001.
Moore, Charles. Telephone interview, December 2009.

Moore, Deacon John. Telephone interview, September 2003.

Moore, Rudy Ray. In-person interview, February 2002.

Palmer, Earl. Telephone interview, March 2001.

Parker, Robert. Telephone interview, April 2002.

Porter, George, Jr. Telephone interview, July 2001.

Rebennack, Mac (aka Dr. John). Two telephone interviews, June 2003.

Ripley, Steve. Telephone interview, March 2001.

Rivers, James. Telephone interview, June 2001.

Rogan, Davis. Telephone interview, January 2002.

Russell, Jim. Telephone and in-person interviews, February 2002.

Sandmel, Ben. Telephone interview, June 2001.

Smith, Huey P. Weekly in-person interviews, January 2001–September 2001.

Thomas, Jesse. Telephone interviews, March 2001 and January 2002.

Toledano, Suzette Becker. Telephone interview, April 2001.

Williams, Ike "Diz." Telephone interview, July 2008.

Williams, Mary. In-person interview, March 2010.

OTHER INTERVIEWS

Coleman, Rick. Unpublished interview with Huey "Piano" Smith. April 2, 1988.

Foose, Jonathan. Unpublished interview with Bobby Marchan. January 16, 1981. Hogan Jazz Archive, Tulane University, New Orleans, La.

———. Unpublished interview with James Booker. December 17, 1981. Hogan Jazz Archive, Tulane University, New Orleans, La.

Ford, Frankie. New Orleans Jazz and Heritage Festival Heritage Stage interview. April 26, 1996. New Orleans Jazz and Heritage Foundation Archive, New Orleans, La.

Hannusch, Jeff [pseud. Almost Slim]. WWOZ interview with Earl King. June 22, 1988. New Orleans Jazz and Heritage Foundation Archive, New Orleans, La.

Palmer, Earl. Rock and Roll Hall of Fame interview. February 11, 2004. Foster Theater, Rock and Roll Hall of Fame and Museum, Cleveland, Ohio.

Price, Lloyd. New Orleans Jazz and Heritage Festival Heritage Stage interview. May 5, 1996. New Orleans Jazz and Heritage Foundation Archive, New Orleans, La.

Roberts, Will. WBRH-FM interview with Huey "Piano" Smith. October 26, 2000.

Sandmel, Ben. Interview with Bobby Marchan. New Orleans Jazz and Heritage Festival Heritage Stage Interview. April 30, 1998. New Orleans Jazz and Heritage Foundation Archive, New Orleans, La.

Soul-Patrol.net. Interview with Huey P. Smith. September 6, 2000.

Tyler, Alvin "Red." New Orleans Jazz and Heritage Festival Heritage Stage Interview. April 28, 1995. New Orleans Jazz and Heritage Foundation Archive, New Orleans, La.

WWOZ. Interview with Chuck Carbo and Earl King. May 1, 1982. New Orleans Jazz and Heritage Foundation Archive, New Orleans, La.

———. Interview with Frank Fields. May 1, 1982. New Orleans Jazz and Heritage Foundation Archive, New Orleans, La.

CORRESPONDENCE

Biederman, Don. Letter to Margrette R. James. February 22, 1995.

Brody, Ray. Letter to Chuck Rubin. August 17, 1984.

Butler, Doretha F. Letter to Huey P. Smith. September 16, 2001.

Chief Deputy Clerk, U.S. District, Middle Court of Louisiana, letter to Huey P. Smith, August 20, 1991.

Internal Revenue Service. Letter to Huey P. Smith Sr. and Margrette Smith. June 19, 2000.

———. Notice to Huey P. and Margrette Smith. December 11, 2000.

———. Letter to Huey P. Smith and Margrette R. Smith. January 8, 2001.

James, Margrette R. Letter to Don Beiderman. February 22, 1995.

Levy, Charles, Jr. Letter to Johnny Vincent regarding sale of four Huey P. Smith songs to Cotillion Music. September 12, 1972.

Murray, Dwayne M. Letter to Huey and Margrette Smith. January 27, 2000.

Rubin, Chuck. Letter of introduction to Huey P. Smith. March 12, 1982.

———. Letter from Artists Rights Enforcement Corporation to Clifford Levy. May 7, 1982.

———. Letter from Artists Rights Enforcement Corporation to Ms. Jane Alshuler. May 7, 1982.

———. Letter to Jerry Bursey, Cotillion Music. August 15, 1984.

Rudin, Milton A. Letter to Ralph E. Hood. July 19, 1993.

———. Letter to Margrette R. James. April 10, 1995.

Smith, Huey P. Email to Gary Roth, BMI, Inc. January 26, 2001.

———. Emails to the *Baton Rouge Advocate*. February 15, 21, 2002.

———. Letter to Dwayne M. Murray, bankruptcy trustee. September 14, 2000.

———. Letter to U.S. Rep. Richard Baker. Undated.

———. Letters to Judge Louis Phillips. November 14, 1997, September 4, 1998, December 14, 1998.

———. Telegram to U.S. District Clerk of Court, Middle District of Louisiana, August 19, 1991.

———. Western Union mailgram to Artists Rights Enforcement Corporation, copied to Richard Linn. May 25, 1984.

———. Western Union mailgram to Chuck Rubin. April 1, 1982.

Smith, Huey P., and Margrette Smith. Letter to Internal Revenue Service. June 19, 2000.

———. Letter to Judge Louis M. Phillips. November 11, 1997.

Vincent, Johnny. Letter to W. Steven Mannear, December 16, 1988. (Re. Huey P. Smith; Your File: 1430.8.)

PUBLISHED OR PRINTED SOURCES

"Ace Rejects 25G Bid for 'Know It' Master." *Billboard,* March 3, 1958, 3.

Act No. 579. *Acts of the State of Louisiana Regular Session* (1956): 1054–1055.

"Alimony Blues Sung for Judge." *New Orleans Times-Picayune,* May 5, 1965, 11.

Almost Slim (pseud.). See Hannusch, Jeff.

"And the Last Shall Be First." *The Third Branch: Newsletter of the Federal Courts* 32, no. 2. (February 2000).

Artists Rights Enforcement Corp. against Cotillion Music, Inc., and Huey P. Smith. Supreme Court of the State of New York, County of New York. March 23, 1988. (Complaint.)

Artists Rights Enforcement Corp. against Cotillion Music, Inc., and Huey P. Smith. Supreme Court of the State of New York, County of New York. August 5, 1988. (Affidavit of Huey P. Smith.)

Artists Rights Enforcement Corp. against Cotillion Music, Inc., and Huey P. Smith. Supreme Court of the State of New York, County of New York. November 1, 1988. (Deposition of Huey P. Smith.)

Artists Rights Enforcement Corp. against Cotillion Music, Inc., and Huey P. Smith. Supreme Court of the State of New York, County of New York. March 17, 1989. (Order.)

Artists Rights Enforcement Corp. v. Huey P. Smith. U.S. District Court, Middle District of Louisiana. September 22, 1989. (Complaint.)

Artists Rights Enforcement Corp. v. Huey P. Smith. U.S. District Court, Middle District of Louisiana. April 11, 1990. (Affidavit of Chuck Rubin in support of plaintiff's motion for summary judgment.)

Artists Rights Enforcement Corp. v. Huey P. Smith. U.S. District Court, Middle District of Louisiana. July 13, 1990. (Ruling on motion for summary judgment.)

Artists Rights Enforcement Corp. v. Huey P. Smith. U.S. District Court, Middle District of Louisiana. September 12, 1991. (Motion to change purpose of scheduled conference and to continue scheduled pretrial conference.)

Artists Rights Enforcement Corp. v. Huey P. Smith. U.S. District Court, Middle District of Louisiana. November 13, 1991. (Declaration of Richard Linn.)

Artists Rights Enforcement Corp. vs. Huey P. Smith. U.S. District Court, Middle District of Louisiana. November 14, 1991. (Declaration of Chuck Rubin in support of plaintiff's renewed motion for summary judgment.)

Artists Rights Enforcement Corp. v. Huey P. Smith. U.S. District Court, Middle District of Louisiana. January 7, 1992. (*Ex parte* motion to reconsider decision.)

Artists Rights Enforcement Corp. v. Huey P. Smith. U.S. District Court, Middle District of Louisiana. January 7, 1992. (*Ex parte* motion to continue trial.)

Artists Rights Enforcement Corp. v. Huey P. Smith. U.S. District Court, Middle District of Louisiana, January 9, 1992. (Order.)

Artists Rights Enforcement Corp. versus Huey P. Smith. U.S. District Court, Middle District of Louisiana. February 5, 1992. (Trial transcript.)

Artists Rights Enforcement Corp. v. Huey P. Smith. U.S. District Court, Middle District of Louisiana. March 6, 1992. (Ruling.)

Artists Rights Enforcement Corp. v. Huey P. Smith. U.S. District Court, Middle District of Louisiana. March 6, 1992. (Notice of appeal.)

Artists Rights Enforcement Corp. v. Huey P. Smith. U.S. Court of Appeals for the Fifth Circuit. November 9, 1992. (Ruling.)

Artists Rights Enforcement Corp. v. Huey P. Smith. U.S. District Court, Middle District of Louisiana. November 9, 1993. (Fix amounts due under final judgment.)

Artists Rights Enforcement Corp. v. Huey P. Smith. U.S. District Court, Middle District of Louisiana. October 11, 1993. (Declaration of Chuck Rubin.)

Artists Rights Enforcement Corp. v. Huey P. Smith. U.S. District Court, Middle District of Louisiana. September 28, 1995. (Trial transcript.)

Artists Rights Enforcement v. Huey P. Smith and Margrette R. James. U.S. District Court, Middle District of Louisiana. September 28, 1995. (Judgment annulling the transfer of four songs from Huey P. Smith to Margrette R. James.)

Artists Rights Enforcement Corp. v. Huey P. Smith. Supreme Court of the State of New York, County of New York. November 28, 1995. (Execution with notice to garnishee BMI. Re: Huey P. Smith.)

Baughman, Christopher. "Landry Hinted of Suicide to Family." *Baton Rouge Advocate,* August 7 1995, 1A.

Berry, Jason. "Davell Crawford Comes of Age." *Offbeat,* December 1995, 44.

Berry, Jason, Jonathan Foose, and Tad Jones. "Huey 'Piano' Smith and Guitar Slim." *Living Blues,* no. 72 (1986): 22.

———. *Up from the Cradle of Jazz: New Orleans Music since World War II.* New York: Da Capo Press, 1992.

"The Billboard Spotlight Winners of the Week." *Billboard,* November 10, 1958, 36; December 22, 1958, 38.

"Bobby Marchan Almost Gave Up; Now a 'Name.'" *Chicago Defender,* March 30, 1957, 8.

Bordowitz, Hank. *Every Little Thing Gonna Be Alright: The Bob Marley Reader.* Cambridge: Da Capo Press, 2004.

Broven, John. *Cruisin' with Frankie Ford: The Imperial Sides and London Session,* CD notes. Ace Records, 1998.

———. *Record Makers and Breakers: Voices of the Independent Rock 'n' Roll Pioneers.* Urbana: Univ. of Illinois Press, 2009.

———. *Rhythm and Blues in New Orleans.* Gretna, La.: Pelican, 1983.

Brown, Ruth, and Andrew Yule. *Miss Rhythm: The Autobiography of Ruth Brown, Rhythm and Blues Legend.* New York: Donald I. Fine Books, 1996.

"Bumper Crop of 45s Sold in '58." *Billboard,* January 5, 1959, 4, 10.

Bundy, June. "Avalon a Standout in Feld's New R&R Pkge." *Billboard,* April 21, 1958, 7.

Charles, Ray, and David Ritz. *Brother Ray: Ray Charles' Own Story.* New York: Dial Press, 1978.

"Charles Brown, Amos Milburn Open La. Tour." *Louisiana Weekly,* January 31, 1959, 15.

City of New Orleans. "Ponchartrain Park Neighborhood Profile." December 1979. 3.01–3.02. New Orleans Public Library.

Clark, Anthony, and Keith Spera. "The Blues Brothers." *Offbeat,* January 1992, 17

Clayton, James E. "Crusader or Opportunist? Battle over New Orleans Vice Arrays Stubborn DA against Stubborn Judge." *Washington Post/Times Herald,* February 10, 1963, A1, A6.

Coleman, Rick. *Blue Monday: Fats Domino and the Lost Dawn of Rock 'n' Roll.* Cambridge: Da Capo Press, 2006.

———. "Jim Russell's Records." *Wavelength,* July 1986, 22.

———. *Little Richard: The Specialty Sessions,* box set notes. Specialty Records, 1989.

———. *Taking Inventory,* album notes. Charly Records, 1988.

Coleman, Rick, and Jason Kruppa. *The Sweethearts of the Blues,* box set notes. Bear Family Records, 1997.

Coleman, Rick, and Jeff Hannusch. *Shame, Shame, Shame,* box set notes. Bear Family Records, June 28, 1994.

Cost, Jud. *Supersnazz,* CD notes. Sundazed Music, 2000.

Dahl, Bill. "Fats Domino: The King of Blueberry Hill." *Goldmine,* June 29, 2001, 14–17, 71.

———. *Motown: The Golden Years.* Iola, Wisc.: Krause Publications, 2001.

Delle, Billy. "Wavelength Interview: Robert Plant." *Wavelength,* November 1990, 7.

Dr. John (Mac Rebennack). *Goin' Back To New Orleans,* CD notes. Warner Bros. Records, 1992.

Dr. John (Mac Rebennack) with Jack Rummel. *Under a Hoodoo Moon: The Life of the Night Tripper.* New York: St. Martin's Press, 1994.

"Eddie 'Guitar' Slim Sued Here for $4600." *Louisiana Weekly,* May 30, 1953, 3.

Eddy, R. U. "Baton Rouge Billboard." *Baton Rouge Morning Advocate,* April 3, May 1, May 15, 1981; June 11, 1982.

Edwards, Pearl Louise Smith. Obituary. *New Orleans Times-Picayune,* December 7, 2001, B-4.

Emery, Joe. "Dig Me! . . ." *Louisiana Weekly,* August 17, 1968, section 1, page 10.

"Fats Domino's New Plush Dream House." *Louisiana Weekly,* July 2, 1960, 15.

Foose, Jonathan. "Lord have mercy that was a good man!" *Living Blues,* no. 72 (1986): 22.

Ford, Frankie. "Ace up His Sleeve." *Offbeat,* April 2000, offbeat.com archives.

Fried, Stephen. "The Three Mrs. Lymons." *Philadelphia,* July 1989, 108.

———. "You're Cheatin' Art." *GQ,* January 1990, 60, 63.

Fumar, Vincent. "Music—Huey 'Piano' Smith." *New Orleans States-Item,* November 11, 1978, Lagniappe, 6, 28.

———. "'Piano Prince of N.O' James Booker Dies at 43." *New Orleans Times-Picayune,* November 9, 1983, section 1, page 1.

———. "Rapping with Ray." *New Orleans States-Item,* June 13, 1980, 116.

Gardner, Carl. *Yakety Yak I Fought Back: My Life with the Coasters.* Bloomington, Ind.: AuthorHouse, 2008.

Garner, Bryan A., ed. *Black's Law Dictionary.* St. Paul: Thomson Reuters, 2009.

Gould, Jonathan. *Can't Buy Me Love: The Beatles, Britain, and America.* New York: Harmony Books, 2007.

Grady, Bill. "Bluesman's Done Got over Bad Luck, Trouble; The Things He Used to Do He's Not Doing Anymore." *New Orleans Times-Picayune,* February 4, 2001, Metro, 1.

———. "Singer Gave Voice to R&B Original: Marchan Takes Care of Business." *New Orleans Times-Picayune,* May 5, 1995, B-1.

Grevatt, Ren. "On the Beat." *Billboard,* May 4, 1959, 30.

"Guitar Slim Bows at Painia's: Held Over for 2nd Big Uptown Week." *Louisiana Weekly,* September 2, 1950, 14.

Gumbo, Phil A. *Rockin' and Jivin',* album notes. Charly Records, 1981.

Guralnick, Peter. *Last Train to Memphis: The Rise of Elvis Presley.* Boston: Little, Brown, 1994.

Guy, Buddy, and David Ritz. *When I Left Home: My Story.* Boston: Da Capo Press, 2012.

The Guy Mitchell & Betty J. Mitchell Family Trust v. Artists Rights Enforcement Corporation. U.S. District Court, Eastern District of Washington, Spokane. January 19, 2011. (Complaint.)

Hannusch, Jeff [pseud. Almost Slim]. "Backtalk: James 'Sugarboy' Crawford." *Offbeat,* February 2002, 100.

———. "Bobby Marchan, 69, Noted N.O. R&B Artist." *New Orleans Times-Picayune,* December 15, 1999, B-4.

———. "Cosimo Matassa: Keeping It Simple, Making It Great." *Offbeat,* February 2000, 58.

———. "Huey 'Piano' Smith: So You Want to Be a Rock 'n' Roll Star." *Wavelength,* June 1981, 20.

———. *I Hear You Knockin': The Sound of New Orleans Rhythm and Blues.* Ville Platte, La.: Swallow Publications, 1985.

———. "Johnny Vincent Imbragulio, 1927–2000." *Offbeat,* March 2000, 94.

———. "Lawrence Cotton: Guitar Slim's Piano Player." *Offbeat,* June 2000, 29.

———. "Marshall Sehorn." *Wavelength,* May 1982, 50.

———. "Masters of Louisiana Music: Earl Silas Johnson IV." *Offbeat,* June 2003, 21.

———. "Percy Stovall, 'Rural Bandit,' Dies at 77." *Wavelength,* April 1984, 7.

———. *The Soul of New Orleans: A Legacy of Rhythm and Blues.* Ville Platte, La.: Swallow Publications, 2001.

———. "Talkin' 'bout New Orleans." *Offbeat,* August 1996, 26.

———. "Talkin' 'bout New Orleans." *Offbeat,* October 1998, 25.

———. "Talkin' 'bout New Orleans: Bobby Marchan—The Ace Years." *Offbeat,* November 1998, 65.

———. *That'll Get It (Even More of the Best),* CD notes. Westside, 1999.

Hannusch, Jeff, Ben Sandmel, and Hayes Ferguson. "Anatomy of a Carnival Song." *New Orleans Times-Picayune,* January 27, 1989, L-17.

Hawkins, Martin. *A Shot in the Dark: Making Records in Nashville, 1945–1955.* Nashville: Vanderbilt Univ. Press and Country Music Foundation Press, 2006.

Hilburn, Robert. "Bartholomew: The Man Behind the Fat Man." *Los Angeles Times,* September 1, 1985, 52

Hoskyns, Barney. *Across the Great Divide: The Band and America.* Milwaukee, Wisc.: Hal Leonard, 2006.

"Hot 100 Adds 15." *Billboard,* January 5, 1959, 4.

Huey P. Smith v. John V. Imbragulio. U.S. District Court, Eastern District of Louisiana. January 1, 1974.

"Huey Smith, to the First Degree." *Baton Rouge Morning Advocate,* June 11, 1982, Fun section, 4.

Hughes, Jennifer. "Blues Star's Widow Suing for Royalties: Dispute with Label, Collection Agency." *Record,* May 23, 2001, L1.

Hychew, Elgin. "Dig Me!" *Louisiana Weekly,* March 12, 1960, 7

———. "Dig Me!" *Louisiana Weekly,* March 26, 1960, 7.

"Interview with Huey 'Piano' Smith." *Louisiana Magazine,* WRBT-TV, Baton Rouge, 1978.

"Irma's Heavenly, But Where's Huey?" *Baton Rouge Morning Advocate,* April 3, 1981, Fun, 4.

James, Fred. *The Bullet Records Story,* CD notes. Blue Label/SPV GmbH, 2011.

Jennings, Nicholas. "The Fight over Golden Oldies." *Maclean's,* March 2, 1987, 36.

"Jim Crow Spectre Nearly Floors Rock & Roll Show." *Louisiana Weekly,* August 10, 1957, 1, 8.

Jones, Tad. "Charles 'Hungry' Williams." *Wavelength,* November 1983, 22–24.

———. "Drummer 'Hungry' Williams Dies in N.Y.C." *Wavelength,* October 1986, 7.

———. "Earl King." *Living Blues,* no. 38 (May/June 1978): 19.

———"Living Blues Interview: Earl King." *Living Blues,* no. 39 (July/August 1978): 19.

———. "Living Blues Interview: Professor Longhair." *Living Blues,* no. 26 (March/April 1976): 28.

Jordan, Scott. "Levon Helm: Backtalk." *Offbeat,* December 1998, 89.

———. "Ray Charles: An Offbeat Interview." *Offbeat,* May 1995, 64–65.

"Judge Acquits Zachary Scott in N.O. Court." *Baton Rouge State Times/Advocate,* November 17, 1952, 1, 6.

Katz, David. *Solid Foundation: An Oral History of Reggae.* New York: Bloomsbury, 2003.

Koch, Ed. "Fund-Raiser to Help Pay Costs of Singer's Burial." *Las Vegas Sun,* November 19, 2002.

Krasilovsky, M. William, and Sidney Shemel. *This Business of Music.* New York: Billboard Books, 2000.

"La. Supreme Court Disbars BR Lawyer." *Baton Rouge Advocate,* December 19, 1998, 6B.

Lee, Vincent. "Chief's Funeral Held Saturday." *New Orleans Times-Picayune,* March 12, 1972, section 1, page 22.

"Lifelines." *Billboard,* January 18, 1986, 61.

Lomax, Alan. *The Land Where the Blues Began.* New York: Pantheon Books, 1993.

Long, Huey P. "Carry Out the Command of the Lord." *Congressional Record,* February 5, 1934.

Mabry, Donald J. "An Interview with Johnny Vincent of Ace Records." HistoricalText Archive.com. October 17, 1987.

———. "The Rise and Fall of Ace Records: A Case Study in the Independent Record Business." *Business History Review* (Autumn 1990): 411–450.

"Making a Hit: The Rise and Fall of New Orleans Music Parallels the History of Ace Records." *Figaro,* December 1980, 32–37.

"A Marchan Band." *New Orleans Times-Picayune,* January 9, 2000, A-29.

Marcus, Greil, ed. *Stranded: Rock and Roll for a Desert Island.* New York: Da Capo Press, 1996.

Marsh, Dave. *Louie Louie.* New York: Hyperion, 1995.

———. "No Future for Who?" Syndicated column. January 14, 2002.

"A Martyr to Freedom." *Louisiana Weekly,* November 30, 1963, 1, 12.

Matthews, Bunny. "Bob French: It's That Beat." *Offbeat,* August 1999, 25.

———. "Masters of Louisiana Music: James Carroll Booker III." *Offbeat,* August 2000, 22–24.

———. "Vreeland-King Top Big Music Weekend." *New Orleans Times-Picayune/States-Item,* July 17, 1981, 8.

McNutt, Randy. *Guitar Towns: A Journey to the Crossroads of Rock 'n' Roll.* Bloomington: Indiana Univ. Press, 2002.

Moore, June "Curley." Obituary. *New Orleans Times-Picayune/States-Item,* December 27, 1985, A-23.

Moore, Rudy Ray. *Hully Gully Fever,* CD notes. Norton Records, 2000.

"More Huey Smith and the Clowns?" *Baton Rouge Morning Advocate,* May 15, 1981, Fun, 4.

Morris, Chris. "Legendary Screamin' Jay Hawkins Dies at 70." *Billboard,* February 26, 2000, 8.

"Negro Says He Will Seek Post of Governor." *Baton Rouge Morning Advocate,* June 14, 1951, 8A.

Neville, Art, Aaron Neville, Charles Neville, and Cyril Neville, with David Ritz. *The Brothers Neville*. Boston: Little, Brown, 2000.

"New Orleans Jazzman 'Red' Tyler Dies." *Baton Rouge Advocate*, April 6, 1998, 6A.

New Orleans Soul '60s: Watch Records, CD notes. Mardi Gras Records, 2000.

"New Show Opens Friday, Band on Stand Nitely at Dew Drop." *Louisiana Weekly*, May 30, 1953, 4-B.

"Newsline. . . ." *Billboard*, July 26, 1997, 46.

"New York Beat." *Jet*, June 19, 1958, 64.

"N.O. Shooting Victims Identified." *New Orleans Times-Picayune/States-Item*, December 17, 1985, A-22.

"N.O. Twist Gives Way to Popeye Muscles." *Billboard*, January 20, 1962, 1.

"On Tour." *Louisiana Weekly*, February 6, 1954, 6-B.

Oumana, Elena. *We Are All One: The Best of Jimmy Cliff*, CD notes. Columbia/Legacy, 2002.

Palmer, Robert. *Deep Blues*. New York: Penguin Books, 1982.

Pareles, Jon. "Tracing Lost Royalties: A White Knight of Rock." *New York Times*, December 2, 1986, C-13.

Pattison, Terry. "Chris Kenner." *Living Blues*, no. 26 (March–April 1976): 8.

Payne, Jim. *The Great Drummers of R&B, Funk and Soul*. Pacific, Mo.: Mel Bay Publications, 2006.

Penny, Dave. *The Chronological Larry Darnell, 1949–1951*, CD notes. Classics Records, 2005.

"Radio-TV Programming." *Billboard*, June 22, 1968, 79.

"R&B Territorial Best Sellers." *Billboard*, July 8, 1957, 57.

"Ray Charles, 1930–2004." *Offbeat*, July 2004, 47.

"Record Ramblings." *Cash Box*, February 3, 1962, 18.

"Regional Breakouts." *Billboard*, June 15, 1968, 34.

"Reviews of New R&B Records." *Billboard*, October 9, 1954, 61.

Richardson, Clive. "The 'Comeback' of Huey Smith, 1979–1980." *Juke Blues*, December 1985, 15.

Robertson, Robbie. "Fifty Artists Pick Their Personal Top 10s." Rollingstoneextras.com /playlists. November 21, 2010.

Robinson, Bobby. *The Fire/Fury Records Story*, box set notes. Capricorn Records, 1992.

"Rock-Jamaica-Rock." *Daily Gleaner*, July 15, 1959, 7, July 30, 1959, 7.

Rosalind Ashford Holmes et al. v. Artists Rights Enforcement Corp. et al. U.S. District Court for the Eastern District of Michigan, Southern Division. March 3, 2004. (Judgment.)

Rosalind Holmes and Annette Beard Sterling v. Artists Rights Enforcement Corp., Charles Rubin, Summit Rovins & Feldesman, and Ira Greenberg. U.S. District Court, Eastern District of Michigan. October 20, 2003. (Deposition of Charles David Rubin.)

Rosalind Holmes and Annette Beard Sterling v. Artists Rights Enforcement Corp., Charles Rubin, Summit Rovins & Feldesman, and Ira Greenberg. U.S. District Court, Eastern

District of Michigan. January 8, 2004. (Declarations of Rosalind Holmes and Annette Sterling.)

Rosemary Prater against Artists Rights Enforcement Corp. and Atlantic Recording Corp. Superior Court of New Jersey. May 21, 2001. (Complaint.)

Sandmel, Ben. *Ernie K-Doe: The R&B Emperor of New Orleans.* New Orleans: Historic New Orleans Collection, 2012.

Saperstein, Stephen. *The Best of Spinett,* CD notes. Night Train International, 1998.

Scherman, Tony. *Backbeat: Earl Palmer's Story.* Cambridge: Da Capo Press, 2000.

Schiffman, Jack. *Uptown: The Story of Harlem's Apollo Theatre.* New York: Cowles Book Company, 1971.

Scott, Hammond. "New Orleans' Cousin Joe." *Living Blues,* no. 19 (January–February 1975): 22.

Sebastian, John. *The Lovin' Spoonful Anthology,* CD notes. Rino Records, 1990.

"Shirley, Lee and Co. Here Jan. 6th." *Louisiana Weekly,* January 5, 1957, 10.

Shirley Goodman v. Audrey Lee, et al. U.S. District Court, Eastern District of Louisiana. August 13, 1991.

Shirley Goodman vs. Capitol Records, Inc., et al. Superior Court of the State of California. March 28, 1994. (Judgment.)

Smith, Huey P., and Margrette R. Smith bankruptcy. U.S. Bankruptcy Court, Middle District of Louisiana. November 21, 1997. (Hearing transcript.)

———. U.S. Bankruptcy Court, Middle District of Louisiana. December 16, 1997. (Hearing transcript.)

———. U.S. Bankruptcy Court, Middle District of Louisiana. April 27, 1998. (Order declaring 50 percent of Huey P. Smith's songwriter publishing royalties are not the property the Smiths' bankruptcy estate and are payable pursuant to the judgment rendered March 5, 1992, in favor of Artists Rights Enforcement Corporation, directly to Artists Rights.)

———. U.S. Bankruptcy Court, Middle District of Louisiana. November 20, 1999. (Order approving engagement of attorney for special purpose.)

———. U.S. Bankruptcy Court, Middle District of Louisiana. March 17, 2000. (Order signed by Judge Louis M. Phillips approving motion for bankruptcy trustee Dwayne M. Murray to receive a $200,000 advance for possible royalties.)

———. U.S. Bankruptcy Court, Middle District of Louisiana. August 18, 2000. (Hearing transcript.)

Snowden, Don. "Fighting for Artists' Publishing Rights." *Los Angeles Times,* March 1, 1987, Calendar, 82.

Soocher, Stan. "Attorneys Make Tracks for Rockers' Royalties." *National Law Journal* (June 8, 1987): 1.

"Specialty Buys Out Champion, Opens Brand." *Billboard,* April 4, 1953, 17, 48.

Spera, Keith. "The Comeback That Wasn't." *New Orleans Times-Picayune*, May 2, 2002, E-1, E-3.

———. "Heirs Fight to Reclaim Rights; La Musicians Often Exploited." *New Orleans Times-Picayune*, June 7, 1998, A-1.

———. "Jazzfest Changes." *New Orleans Times-Picayune*, April 5, 2002, Lagniappe, 29.

———. "A Little Bit of . . . Little Richard." *Wavelength*, June 1993, 27.

———. "Rest in Peace." *New Orleans Times-Picayune*, January 7, 2000, Lagniappe, 11.

———. "Spare Notes: Jazzfest changes." *New Orleans Times-Picayune*, April 5, 2002, Lagniappe, 29.

Spitz, Bob. *The Beatles: The Biography*. New York: Little, Brown, 2005.

"Spotlight Singles." *Billboard*, April 20, 1968, 73.

Steffens, Roger. "In the Tracks of the Stepping Razor: The Peter Tosh Biography." *Honorary Citizen*, CD box set notes. Columbia/Legacy, 1997.

"Strong Sales Potential." *Billboard*, December 15, 1962, 16.

Stroup, Shelia. "'Jock-A-Mo' Composer Will Sing at Jazz Fest." *New Orleans Times-Picayune*, May 6, 2012, D-4.

Swindle, Michael. "Half-Frettin' with George Porter." *Wavelength*, May 1990, 48.

Talley, Tim. "Attorneys Rate Federal Magistrate Best: Survey Finds Differing Opinions of Officials on Federal Bench." *Baton Rouge Sunday Advocate*, July 26, 1992, 1A.

"This Week's R&B Best Buys." *Billboard*, July 8, 1957, 56.

"Thomas Porteous Is the Eighth Federal Judge to Be Convicted and Removed from Office by the Senate." *New Orleans Times-Picayune*, December 8, 2010.

Tosches, Nick. *Hellfire: The Jerry Lee Lewis Story*. New York: Dell, 1982.

———. *Where Dead Voices Gather*. Boston: Little, Brown, 2001.

"Up to His Ears in Tunes," *New Orleans Times-Picayune, Dixie Roto*, June 21, 1959, 16, 19.

Vera, Billy. *The Specialty Story: 1944–1964*, CD box set notes. Specialty Records, 1994.

Webber, Bruce. "Dick Clark, 1929–2012: From 'Bandstand' to Host of New Year's Eve." *New York Times*, April 19, 2012, A1, A24.

Wein, George, and Nate Chinen. *Myself among Others: A Life in Music*. Cambridge: Da Capo Press, 2003.

Weinraub, Bernard. "Pioneer of a Beat Is Still Riffing for His Due." *New York Times*, February 16, 2003.

Wexler, Jerry, and David Ritz. *Rhythm and the Blues: A Life in American Music*. New York: Knopf, 1993.

Whitburn, Joel. *Joel Whitburn Presents Billboard Singles Reviews 1958*. Menomonee Falls, Wisc.: Record Research, 1994.

———. *Top R&B/Hip-Hop Singles: 1942–2004*. Menomonee Falls, Wisc.: Record Research, 2005.

White, Charles. *The Life and Times of Little Richard: The Authorised Biography*. London: Ominbus Press, 2003.

Winslow, Vernon, aka Dr. Daddy-O. "Boogie-Beat Jive" column. *Louisiana Weekly,* January 7, 1950, 13.

Wirt, John. "Connie Francis Is Everybody's Baby but the Hit-Maker Is Nobody's Fool." *Baton Rouge Advocate,* February 14, 1997, Fun, 8.

———. "Cosimo Matassa: Studio Owner Recorded His Way into Louisiana Music History." *Baton Rouge Advocate,* October 19, 2001, Fun, 10, 16.

———. "Dr. John Prescribes Zone's Voodoo Brew." *Baton Rouge Advocate,* August 14, 1998, Fun, 8, 17.

———. "Earl King: New Orleans Music Royalty Performs Sunday." *Baton Rouge Advocate,* October 9, 1998, Fun, 10, 17.

———. "Easterling an Unsung Regional Music Standout from '60s." *Baton Rouge Advocate,* April 23, 2004, Fun, 18.

———. "'50s Teen Idol Frankie Ford Cruises in BR." *Baton Rouge Advocate,* July 20, 2001, Fun, 9.

———. "Ford Has Lifetime Ticket aboard 'Cruise.'" *Baton Rouge Advocate,* October 16, 1998, Fun, 10.

———. "Jazz Lives in Eddie Bo." *Baton Rouge Advocate,* April 27, 2001, Fun, 12.

———. "Jett Williams' Life Story Straight out of a Country Song." *Baton Rouge Advocate,* July 4, 2003, Fun, 8.

———. "K-Doe and 'Mother-in-Law' Ready to Go Another Round." *Baton Rouge Advocate,* February 20, 1998, Fun, 8.

———. "Louisiana Talent Rocked Final Day of Popular Music Event." *Baton Rouge Advocate,* May 11, 2001, Fun, 10.

———. "N.O. Jazz Festival—Fans Rock to Music, Atmosphere, Food." *Baton Rouge Advocate,* April 29, 2001, 1A.

———. "Parker Will Be 'Barefootin' All Day Long at Jazz Fest." *Baton Rouge Advocate,* April 26, 2002, Fun, 21, 24.

———. "Smith's Legacy Rooted in '50s Rock 'n' Roll." *Baton Rouge Advocate,* September 22, 2000, Fun, 10, 20, 21.

———. "Sour Notes." *Baton Rouge Advocate,* July 8, 2001, Magazine, 14, 16.

———. "Symposium Gives Angola Inmates Musical Encouragement." *Baton Rouge Advocate,* November 30, 2001, Fun, 10.

———. "Teen Idol Jimmy Clanton Still Rocking, Rolling." *Baton Rouge Advocate,* December 11, 1998, Fun, 9.

———. "Time Really Is on Irma Thomas' Side." *Baton Rouge Advocate,* May 5, 1995, Fun, 8.

"Woman Is Shot to Death Mistakenly by Husband." *New Orleans Times-Picayune,* March 5, 1972, section 1, page 2.

Wright, Earl M. "Mardi Gras Sad Day for Prof. Long Hair." *Louisiana Weekly,* March 19, 1960, 1, 15.

Wyckoff, Geraldine. "Marchan Memories." *Gambit Weekly,* January 18, 2000, 37.

"Zachary Scott Booked in Raid: Nine Held for Drinking in Negro Establishment." *New Orleans Times-Picayune*, November, 17, 1952, 19.

Zappa, Frank, and Peter Occhiogrosso. *The Real Frank Zappa Book*. New York: Poseidon Press, 1989.

WEBSITES

JohnnyRivers.com.

U.S. Federal Courts website. www.uscourts.gov/FederalCourts/Bankruptcy.

OTHER

Akerman, David. "Who Killed Lumumba?" BBC News World Edition, October 21, 2000.

Brock, Jerry. Unpublished, undated manuscript about James Booker.

Contract between Artists Rights Enforcement Corp., and Martha and the Vandellas, January 12, 1984.

Cotillion Music, Inc., c/o Warner/Chappell Music, Inc. Contract for the sale of four Huey P. Smith compositions by Dwayne M. Murray, trustee in bankruptcy, to Cotillion Music, Inc., c/o Warner/Chappell Music, Inc.

Frame, Pete, and Kevin Howlett. *In His Own Words: Art Rupe—The Story of Specialty Records*. Ace Records Ltd., 1998.

Levy, Charles, Jr. Contract for legal representation of Huey P. Smith. January 31, 1973.

McDaniel, E. M. Assignment of copyright for four Huey P. Smith compositions to Ace Publishing Co., Inc. February 21, 1972.

Palfi, Stevenson. *Piano Players Rarely Ever Play Together* (DVD). Stevenson Productions, 1982.

Rescission, reconveyance, and reassignment agreement between Huey P. Smith, Marjorie A. Levy, aka Jane Alshuler, the estate of Charles A. Levy Jr., Charles A. Levy III, Richard A. Levy and Clifford J. Levy. September 9, 1982.

Smith, Huey P. Biography prepared for the Rhythm and Blues Foundation. June 2000.

Smith, Huey, and Margrette Smith. "High-Tech Copyright Piracy in the Rocking Pneumonia Rip-Off," undated.

Succession of Charles A. Levy Jr. Civil District Court for the Parish of Orleans, State of Louisiana. November 26, 1980. (Sworn descriptive list of assets and liabilities.)

Vincent, Johnny. Assignment of copyright. (Assigns right, title and interest in four Huey P. Smith songs to Cotillion Music, Inc.) February 29, 1972.

GENERAL INDEX

INDEX OF SONG TITLES